Ombudsmen

Public Services and
Administrative Justice

Law in Context

Below is a listing of the more recent publications in the Law in Context Series

Editors: William Twining (University College, London) and Christopher McCrudden (Lincoln College, Oxford)

Ombudsmen

Public Services and Administrative Justice

Mary Seneviratne

Professor of Law, Nottingham Trent University

Butterworths
LexisNexis™

Members of the LexisNexis Group worldwide

United Kingdom	LexisNexis Butterworths Tolley, a Division of Reed Elsevier (UK) Ltd, Halsbury House, 35 Chancery Lane, LONDON, WC2A 1EL, and 4 Hill Street, EDINBURGH EH2 3JZ
Argentina	LexisNexis Argentina, BUENOS AIRES
Australia	LexisNexis Butterworths, CHATSWOOD, New South Wales
Austria	LexisNexis Verlag ARD Orac GmbH & Co KG, VIENNA
Canada	LexisNexis Butterworths, MARKHAM, Ontario
Chile	LexisNexis Chile Ltda, SANTIAGO DE CHILE
Czech Republic	Nakladatelství Orac sro, PRAGUE
France	Editions du Juris-Classeur SA, PARIS
Hong Kong	LexisNexis Butterworths, HONG KONG
Hungary	HVG-Orac, BUDAPEST
India	LexisNexis Butterworths, NEW DELHI
Ireland	Butterworths (Ireland) Ltd, DUBLIN
Italy	Giuffrè Editore, MILAN
Malaysia	Malayan Law Journal Sdn Bhd, KUALA LUMPUR
New Zealand	LexisNexis Butterworths, WELLINGTON
Poland	Wydawnictwo Prawnicze LexisNexis, WARSAW
Singapore	LexisNexis Butterworths, SINGAPORE
South Africa	Butterworths SA, DURBAN
Switzerland	Stämpfli Verlag AG, BERNE
USA	LexisNexis, DAYTON, Ohio

© Reed Elsevier (UK) Ltd 2002

A CIP Catalogue record for this book is available from the British Library.

ISBN 0 406 94676 0

Printed and bound in Great Britain by Thomson Litho Ltd, East Kilbride, Scotland

Visit Butterworths LexisNexis *direct* at www.butterworths.com

Preface

The growth of ombudsmen schemes in both the public and private sectors has been a feature of modern life. In the United Kingdom, these schemes originated in the public sector, with the establishment of the Parliamentary Commissioner for Administration in 1967. Since then, the public sector has acquired ombudsmen for local government and the health service, and systems for the independent investigation of police complaints. Ombudsmen in the public sector are one among many mechanisms available for securing administrative justice, providing remedies for citizens with grievances against public bodies. Despite their important role in relation to public services, there is still widespread ignorance and confusion about their work. This confusion is exacerbated by the fact that there are different ombudsmen dealing with different aspects of public services. Devolution has further complicated the picture. In addition, there has been a proliferation of internal complaints adjudicators within the public sector, leading to an intermediate layer of complaint handling.

Although it is some 35 years since the first public sector ombudsman was established, there are still few readily accessible sources of information about their work. This book is intended to dispel some of the confusion, by providing a description and evaluation of the public sector ombudsman system as it applies in the UK, setting their work within the context of other mechanisms of administrative justice. It describes and evaluates the work of the Parliamentary, Health Service and Local Government Ombudsmen in England. In addition, it examines briefly the public sector ombudsman systems in Scotland, Wales and Northern Ireland, dealing in particular with the new arrangements that have occurred as a result of devolution. Finally, it explains the systems for dealing with complaints against the police.

In researching this book, I have been fortunate to receive the help of individual ombudsmen, and others involved in their work, and I am very grateful to those who have given so generously of their time to discuss their work with me. These discussions have given me greater insight into the work of ombudsmen in the public sector. I would therefore like to thank Sir Michael Buckley, Tom Frawley, Sir Alistair Graham, Walter Merricks, Elwyn Moseley, Nuala O'Loan, Malcolm Ostermeyer, Tony Redmund, Hilary Scott, Stephen Shaw, Ian Smith, Pat Thomas, Jerry White and Robert Whittaker. I would also like to record here my thanks to the Nuffield Foundation for providing the funds which facilitated these interviews. Terry Hanstock, the law librarian at Nottingham Trent University, provided invaluable assistance by tracking down numerous references for me. I am also grateful to Julie Waplington, who gathered and collated various source materials. Above all, my biggest thanks go to my family: to Anna, Sarah and Christopher, for tolerating my occasional neglect of them; and especially to Ian Brownlee, who not only gave me immense support and encouragement, but also painstakingly read all the drafts. His help has been invaluable.

Mary Seneviratne

July 2002

To Ian

Contents

Chapter 5

The Health Service Ombudsman   159

Chapter 6

The Local Government Ombudsman   197

Chapter 7

Devolution   239

Chapter 8

The police service   275

Chapter 9

Conclusions   301

Table of statutes

Table of statutory instruments

List of Cases

S

Table of
House of Commons Papers

Table of Command Papers

Chapter 1

Ombudsmen – a worldwide phenomenon

'Ombudsman'[1] is a Swedish word, meaning a representative or agent of the people, or group of people[2]. Sweden introduced the first ombudsman at the beginning of the nineteenth century, but it was not until the middle of the twentieth century that other countries began to establish ombudsman schemes. It was the introduction of an ombudsman in New Zealand, a common law country, in 1962 that sparked off a great deal of interest in the ombudsman concept. By the 1970s, ombudsmen had appeared in many parts of the world, and by the 1980s, the ombudsman idea had been accepted by almost every country in Western Europe. In the past 30 years, there has been an extraordinary spread of ombudsman systems across the world, with an estimated 90 countries having ombudsman offices at the end of the 1990s[3]. Not only have ombudsmen multiplied, but they have also diversified. They are now to be found in the private sector, operating as consumer redress mechanisms. The concept has been readily adopted

[1]   It appears to have been accepted that 'ombudsman' is a gender-neutral name. A number of women have held and do hold such posts in the UK, but they are always referred to as 'ombudsman' rather than 'ombudswoman', and there has been little call for the office-holder to be referred to as 'ombudsperson' or 'ombud'. The author has however seen reference to an 'ombudsfrau' in Austria.

[2]   The word is said to have originally derived from Germanic tribes 'where the term was applied to a third party whose task was to collect fines from remorseful culprit families and give them to the aggrieved families of victims' (H H Kircheiner 'The Ideological Foundation of the Ombudsman Institution' in G E Caiden (ed) *International Handbook of the Ombudsman* (1983) Greenwood Press).

[3]   R Gregory and P Giddings 'The Ombudsman Institution: Growth and Development' in R Gregory and P Giddings (eds) *Righting Wrongs: The Ombudsman in Six Continents* (2000) IOS Press.

in emergent democracies, as a mechanism for protecting human rights[4]. Thus the ombudsman concept, first introduced at the beginning of the nineteenth century, after being 'basically forgotten until the second half of the 20th century', now appears to have 'conquered the world'[5].

The ombudsman concept is based on the idea that citizens should be entitled to complain against specific acts of their rulers, and that their complaints should be independently investigated. This idea goes back thousands of years[6]. Indeed, there are rudiments of the ombudsman concept to be found in the Roman Republic[7]. However, the establishment of a specific office to investigate citizen complaints against public officials is relatively recent. It was in 1809 that Sweden introduced the institution of the Justitieombudsman with the task of prosecuting culpable administrators and judges. The present day Justitieombudsman is appointed by the legislature to handle complaints against administrative and judicial action, in effect ensuring that those who hold public office respect the law and properly fulfil their obligations.

Over 100 years passed before the idea was taken up elsewhere, and even then the institution remained within Scandinavia. Finland became the second country to create an ombudsman, when, in 1919, provision was made in the constitution for two appointments, a Parliamentary ombudsman and a chancellor. The chancellor's role was to ensure that authorities and officials complied with the law and performed their duties. The ombudsman was to supervise observance of the law in the proceedings of courts and other authorities. Some 35 years passed before Denmark established their Folketingets ombudsman in 1955. Norway completed the Scandinavian quartet in 1963 by setting up an ombudsman for civil administration, the Stortingets ombudsman, using the Danish ombudsman as a model. Indeed,

---

[4]   See also B Von Tigerstrom ('The Role of the Ombudsman in Protecting Economic, Social and Cultural Rights' in International Ombudsman Institute and L C Reif (eds) *The International Ombudsman Yearbook* (1998) Kluwer Law International), who argues that the ombudsman institution may be of assistance in the protection and promotion of economic, social and cultural rights.

[5]   K Heede *European Ombudsman: redress and control at Union level* (2000) Kluwer Law International.

[6]   See C Bell and J W Vaughan 'The Building Societies Ombudsman: a customers champion?' (1988) 132 Solicitors Journal 1478; see also G E Caiden 'The Institution of Ombudsman' in G E Caiden (ed) *International Handbook of the Ombudsman: Evolution and Present Function* (1983) Greenwood Press p 9.

[7]   See C Adam 'In Quest of the Ombudsman in the Mediterranean Area' (1968) (May) The Annals 98.

it was the introduction of the Danish ombudsman, in 1955, which marked the beginning of a worldwide interest in such schemes[8]. The Danish ombudsman was also the model for the New Zealand ombudsman, created in 1962, the first country outside Scandinavia to set up such a scheme[9].

Proliferation of Ombudsmen

As indicated above, there are ombudsmen systems in countries throughout the world. They operate in about 90 countries on a national, state[10], regional or municipal level. There is even a supra-national ombudsman, the European

---

[8] This interest is often attributed in part to the first Danish Ombudsman, Professor Stephen Hurwitz, because of the enthusiasm with which he 'described his work and its fruits' (see W Gellhorn *Ombudsmen and Others. Citizens' Protectors in Nine Countries* (1967) Harvard University Press p 5).

[9] The experience of New Zealand was instrumental in proving to the English-speaking world the value of such a system. The first New Zealand Ombudsman, Sir Guy Powles, a distinguished lawyer and 'highly esteemed administrator-diplomat', probably aided this process (see L B Hill *The Model Ombudsman: Institutionalizing New Zealand's Democratic Experience* (1976) Princeton University Press pp 75-76; see also J F Northey 'New Zealand's Parliamentary Commissioner' in D C Rowat (ed) *The Ombudsman: Citizens Defender* (1968) George Allen and Unwin).

[10] Ombudsmen are not common in federal states, at national level. For example, the US, Canada and Germany only have general competent ombudsmen at state level. There is no theory on why this is so, but in the US it is thought to be because of the congressional style of government, with its strict theory of separation of powers. It is felt that executive departments would regard an ombudsman with suspicion as a biased agent of Congress (see K Heede *European Ombudsman: redress and control at Union level* (2000) Kluwer Law International p 84). Others have attributed it to the availability of other channels for American citizens to have their grievances with the government redressed (see D M Gottehrer, M D Fergusen and S E Aufrecht 'Ombudsman Officers in the United States' in R Gregory and P Giddings (eds) *Righting Wrongs: The Ombudsman in Six Continents* (2000) IOS Press p 369). Although there are no national ombudsmen in the US with general jurisdiction for the various agencies of federal government, there are ombudsmen for five states, and a number of ombudsmen at local level. Apparently, there was some discussion in the 1960s in the US about creating an ombudsman for the country, but this did not get very far (see L D Mankin 'The Role of the Ombudsman in Higher Education' (1996) 51 Dispute Resolution Journal 46-49) and these attempts to establish national ombudsmen have not been repeated (see D M Gottehrer, M D Fergusen and S E Aufrecht 'Ombudsman Officers in the United States' in R Gregory and P Giddings (2000) p 355).

Ombudsman. This office was established in 1995 to deal with complaints about maladministration by European Union institutions and bodies[11]. There have also been calls for another ombudsman in Europe, this time for the private sector, to advise on trans-frontier disputes within the European Union[12]. Another suggestion for a trans-state ombudsman is an ombudsman for humanitarian assistance, whose role would be to provide a mechanism for raising and addressing the concerns of people affected by disaster and conflict within the humanitarian community[13]. There are clearly problems obtaining international jurisdiction for such an ombudsman. However, that such a proposal is made illustrates the perceived success of ombudsmen in righting wrongs. It also indicates a belief in the ability of the concept to be adapted and modified as circumstances demand. A similar belief must account for the suggestion that an ombudsman for the scientific community be established to investigate fraud and dishonesty in scientific research, or where work is not being conducted according to the interests of good scientific practice[14].

The ombudsman concept has been successfully transplanted to the private sector. In the UK in the 1980s and 1990s private sector ombudsman schemes proliferated[15]. Although based on the public sector model, these private sector systems were a modification of the original concept, operating in many cases like arbitration schemes. Some were established on a voluntary

[11]   For details see: K Heede *European Ombudsman: redress and control at Union level* (2000) Kluwer Law International; M Seneviratne 'The European Ombudsman' (1999) 21(3) JSWFL 269-278; M Seneviratne 'The European Ombudsman – The First Term' (2000) 22(3) JSWFL 329-337.

[12]   Such an ombudsman would also identify when jurisdiction should be within the European Courts and when at national level. Where appropriate, the ombudsman could act as an arbitrator, investigating cases and informing consumers and their associations how to obtain redress (European Community Group, *A Briefing Paper from the European Community Group*, August 1990). See also the Green Paper published by the European Commission, *Access to Justice and the Settlement of Consumer Disputes in the Single Market* (1993, Com (93) 576).

[13]   See J Mitchell and D Doane 'An Ombudsman for Humanitarian Assistance?' (1999) 23(2) Disasters 115-124. See also I Christoplos 'Humanitarianism, Pluralism and Ombudsmen: Do the Pieces Fit?' (1999) 23(2) Disasters 125-138.

[14]   This is proposed by the Deutsche Forschungsgemeinschaft, the central self-governing organisation of science and humanities in the Federal Republic of Germany. See 'An ombudsman for the Scientific Community?' (1997) 2(3) German Research 24-25.

[15]   See, generally, R James *Private Ombudsmen and Public Law* (1997) Dartmouth.

basis to improve the image of the industry, although for some, it was the threat of statutory intervention which encouraged their introduction. For all of them, their introduction and success is largely a result of the failures of the court system to address consumer interests. The first private sector scheme, the Insurance Ombudsman's Bureau, was set up in 1981 by the insurance industry[16]. The banks followed in 1986, with the Office of the Banking Ombudsman, 'encouraged' to do so to avoid a statutory scheme[17]. These voluntary schemes were set up by the industries concerned to deal with disputes between consumers and firms. Building societies did not set up a voluntary scheme in the same way and, in 1987, a statutory scheme[18] was imposed on them[19].

In the 1990s, the use of ombudsmen schemes was extended to other private sector industries. In 1990, a group of corporate estate agents set up an ombudsman scheme, anxious to improve the image of estate agency practice[20]. In 1998, the scheme was extended to all estate agents who wished to join[21], but it only covers about 35% of the industry[22]. In 1994, the Funeral Ombudsman scheme was set up to investigate complaints against the funeral directors and private crematoria who are members of the scheme.

[16] See, generally, J Birds and C Graham 'Complaints Mechanisms in the Financial Services Industry' (1998) Civil Justice Quarterly 313; P E Morris 'The Insurance Ombudsman Bureau and Judicial Review' (1994) Lloyd's MCLQ 358.

[17] See generally, P Morris 'The Banking Ombudsman' (1987) Journal of Banking Law 133; P Morris 'The Banking Ombudsman – five years on' (1992) Lloyd's MCLQ 227; C Graham, M Seneviratne and R James 'Publicising the Bank and Building Societies Ombudsman Schemes' (1993) 3(2) Consumer Policy Review 85.

[18] This was by means of the Building Societies Act 1986, Pt IX and Schs 12-13.

[19] See, generally, C Graham, M Seneviratne and R James 'Publicising the bank and building societies ombudsman schemes' (1993) 3(2) Consumer Policy Review 85; C Graham, R James and M Seneviratne 'Building Societies, Consumer Complaints, and the Ombudsman' (1994) 23(2) Anglo-Am LR 214.

[20] See, generally, P E Morris 'The Ombudsman for Corporate Estate Agents' (1994) Civil Justice Quarterly 337; R James 'The Ombudsman for Corporate Estate Agents – Putting Half the House in Order' (1995) 3(5) Consumer Law Journal 188; M Seneviratne 'Estate Agents, the Consumer and the Ombudsman for Corporate Estate Agents' (1997) Consumer Law Journal 123-133.

[21] The scheme is open to all firms with a principal, director or partner who is a member of the National Association of Estate Agents or Royal Institute of Chartered Surveyors, all corporate estate agents, and other estate agents who are sponsored and seconded by existing members.

[22] See The Ombudsman for Estate Agents Annual Report 2001-02 p 9; The Ombudsman (2002) (March) p 2.

Although voluntary, it covers a substantial proportion of the UK funeral profession. An ombudsman was also established in 1994 to deal with complaints about investments[23].

The 1990s also saw the development of ombudsmen who combined the public and the private. For example, the Legal Services Ombudsman scheme, set up in 1990, is more properly described as a 'hybrid' rather than a private sector scheme[24]. It was established by statute[25], is publicly funded and accountable through the Lord Chancellor to Parliament[26]. However, the ombudsman's remit is over the legal profession, which operates mainly in the private sphere. Another scheme, which is not easily classified into public or private, is the Pensions Ombudsman. This scheme, established by statute in 1990[27], was set up to consider complaints in relation to the pensions industry in both the public and private sectors. Not only is it a hybrid scheme, but also, it has been argued, it is more like a tribunal than an ombudsman, and the ombudsman's work is partly subject to the supervision of the Council on Tribunals[28]. The Independent Housing Ombudsman is another hybrid scheme[29]. This statutory scheme[30] deals with complaints about registered social landlords[31] and some private sector landlords[32]. The statutory scheme replaces the former Housing Association

---

23   The Personal Investment Authority was set up as a self-regulatory body under the Securities and Investment Board, and was within the regulatory framework set out in the Financial Services Act 1986. The Authority set up the Personal Investment Authority Ombudsman Bureau to deal with complaints against its members. The Investment Ombudsman dealt with disputes between members of the Investment Management Regulatory Organisation and their customers.

24   See R James and M Seneviratne 'The Legal Services Ombudsman: Form versus Function?' (1995) 58(2) MLR 187-207; M Seneviratne *The Legal Profession: Regulation and the Consumer* (1999) Sweet and Maxwell Ch 6.

25   Courts and Legal Services Act 1990, s 21.

26   The status of the Office of the Legal Services Ombudsman is analogous to that of a non-departmental public body, funded from money voted to the Lord Chancellor's Department.

27   Social Security Act 1990, s 12 and Sch 3, consolidated in the Pensions Schemes Act 1993, and amended in the Pensions Act 1995.

28   R James *Private Ombudsmen and Public Law* (1997) Dartmouth p 154.

29   See M Seneviratne 'Ombudsmen and Social Housing' (2002) 24(3) JSWFL (forthcoming).

30   Housing Act 1996, s 51 and Sch 2.

31   These were formerly known as housing associations. They are not public bodies, although they share the same characteristics of public sector landlords.

32   In March 2001, there were 42 voluntary private landlord members of the scheme. The total membership at that time was 2,284 landlords.

Tenants Ombudsman Scheme, which was established on a non-statutory basis in 1993.

This proliferation has resulted in a new phase of ombudsman development in the UK: rationalisation and integration. In 2000, the eight separate schemes dealing with financial services[33] were integrated to produce a single Financial Ombudsman Service[34]. This new scheme should result in less confusion for consumers of financial services, and the removal of jurisdictional overlaps and gaps. This statutory scheme operates under the supervision of the Financial Services Authority, and its creation has removed more ombudsmen schemes from the 'private' classification into the 'hybrid' category. Although a creature of statute, it has jurisdiction over private sector organisations. Now that there are so many ombudsman schemes established by statute, it appears that there are few truly private sector schemes left — perhaps only the funeral and estate agents ombudsmen.

What is an Ombudsman?

The proliferation of ombudsmen worldwide and in the public and private sectors has focused attention on the essential characteristics of an ombudsman. While there are different interpretations of the functions of ombudsmen, and a number of problems of comparison, some definitions may be useful. Although there are considerable differences according to national background, their common features were recognised some years ago by the International Bar Association, when it resolved that an ombudsman was:

---

[33] These were the Banking Ombudsman, the Building Societies Ombudsman, the Insurance Ombudsman, the Investment Ombudsman, the Personal Investment Authority Ombudsman, the Personal Insurance Arbitration Scheme, SFA Complaints Bureau and arbitration scheme, the Financial Services Authority Direct Regulation Unit and Independent Investigator.

[34] Financial Services and Markets Act 2000. As the Act did not fully come into force until 1 December 2001, the Financial Ombudsman Service existed in shadow form since early 2000. For a discussion of the new scheme see: R James and P Morris 'The new Financial Ombudsman Service Scheme' (2000) 1(2) Financial Services Bulletin 1, 3-5; R James and P Morris 'The New Financial Ombudsman Service in the UK' in C E F Rickett and T G W Telfer (eds) *International Perspectives on Consumers Access to Justice* (2002) Cambridge University Press.

An office provided for by the constitution or by an action of the legislature or parliament and headed by an independent, high-level public official who is responsible to the legislature or parliament, who receives complaints from aggrieved persons against government agencies, officials, and employees or who acts on his own motion, and who has the power to investigate, recommend corrective action, and issue reports.[35]

This comprehensive, if unwieldy, definition describes traditional or classical ombudsman schemes. It is clearly not an appropriate description for the private sector or hybrid schemes. Even in respect of the traditional ombudsmen, it has been noted that the search for definitions disguises the fact that there are 'significantly different interpretations of what exactly the Ombudsman's functions are' in the world community[36]. The focus in the UK is on maladministration, whereas in some countries, the emphasis is on human rights. This latter role is often adopted in emergent democracies, where ombudsmen are seen as 'instruments of good government', 'protectors of human rights' and leaders of the 'fight against corruption that is endemic in many developing and transitional economies'[37].

Hill provides another definition, which includes the fact that the office can use its 'extensive powers of investigation in performing a post-decision administrative audit'[38], that the findings are reported publicly, but that it cannot change administrative decisions. Another definition recognises the dual role of the ombudsman, as a protector of the rights of individuals, and also as protecting the supervising right of the parliament. Thus an ombudsman is:

A reliable person who for the purposes of legal protection of individuals as well as parliamentary control supervises almost all administrative bodies

---

[35]   Quoted in W Haller 'The place of the ombudsman in the world community' (1988) *Fourth International Ombudsman Conference Papers* p 29.

[36]   K Friedman, 'Realisation of ombudsman recommendations' (1988) *Fourth International Ombudsman Conference Papers* p 107.

[37]   G Drewry 'The Ombudsman: Parochial Stopgap or Global Panacea?' in P Leyland and T Woods (eds) *Administrative Law Facing the Future: Old Constraints and New Horizons* (1997) Blackstone Press p 94.

[38]   L Hill *The Model Ombudsman: Institutionalizing New Zealand's Democratic Experiment* (1976) Princeton University Press p 12.

and civil servants. He cannot correct their decisions, but — based on submitted complaints or on own initiatives — he may criticise them.[39]

Others have listed the characteristics of ombudsmen. For some[40], these are essentially independence, wide jurisdiction, direct access, effective redress mechanisms. The characteristics necessary for a parliamentary ombudsman include the fact that, although the office is responsible to the parliament, the holder of the office is not a parliamentarian. Such an office should have a generally defined mandate, with its purpose being the protection of the rights of individuals and/or to assist parliamentary control. The office has investigative powers, the power to seek correction of the investigated activity but without the power to issue decisions with legally binding force[41].

Ombudsmen constitute the subjects of interest for the International Ombudsman Institute at Alberta, Canada, and the European Ombudsman Institute at Innsbruck. The International Ombudsman Institute[42] lists a number of distinguishing features for ombudsmen. They investigate administrative matters, and complaints against government departments and agencies. They are independent of the organisations over which they have jurisdiction. They can make recommendations for remedial action, and can report to the legislature on matters they have investigated[43].

It is difficult to make worldwide comparisons, as these may depend upon the extent to which procedures exist for the resolution of disputes before a formal complaint is made. In a well-established ombudsman system, the ombudsman is at the apex of a pyramid of grievance resolving machinery, and is the last port of call when other procedures are exhausted. Indeed, a significant development, alongside the creation of ombudsman institutions,

---

[39]   Hansen *Die Institution des Ombudsman* (1972) Athenaum Verlag p 2. Referred to and translated in K Heede *European Ombudsman: redress and control at Union level* (2000) Kluwer Law International p 8.

[40]   I Scott 'Reforming the Commissioner for Administrative Complaints Office in Hong Kong' (1994) PL 27-38.

[41]   K Heede *European Ombudsman: redress and control at Union level* (2000) Kluwer Law International p 9.

[42]   This was an organisation established in 1978 to promote the ombudsman concept, and encourage its development throughout the world.

[43]   International Ombudsman Institute, Edmonton, Alberta, Membership By-Laws (1978).

is the introduction of 'in-house' dispute resolution procedures[44]. Furthermore, comparisons are difficult because not all those who fit the definitions are called 'ombudsmen'. In the UK, the statutory term used for the public sector ombudsmen has traditionally been 'commissioner', although they are popularly known as 'ombudsmen'[45]. In some countries, they are known as citizens' or people's defenders, or citizens' protectors[46]. In South Africa, there is a Public Protector. France has a 'Mediator', which emphasises the mediation and conciliation function of the office. Some countries emphasise the human or civil rights aspects of their role, by having titles such as the 'Parliamentary Commissioner for Human Rights', and the 'Commissioner for Civil Rights Protection'[47]. However, worldwide, ombudsmen have two distinguishing features: constitutional independence and extensive powers of investigation[48].

Popularity of Ombudsman Schemes

Why has the institution of ombudsmen, established nearly 200 years ago and unheard of outside Scandinavia until 50 years ago, proliferated to the extent it has during the second half of the twentieth century? One explanation is the expansion of state activity during and after the 1939–45 war, the new concern for the protection of human rights, and the growth of public education and participation. It was these social conditions, together with the activities of the International Commission of Jurists and the United Nations, which favoured the interest in ombudsmen[49]. Ombudsmen came to be seen as useful in helping to meet the problem of an expanded bureaucracy in the modern welfare state, the activities of which had grown in range and complexity. The increase in the powers of discretion given to

---

[44]   V Moore 'Some reflections of the role of the ombudsman' (1991) *International Institute of Administrative Sciences Conference Paper* pp 7-8.

[45]   The new ombudsman scheme in Scotland, discussed in Chapter 7, uses the term 'ombudsman' in the legislation.

[46]   For example, in Spain this is the terminology used (see A Bradley 'The Role of the Ombudsman in Relation to the Protection of Citizens' Rights' (1980) 39(2) Cambridge Law Journal 304). Italy, Quebec, Madagascar and some South American countries also use this term (see R Gregory and P Giddings 'The Ombudsman Institution: Growth and Development' in R Gregory and P Giddings (eds) *Righting Wrongs: the Ombudsman in Six Continents* (2000) IOS Press p 4).

[47]   These are in Hungary and Poland, respectively.

[48]   V Moore 'Some reflections of the role of the ombudsman' (1991) *International Institute of Administrative Sciences Conference Paper* pp 1-2.

[49]   D Rowat *The Ombudsman Plan* (1985) University Press of America p 131.

the executive side of government led to a need for additional protection against administrative arbitrariness, particularly as there was often no redress for those aggrieved by administrative decisions[50]. Ombudsmen were 'an attractive and available concept' for governments seeking such accountability mechanisms, and they 'effectively solved the problem of providing a citizens' protector'[51].

Ombudsmen are useful for filling gaps in systems for redressing wrongs, and the popularity of the institution can be seen from the way this public sector body has been 'flatteringly copied' by the private sector[52]. On grounds of cost alone, they are valuable mechanisms for dispute resolution. They are free to the users of the schemes, and in terms of the volume of cases they deal with, they are probably cost effective for those funding them. They therefore present good value for money for all the parties. Costs are kept to a minimum because, unlike the courts, legal representation is neither required nor advantageous. The private sector was quick to realise that providing an ombudsman service was a 'quick and effective way for resolving disputes'[53]. Indeed, the advantages of ombudsmen schemes mirror the disadvantages with the traditional dispute resolution forum, the courts. Court processes are notoriously slow and expensive, and do not always provide an effective remedy. Some of the problems of the civil justice system can therefore be side-stepped by the use of ombudsmen[54].

Ombudsman schemes thus present an attractive alternative to the courts. Not only do they overcome the procedural difficulties associated with litigation, but they also provide remedies where none may be available in the courts. In the public sector, ombudsmen are concerned with issues about the administration, where there is no legal remedy when things go wrong. In the private sector, ombudsmen are not confined to issues of maladministration, and they frequently deal with issues of a contractual nature. In this sense, they do represent a genuinely alternative dispute

---

[50]   D Rowat *The Ombudsman Plan* (1985) University Press of America pp 3, 49.
[51]   Sir John Robertson 'The Ombudsman Around the World' in International Ombudsman Institute and L Reif (eds) *The International Ombudsman Yearbook 1998* (1999) Kluwer Law International pp 114-115.
[52]   H Woolf *Protection of the Public – A New Challenge* (1990) Stevens p 87.
[53]   T Holland 'Legal Aid R.I.P.' (1999) International Legal Practitioner 24-28, at p 27.
[54]   However, ombudsmen schemes do not always overcome the problems associated with litigation. Although the problems of cost and complexity are often overcome, many ombudsman systems suffer from problems of delay.

resolution mechanism to the courts, because although litigation is theoretically possible, it may be inappropriate because of the small amount of money at stake. In the private sector schemes too, the ombudsmen often provide remedies where none would be available in the courts, because their remits go beyond issues of illegality.

The operating methods of ombudsmen also account for their success and popularity. Each scheme has a different way of operating, but they can all be characterised by two concepts — informality and flexibility. Ombudsmen must act fairly, but they are not constrained by rules of evidence. Their procedures are inquisitorial rather than adversarial. They can thus obtain evidence in ways that the courts are ill-equipped to do. They can attempt negotiated settlements, and can use conciliation techniques. This contrasts with the courts, where the procedure is often confrontational and adversarial, with the aim of producing a winner and a loser. Ombudsmen aim to achieve results acceptable to both parties. They also aim to be accessible and user-friendly. Ombudsmen also have more flexibility in providing remedies than the courts. Sometimes an apology is recommended as appropriate redress, sometimes some monetary compensation. In addition, and this is where their superiority over the courts is most evident, they can recommend improvements to administrative systems and procedures, in order to prevent recurrent problems.

Ombudsman Models

As we have seen, the ombudsman concept originated almost 200 years ago and its modern equivalents have been adapted to suit local conditions. They reveal a range of different types of institutions, varying from country to country, which is not surprising, given the different constitutional positions[55] into which the ombudsmen have to fit. Even within jurisdictions, there can be different types of ombudsmen, with varying operating methods and objectives. What this reveals is how remarkably flexible and adaptable the ombudsman concept has proved to be. Of course, whatever their differences, ombudsmen schemes have many common characteristics. It

---

[55]   For example, in Scandinavian countries, most of the administration is conducted through agencies rather than government departments. In Sweden public administration is 'subject to scant ministerial or parliamentary control' (see W Gellhorn *Ombudsmen and Others. Citizens' Protectors in Nine Countries* (1967) Harvard University Press p 197).

is, therefore, worth examining the different models which may exist for ombudsmen schemes. Ombudsmen are established to fulfil certain functions. Before any meaningful evaluation can be made of a scheme, the purpose for which it was established must be explored. For example, the system may be needed to provide an oversight function of already established procedures of control and redress. It may be an office that replicates existing redress mechanisms, but with more extensive powers to do so. Alternatively, it may be established to deal with matters outside the competence of the existing control and redress mechanisms. The functions for which the office is established will determine the model adopted, with corresponding powers and procedures.

Two main models, or ideal types, for ombudsmen systems have been identified: redress and control[56]. The primary function of a redress ombudsman is to offer and facilitate alternative dispute resolution. The control ombudsman's primary function is general supervision of state authorities, rather than the resolution of disputes. Redress model ombudsmen are created when the traditional means of redress are perceived to be insufficient. Thus, additional means are sought for the regulation of the relationship between the administration and the individual. This insufficiency could arise because the matters are not justiciable, or because of the obstacles inherent in the court process. Ombudsmen schemes adopting this model are often seen as advocates for citizens. Sometimes these ombudsmen are given powers to conduct own-initiative investigations, but this is an adjunct to their redress function. Own-initiative investigations are triggered by complaints, which draw attention to problems that need to be investigated on a large scale.

The control-type of ombudsman is fundamentally different. These schemes are created primarily to regulate the way standards are created and understood by a public authority. These ombudsmen therefore supervise the rules and the way they are interpreted. Their concern is with issues of supervision and accountability. For these ombudsmen, the ability to conduct own-initiative investigations is of major importance and complainants are informants only. Nor need there be any suspicion of a wrongful act in order for the ombudsmen to examine the functioning of the administration, as the focus is the prevention of administrative failures.

---

[56] See K Heede *European Ombudsman: redress and control at Union level* (2000) Kluwer Law International pp 79-112.

The concern of these ombudsmen is the general protection of fundamental rights and individual liberties.

Within these two ideal types, there are sub-sets. Control ombudsmen fall into three categories depending on the bodies they are established to investigate. They may focus on bodies which are not supervised by parliament; all bodies with public power; or the executive. Two types of redress ombudsmen are identified, depending on whether the ombudsman is to deal with cases that courts are not equipped to deal with, or whether the aim is to give remedies for non-legally enforceable rights. In the first of these models[57], the ombudsman is ensuring that all legal rights are enforceable in practice. The ombudsman conducts a legality review of administrative decisions. The latter[58] gives additional remedies where none were available before.

Every system creating an ombudsman will have to decide which function — control or redress — should predominate, and how it should relate to the existing means of redress. The model adopted will depend on whether the ombudsman is primarily concerned to provide redress or supervision of the state's activities. Of course, these models are ideal types. Schemes can and will have primary and secondary purposes, and ombudsmen systems utilise the best features of all the models, in order to fulfil their purposes.

What model best fits the UK public sector ombudsmen? These schemes would appear to conform to the second type of redress model, being established to provide redress for activity that is not susceptible to adjudication, and therefore not dealt with by the courts. For example, as we shall see, these ombudsmen deal with the classic examples of maladministration: rudeness, delay and poor advice. The ombudsmen create and enforce non-legally binding principles of good administrative behaviour. There are also elements of the first type of redress function within the system, as these ombudsmen do often address the legality of decisions. As we shall see, the Parliamentary Ombudsman, which was the model for the public sector ombudsman system in the UK, was set up to assist the Parliamentary process. It could therefore be argued that the

---

57 This is referred to as the 'discount alternative ombudsman' model by Heede (see p 101), as its aim is to lower the threshold of access to the judiciary.

58 This is referred to as the 'extra judicial ombudsman' model by Heede (see p 101), as here the ombudsman is giving remedies for non-legally enforceable rights.

system also has elements of the control model. However, the assistance it is intended to offer is to individual members of Parliament, in order to perform more effectively their grievance remedial function. In addition, the model of a parliamentary control ombudsman is based on the assumption that the ombudsman is supervised by the parliament. The UK public sector ombudsmen are subject to the supervisory jurisdiction of the courts, as their activities can be judicially reviewed.

The Danish Ombudsman

The United Kingdom Parliamentary Ombudsman draws to a large extent on the Danish model[59]. This was the model used for many other systems, including New Zealand, the first common law jurisdiction to establish an ombudsman. The Danish model has been described as 'the primary reference for all the subsequent parliamentary ombudsman plans in the world'[60]. Because of this, it may be worth examining some of its features. The Danish scheme was established in response to the fear that state interference in the daily lives of citizens was increasing. It was also felt that the courts were not appropriate to deal with this. The remit of the Danish ombudsman is the supervision of civil and military central government administration, apart from the courts. The jurisdiction covers ministers, civil servants and all other persons acting in the service of the state, except those engaged in judicial administration. Although the ombudsman can comment on the quality of administration, there is no power to change decisions, so he or she cannot overturn the results of poor administration.

There are a number of parallels with the Danish system and that of the UK. Firstly, like the UK, Denmark does not have a general competent administrative court to adjudicate on the merits of discretionary decisions taken by public bodies. It had been envisaged that these courts would be created alongside the ombudsman, but they were not. Again, this is what had been recommended for the UK[61]. As in the UK, the main argument

---

59 Although, while the Bill creating the Parliamentary Ombudsman in the UK was being debated in Parliament, ministers were at pains to deny that they were creating an ombudsman on the Scandinavian model.

60 K Heede *European Ombudsman: redress and control at Union level* (2000) Kluwer Law International p 25.

61 See Justice *The Citizen and the Administration: the Redress of Grievances* (1961) Stevens.

against setting up an ombudsman scheme in Denmark was that it could interfere with political processes, in particular, ministerial responsibility. Like the scheme in the UK, the Danish scheme was established to examine individual grievances from citizens about administrative practices. Its task is to ensure the protection of citizens' rights in the modern welfare state and to restore equality between citizens and state authorities. It is an institution that supervises administrative decisions, and is easily and freely accessible to citizens. The Danish ombudsman cannot overturn decisions, but can only express criticism and issue recommendations.

The Danish scheme, however, does differ in many ways from that in the UK. For example, the Danish ombudsman has the power to conduct own-initiative investigations, as well as responding to individual complaints[62]. The Danish ombudsman has a very wide remit, which includes central and local government and the police. Most of the work is concerned with examining the merits of decisions. The office operates as a quasi-administrative court, like a court of appeal against administrative decisions. Ombudsmen in the UK are prevented from examining the merits of decisions taken without maladministration. The Danish ombudsman however does not recommend compensatory measures, so the scheme is not used as a small claims court. This contrasts with the UK system where compensatory awards are often made. Thus, although both systems follow the redress model, they have many fundamentally different features.

The Role of Ombudsmen

The ombudsman institution, particularly one which is based on the redress model, has been described as 'primarily a client-oriented office, designed to secure individual justice in the administrative state'[63]. However, even these types of ombudsmen do not confine their work to addressing individual issues. The individual cases investigated may highlight weaknesses in procedures, practice, rules or attitudes. Ombudsmen are concerned that these administrative failures are rectified, to reduce the risk of the same mistakes being made in the future. Those who have not complained will also be helped by the process of uncovering wrongdoing and poor administration. As well as obtaining redress for the individual complainant, ombudsmen are thus concerned with improving public

---

[62] This power is used very rarely, making up only about 1% of the cases investigated.
[63] K Friedmann 'Realisation of ombudsman recommendations' (1988) *Fourth International Ombudsman Conference Papers* p 110.

administration, so that future injustice and maladministration will be prevented.

Ombudsmen therefore have two roles. They provide redress for individual grievances, but they are also concerned to improve standards[64]. Thus, an ombudsman is not merely an instrument of redress, but also has the function of quality control[65]. By investigating individual cases, ombudsmen may highlight more generalised weaknesses in practices, rules and attitudes. Uncovering these weaknesses is advantageous to individuals who have not complained, because the resulting improvement in the system is a generalised benefit. It is this 'orientation towards systems change' that prevents the ombudsman from being little more than 'a glorified complaint department'[66]. This ability to identify systemic problems is what makes ombudsmen such important mechanisms in remedying administrative defects. The two functions need not conflict. Indeed, it could be argued that anyone who handles complaints is only performing half the task if they are not using the casework function to provide feedback to the organisation concerned. This feedback can relate to improvements in the way the organisation deals with complaint handling internally, so that fewer cases need to involve the ombudsman. It can also relate to improvements in other procedures, where the complaints reveal a failure in the system.

Although there is no need for the two roles to conflict, and there is clearly strong linkage between the two, decisions have to be made about which functions should take precedence. This is important because the ombudsmen have to decide whether to devote their main energies into resolving individual cases, or to tackling the systemic faults in public administration which produce such cases. Most individual ombudsman

---

[64] In a worldwide survey of ombudsmen, conducted in 1988, 41 of 43 ombudsmen throughout the world said that one of their functions was to improve administrative practices. The same number included proposals for improving legislation and administrative rules as one of their functions. Indeed, only six respondents to the survey regarded the seeking of satisfactory action for the individual as their prime task. The majority (27) believed that this task was as important as ensuring that the authorities within their jurisdiction fulfilled their duties (W Haller 'The place of the ombudsman in the world community' (1988) *Fourth International Ombudsman Conference Papers* p 29).

[65] G Drewry 'The Ombudsman: Parochial Stopgap or Global Panacea?' in P Leyland and T Woods (eds) *Administrative Law Facing the Future: Old Constraints and New Horizons* (1997) Blackstone Press pp 88-89.

[66] E J Waxman and H Gadlin 'A Breed Apart' (1998) 4 Dispute Resolution Magazine 21-24, p 23.

cases have limited significance. On the other hand, ombudsmen can with justification be categorised as a 'deterrent to maladministration', and cumulatively their decisions 'help to propagate principles of good administrative practice'[67]. In view of this, it can be argued that ombudsmen should see their main task as seeking out systemic causes of injustice in a way courts and tribunals are ill-equipped to do[68]. Raising standards is the most appropriate way of improving the position of the consumers of public services in general. The resolving of individual disputes, while clearly of great importance, should be one of the means to this end, rather than an end in itself.

Ombudsmen in the UK see the dispute resolution function as being the primary role[69]. For example, the present Parliamentary Ombudsman notes that his 'primary objective is to obtain a remedy for those who have suffered injustice'; working to ensure good public administration is 'another important aim'[70]. The ombudsmen, quite rightly, emphasise the importance of the informal settlement of grievances. In these situations, if an acceptable settlement is reached, ombudsmen often consider that nothing further needs to be done on the issue in point. One ombudsman has remarked that in these cases it is 'unnecessary to draw further attention to the defect which has been discovered'[71]. However, although in these cases an individual complainant will be satisfied, there will not have been a thorough investigation of the authority's or department's procedures, which may have uncovered systemic defects.

Where ombudsmen identify injustice to individual citizens, then clearly the authority concerned should take heed by improving its administration, if only to ensure that the same circumstances do not recur. However, the public sector ombudsmen system in the UK has limitations in its function as a general panacea for bad administration. This is because there is no

---

[67]   G Drewry 'The Ombudsman: Parochial Stopgap or Global Panacea?' in P Leyland and T Woods (eds) *Administrative Law Facing the Future: Old Constraints and New Horizons* (1997) Blackstone Press p 83.

[68]   N Lewis *The Classical Ombudsmen* (1992) University of Sheffield p 4.

[69]   Indeed, the British and Irish Ombudsman Association, which will be discussed later in the chapter, defines the core role of an ombudsman as being 'to investigate and resolve, determine or make recommendations with regard to complaints against those whom the Ombudsman is empowered to investigate . . .' (*Rules of the Association*, sch 1, s B).

[70]   M Buckley 'The Parliamentary Ombudsman' (1998) 68 Adviser 6-8, p 7.

[71]   D Yardley 'Local Ombudsmen in England: Recent Trends and Developments' (1983) PL 522, p 526.

roving commission to investigate bad administration[72]. Action can only be taken when a specific individual complaint is made. If the primary function of the ombudsmen were to be administrative improvement, this could only be effectively achieved if the ombudsmen were given power to conduct investigations on their own volition, without the need for a complaint. Of course, this might result in a different relationship with public bodies, which might be happy to co-operate with individual grievance redress, but not so happy if the ombudsman had a roving commission to comment upon their procedures.

The UK model is basically one of compromise, with some attempt to improve procedures where possible. Indeed, it has been said that there has 'never been full agreement over the proper role and function' of the Parliamentary Ombudsman in the UK[73]. Although the Parliamentary Ombudsman was set up as a method of handling individual grievances, the rigour in which complaints were investigated militated against large numbers of complaints being addressed. If more complaints were to be dealt with, the quality of the investigation may suffer. This may make it more difficult to uncover systemic problems. This dilemma is made more difficult because there are differences of opinion as to how far the ombudsmen should be involved in improving administration. For example, some believe that an efficiency audit is a 'substantial function in its own right' which needs to be carried out by an ad hoc body rather than being 'tied to or seen as a spin-off benefit from investigation into individual complaints'[74]. On the other hand, it can be argued that one of the primary functions of an ombudsman is to seek out causes of injustice at the systemic level, in the way that a court of law could never do.

Harlow and Rawlings characterise the two different functions of ombudsmen in terms of fire-fighters and fire-watchers[75]. The fire-fighting

---

[72] Although, as we shall see in Chapter 2, the Parliamentary Ombudsman was given the same status as the Comptroller and Auditor General, it was never envisaged that the ombudsman would conduct audits of administrative procedures, in the same way that the Comptroller and Auditor General audits the accounts of government departments.

[73] C Harlow and R Rawlings *Law and Administration* (2nd edn, 1997) Butterworths p 427.

[74] V Moore 'Some Reflections of the Role of the Ombudsman' *International Institute of Administrative Sciences Conference Paper* (1991) p 13.

[75] C Harlow and R Rawlings *Law and Administration* (2nd edn, 1997) Butterworths pp 423-455.

role is similar to that of the courts, the ombudsman functioning as a small claims court, providing remedies for individual grievances. The fire-watching function is that of inspection and audit, and the ombudsman performs this role when conducting large-scale investigations about systemic problems. Ombudsmen perform both these functions. They resolve grievances (fire-fighting), but they take a more direct interest than the courts in stimulating administrative improvements (fire-watching). They perform their functions not only by making judgments and recommendations, but also by less formal negotiations or consultations.

The fire-fighting role of the UK public sector ombudsmen was largely set by the report which preceded the establishment of the Parliamentary Ombudsman[76]. This had recommended that an impartial officer should investigate and report on complaints of maladministration. It took a narrow, grievance redressing view of the function of an ombudsman, and did not even consider the objective of identifying and eradicating administrative inefficiency. Harlow has argued that the Parliamentary Ombudsman should adopt a more elitist, strategic role[77]. Her concern is that the exhaustive investigative process for complaints is wasted if the ombudsman is simply a small claims court. The fire-watching role could be made more effective if trivial complaints were filtered out, and the ombudsman reserved for the 'apex of a genuinely pyramidal structure'[78].

This approach would firmly establish the ombudsmen as mechanisms primarily intended to improve administration. Their role in the system of administrative justice would then principally be that of an independent and unattached investigator, with a mandate to identify maladministration, recommend improved procedures and ensure their implementation. The

---

[76]   Justice *The Citizen and the Administration: the Redress of Grievances* (1961) Stevens. More recently, the Select Committee on the Parliamentary Commissioner for Administration (as it then was) endorsed this view, considering that 'the investigation of the individual complaint should remain the priority of the Ombudsman's work' ((HC Paper 33-I (1993-94)) (The Powers, Work and Jurisdiction of the Ombudsman) para 10).

[77]   C Harlow 'Ombudsmen in Search of a Role' (1990) 53 MLR 745. The present Parliamentary Ombudsman has noted however that he needs a reasonable number of cases coming through the system in order to conduct an effective administrative audit.

[78]   C Harlow and R Rawlings *Law and Administration* (2nd edn, 1997) Butterworths p 455.

individual complaint would then become a mechanism which draws attention to more general administrative deficiencies. There are problems with this approach. First, if the complaint is unjustified, and hence rejected at an early stage, there will be no resulting administrative improvements. Also, as it relies on individuals complaining, it is a random and imperfect mechanism for highlighting administrative defects. In order to be effective in this aspect of their role, ombudsmen need the power to carry out investigations on their own initiative, without the need for an individual complaint. In fact, none of the public sector ombudsmen in the UK are empowered to conduct 'own initiative' investigations, and in this respect they are out of line with ombudsmen in other systems[79].

Public Sector Ombudsmen in the UK

Ombudsmen were introduced into the public sector in the UK in the 1960s and 1970s. Their emergence at this time was a result of the same concerns that caused their establishment worldwide. These included a growing awareness within government of public disquiet over the ability of the institutions of central and local government to handle and respond to complaints about their activities in a fair and responsive manner[80]. Britain's interest in the ombudsman concept is normally associated with an influential report by Justice in 1961[81]. This report resulted in the establishment of the Parliamentary Ombudsman in 1967, which formed the model on which the other public sector ombudsmen were based.

The ombudsman created in 1967 was very much a 'Parliamentary' ombudsman, whose remit was restricted to central government

---

[79] W Haller 'The place of the ombudsman in the world community' (1988) *Fourth International Ombudsman Conference Papers* pp 41-43. The Select Committee on the Parliamentary Commissioner for Administration has recommended that the Parliamentary Ombudsman be given the power to initiate investigations at the recommendation of the Select Committee ((HC Paper 33-I (1993-94)) (The Powers, Work and Jurisdiction of the Ombudsman) para 44). This suggestion has not been acted upon.

[80] P Birkinshaw *Grievances, Remedies and the State* (2nd edn, 1994) Sweet and Maxwell p 188.

[81] Justice *The Citizen and the Administration* (1961) Stevens. This is sometimes referred to as the Whyatt Report.

departments[82]. Local authorities were not within the remit, an exclusion that was widely criticised during the legislative process by members in both Houses of Parliament. It was not until 1974 that local authorities became the subject of ombudsman investigations, and then this was by means of the creation of a separate local government ombudsman scheme, rather than an extension of the Parliamentary Ombudsman's remit. Separate ombudsmen schemes were established for local government in Scotland, Wales and Northern Ireland. A separate Health Service Ombudsman scheme was established in 1973 to investigate administrative action by hospital authorities[83].

The system, having been in existence for over 30 years, is now experiencing problems. One of these problems is fragmentation. The schemes developed when complaints could be easily identified as being within the remit of a particular ombudsman. The legislation establishing the various schemes assumed that any publicly provided service would be the discrete responsibility of central government, local government or the National Health Service. This is no longer a valid assumption, and there are complaints which cross these jurisdictional boundaries. Public services are now being 'joined-up' and this has raised the question of whether ombudsmen should be joined-up too. Service delivery is now more fluid, with greater emphasis on partnerships, so as to achieve better assessment of client needs and the delivery of services to meet them. The present jurisdictions of the ombudsmen do not sit easily with this trend. Not only can it cause jurisdictional issues for the ombudsmen, but it can also cause confusion among complainants.

Devolution also compounds the confusion and problems. Before devolution, there were seven public sector ombudsmen in the UK[84]. After devolution, there were separate Health Service Commissioners for Wales,

---

[82]   A separate scheme was established for Northern Ireland.

[83]   Hospital authorities were excluded from the remit of the Parliamentary Ombudsman scheme. Since the inception of the Health Service Ombudsmen scheme the Parliamentary Ombudsman has combined this role with that of the Health Service Ombudsman for England, Wales and Scotland.

[84]   The Parliamentary Ombudsman, who is also the Health Service Commissioner; three Local Government Ombudsmen for England, one for Wales and one for Scotland; the Northern Ireland Parliamentary Commissioner for Administration, who is also the Commissioner for Complaints.

Scotland and England[85], and additional ombudsmen for the Scottish Parliament and Welsh Assembly[86]. The United Kingdom Parliamentary Ombudsman still has jurisdiction over all central government departmental functions in England, and reserved matters[87] in the devolved administrations. The situation is ripe for confusion and overlap.

There are now proposals to address both the problems of fragmentation, and the confusion caused by the arrangements after devolution. The ombudsman system in England was the subject of a review by the Cabinet Office[88]. That review, which reported in April 2000, proposed that the three schemes in England (the Parliamentary, Local Government and Health Service Ombudsmen) should be integrated to form one ombudsman service. This can only be achieved by legislation, and although the proposals have been welcomed in all quarters[89], legislation is not anticipated before 2003[90]. A similar review was carried out in Scotland, with similar proposals for an

---

[85] At present these offices are held by the same person, who is also the Westminster Parliamentary Commissioner, but reports are made separately to the Westminster and Scottish Parliaments and the Welsh Assembly.

[86] Transitional arrangements provide for these duties to be performed by the Parliamentary Ombudsman until new arrangements are put in place.

[87] Matters reserved for the Westminster Parliament include defence, foreign affairs and taxation.

[88] *Review of the Public Sector Ombudsmen in England* (2000) a report by the Cabinet Office, conducted by P Collcutt and M Hourihan. The review was announced in the White Paper *Modernising Government* Cm 4310 (1999). A consultation paper based on the review was issued in June 2000 (*Review of the Public Sector Ombudsmen in England: A Consultation Paper* (2000)). For a discussion, see M Seneviratne '"Joining up" the Ombudsmen – the Review of the Public Sector Ombudsmen in England' (2000) PL 582-591; B Thompson 'Integrated Ombudsmanry: Joined-up to a Point' (2001) MLR 459-467; D Lewis and R James 'Joined-up Justice: review of the Public Sector Ombudsman in England' (2000) 4 International Ombudsman Yearbook 109-140. See also M Seneviratne 'Ombudsmen 2000' (2000) 9(1) Nottingham Law Journal 13-24.

[89] It was welcomed by the public sector ombudsmen in England. The Select Committee on Public Administration subsequently reviewed the Collcutt report and proposed further changes (see (HC Paper 612 (1999-2000)) (Review of Public Sector Ombudsmen in England)).

[90] The government announced in July 2001 that it intended to introduce legislation to rationalise the three public sector ombudsmen in England, in response to a Parliamentary question (see Written Answers by the Deputy Prime Minister, 20 July 2001). Consultations are now taking place in order to progress the matter, but it is unlikely that there will be a Bill for the next session of Parliament. It may be after 2004 before the necessary legislation is forthcoming.

integrated system[91]. There, however, legislation has now been passed[92] and its implementation is in process. There is also to be a review of the systems in Wales and Northern Ireland. These proposals, taken as a whole, will have far reaching consequences for the ombudsman system in the UK.

Protection of the 'Ombudsman' Title

Another matter of concern to the ombudsman community in the UK is the use of the term 'ombudsman'. This term is not used in the statutory title of the public sector ombudsmen[93] in the UK[94]. Their title usually includes the word 'commissioner', and this is so 'whether or not there is a corresponding Commission'[95]. The term 'ombudsman', however, is readily understood, and it was used for all the schemes in the private sector. The hybrid schemes, established by statute, sometimes use the term. For example, the word 'ombudsman' is used in the legislation establishing the Legal Services Ombudsman[96], and the recently established Financial Ombudsman Service[97]. The Pensions Ombudsman is referred to in the statute[98] as a 'commissioner to be known as the Pensions Ombudsman'. This has caused the comment that 'the draftsman apparently could not quite bring himself to abandon the hallowed word'[99].

---

[91]   There are however important differences in the type of integrated system envisaged. See M Seneviratne '"Joining Up" the Scottish Ombudsmen' (2002) 24(1) JSWFL 89-98.

[92]   Scottish Public Services Ombudsman Act 2002.

[93]   The Select Committee on the Parliamentary Commissioner for Administration recommended that at the earliest opportunity, the relevant statutes be amended to refer to the 'Parliamentary Ombudsman' and 'Health Service Ombudsman' ((HC Paper 33-I (1993-94)) (The Powers, Work and Jurisdiction of the Ombudsman) para 26).

[94]   Scotland is now the exception, the new Act referring to the 'Public Services Ombudsman'. Northern Ireland also has an Assembly Ombudsman, but originally the office was called the Northern Ireland Parliamentary Commissioner for Administration. The other public sector ombudsmen are popularly known as 'ombudsmen' and any future legislation will need to address this issue.

[95]   M Buckley 'Remedies, Redress and "Calling to Account": Some Myths about the Parliamentary Commissioner for Administration' (1998) Denning Law Journal 29-47, p 29.

[96]   Courts and Legal Services Act 1990.

[97]   This was established by the Financial Services and Markets Act 2000.

[98]   Pensions Schemes Act 1993, s 145(1).

[99]   M Buckley 'Remedies, Redress and "Calling to Account": Some Myths about the Parliamentary Commissioner for Administration' (1998) Denning Law Journal 29-47, p 29, fn 1.

The proliferation of ombudsman schemes, particularly in the private sector in the 1980s, focused attention on the characteristics which must be displayed by complaint-handling schemes before they were deemed to be worthy of the title. There was concern about how far the ombudsmen in the private sector displayed the necessary characteristics of an ombudsman and whether the existence of ombudsmen beyond the public sector represented a strengthening or dilution of the concept. In New Zealand, a law was passed restricting the use of the title to the Parliamentary ombudsman there. There are no such restrictions in the UK, although there have been calls to restrict its use[100]. In 1991, the United Kingdom Ombudsman conference discussed the characteristics of the public sector, or classical, ombudsmen. It was accepted that it was:

> an office created by statute, reporting to the legislature, with tenure, accessible to the citizen, with powers of discovery, protected by privilege, and with powers to investigate and make recommendations.[101]

It was thought that ombudsmen in the private sphere should have as many as possible of the characteristics of the classical ombudsmen. That is, they should be created by statute and be independent of the body investigated, and there should be ease of access for complainants. They should have powers to investigate, the ability to make recommendations and the moral if not the legal authority to secure redress. Without these characteristics, the ombudsman becomes at best an institutional trouble-shooter and at worst an extension of the normal public relations activity of an organisation[102].

Following this conference, a working party[103] was set up to agree criteria for the use of the term 'ombudsman'. Four key criteria were identified:

[100] The Select Committee on the Parliamentary Commissioner for Administration recommended that the term 'ombudsman' should not be used to describe complaints officers if that body came within the jurisdiction of any statutory ombudsman ((HC Paper 33-I (1993-94)) (The Powers, Work and Jurisdiction of the Ombudsman) para 28). The Consumers Association also noted that the ombudsman title needed protection to ensure that it was only used by bodies meeting strict independence criteria (*Ombudsmen* (1997) p 25).

[101] M Hayes 'Emerging issues for ombudsmen' (1991) *United Kingdom Ombudsman Conference Paper* p 5.

[102] M Hayes 'Emerging issues for ombudsmen' (1991) *United Kingdom Ombudsman Conference Paper* p 6.

[103] The working party consisted of five members: the Secretary of the Commission for Local Administration, the Scottish Local Government Ombudsman, the Director of the National Consumer Council, an academic and the Banking Ombudsman, who chaired the group.

independence from those investigated, effectiveness, fairness and public accountability. In order to be effective, the ombudsman should be accessible, the right to complain should be adequately publicised, and those complaining should be able to do so free of charge. Ombudsmen should have adequate powers of investigation, with the ability to make recommendations. Where ombudsmen do not possess the authority to make binding awards, they should have the moral authority to secure redress. In other words, there should be a reasonable expectation that those investigated would comply with the ombudsman's decisions. Independence is a very important characteristic of ombudsman schemes. Ombudsmen in the UK do not see their role as consumer champions, or complainants' advocates. It is the fact that they are impartial that gives them their authority, and the respect of those who are the subject of their investigations.

It was also suggested by the working party that an association be set up, with the main task of ensuring that the currency of the title 'ombudsman' was not devalued. As a result, in 1993, the British and Irish Ombudsman Association (BIOA) was formed[104], on a self-regulatory basis, originally with 14 members. It is an unincorporated association with a small secretariat, and it is funded by subscriptions from members. There are different categories of membership. Full voting membership is restricted to those ombudsman schemes that meet the criteria set out by the BIOA. There is a category of 'ordinary' membership, which is for individuals who are, or have been, office holders, employees or officers of a voting member scheme. In addition, there are three classes of corporate associate membership. Category A is for trade and professional associations and category B is for consumer organisations. Category C is for complaint handling bodies, and it includes those organisations which do not qualify as 'proper' ombudsmen, because they do not possess all the criteria outlined above[105]. There is a further category for individual members, who typically are academics, consumer representatives, or individuals who belong to schemes which are not voting members.

---

[104]   It was originally set up as the United Kingdom Ombudsman Association, the name being changed in 1994, following the inclusion of three ombudsman schemes from the Irish Republic as members.

[105]   As will be seen later, this includes the Prisons and Probation Ombudsman, because he lacks conspicuous independence and the office is also subject to the jurisdiction of the Parliamentary Ombudsman.

There are voting members of the BIOA who carry out ombudsman functions but do not bear the name 'ombudsman'[106] or even 'commissioner'. For example, the organisation dealing with complaints against the police in England and Wales is the Police Complaints Authority[107]. This is unlike the organisation in Northern Ireland, which does use the title 'ombudsman'. This variety of nomenclature may cause confusion, and it has been suggested that any organisation or individual admitted to full membership of the British and Irish Ombudsman Association should be required to take the title 'ombudsman'[108].

Evaluating Ombudsman Schemes: the BIOA Criteria

The criteria set out by the BIOA for ombudsman schemes are aimed at ensuring that such schemes are effective. Of prime importance is independence. One of the great strengths of ombudsman schemes is the impartial investigation of grievances. Therefore, an ombudsman must be independent of the executive and any partisan influence. This independence can be safeguarded in a number of ways. For example, the jurisdiction, powers and method of appointment of an ombudsman should be a matter of public knowledge. Those who appoint the ombudsman should be independent of those who will be subject to investigation, and the appointment must not be subject to premature termination apart from incapacity, misconduct or other good cause. The office should be adequately staffed and financed. Only if the office of a public sector ombudsman is seen to be independent will there be increased public confidence in public administration, and a reassurance for the public that official wrongs when discovered will be corrected.

In order to be effective, the ombudsman must have adequate powers of investigation and as wide a jurisdictional coverage as possible. Ideally, there should be an ombudsman to cover all types of administrative agencies and all levels of government[109]. There should be the right to require the

---

[106] This is true of the public sector ombudsmen, but they are known unofficially by the title 'ombudsman'.

[107] As will be seen in Chapter 8, this is to be renamed the Independent Police Complaints Commission.

[108] J Farrand *Symposium on Consumer Redress* (1995) Office of Fair Trading.

[109] D Rowatt *The Ombudsman Plan* (1985) University Press of America p 183.

production of all the relevant information and documents to ensure that a thorough examination of the case can be made.

The ombudsman should be able to ensure that there is an effective remedy where administrative shortcomings are found. The public sector ombudsmen in the UK do not make legally binding decisions, but only recommendations[110]. This is not out of line with ombudsmen worldwide, and it is thought that if there were decision-making powers, the institution would become 'entirely and radically different'[111]. If the ombudsman's recommendations are not legally binding, there should be a reasonable expectation that there should be compliance with them, and where there is non-compliance this should be publicised.

Another requirement for an effective ombudsman scheme is accessibility. There is differential use of ombudsmen throughout the world, but in essence 'almost everywhere in the world it is a free public service available at no cost to the complainant'[112]. One of the great advantages of an ombudsman over other methods of grievance redress is the fact of easy access. The procedures adopted by the ombudsmen must be such that complainants can use them easily. Care should be taken when imposing particular requirements (for example, that complaints must be in writing) to ensure that they do not present unreasonable obstacles for complainants.

As well as being easily accessible, in order to be effective the ombudsman should be widely known among the general public, and ombudsmen must make every effort to publicise their services. Ombudsmen worldwide are afflicted by the scarcity of public resources, and it is claimed that they 'cannot be as active as they would like in outreach programmes'[113]. Ombudsmen may be reluctant to publicise their services for fear of being overloaded with complaints, and thus subject to the same kinds of delay and bureaucracy that they are supposed to be curing in the administration. If this is so, mechanisms must be found to rectify this, as otherwise the institution, by default, could become another middle class instrument, rarely

---

[110]   As we shall see in Chapter 7, this is not the situation in Northern Ireland.
[111]   K Friedman 'Realisation of Ombudsmen Recommendations' (1988) *Fourth International Ombudsman Conference Papers* p 128.
[112]   V Moore 'Some Reflections of the Role of the Ombudsman' (1991) *International Institute of Administrative Sciences Conference Paper* p 6.
[113]   G E Caiden 'The Challenge of Change' (1988) *Fourth International Ombudsman Conference Papers* p 7.

used by the disadvantaged and powerless in society. Where there is ignorance about the work of ombudsmen, serious consideration should be given to raising their profile, by means of outreach work and advertising.

Conclusion

Ombudsmen are a feature of modern life. From its origins in Sweden, the ombudsman concept has proliferated around the world. This 200-year-old institution has developed into new territories from its origins in the establishment of an officer appointed by one pole of government, the legislature, to handle complaints against the other poles, administrative and judicial action. Its modern equivalents have adapted to suit local conditions. The ombudsmen themselves, and their operating methods and objectives, vary from country to country, which is not surprising, given their different constitutional positions. The concept has proved to be flexible and versatile, adapting to suit local conditions and the task it is required to perform.

The institutions established for the public sector ombudsmen schemes in the UK were themselves an adaptation of the Swedish model, designed to fit the particular constitutional arrangements. One noteworthy feature of the system in the UK is that there is no overall ombudsman scheme for the public sector. The system has developed piecemeal, to rectify gaps as particular needs were perceived and as circumstances allowed. This presents some difficulties with evaluating the system. Individual schemes may be effective, but the system as a whole may not. Problems of evaluation are not new. In 1976 Danet, noting the need for an empirical method for the evaluation of the ombudsman's role, admitted that such evaluations were difficult because the 'vagueness of goals' of ombudsmen systems led to 'difficulties in specifying criteria to evaluate effectiveness'[114].

In this book, each of the public sector ombudsman schemes discussed will be evaluated in terms of the criteria established by the BIOA for the recognition of ombudsman schemes: independence from those investigated; effectiveness; fairness; and accountability. Each scheme will also be evaluated in terms of its fitness for the purpose for which it was

---

[114] B Danet 'Toward a Method to Evaluate the Ombudsman Role' (1978) 10(3) Administration and Society 335-370 p 341.

established, and its purpose in the changed context in which it now exists. The system as a whole will then be examined to evaluate how effective it is, and how effective it may become as a result of the proposals for reforms. Before each of the schemes is examined, the following two chapters will look in more detail at the special features of the public sector ombudsman system in the UK, and will examine its role in delivering administrative justice for citizens as consumers of public services.

Chapter 2

Ombudsmen and administrative justice

As we have seen, the growth of ombudsman schemes in both the public and private sectors has been a feature of modern life. They emerged in the public sector in the UK in the 1960s and 1970s, amid concerns about the inadequacies of the available mechanisms for the redress of grievances against the administration. The ombudsmen were therefore established to provide remedies for administrative wrongs, in particular to address the gaps in the system of administrative justice that existed at the time. This chapter will outline the development of the public sector ombudsman system in the UK, and discuss some of its essential features. It will also indicate its relationship to other mechanisms available for securing administrative justice.

The Origins of the United Kingdom Ombudsmen

The origins of the public sector ombudsmen[1] is normally traced to the report by Justice[2] in 1961[3], which was instrumental in establishing the office of

---

[1]   For a discussion of the background to the ombudsman's proposals see G Marshall 'The United Kingdom' and L Blom-Cooper 'The Case for an Ombudsman' both in D C Rowat (ed) *The Ombudsman: Citizens Defender* (1968) George Allen and Unwin.

[2]   Justice has been 'the most prominent and influential of the pressure groups to campaign for an Ombudsman in Britain' (F Stacey *The British Ombudsman* (1971) Clarendon Press p 28).

[3]   Justice *The Citizen and the Administration: the Redress of Grievances* (1961) Stevens. It is sometimes referred to as the Wyatt Report.

the Parliamentary Ombudsman[4] in 1967. The inquiry by Justice was set up as a result of the feeling that the arrangements that existed for redressing grievances or remedying maladministration were inadequate[5]. These inadequacies had previously been highlighted by the Franks Committee on Administrative Tribunals and Inquiries[6], which had reported in 1957. The Franks Committee had itself been established because of the crisis of public confidence that resulted from the Crichel Down affair in the 1950s. That affair 'exposed a world of administrative policy and decision-making apparently immune from political and parliamentary controls'[7]. Briefly[8], it concerned land acquired before the 1939–45 war by the Air Ministry for use as a bombing range, which was later transferred to the Ministry of Agriculture. The Ministry then tried to let it as a single unit to a tenant, rather than offering it to its original owners to buy back. The original owners' objections resulted in a public inquiry.

As a consequence of the affair, the government set up the Franks inquiry, to review the procedure in tribunals and inquiries. Its remit was to inquire into disputes where formal machinery for appeal or review already existed, and to suggest improvements in that machinery. This remit had the effect of confining the inquiry to an examination of existing appeal and review mechanisms. It was not therefore able to inquire into the wider problem of effective machinery for citizen grievances against public authorities, where there was no appeal to an administrative tribunal. The Franks report noted the redress mechanisms available for complaints by citizens. Some could be referred to the ordinary courts; some could be dealt with by tribunals set up under statute; and some could be referred to a minister after a special procedure had been followed. However, the report drew attention to the fact that 'over most of the field of public administration' there was no formal

---

4   The title used in the Parliamentary Commissioner Act 1967 is the Parliamentary Commissioner for Administration. The office holder has subsequently become popularly known as the Parliamentary Ombudsman.

5   K C Wheare *Maladministration and its Remedies* (1973) Stevens p 112. See also J D B Mitchell 'Administrative Law and Parliamentary Control' (1967) 38(4) Political Quarterly 360–374.

6   *Report of the Committee on Administrative Tribunals and Enquiries* (Cm 218, 1957).

7   C Harlow and R Rawlings *Law and Administration* (2nd edn, 1997) Butterworths p 76.

8   For details see J Griffith 'The Crichel Down Affair' (1955) 18 MLR 557.

procedure for 'objecting or deciding on objections'[9]. Although the Franks report contained extensive proposals for the improvement of inquiry and tribunal procedures, it provided no answers to the problem of grievances which had no remedy in the existing administrative or court processes.

It was to deal with this gap in procedures that the Justice inquiry was set up. Its terms of reference were to:

> inquire into the adequacy of the existing means for investigating complaints against administrative acts or decisions of Government Departments and other public bodies, where there is no tribunal or other statutory procedure available for dealing with the complaints; and to consider possible improvements to such means, with particular reference to the Scandinavian institution known as the Ombudsman.

The inadequacies of the existing system were not difficult to discover. The use of the courts in the form of judicial review was considered too limited. Not only was expense an issue, but the procedure did not cover maladministration, that is, where an administrative authority fails to act in accordance with proper standards of administrative conduct. Parliamentary procedures were considered ineffective. The use of such methods as adjournment debates and Parliamentary questions to control the executive were identified as uneven contests, as only the executive possessed all the relevant information. Ad hoc inquiries were little used, which was not surprising given that this was an elaborate and costly procedure, unsuited to everyday matters.

Justice proposed two reforms to remedy the inadequacies, and in doing so drew a distinction between maladministration and disputes about the merits of decisions. For the latter, Justice concluded that there was substantial scope for subjecting a large number of administrative decisions involving discretion to some kind of appeal. Thus, new specialised tribunals and a general tribunal were proposed, to provide a forum for challenging administrative decisions. The other proposal was for the appointment of an ombudsman, to act as a check on discretionary power, without being an appeal on the merits of discretionary decisions. The ombudsman was therefore to deal with complaints of maladministration. This proposed institution was not to be 'simply the "watchdog" of the public nor the

---

[9] *Report of the Committee on Administrative Tribunals and Enquiries* (Cm 218, 1957) para 10.

apologist of the administration', but 'the independent holder of the highest standards of efficient and fair administration'[10].

An appropriate model for such a new institution was sought. This was found in the Comptroller and Auditor General, an office established by the Exchequer and Audit Act 1866, with the primary function of auditing the accounts of government departments and certifying them correct or otherwise. She or he is independent of government and exercises control in financial matters, in effect investigating financial maladministration. It was recommended therefore that the ombudsman should have the same status[11]. Like the Comptroller and Auditor General, the ombudsman would be answerable to Parliament, but independent of the executive. Despite the identification with the Comptroller and Auditor General, the Justice Committee did not envisage the ombudsman acting as an auditor general or government inspector. Rather, Justice saw the ombudsman's role as more on the lines of an 'administrative small claims court'[12]. A Parliamentary officer was chosen as the model to assuage the fears of members of Parliament and ministers. Justice was aware that members might see the ombudsman as usurping their traditional role as grievance mechanisms, and that ministers might see the office as a threat to the doctrine of ministerial responsibility. It was for this reason that the proposal was modelled on a system that supported and strengthened the Parliamentary process[13].

---

[10] Justice *The Citizen and the Administration* (1961) Stevens p 77. This would seem to suggest a 'control' type of ombudsman, as discussed in Chapter 1. However, in reality, Justice placed more emphasis on the redress aspects of the office, rather than the auditing and inspectorate ones.

[11] Although having the same status, the analogy between the two offices is not entirely accurate. The Auditor General does not investigate the grievances of individual citizens and investigations are not dependent on citizen's complaints or on MP referrals. On the other hand, the Parliamentary Ombudsman cannot investigate administrative systems, except within the context of an individual complaint (see M Buckley 'Remedies, Redress and "Calling to Account": Some Myths about the Parliamentary Commissioner for Administration' (1998) Denning Law Journal 29–47 p 38). In addition, the Comptroller and Auditor General is in 'no way an adversary, but rather an ally of departments', whereas the Parliamentary Ombudsman's role is to investigate 'a charge against the department' (J D B Mitchell 'The Ombudsman Fallacy' (1962) PL 24–33, p 28).

[12] C Harlow and R Rawlings *Law and Administration* (2nd edn, 1997) Butterworths p 428.

[13] See A Le Sueur and M Sunkin *Public Law* (1997) Longman p 411.

Establishing the Ombudsman

These proposals were fairly modest[14], but were nevertheless rejected by the Conservative government at the time on the grounds that they were a threat to the Parliamentary system, and would undermine the ability of the government to govern efficiently. It was felt that to accept the recommendations would 'seriously interfere with the prompt and efficient despatch of public business'[15]. The succeeding Labour government[16], however, had committed itself to the proposal in its election manifesto. This had promised to 'humanise the whole administration of the state' and to set up the new office of Parliamentary Ombudsman 'with the right and duty to investigate and expose any misuse of government power as it affects the citizen'[17]. Although pledged to introduce this reform, the Labour administration did experience difficulties in introducing the legislation. This was despite the fact that the White Paper[18] had emphasised that the office was intended to enforce the existing constitutional arrangements for protecting individuals, rather than to create a new institution that would erode the function of members of Parliament as grievance mechanisms[19].

When the Bill was being debated in Parliament, ministers were at pains to deny that they were creating an ombudsman on the Scandinavian model[20],

---

[14]   The 'unnecessarily conservative proposals' of the Justice Report attempted to make the scheme 'more palatable to members who feared loss of contact with their constituents' (D C Rowat *The Ombudsman Plan* (2nd edn, 1985) University Press of America p 135).

[15]   666 HC Official Report col 1124.

[16]   Although it was the Labour government that showed such commitment, there appears to be 'no necessary connection between left of centre political attitudes and support for the idea of an Ombudsman' (F Stacey *The British Ombudsman* (1971) Clarendon Press p 37).

[17]   *Let's Go with Labour for a New Britain* Manifesto for the 1964 General Election (1964) p 3.

[18]   *The Parliamentary Comr for Administration* (Cm 2767, 1965).

[19]   See, for example, the White Paper (Cmnd 2767, 1965) para 4, which states: 'In Britain, Parliament is the place for ventilating the grievances of the citizen … It is one of the functions of the elected Member of Parliament to try to secure that his constituents do not suffer injustice at the hands of the Government … We shall give Members of Parliament a better instrument which they can use to protect the citizen, namely, the services of a Parliamentary Commissioner for Administration'.

[20]   See, for example, 734 HC Official Report col 49 (18 October 1966), where Mr Richard Crossman said: 'I want to start by repudiating a notion . . . that in this Bill we are borrowing from other countries and trying to force into our British

and the emphasis was upon the ombudsman's Parliamentary context[21]. Members of Parliament were to refer cases to the ombudsman, who would investigate and report back to them and the House of Commons[22]. As a result, the ombudsman scheme introduced in Britain was transformed from a public institution readily and directly available to the citizen. Instead, it became a 'wholly Parliamentary institution, in essence an instrument at the disposal of M.P.s and designed to help them carry out more effectively their traditional functions on behalf of the citizen'[23]. The office is not a citizen's friend and protector, as it is in Scandinavia and New Zealand[24].

An important feature of the Parliamentary Ombudsman system, and one that reinforced its Parliamentary context, was the establishment of a Parliamentary select committee to oversee its work. This was established in 1967, as the Select Committee on the Parliamentary Commissioner for Administration, its remit being to examine the reports of the ombudsman and any matters in connection with them. In 1997, the committee was merged with the former Public Services Committee of the House of Commons to form a new Public Administration select committee[25]. The select committee does not re-investigate cases, but has the power to obtain evidence from civil servants and others, and to call for papers and records. It can also appoint people with technical knowledge to supply information or to elucidate matters of complexity. Its remit is confined to the work of the Parliamentary and Health Service ombudsmen, and it has no jurisdiction over the work of the Local Government Ombudsmen[26].

---

constitutional mould the notion of the Ombudsman which has been the pride of Sweden for 150 years'. See also, M Buckley 'Remedies, Redress and "Calling to Account": Some Myths about the Parliamentary Commissioner for Administration' (1998) Denning Law Journal 29–47.

[21]   '. . . we have decided unequivocally that the Parliamentary Commissioner must remain permanently a servant of the House' (Mr Crossman, 734 HC Official Report col 49 (18 October 1966)).

[22]   The Commissioner was to be 'an extremely sharp and piercing instrument of investigation' for establishing facts and reporting them to the referring MP (Mr Crossman, 734 HC Official Report, col 60 (18 October 1966)).

[23]   R Gregory and P Hutchesson *The Parliamentary Ombudsman. A Study in the Control of Administrative Action* (1975) George Allen & Unwin p 88.

[24]   R Gregory and P Hutchesson p 137.

[25]   The extended remit now covers matters relating to the quality and standards of administration provided by civil service departments, and of the civil service more generally.

[26]   When there was direct rule in Northern Ireland, it also had oversight over the work of the Northern Ireland Parliamentary Ombudsman.

Within its remit, the select committee was left to establish its own role[27]. Its work has tended to focus on examining the extent to which the ombudsman's recommendations are being implemented in departments[28], and the effects of the investigations on administration within the departments. If a department refused to follow the ombudsman's recommendation, the select committee would report this to Parliament. The fact that there is this power, and that the ombudsman commands the support of the select committee, has resulted in a situation where departments have been reluctant to ignore recommendations[29]. Where the ombudsman has found faults in the operation of an administrative system, the select committee has conducted an examination of the department concerned to see what steps had been taken to identify and remedy the defects. More generally, the select committee has addressed the issue of whether the ombudsman's powers of investigation should be strengthened or jurisdiction widened, generally tending to favour a widening of jurisdiction and a strengthening of powers[30].

There is a general consensus that the establishment of the select committee has been very valuable, and that it has enhanced the effectiveness of the ombudsman. Successive ombudsmen have 'greatly valued the select committee connection'[31]. In any new, integrated ombudsman system, the role of the select committee will need to be addressed, as at present the

[27]   P Birkinshaw *Grievances Remedies and the State* (2nd edn, 1994) Sweet and Maxwell p 205.

[28]   It seems that the select committee has given sufficient support to the ombudsman when departments have raised difficulties about implementing recommendations. An early success was in 1975, when the government was persuaded to change the law to allow the Inland Revenue to pay interest on tax which had been overpaid after there had been some delay in its repayment.

[29]   Justice recognised the important work of the select committee in bringing pressure on departments to conform to the ombudsman's recommendations (*Administrative Justice: Some Necessary Reforms* (1988) Clarendon Press p 87).

[30]   For example, the select committee has encouraged the ombudsman to take a broad view of the concept of maladministration. It has however had little success in persuading the government to broaden jurisdiction, and some of its recommendations are ignored. One success was the recommendation that over 50 non-departmental public bodies should be included within the ombudsman's jurisdiction (*Fourth Report of the Select Committee on the Parliamentary Comr for Administration* (HC Paper 619 (1983–84)). This recommendation was substantially implemented by the Parliamentary and Health Service Commissioners Act 1987.

[31]   P Giddings 'The Parliamentary Ombudsman: a successful alternative?' in D Oliver and G Drewry (eds) *The Law and Parliament* (1998) Butterworths p 135.

committee has no remit in connection with the work of the Local Government Ombudsman[32]. Surprisingly, the review of the public sector ombudsmen in England[33] makes no recommendations in relation to this, although it did recommend that the integrated ombudsman system be accountable to Parliament. The ombudsmen themselves have suggested that the new integrated body should be answerable to a select committee for the general conduct of its activities, but not in relation to the investigation of individual complaints[34].

The Function of the Ombudsman

The public sector ombudsman system originally established in Britain thus differed from the Scandinavian model. The Parliamentary Ombudsman scheme was set up as an adjunct to Parliament, rather than as an agency independent of political and administrative regimes. It was to be 'a new and powerful weapon with a sharp cutting edge to be added to the existing antiquated armoury of parliamentary questions and adjournment debates'[35]. The office was designed to improve the process whereby members of Parliament acted to redress citizens' grievances. This Parliamentary function was emphasised by the requirement that the Parliamentary Ombudsman could only investigate complaints referred by a member of Parliament[36].

The ombudsman system was established to deal with complaints about poor administration. The Justice report had drawn a distinction between these complaints and those concerning the merits of decisions. The

---

[32]   There have always been sensitivities about a Parliamentary committee having jurisdiction in relation to the work of local government.

[33]   *Review of the Public Sector Ombudsmen in England* (2000) Cabinet Office.

[34]   *Review of the Public Sector Ombudsmen in England* p 83. See also M Buckley 'Remedies, Redress and "Calling into Account": Some Myths about the Parliamentary Commissioner for Administration' (1998) Denning Law Journal 29–47, p 47.

[35]   G Drewry and C Harlow 'A Cutting Edge? The Parliamentary Commissioner and MPs' (1990) 53 MLR 745–769, p 746.

[36]   Justice had recommended that complaints be filtered in this way, but the 'filter' was seen as experimental, and was to be reviewed after five years. The original proposal had also included members of the House of Lords as having the power to refer complaints (*The Citizen and the Administration: the Redress of Grievances* (1961) Stevens pp 75–76). The latter proposal was never taken up.

ombudsman's remit was confined to maladministration. Thus, the function of the Parliamentary Ombudsman is the investigation of complaints (from members of Parliament) that citizens have suffered injustice as a result of maladministration by public authorities. Remedies are only provided where injustice has been caused by maladministration, and the ombudsman cannot investigate complaints about the merits of decisions or policy matters[37]. It is worth noting that Justice had also recommended the setting up of a comprehensive system of administrative tribunals, so that there could be impartial adjudication of the merits of administrative decisions. As this was never done, there is no general appeal on the merits of such decisions to complement the ombudsman's role.

The ombudsman system, as originally conceived, was therefore essentially to provide remedies for maladministration, rather than to adjudicate legal claims or appeals against the merits of discretionary decisions. The Act establishing the Parliamentary Ombudsman makes this distinction very clear. The ombudsman is empowered to investigate complaints arising out of 'injustice in consequence of maladministration in connection with . . . action taken by or on behalf of a government department or authority in the exercise of administrative functions'[38]. The ombudsman is not authorised or required 'to question the merits of a decision taken without maladministration'[39]. There is a similar provision in the legislation establishing the Local Government Ombudsmen[40]. The Health Service Ombudsman was given a wider frame of reference in the legislation establishing this office. This ombudsman can investigate 'an alleged failure in a service' or 'an alleged failure . . . to provide a service' where the complainant has suffered injustice or hardship as a result of this failure or as a result of maladministration[41].

---

[37] Although, as we shall see, the Health Service Ombudsman does have a wider remit.

[38] Parliamentary Commissioner Act 1967, s 5(1).

[39] Parliamentary Commissioner Act 1967, s 12(3). Marshall notes that this section might 'Conceivably . . . be understood to imply that he *may* question the merits of a decision that does embody maladministration, the maladministration being precisely its injustice and lack of merits. Clearly, however, in the light of the Wyatt Committee discussions and the White Paper that was not the intention' ('Maladministration' (1973) PL 32–44, p 33).

[40] Local Government Act 1974, s 34(3).

[41] National Health Services Reorganisation Act 1973, s 115.

Maladministration

The primary task of the public sector ombudsmen is to investigate allegations of maladministration[42]. Justice had recommended that the ombudsman's jurisdiction be limited to maladministration but had admitted that the term was 'not one of precise meaning'. It had also confessed that, from the communications received during the course of its inquiry, there was 'considerable confusion as to what matters fall within its scope'[43]. Maladministration is the key concept in the system of public sector ombudsmen, and its meaning is crucially important. The Justice report concluded that it should cover situations where 'an administrative authority has failed to discharge the duties of its office in accordance with proper standards of administrative conduct'[44].

Despite its use in the statutes establishing all the public sector schemes, maladministration is not defined in any of the legislation. However, there was much discussion about what it might mean during the Parliamentary debates on the Bill establishing the Parliamentary Ombudsman. It was during these debates that the famous 'Crossman Catalogue' set out the kinds of activities which may come within the ambit of maladministration:

> We might have made an attempt in this clause to define, by catalogue, all of the qualities which make up maladministration, which might count for maladministration by a civil servant. It would be a wonderful exercise – bias, neglect, inattention, delay, incompetence, ineptitude,[45] perversity, turpitude, arbitrariness, and so on.[46]

The decision not to define it was deliberate, as there was a fear that a statutory definition would limit the ability of the ombudsman to develop it as a concept[47]. The ombudsman was not to be concerned about the

---

[42]   Although, as indicated above, the Health Service Ombudsman's remit goes beyond this.

[43]   Justice *The Citizen and the Administration: the Redress of Grievances* (1961) Stevens p 34.

[44]   Justice *The Citizen and the Administration* p 35.

[45]   Hansard (754 HC Official Report col 51 (18 October 1966)) shows this as 'inaptitute', although commentators have repeatedly substituted the word 'ineptitude', presumably on the basis that it was a misprint.

[46]   Richard Crossman, presenting the Second Reading of the Parliamentary Commissioner Bill in the House of Commons (754 HC Official Report col 51 (18 October 1966)).

[47]   A Le Sueur and M Sunkin *Public Law* (1997) Longman p 422.

technical correctness of decisions, but about their administrative quality[48]. Efforts were made therefore to avoid any legalistic overtones when describing the ombudsman's function[49]. The meaning of maladministration was to be 'filled out by the practical consequences of the case work'[50]. Successive ombudsmen have therefore been left to define its scope, although the first Parliamentary Ombudsman admitted that '[n]obody can define maladministration in plain terms'[51]. Indeed, a more recent ombudsman believed that 'to define maladministration is to limit it', as it could effectively prevent those with legitimate grievances which were outside the definition obtaining a remedy[52].

The first ombudsman in Northern Ireland, in his first annual report presented a definition, which has been described as 'a short statement which epitomises, in fairly general terms' the meaning of maladministration[53]:

administrative action (or inaction) based on or influenced by improper considerations or conduct. Arbitrariness, malice or bias, including discrimination, are examples of improper considerations. Neglect, unjustifiable delay, failure to observe relevant rules and procedures, failure to take relevant considerations into account, failure to establish or review procedures where there is a duty or obligation on a body to do so, are examples of improper conduct.[54]

In practice, maladministration often includes fairly minor matters, for example, losing a file or a letter, mistakes in calculations, or some other human error. It can cover administrative action or inaction, based on or influenced by improper considerations or conduct. Such improper

---

48 See P Giddings, who notes that '[as] long as there is administration, there will be maladministration' ('The Ombudsman in a Changing World' (1998) Consumer Policy Review 202–208, p 207).

49 P Birkinshaw *Grievances, Remedies and the State* (2nd edn, 1994) Sweet and Maxwell p 191.

50 734 HC Official Report cols 51–52 (18 October 1966).

51 This was the response of Sir Edmund Clothier, in answer to a question by a member of the select committee in 1968 (*Second Report of the Select Committee on the Parliamentary Comr for Administration* (HC Paper 350 (1967–68)) (Minutes of Evidence) Q 151).

52 Sir William Reid in his annual report for 1993 (HC Paper 112 (1993–94)) para 7).

53 K C Wheare *Maladministration and its Remedies* (1973) Stevens p 11.

54 First Annual Report of the Northern Ireland Commissioner for Complaints (1970) para 20.

considerations would include arbitrariness, malice, bias or unfair discrimination. Neglect, unjustifiable delay, incompetence, failure to observe relevant rules and procedures, and failure to take relevant considerations into account, are all examples of improper conduct. Officials must act in compliance with the law and departmental rules, and a failure to establish a review procedure where there is a duty to do so or the use of faulty systems are examples of maladministration. In addition, high standards of integrity, efficiency and honesty are expected from officials.

These are examples of maladministration. Because of the imprecision in meaning, ombudsmen have some flexibility in deciding what actions or inactions will constitute maladministration. It is for each ombudsman to decide in each case when, for example, a delay becomes unjustifiable, and therefore maladministration, or whether a particular error is excusable. An ombudsman's view of maladministration can be influenced by resource restraints and recruitment difficulties. One ombudsman decided that 'unreasonable delay' in itself was not sufficient to constitute maladministration. It would only be so where it was not caused by uncontrollable difficulties in recruitment, 'financial constraints' or 'resource problems beyond the control of the department'. This ombudsman did not feel justified in criticising a department which was doing its best in difficult circumstances[55]. However, the present Parliamentary Ombudsman is concerned not to allow departments to expect their failures to be excused on the grounds that they are doing their best with the resources available[56].

Where actions are clearly contrary to the law this is maladministration, notwithstanding problems of scarce resources. By way of example, the Local Government Ombudsman decided that there was maladministration in a case[57] where a local authority failed to comply with its statutory duty to provide adaptations to the complainant's home. The complainant was registered as disabled and required the adaptations to enable him to continue to live in his council house. The council was constrained by

---

[55]   Sir Cecil Clothier, in his Annual Report for the Health Service Commissioner for 1981–82 (*Third Report* (HC Paper 419 (1981–82)) para 15, and the Parliamentary Commissioner for Administration Annual Report for 1981 (*Second Report* (HC Paper 258 (1981–82)) para 14.

[56]   Annual Report of the Parliamentary Ombudsman 1999–2000 (HC Paper 593 (1999-2000)) p 9.

[57]   Report on an Investigation into Complaint No 99/B/0012 against North Warwickshire Borough Council.

financial considerations[58] not to approve adaptations to council property, but to offer re-housing when suitable property became available. Given that there was a mandatory duty to fund the works, the ombudsman concluded that the council's budgetary allocation was irrelevant. It was not a consideration to be taken into account in deciding not to fund the adaptations that were needed.

The concept of maladministration has been developed pragmatically over the years, as successive ombudsmen have made decisions on the type of conduct which is acceptable. The first Parliamentary Ombudsman rather cautiously interpreted maladministration in procedural terms, being concerned with 'the way the Department acted or . . . reached its decision'[59]. He was clear that his job was 'to review the administration of Government' and that it was not for him 'to substitute [his] decision for the Government decision'[60]. Some 10 years later, however, another ombudsman was able to declare that the concept of maladministration did not prevent his investigation of 'any unjust or oppressive action'[61]. Ombudsmen have not felt constrained by the concept of maladministration, one of them noting that it was a 'wholly adequate basis' for his investigations[62].

As well as interpreting the concept of maladministration in individual cases, sometimes ombudsmen have provided lists of conduct that would constitute maladministration. The type of conduct can now include:

rudeness; unwillingness to treat the complainant as a person with rights; refusal to answer reasonable questions; neglecting to inform a complainant on request of his/her rights or entitlement; knowingly giving misleading or inadequate advice; ignoring valid advice or overruling consideration which would produce an uncomfortable result for the overruler; offering no redress or manifestly disproportionate redress; showing bias re colour,

---

58   The council had a budget of £40,000 for all adaptations for disabled people living in council-owned properties.

59   Sir Edmund Compton 'The Parliamentary Commissioner for Administration' (1968) Journal of the Society of the Public Teachers of Law 101.

60   *Second Report from the Select Committee on the Parliamentary Comr for Administration* (HC Paper 313 (1970–71)), p 10.

61   I Pugh 'The ombudsman – jurisdiction, power and practice' (1978) 56 Public Administration 127, p 132.

62   This was the view of Sir Cecil Clothier, quoted in the Justice–All Souls Review of Administrative Law in the United Kingdom (*Administrative Justice: Some Necessary Reforms* (1988) Clarendon Press p 93).

sex or any other grounds; omitting to notify those who thereby lose a right of appeal; refusing to inform adequately of right of appeal; faulty procedures; failure by management adequately to monitor compliance with procedures; cavalier disregard of guidance which is intended to result in equitable treatment of service users; partiality; failure to mitigate the effects of rigid adherence to the letter of the law where that produces manifestly inequitable treatment.[63]

The flexibility of the concept has meant that the definitions, even taken together, do not produce an exhaustive list. Thus, even a departure from good practice has been held to be maladministration[64], as have cases where the ombudsman could find no reasonable justification for the council's conduct[65]. It will now also encompass human rights issues. Since the Human Rights Act 1998 came into force[66], all public authorities are obliged, not only as a matter of good practice, but also as a matter of law, to consider the possible bearing of the Convention[67] rights on their decisions. Failure to do so will constitute maladministration.

---

[63] Sir William Reid, Parliamentary Ombudsman from 1989 to 1997, in his Annual Report 1993 (HC Paper 112 (1993–94)) para 7. The present Ombudsman, Sir Michael Buckley, includes within the definition of maladministration the 'failure to give proper advice, harassment ... discrimination and failure to handle claims to benefit properly' ('The Parliamentary Ombudsman' (1998) 68 Advisor 6–8, p 8).

[64] For example, in a case decided by the Local Government Ombudsman, there was criticism of the council's treatment of the complainant, who was a homeless person. The council had given the complainant an oral warning about the consequences of certain actions. It was good practice to provide a written explanation. The ombudsman decided that the process leading up to a decision in relation to a statutory duty to a homeless person was so important that the departure from good practice in this case constituted maladministration (Report on an Investigation into Complaint No 98/A/4244 against the London Borough of Enfield).

[65] This was another Local Government Ombudsman case. It concerned an application by a charity for a permit to conduct a street collection. The ombudsman had found that the council had taken irrelevant considerations into account when determining the application, as some of the information it had sought from the applicant were matters for the Charity Commissioners. They were not the council's business and not relevant to the decision about the grant of the permit (Report on an Investigation into Complaint No. 99/B/04467 against Portsmouth City Council).

[66] It came into force on 2 October 2000.

[67] The European Convention on Human Rights.

Should the Focus on Maladministration be Abandoned?

The limitation of the ombudsman's role to maladministration has received criticism. Other countries do not limit their ombudsmen in this way, but allow them to investigate unreasonable action by public authorities or failures of service. In New Zealand, for example, the ombudsman can report on decisions that are 'unreasonable, unjust, oppressive or improperly discriminatory' or even 'wrong'[68]. In Denmark, the ombudsman can criticise mistakes and unreasonable decisions. In Norway, the ombudsman looks at injustice, and can look at discretionary decisions which are clearly unreasonable or otherwise in conflict with fair administrative practice.

An early commentator on ombudsmen felt that the inclusion of the word maladministration in the statute was 'a compound of compromise and confusion', neither of which had 'lessened in the course of its short unhappy life'[69]. Writing some six years after the establishment of the Parliamentary Ombudsman, there was concern that 'nobody knows what [maladministration] means'. Moreover, its meaning had changed from what it was thought originally to be. It was concluded that the word had lost its utility and needed to be abandoned[70]. Other criticisms related to the 'vague and uncertain boundary surrounding the areas of administration'[71]. Preference was expressed for the New Zealand system, where the legislation makes no reference to administration or maladministration, thus avoiding 'frustrating arguments about definitions', while giving the ombudsman wide scope[72].

In 1977, Justice too suggested that the concept of maladministration was too restrictive, and proposed that the ombudsman should not be so limited[73]. It has been suggested that the term 'maladministration' should

---

68 New Zealand Statutes 1962, No. 10, section 19 provides that the Ombudsman can report on any decision, recommendation, act or omission which '(a) appears to have been contrary to law; (b) was unreasonable, unjust, or improperly discriminatory, or was in accordance with a rule of law or a provision of any enactment or a practice that is or may be unreasonable, unjust, oppressive or improperly discriminatory; or (c) was based wholly or partly on a mistake of law or fact; or (d) was wrong'.

69 G Marshall 'Maladministration' (1973) PL 32–44, p 44.

70 G Marshall 'Maladministration' (1973) PL 32–44, p 32.

71 K C Wheare *Maladministration and its Remedies* (1973) Stevens p 6.

72 K C Wheare *Maladministration and its Remedies* (1973) Stevens p 13.

73 *Our Fettered Ombudsman* (1977). It is worth noting that, although the original Justice report (*The Citizen and the Administration* (1961)) had recommended

be replaced by 'unreasonable, unjust or oppressive action'[74]. It was however becoming clear that the flexibility of the concept was allowing the ombudsman considerable latitude. So much so that the select committee at the time of the 1977 Justice report saw no need to change this aspect of the ombudsman's jurisdiction[75]. It accepted that the interpretation of maladministration used by the ombudsman approximated to the proposed reformulation by Justice. Indeed, the concept had proved to be so flexible that by 1988 even Justice accepted that no change was needed to the wording of the statute in relation to maladministration. The concept of maladministration was conceded to be sufficiently flexible and wide-ranging in operation, and its meaning was felt to be sufficiently well understood[76].

The concept of maladministration has proved to be remarkably 'elastic'[77], so much so that criticisms of it seem to have disappeared. As the distinction between the merits of a decision and the manner in which it is made is not always clear cut, it does allow the ombudsmen to stray very close to criticising decisions by public bodies. For example, in one case, the Local Government Ombudsman formed the view that the council's decision 'flew in the face of the facts' and was therefore 'perverse'. This constituted maladministration[78]. It does now appear that the term no longer presents a significant limitation on the ombudsmen's ability to remedy grievances. However, there may still be a problem with it. It could deter potential complainants, because 'the term is likely to be perceived as inherently obscure to the average citizen'[79]. While this may not be so much of a problem for complaints to the Parliamentary Ombudsman, which are

---

that the ombudsman should be confined to maladministration, it had also recommended the setting up of a comprehensive system of administrative tribunals. In the absence of this, there is no system for a general appeal on the merits of administrative decisions. If there were such a system, confining the ombudsman to cases of maladministration would not be so restrictive.

[74] See C Harlow and R Rawlings *Law and Administration* (1st edn, 1984) p 209.

[75] *Fourth Report from the Select Committee on the Parliamentary Comr for Administration* (HC Paper 615 (1977–78)) (Review of Access and Jurisdiction).

[76] *Administrative Justice: Some Necessary Reforms* (1988) Clarendon Press p 138.

[77] See C Harlow and R Rawlings *Law and Administration* (2nd edn, 1997) Butterworths p 425.

[78] Report of an Investigation into Complaints 00/A/0713; 00/A/08675; and 00/A/10234 against the London Borough of Lambeth.

[79] P Giddings 'The Parliamentary Ombudsman: a successful alternative?' in D Oliver and G Drewry (eds) *The Law and Parliament* (1998) Butterworths p 130.

processed through members of Parliament[80], it is an issue for the other public sector ombudsmen, where potential complainants may be confused and deterred[81].

The Cabinet Office review of the ombudsman system in England[82] did not discuss whether the remit of the ombudsman should be extended beyond maladministration. Neither did it address the issue of whether the word would be sufficiently clear to potential complainants. However, issues about its meaning and scope cannot fail to be addressed in the future. At present, the legislation creating the Health Service Ombudsman specifically mentions the investigation of complaints involving hardship and failures of service, and there is now provision for the investigation of clinical judgment. On the other hand, the Parliamentary and Local Government Ombudsmen's remit is confined to maladministration. If the schemes are to be truly integrated, future legislation will need to address the remit for the new service, and how this will be described in the legislation which is to join the three existing schemes[83].

The select committee, when examining the Cabinet Office review[84], did not discuss maladministration. However, a previous select committee considered that the ombudsman's remit should involve investigations into what is fair and reasonable in all the circumstances[85]. The Director General of Fair Trading has also recommended that ombudsmen should be able to take into account 'what is fair and reasonable in all the circumstances'[86].

---

[80]   The proposals to integrate the ombudsman system in England include the abolition of the Member 'filter' (see *Review of the Public Sector Ombudsmen in England* (2000) Cabinet Office).

[81]   E B C Osmotherly expresses the 'hope' that the new Bill on the ombudsmen will 'use less daunting language', and that the terms maladministration and injustice 'could do with modernisation' ('Modernising the Ombudsman Service' (2000) Journal of Local Government Law 41–43, p 41).

[82]   *Review of the Public Sector Ombudsmen in England* (2000) Cabinet Office.

[83]   As we shall see in Chapter 7, in Scotland, the new Public Services Ombudsman's remit will not be restricted to maladministration, but will also encompass failures of service.

[84]   *Third Report of the Select Committee on Public Administration* (HC Paper 612 (1999–2000)) (The Review of Public Sector Ombudsmen in England).

[85]   *First report of the Select Committee on Parliamentary Comr for Administration* (HC Paper 112 (1994–95)). This is the phrase used in the Financial Services and Markets Act 2000 for the Financial Ombudsman Service (s 228).

[86]   This was in a report, *Consumer Redress Mechanisms* in 1991, which contained recommendations for the adoption of criteria for acceptable ombudsman schemes.

There may be some value adapting the phraseology used by the British and Irish Ombudsman Association. Thus, the public sector ombudsmen's remit could be expressed as follows: 'to make reasoned decisions in accordance with what is fair in all the circumstances, having regard to principles of law, to good practice and to any inequitable conduct or maladministration'[87].

Maladministration and the Courts

Although, as we have seen, the concept of maladministration is not defined in legislation, the courts have had cause to investigate its meaning. It has been described as 'faulty administration'[88] and 'bad administration'[89]. The Crossman catalogue has been judicially endorsed, so that 'a discretionary decision, properly exercised, which the complainant dislikes but cannot fault the manner in which it was taken', is excluded from the definition[90]. In contrast to the merits of decisions, administration and maladministration is concerned with 'the manner' in which decisions by public authorities are reached and 'the manner' in which they are or are not implemented. Administration had nothing to do with the nature, quality or reasonableness of the decision itself[91].

Having drawn this distinction between merits and manner, the courts have been reluctant to interfere with ombudsman's assessment, noting in one case that 'the Ombudsman and not the court is the arbiter' of what constitutes maladministration. The court's supervisory role is therefore to ensure that the ombudsman has acted properly and lawfully. It is thus 'likely to be very rare that the court will feel able to conclude that the ombudsman's

---

87 This is contained in the rules of the Association (BIOA, Rules and Criteria, Schedule 1), which sets out the criteria to which schemes must conform in order to be accepted as full, voting members of the Association.

88 *R v Comr for Local Administration, ex p Bradford Metropolitan Borough Council* [1979] QB 289, per Eveleigh J.

89 This was the term used by May J in the High Court.

90 *R v Comr for Local Administration, ex p Bradford Metropolitan Borough Council* [1979] QB 289, per Denning J.

91 *R v Comr for Local Administration, ex p Eastleigh Borough Council* [1988] QB 855, per Lord Donaldson MR. This view was endorsed by Sir John Donaldson MR, in *R v Comr for Local Administration, ex p Croyden London Borough Council* [1989] 1 All ER 1033.

92 *R v Comr for Local Administration, ex p Doy* [2000] EWHC Admin 361, per Morison J.

conclusions are perverse'[92]. Indeed, in one case, the court said that it was not concerned with how maladministration should be defined, but whether the Ombudsman's decision was 'within the range of meaning which the English language and the statutory purpose together make possible'[93]. The courts have endorsed the view that maladministration does not equate with the unlawfulness of a decision. There is overlap between maladministration and illegality, but 'the concepts are not synonymous'[94].

However, despite the wide latitude allowed to the ombudsmen, the court has intervened where the Parliamentary Ombudsman had found that there was no maladministration and injustice. The case, *Balchin (No 1)* and *Balchin (No 2)*[95], concerned the Parliamentary Ombudsman's report into a complaint about planning blight due to a proposed road scheme. The complainants complained because the proposed scheme had an adverse impact on their home. They alleged maladministration on the part of the Secretary of State in approving the scheme without seeking assurance from the local council that it would compensate them. The ombudsman concluded that there was no maladministration on the part of the department. This decision was the subject of a successful judicial review[96]. The court concluded that the ombudsman's decision in relation to maladministration was defective because he had not considered the council's negative attitude to its compensatory powers. Although it was accepted that the ombudsman had no jurisdiction over the council, the court said that he should have considered whether the Department of Transport should have drawn to the attention of the council their power to buy blighted homes.

[93] *R v Parliamentary Comr for Administration, ex p Balchin* [1996] EWHC Admin 152, (25 October 1996); [1997] JPL 917.

[94] *R v Local Comr for Administration in North and North East England, ex p Liverpool City Council* [1999] EWHC Admin 146 [1999] 3 All ER 85. The court refused to interfere with the ombudsman's view that maladministration could be found where the council had failed to act within the National Code of Local Government Conduct. For a criticism of this approach see C Crawford 'Rule of Law, Lawyers or Ombudsmen' (2001) 4 Journal of Local Government Law 73–79.

[95] See *R v Parliamentary Comr for Administration, ex p Balchin* [1996] EWHC Admin 152 (25 October 1996); [1997] JPL 917; *R v Parliamentary Comr for Administration, ex p Balchin (No 2)* [1999] EWHC Admin 484 (24 May 1999); (1999) 79 P & CR 157, [2000] JPL 267. For a discussion of the case see P Giddings '*Ex p Balchin*: findings of maladministration and injustice' (2000) PL 201.

[96] *R v Parliamentary Comr for Administration, ex p Balchin.*

The court asked the ombudsman to reconsider the complaint, although emphasising that the question of whether any given set of facts amounted to maladministration remained 'entirely a question' for the ombudsman[97]. The matter was reconsidered by the Parliamentary Ombudsman[98], who reached the same conclusion, that there was no maladministration. The outcome of the reconsidered complaint was also challenged by way of judicial review[99], the court in the second case criticising the ombudsman's approach to injustice[100]. This judicial intervention has been criticised as imposing a 'very demanding standard' for the ombudsman's findings, which could 'put at risk the essential informality and accessibility of the institution'[101].

Injustice

A finding that maladministration has occurred is not by itself sufficient to result in a remedy for the complainant. Complainants must show that they have sustained injustice and that the injustice has been suffered as a consequence of maladministration. Like maladministration, injustice is not defined in any of the legislation relating to the public sector ombudsmen. Moreover, very little was said about injustice during the passage of the Bill establishing the Parliamentary Ombudsman. It is wider in scope than 'loss' or 'damage', and indeed these terms were avoided because of the legal concepts they implied. It was intended that 'injustice' should be wide enough to cover situations where a person had not suffered financial loss, but had for example suffered a sense of indignation or outrage aroused by unfair or incompetent administration[102]. In practice, it has been given a wide

---

[97] *R v Parliamentary Comr for Administration, ex p Balchin*, per Sedley J, at para 41.

[98] It was reconsidered by a different ombudsman, Sir Michael Buckley, as Sir William Reid had since retired.

[99] *R v Parliamentary Comr for Administration, ex p Balchin (No 2).*

[100] Judicial review proceedings have now been started following the issue of the ombudsman's third investigation report (see Parliamentary Ombudsman Annual Report 2001–02 (HC Paper 897 (2001–02)) p 7.

[101] P Giddings '*Ex p Balchin*: findings of maladministration and injustice' (2000) PL 201–204, pp 203, 204.

[102] Indeed, in the case of *R v Parliamentary Comr for Administration, ex p Balchin (No 2)* [1999] EWHC Admin 484 (24 May 1999), one of the reasons for quashing the ombudsman's finding of no maladministration and injustice was that the ombudsman had not dealt with the matter of 'outrage' where injustice was one of the principal controversial issues.

interpretation by the ombudsmen, and injustice has been found where the effect was annoyance, as well as the more straightforward cases of financial loss or missed opportunity. However, injustice is not found merely because there is a finding that there has been maladministration. There has to be something over and above this. It has been said that the complainant must show some injustice 'which is personal to him and distinguishes him from the generality of the community'[103].

There can thus be findings of maladministration, but no injustice, where, for example, there has been some procedural shortcomings in the way a decision has been reached, but the result would still have been the same without these shortcomings. In other words, the errors had not affected the correctness of the decision. Also, a person may receive more favourable treatment due to some administrative error. Again, there is no question of injustice. However, there are cases where administrative shortcomings have been said to give rise to injustice, even though the final decision may not have been affected. For example, it may be injustice where an individual, through maladministration, has been denied the opportunity to object to development by a third party. This is seen as a loss of a right, and therefore injustice. Indeed, it has been argued that 'if justice requires that "every man be given his due", and if everyone who deals with government departments is entitled to have his case decided in the proper manner, then defective procedure always constitutes at the same time both maladministration and injustice'[104].

As with maladministration, the courts have said that the meaning of injustice is for the ombudsmen to interpret themselves[105], and until recently the meaning of injustice was not subjected to much judicial comment. However, the *Balchin* cases, discussed above, have ensured that the concept of injustice can also be the subject of judicial scrutiny, and that the ombudsman's discretion in this respect will also be constrained by the limits set by public law. In *Balchin (No 1)*, Sedley J disagreed with the ombudsman's view that, as the outcome would have been the same with

---

[103]   C Clothier 'Legal problems of an ombudsman (1984) 81 Law Society Gazette 3108.

[104]   R Gregory and P Hutchesson *The Parliamentary Ombudsman. A Study in the Control of Administrative Action* (1975) George Allen & Unwin p 331.

[105]   *R v Local Comr for Administration, ex p Bradford Metropolitan Borough Council* [1979] QB 287.

or without maladministration, no injustice could have been suffered[106]. In *Balchin (No 2)*, the ombudsman's finding of no maladministration causing injustice was again criticised, and more was said about the meaning of injustice. Its meaning was conceded to be ambiguous, but it was accepted that it was to include wider considerations than financial loss. In particular, a sense of outrage was sufficient to be within the meaning of injustice. The ombudsman was criticised because he had not made it sufficiently clear in his report whether, if there had been maladministration, the outrage at the events would have amounted to injustice[107].

The outcome in *Balchin* can be contrasted to another case in the same year, which concerned complaints about delay in the assessment for special educational needs. In that case, the Local Government Ombudsman concluded that there was maladministration but no injustice, because the delay would have made no material difference. The proceedings for judicial review of the ombudsman's decision[108] were dismissed. This was on the basis that it was not enough that the applicant had felt that she had been unfairly treated, in order to demonstrate that there was injustice. The law permitted the ombudsman to find maladministration without injustice. The court concluded therefore that the mere finding of maladministration could not automatically mean that there must be injustice as well. There must be 'some prejudice to the applicant' before a finding of injustice could properly be made[109].

It is difficult to reconcile these two cases, which were decided without 'any apparent cross-reference to the other's existence'[110]. It is clear that it is not necessary to show any form of pecuniary loss in order to have suffered injustice. It is equally clear that it is possible for there to have been maladministration without any injustice. The latter usually occurs where

---

[106]   *R v Parliamentary Comr for Administration, ex p Balchin* [1996] EWHC Admin 152 (25 October 1996), at para 16.

[107]   *R v Parliamentary Comr for Administration, ex p Balchin (No 2)* [1999] EWHC Admin 484 (24 May, 1999), paras. 42, 47, per Dyson J. Having been remitted once more to the ombudsman, the ombudsman's third report is now also the subject of judicial review proceedings. At the time of writing the outcome of this is not yet known (see *The Ombudsman*, March 2002, Issue 17, p 12).

[108]   *R v Comr for Local Government, ex p S* [1999] Ed CR 123.

[109]   *Ex p S* , at 130–131, per Collins J.

[110]   G Jones and M Grekos 'Great Expectation? The Ombudsman and the Meaning of "Injustice"' (2001) Judicial Review 20–24, p 24.

the ombudsman finds there would not have been a different outcome for the complainant, even if there had been no maladministration. There would be no prejudice to the complainant in such a case. However, *Balchin* seems to require the ombudsman to deal expressly with the question of whether complainants suffered a sense of outrage at the way they were treated, before coming to a conclusion about injustice. Such a requirement imposes a very demanding standard for ombudsmen[111]. It would be unfortunate if this had the effect of putting at risk the informality and accessibility of the institution[112].

Remedies

The Act establishing the Parliamentary Ombudsman scheme did not focus on remedies. The ombudsman's role was primarily to investigate and report, and it was to be for Parliament and constituency members to secure redress[113]. There was even resistance to the ombudsman being empowered to indicate what remedy was considered appropriate, on the grounds that it would 'change the whole character' of the office if it were set up 'as a tribunal to assess compensation'[114]. Successive ombudsmen have however developed the role in providing redress, where injustice is found as a consequence of maladministration. Where remedies are justified, they can include a variety of recommendations. For example, the ombudsman may recommend that the public body apologies or rectifies the maladministration. The remedy may include a review of procedures. There can also be recommendations for compensation, not only for actual loss, but also for distress, inconvenience and delay[115]. The ombudsmen

---

[111] P Giddings '*Ex p Balchin*: findings of maladministration and injustice' (2000) PL 201–204, p 204.

[112] P Giddings '*Ex p Balchin*: findings of maladministration and injustice' (2000) PL 201–204, p 203.

[113] See M Buckley 'Remedies, Redress and "Calling to Account": Some Myths about the Parliamentary Commissioner for Administration' (1998) Denning Law Journal 29–47, p 32. The Labour Party Manifesto for the 1964 General Election did not mention redress, but proposed that the ombudsman would 'investigate the grievance of the citizen and report to a select committee of the House'.

[114] HC Official Report, SC B (Parliamentary Commissioner Bill) col 305.

[115] There is an issue here as to how far the ombudsmen should get out of line with the awards the courts are making in such circumstances. As we shall see, different ombudsmen have different approaches to the amounts awarded, and the Health Service Ombudsman in particular is reluctant to make financial awards.

frequently make recommendations for financial redress, and in this respect the ombudsman remedy contrasts with the remedies for judicial review. Not only are compensation awards in judicial review proceedings rare, but they are unlikely to cover payments for distress and inconvenience[116].

The ombudsmen make recommendations about the appropriate action that a public body should take in order to remedy the injustice. They do not make binding awards. Neither the ombudsman nor the complainant has the power to institute proceedings in court or in a tribunal in order to enforce the recommendation[117]. This is in contrast to the ombudsmen in the private sector, whose awards are generally binding on the industry concerned. It does however conform to international norms for public sector ombudsmen[118].

In most cases, the lack of enforceability presents no problems, and public authorities normally comply with the ombudsmen's recommendations. Indeed, it is seen as one of the 'essential elements of ombudmanship' that the office generates such respect that the acceptability of recommendations is not a problem[119]. So far as the Parliamentary and Health Service Ombudsmen are concerned, the possibility of being called to account by the select committee is considered to be sufficient incentive on departments to follow the recommendations[120]. Local authorities however are not always amenable. Indeed, around 6% of the recommendations of the Local

---

[116] In addition, damages have traditionally not been awarded for breach of statutory duty by public bodies. However, there may now be the possibility of obtaining compensation in such cases, as a result of the Human Rights Act 1998. This would occur where the administrative failing had resulted in a breach of one of the articles of the European Convention on Human Rights (see R Carnwath 'Welfare Services – Liabilities in Tort after the Human Rights Act' (2001) PL 210–219).

[117] The only exception to this is the Northern Ireland Ombudsman.

[118] See M Buckley, 'Remedies, Redress and "Calling to Account": Some Myths about the Parliamentary Commissioner for Administration' (1998) Denning Law Journal 29–47, p 30.

[119] M Oosting 'Essential Elements of Ombudsmanship' in L C Reif (ed) *The Ombudsman Concept* (1995) International Ombudsman Institute.

[120] The Select Committee has rarely involved itself in matters of redress. When it has, this has been a concern about general policy, or 'the treatment of a significant class of complainants' where there was the 'possibility of substantial public expenditure' (M Buckley 'Remedies, Redress and "Calling to Account": Some Myths about the Parliamentary Commissioner for Administration' (1998) Denning Law Journal 29–47, p 46).

Government Ombudsmen have not been followed. Occasionally this is perceived as a cause for concern, and there are discussions about whether the recommendations should be enforceable. The view however continues to be that not only is judicial enforcement not necessary, but that it could also be counter-productive[121].

Ombudsmen and Legal Remedies

Ombudsmen, as originally conceived in the public sector, were not intended to present an alternative dispute resolution mechanism to the courts. They were established to deal with grievances where no remedy was available in court, because the matter was not justiciable, as no legal right had been infringed[122]. As we have seen, the Parliamentary Ombudsman was originally established as an adjunct to Parliament, and thus a part of the political and administrative regimes. The Parliamentary Ombudsman was to supplement the work of members of Parliament in investigating complaints from members of the public about maladministration. The other public sector ombudsmen followed this model to a large extent. Their function is essentially to provide remedies for maladministration, rather than to adjudicate legal claims or appeals against the merits of discretionary decisions. The ombudsmen thus provide additional remedies, rather than an alternative mechanism for pursuing legal rights. This is in contrast to the schemes established in the private sector, which are not confined to issues of maladministration. These schemes frequently deal with issues of a contractual nature, where court action is theoretically possible. In this respect, the private sector schemes do present genuine alternative dispute resolution mechanisms, both for consumers and the industries concerned[123].

---

[121]   It may, for example, make local authorities defensive, and import formal safeguards into the system. This could make the system more lengthy and costly, and less informal and flexible. There are also human rights issues to be addressed if there were to be judicial enforcement. None of the ombudsmen in the public sector wish to have the power to make binding awards. The issues about enforcement in relation to the Local Government Ombudsmen are discussed in Chapter 6.

[122]   Writing in 1971, H W R Wade in his textbook of administrative law noted that the ombudsman was to 'operate beyond the frontier where the law stops' (*Administrative Law* (3rd edn, 1971) Oxford University Press p 12).

[123]   It could be said that both the public and private sector schemes provide an alternative means of obtaining access to justice.

Moreover, the public sector ombudsmen are precluded from investigating complaints where there is a legal remedy. All the legislation establishing the Parliamentary, Health Service and Local Government Ombudsmen explicitly prevents investigations where the complainant has a remedy before a tribunal or court of law. These provisions emphasise the role of the ombudsmen as providing remedies for administrative problems that the courts and other mechanisms of administrative justice cannot effectively resolve. There is provision in all the legislation, however, for investigation where the ombudsman is satisfied that in the particular circumstances it would not be reasonable to use these other remedies. In exercising this discretion, the ombudsmen normally refuse to investigate complaints where the appropriate course of action is to have the case heard before a tribunal or to use a statutory appeal procedure. Similarly, if the complainant is seeking damages for a contractual or negligence matter, the ombudsmen will not investigate.

There are, however, situations where the legal remedy is not in contract or tort but in judicial review. When the ombudsman system was established in the 1960s and 1970s, the rapid rise of judicial review as a remedy against public bodies was not foreseen. Now there is much overlap between the jurisdiction of the ombudsmen and the courts in reviewing the actions of public bodies[124]. As was acknowledged in one case[125]: 'Every procedural irregularity is likely to exhibit maladministration'[126]. How do the ombudsmen exercise their discretion in cases where the complainant may have a remedy in judicial review? One ombudsman has said that if there were any doubt about the availability of a legal remedy, or where the process of law seemed

---

[124]   Even in 1977, H W R Wade in the 4th edition of his administrative law textbook had accepted as inevitable that a certain amount of overlap would exist between the ombudsman and the courts (*Administrative Law* (4th edn, 1977) Oxford University Press pp 73–86). This was also recognised by Bradley in 1980, who noted that the ombudsman and the courts were 'parallel processes' with 'each having certain advantages and disadvantages relative to the other' (A W Bradley 'The Role of the Ombudsman in Relation to the Protection of Citizens Rights' (1980) CLJ 304, p 332.

[125]   *R v Lambeth London Borough Council, ex p Crookes* (1995) 29 HLR 28 at 36.

[126]   This has also been expressed as: 'maladministration and illegality do often meet in a twilight zone' (P Birkinshaw *Grievances, Remedies and the State* (2nd edn, 1994) Sweet and Maxwell p 228).

too cumbersome, slow and expensive for the objective to be gained, he would exercise his discretion in favour of the complainant[127].

On the other hand, in a case in 1989, Lord Woolf said that the legislation[128] made it clear that generally if there were a court remedy by way of judicial review, the complainants should use judicial review. Moreover, the ombudsman should only exercise his discretion to investigate such a complaint in 'particular circumstances'[129]. However, extra-judicially, Lord Woolf has adopted a different approach. He has acknowledged that it is not surprising that the ombudsmen have taken a 'generous view' of the cases which fall within their discretion, especially in situations where there is no right of appeal to a tribunal[130]. Moreover, in his interim report on Access to Justice, he acknowledged that the courts, with their 'broad general jurisdiction', do 'not share the ombudsman's investigative powers'. They are therefore 'less well equipped to take on functions of handling individual grievances and of setting and maintaining standards of good practice'[131].

In practice, the ombudsmen exercise their discretion liberally, where there are alternative legal remedies. Thus, such cases will be investigated, unless it is considered reasonable in the particular circumstances for the complainant to resort to the legal remedy. However, where an alternative legal remedy has already been used, the ombudsman will not investigate. For example, in one case the Local Government Ombudsman refused to investigate a complaint about a local authority's substantive decision not to accept a housing duty to a complainant, because that decision had previously been challenged in the county court[132]. Similarly, the Local Government Ombudsman has refused to investigate a complaint about a

---

127 *Second Report from the Select Committee on the Parliamentary Comr for Administration* (HC Paper 148 (1980–81)) (Parliamentary Commissioner for Administration Annual Report for 1980).

128 The case concerned the Local Government Ombudsman, and he was referring to the Local Government Act 1974, s 26(6).

129 *R v Comr for Local Administration, ex p Croydon London Borough Council* [1989] 1 All ER 1033.

130 H Woolf *The Protection of the Public – a New Challenge* (1990) Stevens p 82.

131 Lord Woolf *Access to Justice* Interim Report to the Lord Chancellor on the civil justice system in England and Wales (1995) p 139.

132 Report of an Investigation into Complaints 00/A/07813; 00/A/08675; and 00/A/10234 against the London Borough of Lambeth. Other aspects of the complaints were investigated.

failure by a local authority to provide suitable education, because the matter had already been dealt with by judicial review proceedings[133].

This of course poses problems for complainants. Sometimes complainants want an ombudsman investigation in order to obtain compensation for the maladministration, as even when successful, damages are not normally awarded in judicial review proceedings. In one of the cases referred to above, the decision of the Local Government Ombudsman not to investigate was itself the subject of judicial review proceedings. The case concerned a complaint about the failure of a local authority to provide education in relation to the special educational needs of the child of the complainant. The matter had already been the subject of successful judicial review proceedings, but the complainant wanted the ombudsman to investigate in order that she might obtain compensation from the council.

The Court of Appeal refused to interfere with the ombudsman's decision not to investigate[134]. In doing so, it approved of the conclusion reached in the lower court that where a party had 'ventilated a grievance by means of judicial review it was not contemplated that they should enjoy an alternative, let alone an additive, right by way of complaint to a local government commissioner'[135]. The court decided that the ombudsman had no discretion to investigate where an alternative remedy had already been pursued through the courts, even where not all the injustice had been remedied by court action[136]. It was noted that if the court had decided

---

133   *R v Comr for Local Administration, ex p H (A Minor)* [1999] ELR 314. On the other hand, an investigation by the ombudsman will not necessarily bar a judicial review application. For example, the Parliamentary Ombudsman was heavily critical when the Home Office demanded extra television licence fees from those who had bought new ones before their old ones had expired in order to evade an increase in fees. However, the ombudsman accepted that the complainants were in no worse position than those who had waited for their existing licences to expire, and no remedy was granted. A complainant then successfully bought judicial review proceedings against the Home Office (*Congreve v Home Office* [1976] QB 629).

134   *R v Comr for Local Administration, ex p H (A Minor)* [1999] ELR 314.

135   Per Turner J.

136   See also *R v Comr for Local Administration, ex p Field* [1999] EWHC Admin 754 (29 July, QBD), where the ombudsman refused to investigate a complaint about a planning case. The complainant had been refused planning permission by the local authority, but this was overturned on appeal to the minister. The complainant wanted an investigation of alleged maladministration by the council, because he wanted some compensation for the cost of the appeal to the minister

otherwise, it would become routine to follow up a successful judicial review application with a complaint to the ombudsman. Thus, it is clearly important that complainants choose the appropriate remedy for their grievance. By taking judicial review proceedings, complainants will then be prevented from the possibility of obtaining compensation as a result of an investigation by the ombudsman.

Judicial review itself is a discretionary remedy. It can be refused where the court considers that there is an alternative remedy which is more appropriate. This issue was discussed in a case concerning an application for judicial review of a local authority's actions in processing housing benefit claims. The authority had delayed the process, which had caused severe financial difficulties to the owner of a bed and breakfast hostel. This type of complaint is clearly within the jurisdiction of the ombudsman[137]. There was a discussion in the court case of whether the ombudsman remedy was more appropriate for this defective administrative action. The court's view was that judicial review would be denied to an applicant where the complaint was essentially one of maladministration. It would not be denied where there were other grounds for the complaint, for example, illegality, proportionality, or irrationality. While accepting that there was overlap, especially in housing cases, it was acknowledged that 'not every act of maladministration will be encompassed by procedural irregularity'[138].

The courts have said that it is for the ombudsman to decide whether to exercise the discretion to investigate[139]. Moreover, the courts have acknowledged that in some cases the ombudsman remedy, with its informal procedure, may indeed be superior to the 'restrictive forensic forum of the courts'[140]. This indicates an acceptance of the ombudsman's generous exercise of discretion in deciding whether cases are within jurisdiction. Further endorsement of the advantages of the ombudsman's remedy is

---

and loss of profits during the appeal process. Despite the fact that the statutory appeal process for planning decisions could not remedy this injustice, the court decided that the ombudsman had no discretion to investigate.

[137] In this case, the Local Government Ombudsman had jurisdiction.

[138] *R v Lambeth London Borough Council, ex p Crookes* (1995) 29 HLR 28 at 36.

[139] *R v Local Comr for Administration in North and North East England, ex p Liverpool City Council* [1999] EWHC Admin 146 [1999] 3 All ER 85, per Chadwick LJ para 40.

[140] *R v Lambeth London Borough Council, ex p Crookes* (1995) 29 HLR 28, per Sir Louis Blom-Cooper QC.

found in the Liverpool City Council case[141]. The case concerned a complaint about the approval of a planning proposal by Liverpool Football Club. The Local Government Ombudsman found maladministration on the grounds that councillors had failed to act in accordance with the National Code of Local Government Conduct in granting planning permission[142].

There was some discussion in the case as to whether the complainants to the ombudsman should have challenged the council's decision by way of judicial review, and thus that the ombudsman should have refused to investigate. The court said that this was 'a clear case' for the application of the ombudsman's discretion to investigate[143]. The ombudsman's investigation was appropriate, as it would not have been reasonable to expect the parties to resort to legal remedies. The complainants were people in modest housing, without the means to pursue a remedy from their own resources. It would have been very difficult, if not impossible, for them to have obtained the necessary evidence to support an application for judicial review. It was only an investigation by the ombudsman which could have uncovered the evidence.

The superiority of the ombudsman method in many circumstances is now recognised, and the ombudsman's generous application of the discretion to investigate where it would not be reasonable to use legal resources has been judicially endorsed. Furthermore, in cases of maladministration, the court may feel that the applicant ought to refer the complaint to the ombudsman, rather than seek judicial review[144]. It is now recognised that

[141]   *R v Local Comr for Administration in North and North East England, ex p Liverpool City Council* [1999] EWHC Admin 146 [1999] 3 All ER 85.

[142]   The code contains a 'reasonable suspicion' test for bias. This finding was challenged by the council, on the basis that the ombudsman should not have used the test in the code to judge the councillors conduct. Instead, the council argued, she should have applied the legal test for bias, found in *R v Gough* [1993] AC 646, which is a 'real danger of bias'. The court decided that maladministration did not equate with the lawfulness of the decision, and that there was no reason why the ombudsman should not find maladministration where there had been a breach of the code.

[143]   Per Henry LJ para 28.

[144]   *R v Lambeth London Borough Council, ex p Crookes* (1995) 29 HLR 28. Another determining factor in deciding on the appropriate remedy is the rules relating to legal aid. The guidance for legal aid in housing matters states that, before advising a client to commence any proceedings, solicitors should consider recourse to an ombudsman. This will be a factor in deciding whether legal aid should be granted. If fewer people will be able to institute civil proceedings, this has implications

the courts and ombudsmen are parallel processes, with relative advantages and disadvantages[145]. In both processes, neither the court nor the ombudsman can substitute their decision for that of the public body concerned. Judicial review has advantages in that it is an enforceable decision. However, it normally only results in a decision being quashed or an order that action be taken. Monetary compensation is only possible in rare circumstances[146]. Ombudsmen cannot enforce their recommendations, but they can recommend a wide range of remedies, including compensation, and, unlike the courts, they can provide mediation between the complainant and the public body concerned.

The dividing line between the courts and ombudsmen, once thought clearly distinct, is now becoming more contentious[147]. Moreover, both are discretionary remedies. If the courts refuse an application for judicial review, on the basis that their remedial powers 'do not significantly improve the situation of the complainant against the local authority'[148], there is a danger that aggrieved citizens may fall between a gap in both of these discretionary remedies. It is no wonder, therefore, that Lord Woolf has called for 'a more closely integrated system of review' and 'partnership between judicial and

---

for the way ombudsmen exercise the discretion to investigate where there is a legal remedy. Also, in April 2000, the Legal Service Commission's guidance on its funding code said that one of its objectives was the wider use of ombudsman schemes, by allowing legal help to be offered to enable clients to pursue complaints (see N O'Brien 'Ombudsmen: fly swatters or lion-hunters?' (2000) 14 (August) The Ombudsman 11).

[145] A W Bradley 'The Role of the Ombudsman in relation to the Protection of Citizens Rights' (1980) CLJ 304, p 332.

[146] There is no general statutory or common law right to damages where a person suffers loss as a result of wrongful administrative action (see M Amos 'The Parliamentary Commissioner for Administration, redress and damages for wrongful administrative action' (2000) PL 21–30).

[147] The potential overlap is more obvious in some areas than others. As we shall see in Chapter 5, the Health Service Ombudsman has jurisdiction in relation to clinical treatment. Although the ombudsman will not investigate where the complainant is seeking compensation for clinical negligence (on the grounds that this should be dealt with by the courts) it may be that the investigation will reveal information that could be used in evidence in negligence proceedings. There would be nothing to prevent a complainant going to court after the ombudsman investigation.

[148] *R v Lambeth London Borough Council, ex p Crookes* (1995) 29 HLR 28 per Sir Louis Blom-Cooper QC p 39.

non-judicial remedies', in order to protect citizens from the abuse of administrative power[149].

Resolving Grievances about Public Administration

As we have seen, there is some overlap between the jurisdiction of the ombudsmen and the courts. Such overlap was not envisaged when the ombudsman system was established in the 1960s and 1970s. Then, it was felt that the problems the ombudsman was established to deal with might not be susceptible to review by the courts. Similarly, it was acknowledged that the other mechanisms available for securing administrative justice were not adequate. Some other avenue for redress was therefore required, and the ombudsman system was to fill this gap. In order to understand the place of ombudsmen in the system for securing administrative justice, it is necessary to look briefly at other mechanisms for resolving grievances about public administration.

The obvious institutions for the resolution of grievances are the courts, these being the traditional protectors of rights. This is true for grievances of individuals against the state, as well as individuals in relation to each other. Legal remedies against the state include actions in contract and tort, as well as various statutory provisions for appeal by those aggrieved by the decisions of public authorities in specific cases. In addition, the decisions of public authorities are subject to judicial review. Traditional legal methods of grievance resolution are problematic, mainly because of the cost, actual or potential, of advice and proceedings. When delay and formality are added to the problem of cost, it is hardly surprising that alternative mechanisms have been introduced for dealing with disputes. As has been noted, there is some overlap between the jurisdiction of the ombudsmen and the powers of the courts in relation to judicial review.

[149]   H Woolf *The Protection of the Public – A New Challenge* (1990) Stevens p 92. Lord Woolf also made proposals for a closer and more fluid relationship between the courts and the ombudsman in his Access to Justice report (Interim Report 1995). He recommended a closer relationship, while preserving the independence of the ombudsman from the court system. Woolf said that an ombudsman decision should not prevent a subsequent application to the courts. The ombudsman should be able to apply to the courts for a ruling on a point of law, without a complainant having to commence proceedings. There was also a suggestion that the courts should be able to refer issues to the ombudsman, with the ombudsman's and the parties' consent, in order to uncover facts. These proposals never got very far.

Judicial review is concerned with illegality, irrationality[150] and procedural impropriety in decision making[151], all of which may be evidence of maladministration. The courts, like the ombudsmen, cannot change decisions with which they disagree on the merits.

If there is a successful challenge by way of judicial review, the decision of the public body concerned is quashed; the decision is declared unlawful and of no effect; or, if the case involves a failure to perform a public duty, the public body can be ordered to perform its duty. However, the courts are not as flexible as the ombudsman and are not always an effective instrument for remedying wrongs in this area. In addition to being costly, cumbersome and slow, they have limited powers of review, being mainly concerned with the legality of decisions. For many minor matters, judicial review can be too burdensome an undertaking. Notwithstanding this, judicial review can be a useful remedy, and the ombudsman and judicial review should be seen as complementary to each other[152]. Indeed, the fact that there is overlapping jurisdiction between the ombudsman and the courts may benefit consumers 'in offering some limited range of review venue'[153].

As an alternative dispute resolution mechanism, the ombudsman has a number of advantages over the courts. The courts operate on an adversarial model of grievance redress, but this has limitations as a method of righting wrongs in administration. As we shall see, the ombudsman uses inquisitorial methods, often operating informally, and his or her investigations do not impede the normal processes of government. The investigation powers given to the ombudsmen can often bring to light cases of bureaucratic maladministration that would otherwise pass

---

[150] The challenge on the basis of irrationality refers to a decision 'which is so outrageous in its defiance of logic or of accepted moral standards that no sensible person who had applied his mind to the question to be decided could have arrived at it' (*Council of Civil Service Unions v Minister for the Civil Service* [1985] AC 374 at 410 per Lord Diplock).

[151] See *Associated Provincial Picture Houses Ltd v Wednesbury Corpn* [1948] 1 KB 223; *Council of Civil Service Unions v Minister for the Civil Service* [1985] AC 374.

[152] See Justice *Administrative Justice: Some Necessary Reforms* (1988) Clarendon Press p 86. See also P Craig and D Fairgrieve '*Barrett*, Negligence and Discretionary Power' (1999) PL 626–662, who discuss the way that the investigations of the Local Government Ombudsmen in particular overlap with recent negligence cases.

[153] D Lewis and R James 'Joined-up Justice: Review of the Public Sector Ombudsman in England' (2000) 4 International Ombudsman Yearbook 109–140, p 129.

unnoticed. On the other hand, there may be a finding that the complaint is without merit, in which case the fact that there has been an impartial and independent investigation may well serve to enhance morale in the public authority investigated.

The ombudsman is impartial, but has a conciliatory approach. It is not the aim of the investigation to antagonise public officials 'but to induce them to internalise fairness and justice values and to accept them as values that legitimately compete with effectiveness and other bureaucratic values for balanced accommodation'[154]. In order to be effective, the ombudsman depends to a considerable extent on voluntary compliance from public officials, so co-operation has to be the norm. The ombudsman can also help to negotiate adjustments to decisions that are not illegal or otherwise subject to criticism, and 'suggest minor adjustments that overcome bureaucratic rigidity'[155]. However, there is no general review of discretion, and criticism is only appropriate where discretion is exercised for unsupportable reasons.

The decisions of public authorities have increasingly been subjected to appeal in tribunals, rather than the courts, but these administrative appeal bodies only cover a small portion of the total field of administrative action. Those which do exist have, on the whole, been very successful, but there is no general administrative appeals tribunal. Because of this, citizens must depend upon individual statutes conceding rights of appeal for particular decisions. There is no general duty imposed upon public administration to produce a grievance system of any sort that could be used by someone to register a complaint.

Elected representatives play an important part in individual grievance resolution. There is a long-established tradition of citizens using members of Parliament when they wish to complain about the actions of central government departments and local government. Indeed, the workload of members of Parliament as a whole in relation to grievance handling is considerable. Research in 1992 revealed that they receive, in total, an estimated 300,000 complaints a year, and write about 50,000 letters to

---

[154]   K Friedmann 'Realisation of ombudsman recommendations' (1988) *Fourth International Ombudsman Conference Papers* p 114.
[155]   W Gellhorn *Ombudsmen and Others* (1967) Harvard University Press p 433.

ministers on behalf of constituents each year[156]. The importance of this work in relation to grievance handling should not be underestimated. Nevertheless, they are restricted by time and expertise, and they do not have access to civil servants and departmental files. These problems are even more acute for local councillors. Being part-time and unpaid, councillors cannot be expected to devote more than a small part of their time to following up grievances of constituents. Ombudsmen can act as an aid to the work of elected members, and because of their wide investigative powers can achieve a resolution where elected members would be powerless.

Other methods of grievance resolution involve the political process. The classical remedy for maladministration in the UK is the individual responsibility of the minister to Parliament. This has its limitations. Parliament itself is preoccupied with legislation and national and international policy, and cannot devote its collective time to individual grievances[157]. The executive is unwilling to investigate itself, and the machinery for controlling it is inadequate. As long ago as 1968, Rowat recognised that the effectiveness of the Parliamentary question and of the adjournment debate was diminishing, as the field of administrative law was broadening[158]. Select committees have a limited role. Although they can call officials before them to account for action in their departments, they do not deal with individual grievances of citizens. They act rather as watchdogs in general, over the conduct of administration in a department.

The inadequacies in the political and legal[159] processes for securing administrative justice led to the establishment of the ombudsman system. The need was felt because of the problems with the other checks in preventing the abuse of power and of resolving grievances. The powers granted to the ombudsmen allow them to address administrative problems that the courts, the legislature and the executive cannot effectively resolve.

---

[156] See R Gregory and J Pearson 'The Parliamentary Ombudsman after twenty-five years: problems and solutions' (1992) 70 Public Administration 469, p 474.

[157] See C Clothier 'The Value of an Ombudsman' (1986) PL 204, p 205.

[158] D C Rowat *The Ombudsman: Citizens Defender* (1968) George Allen and Unwin p 269.

[159] The fact that the ombudsmen operate outside the courts has meant that they have been able 'to approach the dispute resolution task in a way that . . . tackles some of the criticisms often levelled at the courts and judges' (W Merricks 'The Jurisprudence of the Ombudsman' (2001) 41 JBL 654–660, p 659).

As a method of grievance resolution, the ombudsman is ideally placed to protect the interests of all concerned. The procedure is informal, the wide powers of investigation ensure the ability to uncover the facts, and the office is independent and impartial. These unique characteristics render the office capable of addressing many of the concerns left untouched by the traditional bureaucratic control devices. Citizens can feel confident that maladministration will be uncovered, and officials can feel that, where no maladministration is found, official action is vindicated.

Conclusion

In the UK, the ombudsman was initially seen as an adjunct to Parliament, whose role was to assist members of Parliament in their dealings with government agencies on behalf of their constituents. The value of this novel institution was perceived to be its independence, its thoroughness, and its wide powers of investigation. The system was designed to supplement the other mechanisms for securing administrative justice and, in particular, not to usurp the 'historic role' of Parliament 'as a committee of grievances'[160]. The ombudsman's remit was restricted to complaints about maladministration, a restriction which has been criticised. Some argue that there should be the power to criticise the use of administrative discretion where it has clearly been unreasonable. Others are of the view that any extension of remit would involve the ombudsman substituting his or her view, and that this is politically controversial. Notwithstanding these arguments, the concept of maladministration has proved to be sufficiently flexible to encompass a wide range of administrative shortcomings.

Ombudsmen are one form of remedy for administrative action or inaction, in a system which offers a range of mechanisms for administrative justice. However, the ombudsman institution has 'a unique combination of characteristics that gives it advantages over all other types'[161]. Most important is independence, together with the prestige of the office and the powers to investigate and publicise. This gives the institution a strength which non-governmental organisations and members of a legislature cannot match. As we shall see in the following chapters, the methods employed by ombudsmen ensure that they provide a more flexible way of

---

160   K Wheare *Maladministration and its Remedies* (1973) Stevens p 115.
161   D C Rowat *The Ombudsman Plan: The Worldwide Spread of an Idea* (2nd edn, 1985) University Press of America p 185.
162   N O'Brien 'Justice by any other name' (2001) (November) The Ombudsman 7–8, p 7.

obtaining access to justice than the courts. They can mediate and negotiate in order to reach a satisfactory conclusion. Another feature of the system is 'its refusal to be ensnared by traditional judicial forms and precedent'[162]. Ombudsmen provide remedies where none were previously available, in order to address the gaps in the system of administrative justice. Since their establishment, the mechanisms for dealing with grievances against the administration have undergone enormous changes. The next chapter will examine the systems for grievance redress within the public sector, and discuss the role of ombudsmen within this changed system.

Chapter 3

Ombudsmen and public services

As we have seen, the Parliamentary Ombudsman was originally established to be an 'independent holder of the highest standards of efficient and fair administration'[1]. In 1973 and 1974, separate ombudsmen systems were established for the health service and local government, and by 1977, the ombudsman system was being seen as an effective safeguard for the citizen against administrative abuse[2]. Now, the role of the public sector ombudsmen has evolved even further. Their 'modern purpose' is 'to resolve disputes fairly by whatever means are appropriate'[3]. This evolution is a response to the changing environment in which the ombudsmen in the public sector operate. Public services are now delivered very differently to the way they were in the 1960s and 1970s. Expectations about the quality of those services have also changed. In addition, the context of administrative justice has changed. Not only have the decisions of public bodies become more susceptible to review by the courts, but there has also been a rapid rise in the use of extra-judicial remedies. Ombudsmen systems are now 'but one of a plethora of schemes and procedures for complaint-handling' in the public sector[4]. This chapter will outline these changes and discuss the consequences of them for the ombudsman system.

[1] Justice *The Citizen and the Administration: the Redress of Grievances* (1961) Stevens p 77.
[2] Justice *Our Fettered Ombudsman* (1977) JUSTICE.
[3] E B C Osmotherly 'Modernising the Ombudsman Service' (2000) 3 Journal of Local Government Law 41–43, p 41.
[4] P Giddings 'The Ombudsman in a Changing World' (1998) 8(6) Consumer Policy Review 202–208, p 202.

Public Services

The boundary between public services and services provided by the private sector is becoming less distinct. This is due in part to the privatisation of what were once nationalised industries and utilities. In addition, public bodies now contract out many of their functions to the private sector. There is the view that the provision, by private organisations, of services which perform 'a core function essential to the furtherance of economic and social life' involves the private sector in a role with a strong public element[5]. Having said this, it is still possible to note a number of characteristics which differentiate between public and private service providers. The private sector provides services in order to make a profit, or at least not to make a loss, and will judge its effectiveness in terms of profits and market share. In the public sector, citizens are rarely called upon to pay the economic price for the services they receive, and many services are free at the point of delivery. Where public services are concerned, organisations have a duty or a power to provide them, and citizens have a right or expectation to receive them. In some cases, they may even be compelled to receive a service, against their will[6].

Public services are often monopolistic in nature. There is usually no alternative supplier to the services provided, and if there is, it is often not a realistic alternative for the majority of citizens. This means that there is often an inequality of bargaining power in the relationship, which could result in abuses of power by service providers. Where there is a lack of choice in service provision, consumers cannot realistically use the 'exit' option if they are dissatisfied with the service they receive[7]. This lack of

---

[5]   R James *Private Ombudsmen and Public Law* (1997) Dartmouth p 1. See also H Woolf 'Public Law – Private Law: Why the Divide?' (1986) PL 220–238.

[6]   Examples of this include the services provided by local authorities in relation to children and services provided by the police and prisons.

[7]   See A Hirschmann *Exit, Voice and Loyalty: responses to decline in firms, organisations and states* (1970) Harvard University Press. Exit and voice are two options in response to dissatisfaction in a variety of public and private institutional settings. When quality deteriorates, failings are discovered by voice (that is, the organisation receives a growing number of complaints) or exit (that is, consumers choose to go elsewhere for the goods or services) or both. Those most able to exit may also be the most effective at voicing. This applies in the public sector, where those who can articulate their grievances may also be those who can afford to pay for, for example, housing and education. See also S Paul 'Accountability in Public Services: exit, voice and control' (1992) 20(7) World Development   1047–1060.

choice means that other mechanisms must be found for consumers to express their dissatisfaction. One option for consumers is 'voice', that is, making a complaint.

One feature of public services, which we have noted, is that they are usually provided under a legal duty or power, rather than as a result of a commercial or contractual arrangement. Although some aspects of public service are subject to clearly defined rules, much of it relies on discretionary decision making[8]. The reasons for this are not hard to find. They include the complexity of contemporary society, the sheer size and burden of the legislative task, and the growing dependence upon specialist, technical or scientific knowledge and expertise. In the face of all this, legal rules seem 'both inflexible and ill suited as a means of coping with uncertainty and change'[9]. In addition, an element of discretion is inevitable in any system of rules, because of 'the vagaries of language, the diversity of people's circumstances and an indeterminacy in official purpose'[10]. Not only is discretionary decision-making inevitable, but also, as has been noted, the trend in modern legal systems is towards 'a greater reliance upon discretion by lower-level officials and less reliance on clearly defined rules'[11].

Another feature of public sector decision-making is that in many cases it involves the allocation of scarce resources. Questions of allocation are not simply matters for the political process. They involve the administrative process, and they involve 'polycentric' decisions, that is, they have a number of interconnected, linked issues[12]. If one aspect of a decision is changed, it results in unpredictable consequences for other aspects of the service. For example, a decision by a local authority to allocate a council house to one family has consequences for all other families in the housing queue. A decision by a health authority to fund expensive medical treatment to a patient has implications for other medical priorities. Matters of 'justice' in these situations cannot be expressed simply in terms of legal rights.

---

8   For a discussion of the rules versus discretion debate, see K Davis *Discretionary Justice* (1969) Louisiana State University Press.
9   See K Hawkins 'The uses of legal discretion: perspectives from law and social science' in K Hawkins (ed) *The Uses of Discretion* (1992) Clarendon Press p 12.
10   D Galligan *Discretionary Powers* (1986) Oxford University Press pp 64–65.
11   J Allsop and L Mulchay *Regulating Medical Work: formal and informal controls* (1996) Open University Press p 18.
12   See L L Fuller 'The forms and limits of adjudication' (1978) 91 Harv LR 353.

Administrative Justice

The public sector is a major provider of services to the citizen, many through the medium of discretionary powers. Given the distinctive qualities in the provision of public services, mechanisms are needed to ensure that rules are properly applied and discretion is not exercised in an arbitrary fashion. There is a need for checks on the use of power so that individuals who are subjected to decisions of public bodies are safeguarded. This is provided in a number of ways[13]. First, the courts provide a check on public bodies by means of judicial review. The problems with the courts providing administrative justice have previously been addressed. The realisation of their limitations has 'led administrative law in many directions'[14]. Indeed, '[m]uch of the energy of modern administrative law' has been spent in devising alternative mechanisms for resolving these kind of disputes[15]. In particular, new mechanisms were found to be needed to handle disputes that could not be resolved adequately by the courts or the political system[16].

One mechanism for the provision of administrative justice is to be found in tribunals. These emerged during the early part of the twentieth century as mechanisms for challenging administrative decisions[17]. They are statutory bodies, established to provide the primary forum for the resolution of disputes in particular areas of administrative decision making. There are around 70 different administrative tribunals in England and Wales, dealing with such diverse issues as criminal injuries compensation, parking, pensions, special educational needs, mental health and social security. As they decide nearly one million cases each year, their impact on the administrative justice system is immense. Unlike the ombudsman system, they were established to decide on the merits of decisions, providing fora for appeals against individual administrative decisions. They are court-substitutes, rather than alternative dispute resolution mechanisms. The

---

[13]   For a comprehensive review of the mechanisms for raising and resolving complaints in the public sector see N Lewis and P Birkinshaw *When Citizens Complain: Reforming Justice and Administration* (1993) Open University Press.

[14]   C Harlow and R Rawlings *Law and Administration* (2nd edn, 1997) Butterworths p 574.

[15]   C Harlow and R Rawlings *Law and Administration* p 391.

[16]   See J D B Mitchell 'The Ombudsman Fallacy' (1962) PL 24–33.

[17]   For a discussion and evaluation of administrative tribunals see H Genn 'Tribunal Review of Administrative Decision-Making' in G Richardson and H Genn (eds) *Administrative Law and Government Action* (1994) Clarendon Press.

disputes they deal with are specifically allocated to tribunals, rather than the courts, by statute.

Like the courts, tribunals too have 'considerable limits' to their effectiveness 'as a check on administrative decision-making'[18]. Problems with the system include the haphazard way it has evolved. This has resulted in wide variations in practice in tribunals. In addition, there are issues in relation to their independence, as many tribunals are administered by the departments whose decisions are being disputed. In contrast to the claims made for tribunals (that they are quick, informal and non-technical), research has concluded that they are not particularly quick and they have varying degrees of informality. They are often highly technical because they have to deal with complex areas of law and intricate factual situations. In addition, those appearing before them without representation are often disadvantaged[19].

A recent review of tribunals called for important changes in the workings of the system, in order to make it more independent, more coherent, and more user-friendly[20]. The review addressed the question of which matters were appropriate for adjudication by the courts, and which should be allocated to tribunals. It concluded that tribunals were appropriate where the issues were unlikely to be so complex as to prevent users from preparing and presenting their own cases. Tribunals were also useful where expertise was a major issue in the resolution of disputes. Tribunals were also preferred where accessibility to users was important[21]. The review did not engage in a similar discussion about what matters may be more appropriate for ombudsmen rather than tribunals. The focus in the review on the distinction between tribunals and courts is probably not surprising, given that tribunals were established because of their perceived advantages over the courts. The report does make reference to ombudsmen, but only to conclude that their function is different[22]. This begs a rather important

---

[18]   H Genn 'Tribunal Review of Administrative Decision-Making' p 284.

[19]   H Genn 'Tribunal Review of Administrative Decision-Making' p 285.

[20]   *Tribunals for Users: One System, One Service* (2001) Report of the Review of Tribunals by Sir Andrew Leggatt.

[21]   *Tribunals for Users: One System, One Service* (2001) paras 1.10–1.12.

[22]   *Tribunals for Users: One System, One Service* (2001) para 12.12. However, the report does note that the Pensions Ombudsman, who can make binding determinations, is subject to supervision by the Council on Tribunals. It argues that the new Financial Ombudsman Service and Legal Services Ombudsman, which also have such power, should also be supervised in this way (para 12.13).

question. In terms of administrative justice, what is the appropriate function of ombudsmen, and do their methods of working make them more appropriate than tribunals for determining some disputes?[23]

Modernising Public Services

Administrative justice is not only concerned with providing remedies for citizens' grievances. It is also concerned to improve administrative practice, and thus provide better services. The performance of the public sector, like the private sector, is to be judged on the extent to which it meets the needs of the consumers for whom services are provided. If these needs are not met, citizens complain. The 'complaints explosion' probably started in the private sector in the 1970s and 1980s, fuelled by increased consumer awareness together with legislation designed to protect the consumer interest[24]. During this time, consumer groups emerged 'as a political force demanding improved conditions and rights for the population'[25].

This had consequences for the public sector where these same consumers demanded better public services. In turn, this has prompted politicians and administrators to recognise that public services exist for the benefit of those who use them. Public service delivery is now concerned with quality and effectiveness. Indeed, in 1988, the Audit Commission made the assertion that local authorities exist to provide services to the public, the only value

---

[23] See also D Lewis and R James 'Joined-up Justice: Review of the Public Sector Ombudsman in England' (2000) 4 International Ombudsman Yearbook 109–140, p 126, who note that 'questions of what is an "ombudsman" and what are the crucial distinguishing feature as against a tribunal call for an examination'. J Farrand has also compared the roles and practices of tribunals and ombudsmen ('Courts, tribunals and ombudsmen' (2000) 26 Amicus Curiae 3–8).

[24] See T Williams and T Goriely 'A Question of Numbers: Managing Complaints against Rising Expectations' in M Harris and M Partington (eds) *Administrative Justice in the 21st Century* (1999) Hart pp 100–101. Until the 1980s, there was little theoretical or empirical work in relation to grievance redress outside the courts. R Rawlings (*The Complaints Industry: a Review of Socio-Legal Research on Aspects of Administrative Justice* (1986) Economic and Social Research Council) provides a review of the 'complaints industry' that emerged around this time. See also L Mulcahy, R Lickless, J Allsop and V Karn *Small Voices Big Issues: An Annotated Bibliography of the Literature on Public Sector Complaints* (1997) University of North London.

[25] J Allsop and L Mulchay *Regulating Medical Work: formal and informal controls* (1996) Open University Press p 12.

of these services being 'the extent to which they satisfy popular needs'[26]. This approach to public service provision was motivated in part by a desire during the 1980s to hold down public expenditure. It was also fuelled by an ideology which sought to extend market forces to the delivery of public services[27]. It resulted in what has become known as 'new public management', an approach which values high quality, high value public services, delivered with the maximum efficiency, effectiveness and economy. Part of the new managerialist approach was manifested in the establishment of 'next steps'[28] executive agencies[29]. There were also radical changes in the health service, in particular, the creation of hospital trusts. In local government, the market ideology resulted in the contracting out[30], through compulsory competitive tendering[31], of the delivery of many local services.

Although the transformation of public service delivery was underpinned by new right ideologies, the new Labour administration in 1997 did little to change the approach, retaining most of what had been achieved under new public management. In its 'modernising government' agenda[32], there is a commitment to ensuring the delivery of high quality and efficient public services. Part of this commitment involves providing services to meet the needs of citizens, not the convenience of service providers. It includes target setting, and performance monitoring. Within this framework, citizens'

---

[26] *The Competitive Council* (1988) HMSO p 5.

[27] See generally R Gregory and P Giddings 'The Ombudsman and the New Public Management' in R Gregory and P Giddings (eds) *Righting Wrongs: The Ombudsman in Six Continents* (2000) IOS Press.

[28] See Improving Management in Government: the Next Steps (1988) Cabinet Office.

[29] These are autonomous agencies of government departments, which manage their own staff and budgets, and which operate within the terms of framework documents drawn up by departments. Their tasks are to implement policies which are decided by departments (see R Austin 'Administrative Law's Reaction to the Changing Concepts of Public Service' in P Leyland and T Woods (eds) *Administrative Law Facing the Future: Old Constraints and New Horizons* (1997) Blackstone Press p 13; G Drewry 'Revolution in Whitehall: The Next Steps and Beyond' in J Jowell and D Oliver (eds) *The Changing Constitution* (3rd edn, 1994) Oxford University Press).

[30] See I Harden *The Contracting State* (1992) Open University Press.

[31] Compulsory competitive tendering has now been replaced by 'Better Value' principles (see P Vincent-Jones 'Responsive Law and Governance in Public Sector Provision: a Future for the Local Contracting State' (1998) 61 MLR 362).

[32] See *Modernising Government* (Cm 4310, 1999) Cabinet Office.

grievances are used to highlight problems in the system that need to be addressed.

The Charter Programme

An important landmark in charting the changes in the delivery of public services is the introduction of the Citizen's Charter by the Conservative government in 1991[33]. The aims of the charter, expressed in the White Paper which preceded it was to improve the quality of public services and make them more responsive to the needs and wishes of their users. The charter was to be the 'most comprehensive programme ever to raise quality, increase choice, secure better value, and extend accountability'[34]. It was to apply to all public services, including central government departments and agencies, local government, the health service, the courts, and the police. The charter contained a statement of principles of what the citizen was entitled to expect from public services. These six 'principles of public service' included the setting of explicit standards for and information about services, and the provision of choice and consultation. Services were to provide value for money, they were to be provided with courtesy and there was to be effective complaints systems[35]. Public authorities were to give effect to the charter by issuing their own individual charters, and indeed, soon afterwards, these started to emerge. Central co-ordination for the charter, and the emerging departmental charters was placed in the Cabinet Office.

---

[33]   The charter was launched in July 1991, without any statutory enactment. Its status was ambiguous, and as it was not a legislative instrument, many of the remedies it proposed relied on internal processes (see D Cooper 'The Citizen's Charter and Radical Democracy: Empowerment and Exclusion within Citizenship Discourse' (1993) 2 Social & Legal Studies 149–171 p 151). This lack of 'legislative teeth' accorded with the government's view that not only was this not necessary, but that it would have been undesirable. Legislation may have become a constraint in the development of more flexible and responsive public services (see D Goldsworthy 'The Citizen's Charter' (1994) 9 Public Policy and Administration 59, p 63). Interestingly, the Labour Party also published a Citizen's Charter in 1991, just days before the Conservative government published their White Paper.

[34]   *The Citizen's Charter: Raising the Standard* (Cm 1599, 1991) p 4.

[35]   See A Page 'The Citizen's Charter and Administrative Justice' in M Harris and M Partington (eds) *Administrative Justice in the 21st Century* (1999) Hart p 87.

The charter as originally conceived by the Major government has been described as 'rearticulating citizenship with a right-wing discourse' and reconceptualising 'welfare state users as paying customers' within a type of contractual relationship[36]. It adopted a 'rights' approach to ensuring welfare provision for citizens, by placing emphasis on market accountability within the public sector. By introducing a degree of choice, it was anticipated that this would create an enhancement of individual freedom because individuals would be able to realise their preferences. The charter concept was based on the notion that the quality of public services can be improved if service delivery is subject to market forces, because market forces empower the citizen. It was seen as a part of the Conservative government's strategy to either privatise public services, or, if that was not possible, to introduce private sector mechanisms into the public sector[37].

The approach adopted in the charter was that the satisfaction of consumer preferences was the primary objective of service provision. Such an approach has been criticised for implicitly denying that 'the moral basis of such provision, or citizenship itself, could be entitlement based on need'. The rhetoric of the charter suggested that the meeting of needs was no longer be regarded as essential to the ideal of citizenship[38]. Indeed, it has been suggested that the title of the citizen's charter is a misnomer. It perhaps should more properly have been called the 'public customers' charter' because it sought 'to provide remedies for individuals who are forced to be loyal customers to public institutions over which they have very little direct control'[39]. The charter adopted a limited view of citizenship, with a citizen being defined simply as a user of services, and with no corresponding civic and social obligations, which are 'the hallmarks of citizenship'[40].

---

[36] D Cooper 'The Citizen's Charter and Radical Democracy: Empowerment and Exclusion within Citizenship Discourse' (1993) 2 Social & Legal Studies 149–171, p 149.

[37] See A Barron and C Scott 'The Citizen's Charter Programme' (1992) 55 MLR 526, p 357.

[38] A Barron and C Scott 'The Citizen's Charter Programme' (1992) p 544.

[39] R Hambleton and P Hoggett 'Rethinking consumerism in public services' (1993) 3(2) Consumer Policy Review 103–111, p 111.

[40] G Drewry 'Whatever happened to the Citizen's Charter?' (2002) PL 9–12, p 11.

However, despite the cynicism that greeted its introduction[41], the charter programme has 'contributed towards a changing culture in the delivery of public services'[42]. Some have concluded that the charter did constitute a potentially useful addition to the machinery of administrative justice, because of its potential for administrative improvement and grievance redress[43]. It did at least 'formulate a concept of citizenship grounded in the use of public services and products'[44]. The importance of this 'for any broad vision of administrative justice should not be undervalued'[45]. Some have praised the charter for being an affirmation by government of the right of the citizen to expect proper standards of public services and to be compensated in the event of a failure[46].

When the Labour government came to power in 1997, it noted that the original charter programme had made a major contribution to the improvement in public services during the 1990s[47]. Soon after taking office, it affirmed its commitment to ensuring the provision of high quality public services. As part of this commitment, it conducted a consultation exercise in order to discover how the charter programme might be refocused in order to deliver better and simpler services[48]. In June 1998, the government re-launched the charter programme, renaming it 'Service First – a new Charter programme', on the basis that this better reflected the programme's

---

[41] 'The way in which the Citizen's Charter was launched by the previous Conservative Government was pretty inept and engendered much cynicism' (M Harris and M Partington 'Introduction' in M Harris and M Partington (eds) *Administrative Justice in the 21st Century* (1999) Hart Publishing p 6).

[42] P Giddings 'The Ombudsman in a Changing World' (1998) 8(6) Consumer Policy Review 202–208, p 202.

[43] A Page 'The Citizen's Charter and Administrative Justice' in M Harris and M Partington (eds) *Administrative Justice in the 21st Century* (1999) Hart Publishing.

[44] D Cooper 'The Citizen's Charter and Radical Democracy: Empowerment and Exclusion within Citizenship Discourse' (1993) 2 Social & Legal Studies 149–171 p 166.

[45] M Harris and M Partington 'Introduction' in M Harris and M Partington (eds) *Administrative Justice in the 21st Century* (1999) Hart Publishing p 6.

[46] M Hayes 'Emerging Issues for Ombudsmen' (1991) Paper presented to the United Kingdom Ombudsman Conference p 14.

[47] See Service First: the new charter programme (1998) Cabinet Office para 2.1. It also noted that the original charter idea had been pioneered in local government by Labour-run authorities (p 1).

[48] *The Citizen's Charter: A Consultation Exercise* (1997) Cabinet Office, Office of Public Service.

emphasis on providing responsive public services[49]. The reforms to the charter programme 'reinforce much of the approach and style' of the previous citizens' charter programme, but there is a move away from its 'most controversial' aspects, notably its 'avowedly consumerist and market ideology'[50]. Although the original Citizen's Charter has now disappeared, its 'spirit . . . lives on', as part of 'a wider agenda of "modernisation" and "consumer focus"'[51]. The concept of charters for citizens is now very much a part of our national life.

The Charter Programme, Adjudicators and Ombudsmen

The original charter made little reference to the ombudsman system[52]. It has been suggested that one reason for this omission was that the government at the time might not have welcomed the 'potential contribution that a more flexible and responsive model of the existing Ombudsman' might

[49] Service First (1998) para 1.7. The new programme has nine new principles of public service delivery, representing what the public service should be striving to achieve. First, every public service should set clear standards of service. Second, they should be open and provide full information about services. Consultation and involvement of service users is the third principle. The fourth principle is the encouragement of access and the promotion of choice. Public services are to treat all people fairly, respecting their privacy and dignity, and being helpful and courteous. They are to provide effective redress mechanisms, and have a clear, well publicised complaints procedure. The seventh principle is that public services are to use resources effectively, in order to provide best value for taxpayers and users. The service must innovate and improve, and finally, it should work with other providers to ensure that services are simple to use, effective and co-ordinated (para 2.8). The Service First programme has a website, with links to the charters of service providers.

[50] C Scott 'Regulation inside government: re-badging the Citizen's Charter' (1999) PL 595–603, p 602.

[51] G Drewry 'Whatever happened to the Citizen's Charter?' (2002) PL 9–12, p 12.

[52] In all of the 51 pages of the White Paper (Cm 1599, 1991), there is only a brief recognition of the Health Service Ombudsman's role in hospital complaints, and a brief reference to the Health Service and Parliamentary Ombudsmen in providing an external remedy, should the internal procedures fail (see A W Bradley 'Sachsenhausen, Barlow Clowes – and then' (1992) PL 353, p 356). Commentators at the time of the charter's inception similarly ignored the ombudsman system, even in discussions about empowering citizens by extending complaints mechanisms (see, for example, an article by A Barron and C Scott 'The Citizen's Charter Programme' (1992) 55 MLR 526).

have made to meeting citizens' expectations[53]. The Citizen's Charter was to introduce new forms of redress where these could be made 'to stimulate rather than distract from efficiency'[54]. It was also concerned with the need within public services to 'increase both choice and competition'[55]. The omission of ombudsmen from this project may have represented a veiled criticism of the ombudsman system. It could at the very least have indicated that the government was ambivalent about ombudsmen[56]. The present charter programme, Service First, is similarly silent on the role of ombudsmen in the new programme. It does advise that complaints systems should have mechanisms for independent review where possible, but does not refer to the ombudsman's function in providing external oversight. The Service First website does however have a link to ombudsmen and the British and Irish Ombudsmen Association websites.

It is clear, however, that the charter programme does have implications for the ombudsman system[57]. The programme provides an opportunity to raise standards in public services, which is an aim ombudsmen would support. Furthermore, the standards set out in individual departmental charters will provide the ombudsman with some benchmarks against which to determine any alleged maladministration[58]. As the charter programme attaches great importance to the effectiveness of internal complaints procedures in the public sector, this may have the effect of reducing the numbers of complaints reaching the ombudsman[59]. What the charter programme does not do is make the ombudsman system redundant. Even when public services have effective internal complaints procedures, there is still a need

---

53   A W Bradley 'Sachsenhausen, Barlow Clowes – and then' (1992) PL 353, p 357.
54   Cm 1599, 1991 p 5.
55   Cm 1599, 1991 p 4.
56   A W Bradley 'Sachsenhausen, Barlow Clowes – and then' (1992) PL 353, p 357.
57   This fact was recognised by the Parliamentary Ombudsman at the time of the introduction of the original charter programme. In view of this, in 1991, the Select Committee on the Parliamentary Commissioner for Administration undertook a brief inquiry into the possible implications of the charter for the ombudsman (HC Paper 158 (1991–92)) (the Implications of the Citizen's Charter for the Work of the Parliamentary Commissioner for Administration).
58   Of course, it will still be for the ombudsman to determine whether or not there has been maladministration.
59   In fact, this did happen in some departments. After establishing their own complaints machinery, there was a reduction in the number of complaints to the Parliamentary Ombudsman against the prison service, while the percentage of complaints relating to the Inland Revenue also fell (see Parliamentary Ombudsman Annual Report 1996 (HC Paper 386 (1996–97)) paras 36 and 60).

for an external, impartial investigator, a function performed by the ombudsmen.

There are concerns however that the public may become confused at the proliferation of redress mechanisms that have arisen since the introduction of the charter programme. This is particularly so where there are 'independent' complaints adjudicators. This 'new breed' of complaint-handler[60] has been given various titles, including 'adjudicator', 'examiner' and 'reviewer'. They form an intermediate layer of complaint handling, for those who are dissatisfied with the internal complaints procedures operated by public bodies. Although they are internal departmental appointments, they are operationally independent, a point sometimes emphasised by the use of the word 'independent' in their title. Their appointments have occurred in departments and agencies which have traditionally had high levels of complaints[61]. They provide an independent mechanism for dealing with complaints which are essentially about maladministration, so their work obviously has implications for ombudsmen. Before discussing these implications, there will be a brief overview of the work of some of these bodies.

Independent Departmental Complaints Mechanisms

The Adjudicator

The Adjudicator deals with complaints about the Inland Revenue, the Tax Credit Office, the Contributions Agency, the Valuation Office Agency, Customs and Excise, and the Public Guardianship Office. The forerunner of the Adjudicator scheme, the Revenue Adjudicator, was established in 1993 by the Inland Revenue, a department that traditionally accounted for a high level of complaints to the Parliamentary Ombudsman[62]. It was the

---

[60] See D Oliver 'The Revenue Adjudicator – A New Breed of Ombudsperson?' (1993) PL 407; P Morris 'The Revenue Adjudicator – The First Two Years' (1996) PL 309, p 309.

[61] These 'complaint-prone' organisations may also have introduced these independent complaints mechanisms to avoid the risk of judicial involvement (see P Giddings 'The Ombudsman in a Changing World' (1998) 8(6) Consumer Policy Review 202–208, p 205).

[62] Its introduction also reflected the Inland Revenue's commitment to the charter standards of service and complaint handling. For a discussion of the work of the office, see D Oliver 'The Revenue Adjudicator – A New Breed of Ombudsperson?'

first of these independent complaints offices to be created. No legislation was needed for its creation, as it was based on a contractual arrangement between the office holder[63] and the department. It was funded by the Inland Revenue, with its own independent budget[64]. In 1995, the remit was extended to Customs and Excise and the Contributions Agency[65], both of which also had large numbers of complaints to the Parliamentary Ombudsman. The name was then changed to the 'Adjudicator' to reflect this expanded role[66]. In 2001, the Public Guardianship Office came within the remit of the office. The Tax Credit Office is a recent addition to the bodies within jurisdiction and in due course the remit will be extended to child benefit, when the Child Benefit Centre joins the Inland Revenue[67].

The Adjudicator's role is to act as an impartial referee where complainants feel that their affairs have been poorly handled by the organisations within remit. These matters are similar to those dealt with by the Parliamentary Ombudsman. They include excessive delays, mistakes, discourtesy and poor or misleading advice, in effect, the classic examples of maladministration. The Adjudicator cannot investigate complaints about the law or government policy, or matters that are or have been before the courts. Nor can she investigate matters that can be dealt with by a tribunal. This means that she cannot become involved in disputes about an individual's tax assessment, as there are statutory tribunals for these types of disputes[68]. Another exclusion is where the complaint is in relation to a criminal prosecution that is in progress or being investigated. The Adjudicator will not investigate matters which have been, or are being, investigated by the Parliamentary Ombudsman. The converse is not true, and the Parliamentary Ombudsman does investigate complaints that have been dealt with by the Adjudicator.

(1993) PL 407; P Morris 'The Revenue Adjudicator – The First Two Years' (1996) PL 309.

[63]   The first Revenue Adjudicator was Elizabeth Filkin.

[64]   Its current budget runs to around £2 million annually. Three-quarters of this is spent on staffing costs. There are currently 47 staff employed (The Adjudicator's Office Annual Report 2001–02 p 46).

[65]   The Contributions Agency merged with the Inland Revenue in 1999, to become the National Insurance Contributions Office.

[66]   Dame Barbara Mills has been the Adjudicator since April 1999.

[67]   The Adjudicator's Office Annual Report 2001–02 p 5.

[68]   Disputes are heard by the General Commissioners in the case of the Inland Revenue, and VAT Tribunals for Custom and Excise matters.

Complainants are expected to use the department's internal complaints procedure before approaching the Adjudicator. The complaint to the Adjudicator must be in writing, and must normally be referred within six months of the final decision by the department. When accepted, the department is asked for a report on the complaint and all the relevant papers, with the expectation that they will be sent within one month. There is an attempt at mediation, where this seems appropriate. Where settlement in this way is not possible, an adjudication officer makes a thorough review of all the evidence. Although mainly conducted on the papers, visits to complainants and staff are conducted where necessary, and use is also made of telephone contact. Cases are decided according to whether the organisation has followed its published procedures, met the standards of service and acted consistently[69]. The Adjudicator aims to settle all complaints within five months of receipt.

After the investigation, the decision is communicated by means of a detailed letter to the complainant, and a copy is sent to the department. The remedies that the Adjudicator can recommend include apologies and compensation. Compensation will be recommended where the complainant has suffered some financial loss, in which case there will also be reimbursement for the additional costs incurred because of the department's mistake. In some cases, recommendations for small awards are made for the distress and upset caused to the complainant. Sometimes, instead of compensation, the department will forgo some tax or interest due. The recommendations of the Adjudicator have always been followed[70].

The Adjudicator is a free service with accessible, easy-to-use procedures. The caseload of the Adjudicator has shown an overall rise in the numbers of cases dealt with each year. In 2001–2002, the office accepted 551 cases for investigation. Of these, 393 concerned the Inland Revenue. The year brought a 45% increase in the number of complaints about Customs and Excise. These were mainly concerned with seizures of property as a result of the department's actions to prevent the smuggling of alcohol and tobacco. There is a formal appeal mechanism for such cases, but the Adjudicator can examine the manner in which such seizures occurred. Altogether 573 cases were completed, and of these 39% were upheld, 54% were not upheld and 7% were withdrawn. There were 39% of complaints

---

[69]   The Adjudicator's Office Annual Report 2001–02 p 5.
[70]   The Adjudicator's Office Annual Report 2001–02 p 6.

against the Inland Revenue which were upheld, and a total of almost £120,000 was paid by the department to successful complainants. In 65% of all the cases, the resolution of the complaint was by means of a recommendation, with 27% being resolved by mediation. The remaining cases were withdrawn or reconsidered by the organisation[71].

A survey of complainants revealed that 61% of respondents were satisfied with the way the case was handled by the office, a figure that rose to 77% where the complaint was upheld[72]. The Adjudicator also gives feedback to the departments about the complaints received, from which she hopes lessons will be learnt in order to improve performance. There is evidence that changes in administrative practices have been achieved[73].

Evaluations of the work of the Adjudicator have indicated that the office achieves effective outcomes for significant numbers of complainants. However, this has not resulted in a significant reduction in the numbers of cases being referred to the Parliamentary Ombudsman[74]. The scheme has been given 'high' marks for openness, accessibility, fairness and effectiveness. However, it is 'clearly flawed in terms of perceived independence and accountability'[75]. This lack of formal independence has prevented the scheme becoming a full voting member of the British and Irish Ombudsman Association[76].

The Independent Case Examiner

The Independent Case Examiner deals with complaints about the Child Support Agency[77]. Its establishment was a response to the continuing criticism by the Parliamentary Ombudsman of the agency's complaint

---

[71]   The Adjudicator's Office Annual Report 2001–02 p 40.

[72]   The Adjudicator's Office Annual Report 2001–02 p 45.

[73]   P Morris 'The Revenue Adjudicator – The First Two Years' (1996) PL 309 p 321.

[74]   P Giddings 'The Ombudsman in a Changing World' (1998) 8(6) Consumer Policy Review 202–208, p 205.

[75]   P Morris 'The Revenue Adjudicator – The First Two Years' (1996) PL 309 p 321.

[76]   It should also be noted that, as the scheme is within the remit of the Parliamentary Ombudsman, complaints alleging maladministration in the Adjudicator's Office can be made to the Parliamentary Ombudsman.

[77]   The remit also includes the Northern Ireland Social Security Agency.

handling procedures[78]. The government announced its intention to establish the office in December 1996, and the office became operational in April 1997[79]. The remit of the Case Examiner is to act as an independent referee where there are complaints about maladministration by the agencies within her jurisdiction. Typically, complaints are about long delays, mistakes and discourtesy by staff. Delay is 'an endemic feature' of most of the complaints and the most common fault found. Other common complaints are about poor communication; failings in the internal complaint-handling processes; and procedures for dealing with arrears of maintenance[80]. The Case Examiner cannot investigate matters of law in relation to child support, or complaints about the calculations of child maintenance. For these latter disputes, there are separate review and appeal procedures. Nor will she investigate where the matter has been, or is being, investigated by the Parliamentary Ombudsman[81].

Before submitting a complaint, complainants must use the Child Support Agency's internal complaints procedure[82]. Complaints must normally be made within six months of the final decision by the agency. The Case Examiner retains the discretion to reject complaints even when they are within remit. About half of the cases received are not accepted for investigation[83]. Complaints have to be made in writing, but help will be given to complainants where this causes difficulty. Where complaints are investigated, the procedure involves the collection of facts from the agency. There are attempts at mediation, where this seems appropriate. If this is not possible, a formal report is prepared, which is sent to the complainant and the agency. Where the complaint is made out, a variety of recommendations can be made. These include apologies and reviews of

---

[78] P Giddings 'The Ombudsman in a Changing World' (1998) 8(6) Consumer Policy Review 202–208, p 206.

[79] The first office holder was Anne Parker, and the office was supported by 40 staff. In its first year it received over 1,000 complaints, and cleared over 80% of them. In July 2001, Jodi Berg became the office holder, and the staff numbers have increased to 60. The office has an annual budget of around £1 million, 75% of which goes on staffing costs.

[80] Independent Case Examiner Annual Report 1997–98 p 4.

[81] An investigation by the Independent Case Examiner does not preclude an investigation by the Parliamentary Ombudsman.

[82] This is a two-stage process. The complaint must first be made to the Customer Service Manager, and then to the Chief Executive of the Child Support Agency.

[83] The figures were 49% rejected in 2000–01, and 52%, 54% and 57% rejected in the previous three years (see Independent Case Examiner Annual Report 2000–01 p 90).

procedures. There can also be recommendations for compensation for financial loss. In all but the most exceptional cases, the agency has agreed to follow the Case Examiner's findings. If the finding is not followed, the Case Examiner can publicise this fact in her annual report. As with the Adjudicator, the introduction of the Case Examiner has not had much impact on the Parliamentary Ombudsman's workload, and complaints about the Child Support Agency still account for a significant number of reports issued each year[84].

Independent Complaints Reviewer

The Independent Complaints Reviewer deals with complaints against the Land Registry[85], the Public Record Office, the Charity Commission and the Housing Corporation. The Reviewer acts as a fair and independent referee for those with complaints against these bodies, after the internal complaints procedures have failed to achieve a satisfactory outcome. The service was established as a result of Service First's recommendation that organisations have, where possible, independent review arrangements. The Reviewer can deal with complaints about maladministration: for example, failures to meet standards of service, delay, and mistakes. In 2000–01, she dealt with 67 complaints.

The Ombudsman and Adjudicators

The introduction of these independent complaints mechanisms have implications for the ombudsman system. It is clearly better for all concerned that complaints are resolved as quickly and as informally as possible. That is the rationale for internal complaints systems within organisations, where complaints can be addressed at local level. In any well-established complaints system, the ombudsman is at the apex of a pyramid of grievance resolving machinery, and is the last port of call when other procedures are

---

[84]   In 2000–01, they accounted for 32% of the reports (Parliamentary Ombudsman Annual Report 2000–2001 (HC Paper 5 (2001–02)) para 3.1). In 2001–02 they accounted for 24% (Parliamentary Ombudsman Annual Report 2001–02 (HC Paper 897 (2001–02)) p 31).

[85]   The office was first established as the Independent Complaints Reviewer to the Land Registry in 1998. The other bodies were added to her remit in 1999 and 2000. The Independent Complaints Reviewer is Jodi Berg.

exhausted. Notwithstanding the necessity for internal complaints procedures, it is the ombudsman system that provides a completely independent mechanism for those grievances which cannot be resolved at local level.

Independent adjudicators and complaints examiners present an intermediate layer of complaint handling between the internal processes and the ombudsman. Operationally, they appear to be performing exactly the same function as the ombudsman. They investigate complaints of maladministration, they recommend the same kinds of remedies, and they try to improve standards in the organisations within their remit. Some of them have significant budgets, sizeable staff members, and they publish annual reports of their activities. The office holders have been, and are, distinguished people of high calibre who have ensured that these offices command respect. When evaluated, they tend to score highly on the criteria adopted by the British and Irish Ombudsman Association, except in relation to independence. They clearly lack independence, because they are appointed and funded by the organisations which they investigate. However, operationally, they are independent, and they exercise their judgment in an impartial way.

Why is this problematic, particularly if they handle many of the trivial cases which may overburden the Parliamentary Ombudsman? One problem is that they are not restricted to dealing with trivial and simple cases. They deal with cases which may be more appropriate for the Parliamentary Ombudsman, because of their size and complexity. There may also be cases where the internal complaints examiner is constrained in what redress might be sought from the body complained about. The referral of such complaints to independent adjudicators could have the effect of causing considerable delay before cases are eventually referred to the Parliamentary Ombudsman. This presents problems for the conduct of the ombudsman's investigations. It may even put the complaint outside jurisdiction because the time limit for referral has been exceeded[86]. Not only might the intermediate process be a source of delay, but it may also be a source of confusion to the public. Information given to the public by the complaint examiners indicates that the Parliamentary Ombudsman may be approached

---

[86]   The Parliamentary Ombudsman has expressed concern about this, and is anxious that these types of cases are referred to him sooner rather than later (Parliamentary Ombudsman Annual Report 2000–2001 (HC Paper 5 (2001–02)) p 12).

instead of them, and even after they have dealt with the case. However, it may present difficulties for complainants in deciding which body is appropriate. Complainants need to be given sufficient information to make an informed choice of which complaints route is best for them[87].

There is a more fundamental issue to be addressed. What is the value in having duplicate systems? If they are not to duplicate each other's work, what different functions should each be performing? The introduction of these independent complaints handlers may have been a result of the cumbersome and complicated processes of the Parliamentary Ombudsman. As we shall see, these processes are not appropriate for many of the complaints about public services[88]. Without these independent departmental procedures, there would be little chance of a resolution for many complainants. Indeed, in relation to the (then) Revenue Adjudicator, one commentator concluded that her work represented a 'valuable project to humanise and sensitise Revenue administration for the benefit of taxpayers generally'. It was doubted whether this would have been achievable by the Parliamentary Ombudsman[89].

However, when the ombudsman system is reformed in England, what will become of the duplicate systems? The Cabinet Office review[90] favoured the proliferation of these independent complaints examiners, believing that they had an important part to play in the complaints process. If there were problems, the review considered that they could be addressed by better publicity, and collaborative working arrangements. The solution was a management one: the provision of clearer explanations to complainants of the relative roles and status of the mechanisms, and more information about the remit of the adjudicators[91]. It is unfortunate that the review failed to discuss whether there was any value of having duplicate systems.

---

[87] In order to address this problem, the ombudsman has agreed working methods with the Adjudicator and the Independent Complaints Examiner and their staff, with a view to making it easier for individual complainants to decide which complaints mechanism to use (Parliamentary Ombudsman Annual Report 1999–2000 (HC Paper 593 (1999–2000)) para 1.21).

[88] There is also, as we shall see, the additional hurdle of having to have the complaint referred by a member of Parliament, whereas complaints can be made directly to the independent adjudicators.

[89] P Morris 'The Revenue Adjudicator – The First Two Years' (1996) PL 309 p 321.

[90] *Review of the Public Sector Ombudsmen in England* (2000) Cabinet Office.

[91] *Review of the Public Sector Ombudsmen in England* (2000) paras 7.33–7.36.

However, this omission is perhaps not surprising, given that it failed to make any recommendations about the jurisdiction or function of the ombudsmen[92]. It was 'essentially a management exercise' rather than a rational and coherent body of reforms[93].

The issue will need to be addressed in any new system, if it is to be coherent[94]. Is the ombudsman to be at the apex of the system, a safety valve and last resort for cases which have not been dealt with satisfactorily by the adjudicators? If so, should there be a requirement for this procedure to be exhausted before a referral to the ombudsman? The problem with such a requirement is that it results in a long, drawn out process before there is a final decision. In Australia, the approach adopted by the ombudsman is to spend more time on own-initiative systemic investigations, where problems have been highlighted by individual complaints. There, departments are encouraged to set up internal systems, with the ombudsman acting as auditor of the system. In this way, the Australian ombudsman hopes to reduce the large numbers of trivial and premature complaints[95]. There are, however, problems with using the ombudsman system as a kind of vestigial appeal body. In such a role, the office may not receive sufficiently large numbers of cases to enable there to be an assessment of whether public services are performing effectively. This would reduce the ombudsman's ability to comment on and suggest improvements in administrative practice.

---

[92] See M. Seneviratne '"Joining Up" the Ombudsmen – the Review of the Public Sector Ombudsmen in England' (2000) PL 582–591, p 589: D Lewis and R James 'Joined-up Justice: Review of the Public Sector Ombudsman in England' (2000) 4 International Ombudsman Yearbook 109–140.

[93] D Lewis and R James 'Joined-up Justice: Review of the Public Sector Ombudsman in England' (2000) p 119.

[94] Not only will the relationship of the adjudicators with the new system need to be addressed, but there will also need to be some decisions made about how the new system will relate to other internal mechanisms. At present, there is no common pattern with the three public sector ombudsmen. Complainants to the Health Service Ombudsman must exhaust the NHS internal complaints procedure before they can refer their case to the ombudsman. The Local Government Ombudsman makes no such stipulation, although the local authority must have had a reasonable opportunity to respond to the complaint before the ombudsman will accept it.

[95] See The Ombudsman (2001) Issue 16 p 5.

The Penal System and Complaints: the Prisons and Probation Ombudsman

Prisons are administered by the Home Office, and as we shall see, are within the jurisdiction of the Parliamentary Ombudsman. The Parliamentary Ombudsman has therefore always been available to receive complaints from prisoners. In 1994, a separate ombudsman system was introduced to deal with complaints about the prisons service[96]. The introduction of this separate ombudsman system has implications for the work of the Parliamentary Ombudsman and the ombudsman system as a whole. Before discussing the relationship between the Parliamentary Ombudsman and the Prisons and Probation Ombudsman schemes, there will be a brief discussion of the origins and features of the Prisons and Probation Ombudsman office.

An Ombudsman for Prisoners

In 1994, the Prisons Ombudsman scheme was established to provide an independent mechanism for dealing with complaints from prisoners[97]. The reasons for the establishment of such a scheme have been well documented[98]. Briefly, it resulted from concerns, expressed throughout the 1980s, that the mechanisms for dealing with prisoners' grievances were inadequate. These concerns were brought into sharp focus by the Strangeways prison riots in 1990[99]. The inquiry into that riot recommended

---

[96]   This was extended to the probation service in 2001. The Prisons and Probation Ombudsman scheme applies to England and Wales. In Scotland there is an independent adjudicator for the prisons service (see P E Morris and R Henham 'The Prisons Ombudsman: A Critical Review' (1998) 4(3) European Public Law 345–378). Northern Ireland does not have a comparable office.

[97]   As indicated above, the remit was extended on 1 September 2001, to cover complaints from those supervised by the newly created National Probation Service.

[98]   See for example G Wener *A Legitimate Grievance? A Report on the Role of the Ombudsman in the Prison System* (1983) Prison Reform Trust; P E Morris and R J Henham 'The Prisons Ombudsman: A Critical Review' (1998) 4(3) European Public Law 345–378; M Ryan and T Ward 'A Prison Ombudsman of Sorts: The Long Road to Reform' in N Hawke (ed) *The Ombudsman – Twenty Five Years On* (1993) Cavendish.

[99]   The riots began at Strangeways prison in Manchester in April 1990. They spread to other prisons, and lasted for almost four weeks. They resulted in over 200 staff and prisoners being injured, and millions of pounds worth of damage being caused.

the establishment of an independent element in the prisons complaints system[100]. It was felt that this would have a salutary effect on the internal grievance system, increase its validity, and improve standards within prisons.

In January 1993, the Home Office announced its intention to create an independent person to consider grievances from prisoners who had failed to obtain satisfaction from the internal prison complaints system. This person was to be called the Prisons Ombudsman[101], and the first office holder was appointed in 1994[102]. The office of the Prisons Ombudsman was not created by statute and its status and terms of reference were originally to be found in prison service documents[103]. The powers given to the ombudsman in these documents were wide. However, there were differences of opinion between the ombudsman and the prison service about their extent[104]. These differences were resolved by a revision of the terms of reference by the Home Office, which considerably narrowed the ombudsman's remit[105]. Subsequently, however, the Select Committee on

---

100   Lord Justice Woolf Report of an enquiry into the Prison Disturbances of April 1990 (Cm 1456, 1991).
101   This was despite the fact that the Woolf Report had been clear that the 'Complaints Adjudicator would not be a Prisons Ombudsman' (Cm 1456, 1991 p 420).
102   The first Prisons Ombudsman, Peter Woodhead, was appointed in May 1994 and began to receive complaints in October 1994. He retired in October 1999, to be replaced by the present post holder, Stephen Shaw, who was formerly the Director of the Prison Reform Trust.
103   These documents are: Proposal for Ministerial Consideration, December 1992 and Note of Arrangements for the establishment of the post, April 1994. The documents indicated that the remit of the ombudsman was to consider grievances from prisoners after all internal procedures had been exhausted. This included an examination of the merits of decisions, as well as procedures. With a few exceptions, investigations were to be undertaken into all matters affecting individual prisoners for which the Prison Service is responsible, including grievances about disciplinary offences. Excluded from the remit were matters which were the subject of litigation or criminal proceedings, and the actions of individuals or bodies outside the prison service. Also excluded were ministers' exercise of their functions in considering the release of mandatory life sentence prisoners.
104   In his first annual report in 1995, the Prisons Ombudsman noted that much of his attention during the first 14 months of his appointment had been taken up with resolving the differences in interpretation of his remit with the prison service and other bodies.
105   This presented a serious challenge to the ombudsman's independence, as the ombudsman was obliged to accept any changes which the Home Secretary might make to the terms of reference. The Home Secretary was also to determine

the Parliamentary Ombudsman examined the Prisons Ombudsman's role and powers, and concluded that the present non-statutory framework was inadequate. It made a number of recommendations[106], which were not accepted by the previous government.

New terms of reference were agreed after Labour came to power in 1997, which restored the powers of the ombudsman, coming into effect in July 1998. The new terms of reference provide that the ombudsman can investigate all decisions relating to individual prisoners taken by prison service staff, agents of the prison service, and boards of visitors. It also includes decisions taken by the National Probation Service[107]. As with all ombudsmen, there are areas excluded from jurisdiction. First, the ombudsman cannot investigate complaints which relate to policy decisions by ministers and the official advice on which these decisions are based. Also excluded are the merits of decisions taken by ministers except in cases which have been approved by ministers for consideration. The personal exercise by ministers of their function in the setting and review of tariff and the release of mandatory life sentence prisoners is excluded. The ombudsman cannot investigate actions and decisions outside the responsibility of the prison service and the National Probation Service, including for example, the police, judiciary and Crown Prosecution Service. Cases which are the subject of civil litigation or criminal proceedings are also excluded. Nor can the ombudsman investigate matters relating to the clinical judgment of prison doctors or deaths in prison[108].

As indicated above, in September 2001, the ombudsman's remit was extended to cover probation service matters, so that the new office of the

---

unresolved issues about the eligibility of complaints and about interpretation of the terms of reference. The changes to remit meant that the ombudsman no longer had unfettered access to documents, a restriction which is contrary to a fundamental principle of effective complaint handling. The unsatisfactory nature of the revised terms of reference was referred to in the annual reports in 1996 and 1997.

[106] These included extending the ombudsman's remit to include the administrative decisions of ministers and granting unfettered access to relevant documents.

[107] See Prisons and Probation Ombudsman Annual Report 2001–02 p 98. The remit includes contracted out services and the actions of people working in prisons but not employed by the prison service.

[108] Complaints about deaths in prison are within the Parliamentary Ombudsman's remit. There are however discussions taking place about whether this should be added to the Prisons and Probation Ombudsman's remit (see M Seneviratne 'The Prisons Ombudsman' (2001) 23(1) JSWFL 93–101).

Prisons and Probation Ombudsman extends beyond prisoners to those supervised by the probation service or on licence.

The ombudsman is appointed by, and is accountable to, the Home Secretary for a fixed term. The office remains without a statutory basis, a factor which has raised questions about the perceived independence of the office. Indeed, the British and Irish Ombudsman Association[109] has denied the Prisons and Probation Ombudsman the status of 'voting member' of the association on this basis[110]. The ombudsman's terms of reference note that the office is independent of the prison service. Nevertheless, the ombudsman is appointed by and answerable to the minister, who is responsible for that service and it is funded entirely by the Home Office. In this respect, the office has a similar status to the independent adjudicators described earlier[111]. This 'second-class status' within the British and Irish Ombudsman Association has been a cause of some complaint by the Prisons Ombudsman, who maintains that independence and authority are best demonstrated by what the office does, rather than by its governing instrument. He notes that there is nothing second-class or inferior about the service his office provides for prisoners or the way it is regarded by the prison services as a whole[112].

The autonomy, high calibre and personal integrity of the holders of the office have never been doubted. Despite this, the British and Irish Ombudsman Association insists on 'conspicuous independence as a

---

[109] As indicated earlier, the British and Irish Ombudsman Association was established on a self-regulatory basis, as a result of concerns that the title 'ombudsman' was being used inappropriately. The criteria which an ombudsman scheme must meet in order to be a full voting member of the organisation are: independence for those whom s/he has power to investigate; effectiveness; fairness; public accountability.

[110] Another impediment to being given this status is that the Prisons and Probation Ombudsman, like the other independent adjudicators, is subject to the overall jurisdiction of the Parliamentary Ombudsman.

[111] The office is 'squarely located within the rapidly proliferating "new breed" of Adjudicators established pursuant to the Citizen's Charter programme . . . with no statutory underpinning whatsoever' (P E Morris and R J Henham 'The Prisons Ombudsman: A Critical Review' (1998) 4(3) European Public Law 345–378, pp 352–353). Woolf had actually recommended that a Complaints Adjudicator for prisons should be established (Cm 1456, 1991).

[112] S Shaw 'First thoughts of the Prisons Ombudsman' (2000) 14 The Ombudsman 5–6, p 5.

criterion for voting membership[113]. The government has promised that the office will be put on a statutory basis at the earliest opportunity. Although the ombudsman does not believe that this will make 'a jot of practical difference' to the work of the office[114], it will give the office the sort of conspicuous independence which it now lacks. This will reduce the vulnerability of the office to political interference, and promote confidence in the impartiality of the system[115].

Procedures and Practice

The Prisons and Probation Ombudsman investigates complaints from individual prisoners who have failed to obtain satisfaction from the prison service complaints system. The ombudsman also investigates complaints from individuals who are or have been under the supervision of, housed in the accommodation of, or had pre-sentence reports prepared by the National Probation Service, and who have failed to obtain satisfaction from the National Probation Service complaints procedure. The ombudsman can look at merits as well as procedures. The Prisons and Probation Ombudsman is thus at the apex of the prisoner complaints system[116]. Prisoners must first seek redress for their grievances within the established complaints system.

If the prisoner is dissatisfied with the response of the prison service, the matter can be considered by the ombudsman. The ombudsman tries, in appropriate cases, to settle complaints informally, without the need to conduct a full investigation and to issue a formal report[117]. Where this is

---

[113] See the note from Sir Edward Osmotherly, then Chair of the Association (2000) 14 The Ombudsman p 5.

[114] Prisons Ombudsman Annual Report 2000–01 p 2

[115] The ombudsman notes that a 'significant proportion of prisoners' doubt his independence, and that statutory independence 'which remains the office's goal' would help (Prisons and Probation Ombudsman Annual Report 2001–02 p 17).

[116] The numbers of probation complaints has been modest. Almost all were ineligible, as they had not exhausted the internal complaints system. Almost all were from prisoners, not from those currently on licence or other forms of probation supervision (Prisons and Probation Ombudsman Annual Report 2001–02 p 3). Because the bulk of the ombudsman's work relates to prisons, this section will focus on this aspect of the ombudsman's work.

[117] Increasingly, complaints are being resolved through dialogue with the prison service. This means that redress is provided for prisoners with a minimum of

not possible, the ombudsman will conduct a formal investigation. In conducting the investigation, the ombudsman has unfettered access to documents and can interview staff, prisoners[118] and other individuals during the course of the investigation. The ombudsman is able to consider the merits of matters complained of, as well as procedures, and is thus unlike the other public sector ombudsmen. The office thus provides a review of the merits of decisions, as well as a review of administrative procedures. The ombudsman aims to complete investigations within eight weeks of accepting a complaint, and to close cases within 12 weeks of accepting them[119].

Where the complaint is made out, the ombudsman will recommend a remedy. These recommendations, which can be wide-ranging, are made to the director general of the prisons service. Where complaints about loss or damage to prisoners' property is upheld, compensation may be recommended which is designed to return prisoners to the position they would have been in had the loss or damage not occurred. Where there are complaints about disciplinary hearings, the ombudsman can recommend that the findings are quashed and that lost remission is reinstated. Recommendations can be made about the appropriate security categorisation of prisoners. The Director General of the Prison Service does not have to accept the ombudsman's recommendations, although the majority are accepted[120].

---

bureaucracy. Letters sent direct to prisoners rather than formal investigation reports have increasingly become the norm (Prisons and Probation Ombudsman Annual Report 2001–02 p 10).

[118] Visits to prisons by investigators is now becoming more common, and it provides a 'welcome personal touch' and 'tangible reassurance that someone is listening' (Prisons and Probation Ombudsman Annual Report 2001–02 p 3).

[119] See Prisons Ombudsman Annual Report 2000–01 p 10. Only 63% of cases were completed within the target in 2000–01, compared with 73% in the previous year. In 2001–02, this had dropped to 32%. This was partly a result of clearing cases in the accumulated backlog. The ombudsman aims to determine the eligibility of 70% of complaints within 10 days. This target was reached in 80% of cases in 2001–02 (Prisons and Probation Ombudsman Annual Report 2001–02 p 11).

[120] In 2001–02 for example, out of a total of 324 formal recommendations, 99% were accepted. Seven were rejected, but after further representations by the ombudsman, three of these were accepted (Prisons and Probation Ombudsman Annual Report 2001–02 pp 11–12). Five recommendations were rejected in the previous year (Prisons Ombudsman Annual Report 2000–01 p 10).

The numbers of complaints to the ombudsman has increased steadily over the years since the office was established. In 2001–02, there were 2,825 complaints, an increase on the previous year.[121] Only 97 complaints were about the National Probation Service. There was also an increase in the proportion of cases eligible for investigation[122]. Typically, the largest category of complaints concern prison discipline and adjudications. This is not surprising, given the consequences in terms of lost remission for breaking prison rules[123], particularly where prisoners feel that they have not had a fair hearing[124]. There are also large numbers of complaints about loss or damage to prisoners' property. Other complaints relate to transfer and allocations decisions; security classifications; segregation; racial harassment by prisoners; communications and health care.

Prisons and the Parliamentary Ombudsman

As indicated above, prisons are within the jurisdiction of the Parliamentary Ombudsman[125]. However, complaints from prisoners have never formed a major part of the Parliamentary Ombudsman's workload. Sometimes only one or two prisoners' complaints were investigated by the Parliamentary Ombudsman in any one year. A number of explanations were given for the low level of complaints, none of which concluded that it reflected an absence of grievances. Indeed, there was concern that such low numbers could not possibly reflect the extent of maladministration, arguably causing injustice, within the prison system[126]. Justice commented that there were areas of prison life barely touched on by the Parliamentary Ombudsman[127].

---

[121]   Prisons and Probation Ombudsman Annual Report 2001–02 p 7. In 2000–01, there were 2,176 complaints, itself a 12% increase on the previous year (Prisons and Probation Ombudsman Annual Report 2000–01 p 5).

[122]   Prisons and Probation Ombudsman Annual Report 2001–02 p 3. In 2001–02, 43% of complaints met the eligibility criteria.

[123]   Prisoners can have 42 days added to their sentence in lost remission, as a penalty for breaking prison rules. Another penalty is time spent in solitary confinement in the segregation unit.

[124]   There is now some concern that prison disciplinary hearings do not accord with human rights principles.

[125]   Prisons contracted out to the private sector are still within the jurisdiction of the Parliamentary Ombudsman.

[126]   See A W Bradley 'Sachsenhausen, Barlow Clowes – and then' (1992) PL 353, p 355.

[127]   Justice *Our Fettered Ombudsman* (1977) JUSTICE pp 20–21.

One reason advanced for the low number of complaints is the fact that complaints to the Parliamentary Ombudsman have to be filtered through a member of Parliament[128], which acts as a strong disincentive to prisoners. Perhaps more importantly, the Parliamentary Ombudsman can only investigate allegations of maladministration. The Parliamentary Ombudsman cannot therefore be used as an independent mechanism for appeal against the merits of decisions, which is arguably what prisoners are seeking.

The establishment of the Prisons and Probation Ombudsman does not effect the Parliamentary Ombudsman's remit. This still includes prison matters, along with other matters which are within the jurisdiction of the Home Office. Prisoners still, therefore, have a right to approach the Parliamentary Ombudsman, through a member of Parliament, where the matter is one of alleged maladministration. The normal practice, however, is to encourage the use of the Prisons Ombudsman's services for prisoners' complaints[129], and the Parliamentary Ombudsman will refer any such complaints to the Prisons Ombudsman for initial investigation. A prisoner dissatisfied with the Prisons Ombudsman's decision can refer the matter to the Parliamentary Ombudsman, but it is unlikely that there will be a different outcome[130]. The Prisons Ombudsman is unable to investigate deaths in custody, since he is unable to investigate complaints from third parties. However, the Parliamentary Ombudsman can investigate these, where they are properly referred[131].

The recent Cabinet Office review[132] of the public sector ombudsmen in England did not include the Prisons Ombudsman within the new commission, which it recommended for the public sector ombudsmen. The reason given for this was that the Prisons Ombudsman was a 'niche' role,

---

[128] As we will see in the following chapter, there is no direct access to the Parliamentary Ombudsman.

[129] See P E Morris and R J Henham 'The Prisons Ombudsman: A Critical Review' (1998) 4(3) European Public Law 345–378.

[130] P E Morris and R J Henham 'The Prisons Ombudsman: A Critical Review' (1998) p 354.

[131] Neither the Prisons Ombudsman nor the Parliamentary Ombudsman can investigate complaints from prisoners which call into question the clinical judgment of medical staff. It is the Health Service Ombudsman who has jurisdiction over such complaints where treatment has been provided directly by the National Health Service.

[132] *Review of the Public Sector Ombudsmen in England* (2000) Cabinet Office.

with no statutory underpinning, and was more properly 'part of the executive'[133]. The review did acknowledge, however, that the relationship of the Prisons Ombudsman to the proposed new, integrated commission might need to be addressed in the future. At present, there are some issues of overlap with the Parliamentary Ombudsman, but given that the Prisons and Probation Ombudsman is concerned with merits as well as process, they are really addressing different issues. When the office is eventually put on a statutory footing, the relationship with the proposed new commission will have to be addressed, particularly where there may be issues of overlapping jurisdiction[134]. For the present, particularly with the extension of remit to the National Probation Service, it appears that the office of the Prisons and Probation Ombudsman is becoming more 'joined up' with the criminal justice system[135], rather than with the rest of the public sector ombudsman system.

Conclusion

When the ombudsman schemes were first established in the public sector, there were few internal mechanisms for complaint handling and no charter programme. During the 1980s and 1990s, public services became more consumer-orientated, and public service provision is now high on the political agenda. Public services are now delivered in a culture of rights-based entitlement. Citizens have high expectations of public services, and they will voice their discontent if these expectations are not met. The last decade has seen the rise in the provision of internal redress mechanisms within public services, to deal with citizens' grievances. These redress mechanisms include a range of informal and independent reviews. Ombudsmen are part of this new landscape. There are clearly issues as to where ombudsmen fit in this plethora of complaints mechanisms and processes. In this changed environment, where the ombudsmen system is

---

[133]   *Review of the Public Sector Ombudsmen in England* (2000) para 4.7.
[134]   At least, there will be some need to establish protocols.
[135]   See 'Ombudsman's Office Launched', Prisons and Probation Ombudsman (2002) 5 On the Case, which noted that the new office 'constitutes a joined-up Ombudsman's service for both prisons and probation, and is a major step forward in joining up the criminal justice system'. See also, Prisons Ombudsman Annual Report 2000–01 p 2. The ombudsman also notes that '[j]oining up prison and probation complaints procedures reflects real continuities in the penal system' (Prisons and Probation Ombudsman Annual Report 2001–02 p 3).

one among mechanisms of redress, it becomes important to ensure that citizens use the appropriate remedy for their grievance. Ombudsmen are 'a central plank of our system of administrative justice'[136], and they occupy a unique role at the interface between individuals and public services. In the following chapters, the individual schemes that make up the ombudsmen system in the UK will be examined, in order to assess their role in providing administrative justice.

---

[136] D Lewis and R James 'Joined-up Justice: Review of the Public Sector Ombudsman in England' (2000) 4 International Ombudsman Yearbook 109–140, p131.

Chapter 4

The Parliamentary Ombudsman

The office of the Parliamentary Ombudsman was established by the Parliamentary Commissioner Act in 1967. It was the first ombudsman scheme to appear in the UK, and the background to its development has been explained in preceding chapters. As indicated previously, the scheme owes its origins to a report by Justice in 1961[1], although the powers of the ombudsman under the 1967 Act are greater than those envisaged in that report[2]. Justice had been concerned about the lack of remedies for maladministration, and an ombudsman was suggested as a means of rectifying this. Although the terms of reference of the Justice inquiry had specifically referred to the 'Scandinavian institution known as the Ombudsman', what emerged in 1967 was a 'commissioner' whose role was to support and strengthen the Parliamentary process. The office was very different to its Scandinavian counterparts, and it was designed to help members of Parliament secure redress for their constituents. The original focus of the scheme should be borne in mind in the subsequent discussion.

The Scheme

The Parliamentary Commissioner Act 1967, s 1 provides for the appointment of the Parliamentary Ombudsman[3], whose function it is to investigate

---

[1] Justice *The Citizen and the Administration* (1961) Stevens.
[2] See F Stacey *The British Ombudsman* (1971) Clarendon Press p 26.
[3] Although 'commissioner' is used throughout the legislation, the word 'ombudsman' has become the accepted terminology, and will be used throughout this chapter.

administrative action taken on behalf of the Crown. The ombudsman is an independent officer of Parliament, appointed by the Queen, on the advice of the Prime Minister. The office is held during good behaviour, and although the ombudsman may be relieved of office by request, removal from office before retiring age[4] can only be effected by the Queen on addresses from both Houses of Parliament. There is also provision for the removal of an ombudsman, who is incapable for medical reasons of performing the duties of the office, without the need for addresses from both Houses of Parliament[5]. The ombudsman's salary and pension are paid out of the Consolidated Fund[6].

The Parliamentary Ombudsman began to investigate complaints on 1 April 1967. The first ombudsman had previously been the Auditor and Comptroller General, and this reinforced the Parliamentary focus of the office in its early days[7]. Essentially the scheme provides redress for members of the public who have suffered injustice as a result of maladministration by government departments, agencies and other public bodies.

---

[4]   The retirement age is 65.

[5]   Parliamentary and Health Service Commissioners Act 1987, s 2. This amendment to the 1967 Act is to allow removal from office where an ombudsman is so severely incapacitated as to be incapable of resigning, and is included as a precautionary measure.

[6]   The ombudsman's salary is equivalent to that of a High Court judge, whose salaries and pensions are also paid from the Consolidated Fund. Under the 1967 Act, it is for the ombudsman to determine the numbers and conditions of service of the staff of the office, subject to the approval of the Treasury.

[7]   This was Sir Edmund Compton. The present, and seventh, office holder, Sir Michael Buckley, took up office in January 1997, and is to retire in the summer of 2002. The majority of the ombudsmen have been former civil servants, although some have been lawyers. It used to be the case that the entire investigations staff in the office were temporary secondments from government departments or the health service, normally for three years. However, since 1997, staff have been appointed on a permanent basis, although there are still a few secondees from government departments. The Parliamentary Ombudsman does not have a staff legal advisor. The Treasury Solicitor provides legal advice, where necessary, as do the legal advisors of the departments under investigation. Sometimes the ombudsman takes independent legal advice.

Bodies Subject to Jurisdiction

The authorities within the jurisdiction of the ombudsman are those listed in Sch 1 of the Parliamentary and Health Service Commissioners Act 1987[8]. These are essentially government departments and certain non-departmental bodies[9]. The ombudsman is also authorised to investigate actions taken by or on behalf of an authority listed in the schedule[10], a provision which brings within remit bodies with functions delegated to them by government departments. Thus, the 'next steps' executive agencies are subject to the jurisdiction of the Parliamentary Ombudsman, as they act on behalf of a government department[11]. Indeed, there are as many investigations of cases involving departmental agencies as there are of those involving the parent departments themselves[12]. Advisory bodies and tribunals are not included in the schedule, and are therefore not within the ombudsman's jurisdiction[13]. Bodies operating essentially under a contract, rather than an agency relationship are also not within jurisdiction[14].

The 1967 Act specifically lists the bodies within jurisdiction, rather than describing them by means of a generic phrase, such as 'public authority'. Because of this, new bodies must be brought specifically within the jurisdiction of the ombudsman before complaints against them can be

---

[8]   Originally, the authorities within jurisdiction were listed in the Parliamentary Commissioner Act 1967, Sch 2 and were mainly departments of central government. Section 2 of the 1987 Act extended the jurisdiction to include certain non-departmental bodies. This provision was included to honour an undertaking given in the White Paper, Non-Departmental Public Bodies (Cm 9563, 1985).

[9]   These are bodies which have executive or administrative functions that directly affect individuals or groups of citizens, and which would be within the Parliamentary Ombudsman's jurisdiction if carried out by a government department. In addition, they are subject to some degree of ultimate ministerial accountability to Parliament, in that they are dependent for their financing and continued existence on government policy.

[10] Parliamentary Commissioner Act 1967, s 5.

[11] Parliamentary Ombudsman Annual Report 1990 (HC Paper 299 (1990–91)) p 2.

[12] Parliamentary Ombudsman Annual Report 1991 (HC Paper 347 (1991–92)) p 2.

[13] Thus, for example, the Boundary Commission is not listed, as it is deemed advisory only. The Civil Aviation Authority is excluded, as it is deemed a tribunal. Some important bodies are, however, included, for example Urban Development Corporations, and the Commission for Racial Equality.

[14] This excludes, for example, Training and Enterprise Councils.

considered[15]. This is a cumbersome system, and it also results in a situation where it may be difficult to provide a definitive list of the bodies within jurisdiction at any given time. A previous ombudsman and the select committee did suggest that new public bodies should automatically be within jurisdiction, unless the legislation establishing them provided a specific exclusion, but this suggestion was never implemented[16]. The issue was addressed in the Cabinet Office review[17]. The recommendation was for a 'mixed' approach, which would include both generic types together with a list of those organisations which might have doubtful status. Although it was concluded that some generic descriptions, for example, local authorities and NHS Trusts, would be sufficient to cover many public bodies, there were areas of the public sector which could not easily fit a generic description. Therefore, to 'banish all doubt' some organisations would need to be listed. It was felt that to express the remit in terms of a generic word like 'public authority' would be 'undesirable', but no reason was given for this conclusion. Some support for it was drawn, however, from the fact that the Freedom of Information legislation adopted a mixed approach[18]. Finding an appropriate format for describing jurisdiction in any future legislation is obviously of great importance. It is clearly desirable that all public bodies are within the remit of the ombudsman, and a system must be found which reduces the need to list over 250 government departments and public bodies, as is presently the case.

---

[15]   The Parliamentary and Health Service Commissioners Act 1987, s 1 provides for amendments to the schedule to be made by Order in Council, in order to include those bodies where more than half of their running costs come from money provided by Parliament or funds raised under legislative authority (the Parliamentary Commissioners Act 1967, s 4 provides that this includes ministers, members or officers of the authority).

[16]   See Parliamentary Ombudsman Annual Report 1992 (HC Paper 569 (1992–93)) p 7. See also First Report from the Select Committee on the Parliamentary Commissioner for Administration (HC Paper 333 (1993–94)) p xv, which recommended that the bodies subject to jurisdiction should be expressed in terms of exclusion rather than inclusion. The government response to this recommendation was that there should first be an exploration of whether more publicity about the remit might provide a solution to the problem (Fifth Report of the Select Committee on the Parliamentary Commissioner for Administration (HC Paper 619 (1993–94)) (memorandum appended to the report) para 20).

[17]   *Review of the Public Sector Ombudsmen in England* (2000) Cabinet Office.

[18]   *Review of the Public Sector Ombudsmen in England* (2000) Cabinet Office, para 5.8.

Local authorities are not within the Parliamentary Ombudsman's jurisdiction. This exclusion was widely criticised during the passage of the Bill, by members in both Houses, on the basis that this was an area that produced a number of complaints, many of which were brought to members of Parliament. Local authorities are now subject to the jurisdiction of the Local Government Ombudsman. Likewise, other excluded bodies, for example hospitals and the police, later became subject to their own ombudsman or ombudsman-like body. One omission which still remains however is educational establishments[19]. Unlike schools, which are subject to the control of local education authorities and thus within the remit of the Local Government Ombudsman[20], educational establishments for both higher and further education are outside the scope of any ombudsman system[21]. The select committee is of the opinion that education is an area of the public sector where ombudsman schemes remained undeveloped, and that this should be brought within remit when the system is re-structured[22].

Exclusions from Jurisdiction

Not all the activities of the public bodies within the ombudsman's jurisdiction can be investigated. Schedule 3 of the 1967 Act contains a long list of matters that are not to be subject to investigation, even though they are performed by the public bodies within jurisdiction[23]. These 'Schedule 3 exclusions' were criticised during the passage of the Bill[24]. Some have now been remedied, but there are still large areas of government activity which are eliminated from investigation. This contrasts sharply with the position adopted in other countries. For example, in Sweden and

---

[19] See the 1967 Act, s 4, as amended by the Parliamentary and Health Service Commissioners Act 1987.

[20] However, as we shall see, the remit of the Local Government Ombudsman does not extend to the internal affairs of schools.

[21] There has been some discussion about an ombudsman for higher education (see G Evans 'An ombudsman for higher education is long overdue' (2001) Guardian, 29 May). However, rather than establishing a separate ombudsman, the jurisdiction of the Parliamentary Ombudsman could be extended to cover these bodies.

[22] Third Report of the Select Committee on Public Administration (HC Paper 612 (1999–2000)) (Review of Public Sector Ombudsmen in England) para 14.

[23] The Parliamentary Commissioner Act 1967, s 5(3) provides that the ombudsman shall not investigate any action or matter described in Sch 3. Eleven such matters are contained in the schedule.

[24] See F Stacey *The British Ombudsman* (1971) Clarendon Press p 295.

Denmark, there is a presumption in favour of all decisions of public servants being subject to investigation by the ombudsman, unless there is sound reason to the contrary[25]. A similar presumption should and could operate in this country. This would mean that all decisions of civil servants and others within appropriate departments would be subject to investigation, unless there was a constitutional principle that dictated otherwise[26]. The stated aim for establishing the Parliamentary Ombudsman was to strengthen the machinery of Parliamentary surveillance over administrative action by providing members of Parliament with a new instrument for investigating executive action. There can therefore be no case in principle for excluding from the ombudsman's remit anything that members can take up with ministers[27].

Schedule 3 contains a number of exclusions, but the most widely criticised, since the inception of the scheme, are those relating to commercial transactions and personnel matters.

Commercial Transactions

The ombudsman is excluded from investigating actions taken in matters relating to contractual or other commercial transactions by government departments or authorities, except for those relating to the compulsory acquisition or disposal of land[28]. The justification given for the exclusion is that the ombudsman's remit should be limited to complaints against government by an aggrieved citizen, rather than by an aggrieved supplier

---

[25]   See R Gregory and J Pearson 'The Parliamentary Ombudsman after twenty-five years: problems and solutions' (1992) 70 Public Administration 469–498, p 489.

[26]   See First Report from the Select Committee on the Parliamentary Commissioner for Administration (HC Paper 129 (1990–91)) (Report of the Parliamentary Commissioner for Administration for 1989). This approach has received more recent endorsement from the Select Committee (see First Report of the Select Committee for the Parliamentary Commissioner for Administration (HC Paper 33–I (1993–94)) (The Powers, Work and Jurisdiction of the Ombudsman) para 50).

[27]   See R Gregory and J Pearson, 'The Parliamentary Ombudsman after twenty-five years: problems and solutions' (1992) 70 Public Administration 469–498, p 489.

[28]   Parliamentary Commissioner Act 1967, Sch 3, para 9. The exception to the exclusion, in relation to the compulsory acquisition and disposal of land, makes it possible to investigate procedures for compulsory purchase, refusals to purchase in advance of a compulsory purchase programme, and action in connection with blight notices. The Channel Tunnel Rail Link case is a recent example.

of goods and services. Previous governments have proved to be unwilling to have their commercial and contractual relationships subjected to scrutiny by the ombudsman. It has been argued that these matters are not of the very nature of government. Another reason put forward is that these transactions involve a wide measure of commercial discretion[29].

Criticism of this exclusion has a long history, notably by Justice in 1977[30], and the Royal Commission on Standards of Conduct in Public Life in 1976[31]. Previous Parliamentary Ombudsmen have also been critical[32]. The basis of the criticism is that since the relationship between citizens and public bodies is increasingly contractual and commercial in nature, it is unrealistic to distinguish between governmental and commercial activities. Previous select committees on the Parliamentary Ombudsman have not been impressed with the reasons for the exclusion. They have in the past recommended that the ombudsman should be able to investigate some commercial complaints, particularly where a department has been improperly influenced in deciding which firms to include among those entitled to tender for contracts. It was also thought appropriate to allow investigations where decisions have been made in an arbitrary manner; or where a department has acted improperly in connection with the withdrawal of a firm's name from a list of approved tenderers[33]. The select committee has also formed the view that the government has a duty to administer its purchasing policies fairly and equitably, and that complaints about these ought to be investigated[34]. The present select committee has not given its view, except to say that it is appropriate to review all the exclusions[35].

---

[29] Observations by the Government on the Fourth Report from the Select Committee on the Parliamentary Commissioner for Administration (Review of Access and Jurisdictional Session) (Cm 7449, 1977–78).

[30] Justice *Our Fettered Ombudsman* (1977) JUSTICE.

[31] Report of the Royal Commission on Standards of Conduct in Public Life (Cmnd 6524, 1976) pp 82–83.

[32] See for example, Sir Cecil Clothier, in his final report, Annual Report for 1984 (HC Paper 262 (1984–85)) and Sir Anthony Barrowclough, in his Annual Report 1988 (HC Paper 301 (1988–89)).

[33] Fourth Report from the Select Committee on the Parliamentary Commissioner for Administration (HC Paper 615 (1977–78)) (Review of Access and Jurisdiction).

[34] Fourth Report of the Select Committee on the Parliamentary Ombudsman (HC Paper 593 (1979–80)) para 8.

[35] Third Report of the Select Committee on Public Administration (HC Paper 612 (1999–2000)) (Review of Public Sector Ombudsmen in England) para 16.

Clearly there are some contractual matters which are more appropriately dealt with by the courts, but this is not a valid reason for excluding the whole administrative side of contracting from the remit of the Parliamentary Ombudsman. The government is exercising its power, through the medium of contract, and at present there is inadequate supervision of this power[36]. Some have pointed out that 'bearing in mind that commercial activities are likely to attract little political or judicial scrutiny' there is a very strong case for bringing them within jurisdiction[37]. There was at one time particular concern about governments using the award of contracts as a political weapon[38]. Despite the criticisms, there has been little progress in this area, and the exclusion still remains.

The Parliamentary Ombudsman does receive significant numbers of complaints which are outside jurisdiction because they relate to contractual matters[39]. The scope of the exclusion has been limited to some extent by successive Parliamentary Ombudsmen, who have decided that making a charge for a service does not give it the status of 'commercial'. For example, the provision of driving tests and licences, the provision of passports, and the protection of patents, all of which entail the payment of a fee, are not included in this exclusion. It also seems that the exclusion will not apply to cases where the issue is about landlord and tenant relationships, or licences in connection with land. There have been some strained interpretations as to what is within and outside jurisdiction. For example, complaints about the communication of confidential information by one department to another can be investigated, as this involves administrative actions. However, if the information is used to remove a contractor from the list of tenderers, it becomes a commercial matter, and therefore outside jurisdiction.

---

[36]   See P Birkinshaw *Grievances, Remedies and the State* (2nd edn, 1994) Sweet and Maxwell p 200.

[37]   A Le Sueur and M Sunkin *Public Law* (1997) Longman p 426.

[38]   This concern appears to refer to a previous Labour government's policy of not contracting with companies which flouted its pricing policy (A Le Sueur and M Sunkin *Public Law* (1997) p 426). See also G Ganz 'Government and Industry: The provision of financial assistance to industry and its control' (1977) PL 439; Sir Cecil Clothier 'The Value of an Ombudsman' (1986) PL 204, pp 210–211.

[39]   Parliamentary Ombudsman Annual Report 2001–02 (HC Paper 897 (2001–02)) p 13.

Ombudsmen appear to adopt a robust approach to examining complaints in commercially sensitive areas[40]. For example, the exclusion did not prevent the ombudsman investigating the actions of the Department of Trade and Industry in relation to the regulation of investment business[41]. It does appear therefore that this exclusion represents 'something of a grey area'[42].

Personnel Matters

Another exclusion which has attracted criticism is that relating to the investigation of complaints about personnel matters made by civil servants, members of the armed forces, or other people 'in office or employment' under the Crown[43]. The exclusion prevents investigations by the ombudsman of action taken in respect of appointments, removals, pay, discipline, superannuation, promotion or postings. Also excluded are complaints of ex-employees, and complaints arising after the death of an ex-employee. This exclusion has also been interpreted to cover prospective employees, although this is not necessary on a strict construction of the Parliamentary Commissioner Act. The reason given for this exclusion is that the ombudsman scheme is concerned with the relationship between government and the governed, and not between the state as employer in relation to its employees[44]. It has been argued that without this exclusion, civil servants would be a privileged class of employee. Moreover, the existing internal arrangements to deal with staffing issues are said to be more appropriate[45].

---

[40]   See P Birkinshaw *Grievances, Remedies and the State* (2nd edn, 1994) Sweet and Maxwell p 201.

[41]   See R Gregory and G Drewry 'Barlow Clowes and the Ombudsman' (1991) PL 192–214 and 408–442; P Birkinshaw *Grievances, Remedies and the State* (2nd edn, 1994) Sweet and Maxwell p 201.

[42]   Third Report from the Select Committee on the Parliamentary Commissioner for Administration (HC Paper 353 (1989–90)) (Report of the Parliamentary Commissioner for Administration for 1989) para 5.

[43]   Parliamentary Commissioner Act 1967, Sch 3, para 10, as amended.

[44]   See F Stacey *The British Ombudsman* (1971) Clarendon Press p 296.

[45]   See Second Report from the Select Committee on the Parliamentary Commissioner for Administration (HC Paper 385 (1968–69)). In particular, there was a fear that without this exclusion, there could be a risk of 'damage to the non-political character of the Civil Service' (evidence, pp 121–122).

Criticisms of this exclusion focus on the fact that members of Parliament can, and do, take up cases from civil servants in connection with their employment, and ombudsmen in other countries have such power[46]. A previous select committee was particularly concerned that the ombudsman is prevented from investigating complaints about matters prior to appointment to the civil service, and after retirement[47]. The ombudsmen themselves have not been critical, and indeed often express a reluctance to become involved in employment disputes. They generally concur with the view that these matters are not appropriate for investigation, because they do not concern the relationship between government and citizen. In addition, there are now other mechanisms which may be more appropriate for these types of complaints. For example, complaints about superannuation matters can now be dealt with by the Pensions Ombudsman, and issues in relation to the appointments process may be dealt with by the Commission for Public Appointments.

Other Schedule 3 Exclusions

Another area of exclusion is in relation to foreign affairs. Although the Foreign Office is within jurisdiction, matters concerned with the conduct of foreign affairs are outside the remit of the ombudsman[48]. Similarly, action taken outside the territory of the UK, under the authority of the Crown, by British officials is generally excluded[49]. The only exception to this is consular activities. Thus, complaints about the actions of career consular officials overseas in relation to UK citizens are within jurisdiction[50], as are complaints by British citizens resident overseas about the quality of the assistance they receive from consular officials[51]. The ombudsman is prevented

---

[46]   Indeed, for the European Ombudsman, staff matters are the largest category of admissible complaints (see K Heede *European Ombudsman: redress and control at Union level* (2000) Kluwer Law International).

[47]   First Report from the Select Committee on the Parliamentary Commissioner for Administration (HC Paper 129 (1990–01)) (Report of the Parliamentary Commissioner for Administration for 1989) para 9.

[48]   The Parliamentary Commissioner Act 1967, Sch 3, para 1 provides that the Foreign Secretary or other ministers have power to prevent an investigation into a matter which is certified by a minister to affect relations or dealings between the government and other governments or international organisations.

[49]   Parliamentary Commissioner Act 1967, Sch 3, para 2, as amended. The Channel Islands and the Isle of Man are regarded as territories outside the UK, for the purpose of this exclusion.

[50]   Parliamentary Commission Order 1979, SI 1979/915.

[51]   Parliamentary Commissioner (Consular Complaints) Act 1981.

however from investigating action taken in connection with the administration of the government of any country or territory outside the UK, where the UK has jurisdiction, for example dependent territories[52].

There are also exclusions in relation to some of the activities of the Home Office. For example, the ombudsman cannot investigate action taken by the Home Secretary in relation to extradition or fugitive offenders, under the Extradition Act 1989[53]. In addition, there can be no investigation of the actions taken by or with the authority of the Home Secretary in relation to investigating crime or protecting the security of the state[54]. The exclusion specifically refers to the Home Secretary's actions in respect of passports, and thus complaints in relation to the issuing of these cannot be investigated by the ombudsman[55]. Any exercise of the prerogative of mercy by the Home Secretary is excluded from the ombudsman's jurisdiction.

The ombudsman cannot investigate complaints about the commencement or conduct of civil or criminal proceedings before the courts in the UK, proceedings in military courts, and proceedings before any international court or tribunal[56]. This exclusion covers the decision by departments on whether or not to commence proceedings. Originally, the administrative actions of court and tribunal staff were excluded from jurisdiction. This has now changed[57]. The actions of court and some tribunal[58] staff are within

---

52   Parliamentary Commissioner Act 1967, Sch 3, para 3.
53   Parliamentary Commissioner Act 1967, Sch 3, para 4, as amended. This refers to the confirming or rejecting of orders of extradition.
54   Parliamentary Commissioner Act 1967, Sch 3, para 5. It should be noted that the Parliamentary Ombudsman has no power to investigate the actions of the police, and this exclusion therefore relates to certain specific actions by the Home Secretary, for example the authorisation of telephone tapping.
55   The exercise of the power to issue or deny passports is, however, judicially reviewable: see *R v Secretary of State for Foreign and Commonwealth Affairs, ex p Everett* (1987) Independent, 4 December.
56   Parliamentary Commissioner Act 1967, Sch 3, para 6, as amended.
57   The Courts and Legal Services Act 1990, s 110 provides that administrative functions exercisable by a person appointed by the Lord Chancellor as a member of the administrative staff of any court or tribunal shall, in the normal course of events, be subject to the investigation of the Parliamentary Ombudsman. This settles a long-standing dispute between the Parliamentary Ombudsman and the Lord Chancellor's Department, which maintained that the courts, as separate and independent institutions, were outside jurisdiction.
58   These are where the administrative staff are appointed by the Lord Chancellor, or the tribunals specified in the Parliamentary Commissioner Act 1967, Sch 4, as amended.

jurisdiction, unless taken under the direction or authority of a person acting in a judicial capacity or in the capacity as a member of the tribunal. The ombudsman has noted[59] that it is often difficult to identify which of the actions complained about are administrative rather than judicial[60]. Similarly, the ombudsman may not investigate actions in connection with the administration of appeals relating to the Criminal Injuries Compensation Scheme, where these are taken under the direction or authority of an adjudicator appointed to determine these appeals[61]. The granting of honours, awards or privileges within the gift of the Crown, including the grant of Royal Charters, cannot be investigated by the ombudsman[62].

The Department of Health is included in the list of departments subject to investigation and is thus within jurisdiction. What is excluded is action taken by hospital authorities in the National Health Service[63]. This exclusion was defended at the time of the passing of the Parliamentary Commissioner Act on the basis that hospitals are independent, and local, and that they had improved their procedures for dealing with complaints. Another reason was that complaints might also involve general practitioners or a local authority service, neither of which were the direct responsibility of the Ministry of Health[64]. Other reasons advanced for the exclusion were in connection with the problems of clinical judgment and the possibility of negligence actions in court[65]. Despite these justifications, the exclusion was criticised. It was eventually remedied by the introduction of the Health Service Ombudsman in 1973[66].

59   The Parliamentary Ombudsman Annual Report 2000–01 (HC Paper 5 (2001–02)) p 38.
60   One case (C1162/00) investigated by the ombudsman concerned delays in dealing with a claim for costs, where the ombudsman found that there had been a failure to reply to correspondence and to deal properly with a claim for compensation.
61   Parliamentary Commissioner Act 1967, Sch 3, para 6C. This exclusion was not within the original Schedule 3 exclusions, but was inserted by the Criminal Injuries Compensation Act 1995, s 10(2).
62   Parliamentary Commissioner Act 1967, Sch 3, para 11.
63   Parliamentary Commissioner Act 1967, Sch 3, para 8, as amended.
64   Sir Arnold France, Permanent Secretary to the Ministry of Health in evidence to the Select Committee on the Parliamentary Commissioner for Administration, at question 690 (HC Paper 350 (1967–68)) p 119.
65   See F Stacey *The British Ombudsman* (1971) Clarendon Press pp 292–293.
66   The National Health Service Reorganisation Act 1973 and the National Health Service (Scotland) Act 1973 established the office of the Health Service Ombudsman to examine complaints against hospital authorities. This will be discussed in the next chapter.

Courts and Tribunals

The ombudsman is not permitted to investigate any administrative action in respect of which the person aggrieved has or had a right to go before a tribunal or has a remedy in a court of law[67]. This provision is in line with the expressed purpose for establishing the ombudsman, as essentially to provide remedies for maladministration, rather than be an alternative mechanism for pursuing legal rights. The ombudsman does however have discretion here. There can be an investigation where the ombudsman is satisfied that, in the particular circumstances, the individual cannot reasonably be expected to resort to the remedy in the court or tribunal. In practice, where there is a right of appeal to a tribunal, the Parliamentary Ombudsman will normally not investigate the complaint.

Where the only remedy is in court, however, the Parliamentary Ombudsman will normally investigate, unless it is a case which is clearly within the jurisdiction of the court, for example personal injuries[68]. Any doubts about the availability of a legal remedy are normally resolved in favour of the complainant. Equally, where there may be a legal process, but it is considered too cumbersome, slow and expensive for the objective to be gained, discretion is normally exercised in favour of the complainant[69]. An example of the generous exercise of the discretion is the investigation into the collapse of Barlow Clowes, where the Parliamentary Ombudsman investigated, even though the complainants could have pursued the matter through the courts[70].

Discretionary Powers

Even if a complaint is against the bodies within jurisdiction and is not an excluded matter, the Parliamentary Ombudsman has discretion whether or not to investigate. The Act provides that the ombudsman 'may'

---

[67] Parliamentary Commissioner Act 1967, s 5(2).
[68] See Justice *Administrative Justice: Some Necessary Reforms* (1988) Clarendon Press p 95.
[69] Second Report from the Select Committee on the Parliamentary Commissioner for Administration (HC Paper 148 (1980–81)) (Parliamentary Commissioner for Administration Annual Report for 1980).
[70] See R Gregory and G Drewry 'Barlow Clowes and the Ombudsman' (1991) PL 192–214 and 408–442, p 422.

investigate[71], the discretionary nature of the role being further emphasised by the fact that the ombudsman acts 'in accordance with his own discretion', and decides whether a complaint is duly made[72]. The courts are reluctant to interfere with this discretion. In *Re Fletcher*[73], the applicant wanted a court order requiring the ombudsman to hear his allegations of neglect of duty. The House of Lords concluded that they had no jurisdiction to order the Parliamentary Ombudsman to investigate any complaint. They were bound by the Parliamentary Commissioner Act, which gave the ombudsman discretion whether to investigate a complaint or not. They therefore refused to require the ombudsman to investigate the complaint.

This view was later confirmed in *R v Parliamentary Comr for Administration, ex p Lithgow*[74], where the court refused to interfere with the decision of the Parliamentary Ombudsman not to investigate a complaint. Indeed, doubt was expressed by the court, as to whether they would interfere with the ombudsman's decision as to his own jurisdiction in any event[75]. However, in *R v Parliamentary Comr for Administration, ex p Dyer*[76], there was a very clear message that the court was entitled to review the ombudsman's exercise of discretion. There was nothing about the ombudsman's role or the statutory framework 'so singular as to take him wholly outside the purview of judicial review'[77]. Neither was the court's power to review restricted to cases of abuse of discretion by the ombudsman. However, the discretion about whether to undertake an investigation is so wide under the terms of the Act that the courts will not readily interfere with it. In *Dyer*, the court was clear that the ombudsman's refusal to re-open an investigation was not only perfectly proper, but that it was not even a matter for the ombudsman's discretion. The Act does not give the power to re-open an investigation once a report is submitted.

71   Parliamentary Commissioner Act 1967, s 5(1).
72   Parliamentary Commissioner Act 1967, s 5(5).
73   [1970] 2 All ER 527n.
74   (26 January 1990, unreported), QBD.
75   The court in Lithgow drew a distinction between the Parliamentary Ombudsman and the Local Government Ombudsman, whose decisions had been considered by a court where there had been a dispute over jurisdiction. In Lithgow, the court thought that questions relating to the Parliamentary Ombudsman's jurisdiction should not be investigated by the court unless the matter fell within the principles of Wednesbury unreasonableness.
76   [1994] 1 All ER 375.
77   Per Simon Brown LJ, at 379.

There is a time restriction for complaints to the ombudsman. A complaint must be received by the sponsoring member of Parliament[78] within 12 months of the time the complainant became aware, or ought to have become aware, of the matters about which he or she is complaining[79]. This does not bar investigations of actions which have taken place before the previous 12 months, as time only begins to run when the alleged injustice comes to light. The ombudsman has discretion to investigate complaints out of time. This will only be done in certain limited circumstances, for example, where the complainant was prevented from making the complaint through illness. Complaints may also be accepted out of time where a complainant has been unsuccessful in pursuing other remedies. Once the complaint has been received by the member of Parliament, the member can bring it to the ombudsman for investigation at any time.

Maladministration and Injustice

The remit of the Parliamentary Ombudsman, as we have seen, is to provide remedies for those who have suffered injustice through maladministration. The 1967 Act states that the ombudsman may investigate complaints from those who claim to have sustained 'injustice in consequence of maladministration' by a government department, or any other authority named in the Act[80]. Maladministration is not defined, and its meaning and interpretation have been discussed more fully in Chapter 2. The 1967 Act is clear about the area of activity that does not come within the ombudsman's remit. Thus, the ombudsman is not authorised or required 'to question the merits of a decision taken without maladministration by a government department or other authority in the exercise of a discretion vested in that department or authority'[81]. The ombudsman is therefore

---

[78] As we shall see, complainants cannot complain directly to the Parliamentary Ombudsman, but must do so through a member of Parliament.

[79] Parliamentary Commissioner Act 1967, s 6(3).

[80] Parliamentary Commissioner Act 1967, s 5(1).

[81] Parliamentary Commissioner Act 1967, s 12(3). This section is less restrictive than it might have been. An amendment was introduced at the Report Stage of the Bill in order to ensure that maladministration was not given too wide an interpretation. This amendment provided that the powers given to the ombudsman should not be construed as authorising or requiring a review by way of appeal of any discretionary decisions. This was considered too wide a restriction, and it was replaced by what became s 12(3).

explicitly prevented from investigating the merits of discretionary decisions in the absence of administrative failure. The ombudsman cannot be used as an appeal mechanism from administrative decisions. The function of the ombudsman is to check that the decision was reached in the correct manner, following the correct procedures. In the absence of this, the ombudsman cannot substitute his or her own opinion, even where he or she clearly disagrees with it. Even in cases where there has been maladministration in the manner of reaching the decision, all that the ombudsman can do is to request that a fresh decision is made in a properly administered manner. The ombudsman cannot overturn that decision.

The ombudsman cannot investigate a complaint about the terms of a statute, and no authority can be criticised for acting within its provisions. Similarly, disputes about statutory interpretation are outside the ombudsman's remit. The ombudsman is not entitled to investigate matters which call into question the policies of a particular authority. Once ascertained what a particular policy is, all that the ombudsman can do is check that it has been properly applied in the individual case. The ombudsman can criticise where a policy is not properly expressed, or where policies are inconsistent, but cannot question the policy itself. The ombudsman cannot investigate 'political' matters. This has been interpreted as those matters that have been debated in Parliament.

In the ombudsman's investigation reports, the term 'maladministration' is not always used. What are frequently mentioned are 'failings' on the part of departments, or 'administrative faults'. It seems that the ombudsman is not required, by the Act, to say in the report whether 'maladministration' has been found. In most cases, the matters investigated are very clearly 'administrative', involving such matters as unreasonable delays, lost letters, misleading advice and mistakes in calculations. There are however some cases where it is difficult to draw an appropriate line between the manner in which a decision was reached, and the merits of the decision itself. This does involve some pushing at the outer limits of jurisdiction. For example, in the *Barlow Clowes* case[82], the ombudsman criticised the Department of Trade and Industry because improper or insufficient weight had been given to the information or evidence. This course of action has been described as bringing him 'perilously close to the merits' of the

---

[82]   This case is discussed later in the chapter.

department's decision[83]. In the Channel Tunnel link case[84], the ombudsman was accused of exceeding his powers, because he had criticised ministerial policy. The ombudsman's response to this accusation was that his concerns were with the effects of the policy rather than with the policy itself[85].

As previously discussed, the concept of maladministration has been criticised for being too narrow a test. It has however proved to be remarkably flexible and wide-ranging. Even in 1978, the ombudsman could claim that 'any unjust or oppressive action' could be investigated[86]. It does appear that the term now no longer presents a significant limitation on the ombudsman's ability to remedy grievances, and ombudsmen are not pressing for change in this area[87]. The Cabinet Office review did not discuss whether the remit of the ombudsmen in any new system should be extended beyond maladministration[88].

The meaning of injustice has been previously discussed. It is wider in scope than loss or damage, and can cover feelings of indignation and distress. In many cases there will be a financial loss, but this is not necessary for the ombudsman to find injustice. It has been given a wide interpretation, and injustice has been found in many cases where no financial loss has been suffered. For example, in one case, the Benefits Agency, as part of a fraud drive, interviewed the complainant under caution without reasonable

---

83   See P Birkinshaw *Grievances, Remedies and the State* (2nd edn, 1994) Sweet and Maxwell p 202.

84   In this case, the ombudsman criticised the way the Department of Transport had handled compensation claims by those whose property had been blighted by the uncertainty about the proposed route for the high-speed rail link between the Channel tunnel and London (see R James and D Longley 'The Channel tunnel rail link, the Ombudsman and the Select Committee' (1996) PL 38).

85   Fifth Report of the Select Committee on the Parliamentary Commissioner for Administration (HC Paper 193 (1994–95)) para 48.

86   I Pugh 'The ombudsman – jurisdiction, power and practice' (1978) 56 Public Administration 127, p 132.

87   See R Gregory and P Giddings 'The United Kingdom Ombudsman Scheme' in R Gregory and P Giddings (eds) *Righting Wrongs: The Ombudsman in Six Continents* (2000) IOS Press p 29.

88   *Review of the Public Sector Ombudsmen in England* (2000) Cabinet Office. Notwithstanding this omission, some issues about maladministration will need to be addressed in any future legislation to reform the ombudsman system. As we will see, the Health Service Ombudsman, unlike the Parliamentary and Local Government Ombudsmen can investigate complaints involving hardship, failures of service and clinical judgment.

evidence to suspect she had committed benefit fraud. The injustice here was gross inconvenience, severe distress, and gross embarrassment[89]. In another case, the Benefits Agency failed to carry out normal procedures for complaint handling, and misrepresented the outcome of the complaint to the complainant. This was seen as injustice[90].

There can however be findings of maladministration but no injustice, where for example procedural errors have not affected the decision itself. Indeed, in one case, maladministration probably resulted in a benefit for the complainant. This case concerned the Home Office Immigration and Nationality Directorate, which was found to have delayed unreasonably in considering an application for asylum. One unforeseen but fortunate result of this delay was that the complainant had become eligible for consideration under a new scheme for dealing with asylum claims[91]. As a result, she had been granted exceptional leave to remain in the UK. The ombudsman considered that injustices caused by the delay were not sufficient to outweigh this benefit, which was itself the result of the delay[92].

More commonly, injustice has been found because of loss suffered in cases of delay or refusal of benefits, and refusal or delay in returning erroneous payments. Sometimes the injustice is the financial loss caused by misleading advice, or other wrongful action. For example, in one case, the Benefits Agency misinformed the complainant about the effect on her child benefit entitlement of a proposed visit abroad. Acting on this advice, the complainant lost benefit when she returned to the UK[93]. Casting unjustified doubts on a person's honesty or integrity has been held to be injustice, as has unfair and prejudicial treatment in connection with appeals. In one case, the Appeals Service had made several mistakes in handling the arrangements for appeals by the complainant. In particular, the service had overlooked requests for assistance at the hearings because of the complainant's ill-health. This was considered to be an injustice[94].

---

[89]   Case No C 1513/00.
[90]   Case No C 38/01.
[91]   Details of the scheme were discussed in *Fairer Faster and Firmer – A Modern Approach to Immigration and Asylum* (Cm 4018, 1998).
[92]   Case No C 1851/00.
[93]   Case No C 584/01.
[94]   Case No C 11/01.

Procedure and Powers

The 1967 Act allows the ombudsman to determine the procedure to be followed for the receipt and investigation of complaints. However, there are some constraints on this. For example, complaints have to be made in writing by a member of the public to a member of Parliament. The complaint must then be referred by the member to the ombudsman, and it is the member, not the complainant, who makes the request for an investigation. The complainant must consent to the investigation[95]. The Act also requires that the investigation be held in private[96]. Although the procedure does not require legal representation, the ombudsman has discretion to allow representation by a lawyer or otherwise, and this applies not only to the complainant, but to staff in the departments involved in the investigation. The ombudsman may also pay any expenses incurred in connection with an investigation[97]. This includes travelling expenses, and any loss of earnings to attend for interview. In practice, there will be little cause for expenditure, as people are usually interviewed in their own homes or places of work. Where a professional representative is used, the ombudsman has the power to pay the reasonable cost of such representation.

The ombudsman is given extensive powers by the 1967 Act to ensure that a full and thorough investigation can be conducted. Any person, including a minister, can be required to give information, or produce documents which are relevant to the investigation. Witnesses can be compelled to attend and give evidence, in the same way that the High Court can compel, and the ombudsman has the power to administer oaths. There is no obligation on civil servants to maintain secrecy when giving evidence to the ombudsman, and no restriction upon the disclosure of information applies to information disclosed to the ombudsman. Nor can Crown privilege be used to withhold documents or evidence[98]. In order to give backing to these powers, the ombudsman can certify that obstructions, acts or omissions would constitute a contempt of court, if the proceedings were taking place in court[99]. This can then be dealt with by the court, after a hearing, as if it were a contempt of court.

---

[95]   Parliamentary Commissioner Act 1967, s 5(1). The issue of the lack of direct access will be discussed later in the chapter.
[96]   Parliamentary Commissioner Act 1967, s 7(2).
[97]   Parliamentary Commissioner Act 1967, s 7(3).
[98]   Parliamentary Commissioner Act 1967, s 8.
[99]   Parliamentary Commissioner Act 1967, s 9.

The powers of the ombudsman are subject to some restrictions. First, a person cannot be compelled to give evidence or produce documents which he or she could not be compelled to do in proceedings before the High Court[100]. Second, information relating to proceedings of the Cabinet, or any Cabinet committee can be withheld[101]. In these cases, the Secretary of the Cabinet, with the approval of the Prime Minister, can certify that information relates to the Cabinet and this is conclusive. This restriction has apparently not caused any problems in practice. In addition, although the Act gives the ombudsman power to see all relevant documents, ministers have the power to instruct the ombudsman not to disclose their contents, on the grounds that disclosure would be 'prejudicial to the safety of the State or otherwise contrary to the public interest'[102]. This power has been rarely used.

When an investigation is completed, the ombudsman is required to send a copy of the results report to the member of Parliament who requested the investigation of the complaint[103]. A copy has also to be sent to the principal officer of the department concerned, and to the civil servants who were alleged to have taken or authorised the actions complained of. The ombudsman has interpreted this section in such a way that reports are only sent to those required by the Act. Thus, the complainant is not sent a copy of the report, although the practice is to send two copies to the sponsoring member, so that one can be forwarded to the complainant. The result of this is that publicity for the reports is patchy, as it is left to the individual member of Parliament to decide whether or not to publicise it. Some do inform the press, but some do not, and even those who do might only inform a local newspaper. The ombudsman can, and does, report directly to Parliament[104], but there is no power within the Act to report directly to the complainant. It is for members of Parliament to report to the complainants, and for them to decide what publicity, if any, should be given.

---

[100]   Parliamentary Commissioner Act 1967, s 8(5).
[101]   Parliamentary Commissioner Act 1967, s 8(4).
[102]   Parliamentary Commissioner Act 1967, s 11(3).
[103]   Parliamentary Commissioner Act 1967, s 10.
[104]   Under powers contained in s 10(4) of the 1967 Act.

Access to the Ombudsman

As we have seen, complaints cannot be made to the Parliamentary Ombudsman directly, but can only be referred by a member of Parliament. This restriction is almost unique in the world community of ombudsmen, where direct access is the norm[105]. The requirement is in line with the original proposals by Justice in 1961. These proposals had recommended that access to the office should be filtered through members of Parliament, including members of the House of Lords, although this latter recommendation was never taken up. The provision for access was seen as experimental, and it was proposed that it should be reviewed after five years[106]. The original argument for restricting access in this way was that if there was direct access in a country with over 55 million people, the ombudsman would be overwhelmed with cases. However, the number of cases anticipated was greatly overestimated. Contrary to the expected 6,000–7,000 complaints a year[107], there have only just recently been more than 2,000 complaints annually. If the reason for the member filter was to prevent 'swamping', it has proved remarkably successful.

There was also a belief that the majority of members of Parliament wanted the member filter[108]. Certainly, when the Bill was being debated in Parliament, stress was placed on the ombudsman's potential to assist back-bench MPs, and the ombudsman's status as a servant of the House of Commons. To have direct access was seen as undermining the position of members of Parliament in relation to the public.

There is no doubt that indirect access involves a shift in the philosophy of ombudsman schemes. In the UK, there was emphasis on the function of the ombudsman as a means of enhancing the role of back-bench MPs, and

---

[105] Only the French Mediateur has a similar filter on access. The other public sector ombudsmen in the United Kingdom also have direct access.

[106] Justice *The Citizen and the Administration: the Redress of Grievances* (1961) pp 75–76.

[107] See F Stacey *Ombudsmen Compared* (1978) Clarendon Press p 129.

[108] Such attitudes are not uncommon. In Australia, for example, the ombudsman was originally viewed with suspicion by members, fearing that the office would usurp their role, weaken their political leverage with constituents, and dent their profile (see K Wiltshire 'The ombudsman and the legislature' (1988) Fourth International Ombudsman Conference Papers p 146).

making the office very much a matter for Parliamentary control[109]. The office became a 'parliamentary' rather than a 'public' institution[110], an aid to members of the legislature, in their role as a check on the executive. Indeed, when the issue was discussed in the 1970s, the head of the Home Civil Service felt that to allow direct access would change the whole nature of the office. It would no longer be a 'very high-powered office inquiring into a few relatively complex cases', but would become 'a vast citizen's advice bureau'. He concluded that the 'public interest, clearly, would not be served by a transformation of that kind'[111].

This is not a universal view, and the restriction on access has attracted criticism. Justice recommended its removal in 1977[112] and 1988[113], highlighting the fact that the ombudsman was little used, and attaching some blame for this on the member filter. To remove the filter would allow the ombudsman to project himself to the public in a more positive way[114]. Others have criticised this 'undesirable restriction' on the ombudsman's powers, on the grounds that 'many complainants will not wish to take their case to a partisan politician'. The member thus represents 'an extra screen between [complainants] and the administration'[115], and the filter may thus present a barrier to access. This is in addition to the fact that members of Parliament have other work to do. Research in the 1970s revealed that members used the office 'very sparingly indeed by comparison with the frequency with which they employ the established techniques for helping constituents'[116]. Research some 15 years later drew a similar conclusion. In 1986, it was found that 40% of members of Parliament had not referred

[109]   R Gregory and P Hutchesson *The Parliamentary Ombudsman. A Study in the Control of Administrative Action* (1975) George Allen and Unwin p 91.
[110]   G Drewry and C Harlow 'A cutting edge? The Parliamentary Commissioner and MPs' (1990) 53 MLR 745, p 748.
[111]   See Fourth Report from the Select Committee on the Parliamentary Commissioner for Administration (HC Paper 615, 444 (1977–78)) (proceedings of the committee relating to the report and the minutes of evidence taken between 3 May and 5 July 1978 and appendices. Parliamentary Commissioner for Administration (Review of Access and Jurisdiction)), 10 May 1978, Q 143.
[112]   Justice *Our Fettered Ombudsman* (1977) JUSTICE pp 17–18.
[113]   Justice *Administrative Justice: Some Necessary Reforms* (1988) Clarendon Press pp 89–90.
[114]   Although the Parliamentary Ombudsman's role is essentially personal, the ombudsman has never been a familiar public figure.
[115]   D Rowat *The Ombudsman Plan* (1985) University Press of America p 135.
[116]   R Gregory and A Alexander 'Our Parliamentary Ombudsman (Part II)' (1973) 51 Public Administration 48, p 48.

any complaints to the ombudsman, and only 13% had referred three or more complaints. Many members did not hold the office in high esteem, and some were unaware of its scope and functions[117].

Nevertheless, the filter does have some support, as representing an appropriate division of labour, with members of Parliament handling routine cases, and referring the 'tougher nuts' to the ombudsman[118]. The select committee originally felt that the filter was an advantage, and saw no reason to abolish it. Its view in 1978 was that it was advantageous to the complainant because the problem may be resolved quickly by a member of Parliament. It was advantageous to members, because they were kept in touch with constituency problems. The ombudsman also gained, because complaints were only referred where the member was unable to reach a solution[119]. This view was endorsed in 1991, but the select committee did recommend more publicity for members about the ombudsman's work[120]. Indeed the ombudsman did take up the select committee's suggestion, and wrote personally to every member of Parliament enclosing a new revised and re-issued guidance leaflet on his role and functions[121]. In 1994, the select committee agreed that public awareness was vital to the effectiveness of the ombudsman. Nevertheless, it still favoured the

---

[117] G Drewry and C Harlow 'A cutting edge? The Parliamentary Commissioner and MPs' (1990) 53 MLR 645.

[118] R Rawlings 'Parliamentary Redress of Grievance' in C Harlow (ed) *Public Law and Politics* (1986) Sweet and Maxwell p 138. Rawlings recognised the important role of MPs for those with grievances, particularly in relation to problems involving maladministration or general personal difficulties. He believed that the filter should continue, so that MPs can handle routine cases, only bringing in the ombudsman for the difficult ones. But he also wanted MPs to be encouraged to report to the select committee cases or patterns of cases which suggested serious or recurring instances of maladministration. He suggested that the select committee be empowered to identify problem areas and direct the ombudsman to investigate. Such an approach would facilitate a broad, systematic and responsive use of the oversight function of the Parliamentary Ombudsman.

[119] Fourth Report of the Select Committee on the Parliamentary Commissioner for Administration (HC Paper 615 (1977–78)) (Review of Access and Jurisdiction).

[120] First Report of the Select Committee on the Parliamentary Commissioner for Administration (HC Paper 129 (1990–91)) (Report of the Parliamentary Commissioner for Administration) paras 29–30.

[121] Fourth Report of the Select Committee on the Parliamentary Commissioner for Administration (HC Paper 368 (1990–91)) (Report of the Parliamentary Commissioner for Administration for 1990) para 10.

retention of the filter[122], direct access proving to be 'too much of a leap in the dark' for the select committee to contemplate[123].

The Cabinet Office review came out 'strongly' in favour of the abolition of the filter, presenting a large amount of evidence in support of this view. It noted that the 'overwhelming majority' of organisations and individuals who had made contributions to the review proposed the abolition of the filter, as did the existing select committee[124]. However, a survey conducted for the review found that 52% of MPs supported the retention of the filter. This majority has decreased over the years, and Labour and newly elected MPs are generally in favour of its abolition[125]. Despite the lack of member support, the conclusion of the review is that the filter 'can no longer be sustained in an era of joined up government'[126]. If the public sector ombudsmen in England are to be integrated, it would be problematic for one part of the new service to have a filtering process, when the other aspects of the service can be accessed directly.

The select committee now supports the abolition of the filter, believing it to be 'inconsistent with the world of public service charters' and wants it to be replaced with direct access[127]. There are clearly sensitivities in this area[128], with some members of Parliament anxious to retain their undoubted

---

[122] First Report of the Select Committee on the Parliamentary Commissioner for Administration (HC Paper 33–I (1993–94)) (The Powers, Work and Jurisdiction of the Ombudsman) para 76.

[123] R Gregory, P Giddings and V Moore 'Auditing the Auditors: the Select Committee Review of the Powers, Work and Jurisdiction of the Ombudsman 1993' (1994) PL 207–213, p 213.

[124] Review of the Public Sector Ombudsman in England (2000) Cabinet Office para 3.19. In 1997, the Consumers Association concluded that the filter should be removed (Ombudsmen (1997) p 25, recommendation 7).

[125] See B Thompson 'Integrated Ombudsmanry: Joined-up to a Point' (2001) 64 MLR 459–467, p 461.

[126] *Review of the Public Sector Ombudsman in England* (2000) Cabinet Office para 3.52.

[127] Third Report of the Select Committee on Public Administration (HC Paper 612 (1999–2000)) (Review of Public Sector Ombudsmen in England) para 12.

[128] Perhaps these sensitivities were not in the forefront of Lord Lester of Herne Hill's mind when he introduced a Private Members Bill into the House of Lords to abolish the member filter in February 2000. The Parliamentary Commissioner (Amendment) Bill had two clauses, designed to amend the 1967 Parliamentary Commissioner Act to enable the ombudsman to investigate complaints directly from the public. Perhaps not surprisingly, the Bill got no further than this.

important role in complaint-handling[129]. However, these sensitivities must be overcome if the new system is to be coherent. Attention must also be paid to resourcing the office when the filter is removed, as evidence suggests that this will result in an increase in the number of complaints[130].

Initiating Complaints

The ombudsman can accept complaints, referred by members of Parliament, from individuals, companies, partnerships, trustees, amenity groups or interest groups. The person aggrieved must make the complaint, unless unable to act for him or herself, when it can be made on their behalf[131]. A complaint is treated as made by a person if it is made by an employee or agent of that person and complaints have been accepted from solicitors on behalf of clients, and from other professionals and professional bodies. However, complaints cannot be made on behalf of others where there is no question of there being an agency, and where there are no particular links between the complainant and the person aggrieved.

The Act thus prevents the ombudsman investigating on his or her own initiative. This contrasts with the Comptroller and Auditor General, on whom the office was modelled, who does not investigate on the basis of complaints, but on his or her own initiative in the course of carrying out the functions of an auditor. The Parliamentary Ombudsman can only act upon a complaint, and there is no power to act where there is a suspicion that there is something amiss. Indeed, in the absence of a written complaint from a member of the public, members of Parliament cannot act on their own initiative and request the ombudsman to investigate an issue.

Most ombudsmen worldwide are able to conduct investigations on their own initiative. The Swedish ombudsman has power to inspect

---

129   See also R Rawlings 'The M.P.'s Complaints Service' (1990) 53 MLR 22–43 and 149–169. He notes the 'undoubted strength' of the complaint-handling function of members of Parliament (p 165), and sees the service as 'uniquely comprehensive, locally accessible and free at the point of delivery' (p 40).

130   Third Report of the Select Committee on Public Administration (HC Paper 612 (1999–2000)) (Review of Public Sector Ombudsmen in England) para 12.

131   The Parliamentary Commissioner Act 1967, s 6(2) provides for a complaint to be made by the personal representative of a deceased, or by the member of the family or other suitable representative where a person is for any reason unable to act for him/herself.

administrative transactions, and thus acts as a permanent commission on administrative procedure and efficiency. The nearest equivalent we have is the National Audit Office for central government, and the Audit Commission for local government, but their roles are very different to that of ombudsmen. The Austrian ombudsman is entitled to investigate suspected grievances, and the Australian Commonwealth ombudsman has such powers, although they are rarely exercised. A survey conducted in the 1980s indicated that the only ombudsmen not to have this power are the British, the French, the German Federal Petitions Committee, Liechtenstein and the City of Zurich[132]. There seems little justification for denying these powers to the British ombudsmen, and indeed a reason for giving such powers is to protect the interests of those who are too weak and oppressed to protect their own.

The Cabinet Office review rejected the idea of giving the ombudsman power to initiate investigations without a complaint, on the basis that it would make the system 'vulnerable to external pressures to examine alleged systemic weaknesses'. Moreover, it claimed that own-initiative investigations appeared 'inconsistent with impartiality'[133]. These conclusions are not supported by evidence[134]. Nor is the restriction supported by the select committee, which has in the past recommended a limited power of investigation without complaint. For example, one select committee suggested that own-initiative investigations might be appropriate where systemic failings came to light as a result of individual complaints. Subject to its approval, the select committee felt that the ombudsman ought to be permitted to conduct an investigation, in order to identify the causes of a problem, and make recommendations for systemic improvements[135]. The present select committee is of the view that 'there

---

[132]   W Haller 'The place of the ombudsman in the world community' (1988) Fourth International Ombudsman Conference Papers p 40.

[133]   *Review of the Public Sector Ombudsmen in England* (2000) Cabinet Office para 6.15.

[134]   For criticism of the review's conclusions in this respect, see D Lewis and R James 'Joined-up Justice: Review of the Public Sector Ombudsman in England' (2000) 4 International Ombudsman Yearbook 109–140, p 122.

[135]   Fourth Report of the Select Committee on the Parliamentary Commissioner for Administration (HC Paper 615 (1977–78)) (Review of Access and Jurisdiction). This proposal was rejected by the government at the time, on the grounds that such additional powers were not necessary. Moreover, it was felt that they would detract the ombudsman from the task of investigating individual complaints (Observations by the Government on the Fourth Report of the Select Committee

may well be a case for own initiative investigations in certain circumstances', and that it 'may have a role in suggesting some such investigations'[136]. It made no suggestions however as to the appropriate circumstances for this, nor what role it might play in this regard.

Certainly, there seems little justification for this exclusion, and indeed the arguments for it have been described as 'specious in the extreme'[137]. Justice has supported a limited power of own initiative investigation[138]. Where ombudsmen do have this power, it appears that it is sparingly used, but it can have important consequences for a wide range of people[139]. There is certainly no suggestion that that the power undermines confidence in the independence of an ombudsman system[140]. Previous ombudsmen have not sought such a power, sometimes on the pragmatic argument that if there was a suspicion that something needed investigating, it would be easy to find a member of Parliament willing to forward a case. Presumably this would only be possible if a willing complainant was also identified. The present Parliamentary Ombudsman and other public sector ombudsmen support the conclusions of the Cabinet Office review[141]. However, they do not in general appear to be firmly against the power to conduct investigations on their own initiative. They do concede that such investigations would be advantageous in some circumstances, and that the power would only be used sparingly[142].

---

on the Parliamentary Commissioner for Administration (Review of Access and Jurisdiction) (Cm 7449, 1979)).

[136] Third Report of the Select Committee on Public Administration (HC Paper 612 (1999–2000)) (Review of Public Sector Ombudsmen in England) para 11.

[137] K Wiltshire 'The ombudsman and the legislature' (1988) Fourth International Ombudsman Conference Papers p 155.

[138] Justice *Administrative Justice: Some Necessary Reforms* (1988) Clarendon Press p 92.

[139] For example, in New Zealand, there were a number of complaints from Telecom subscribers about Telecom's standard terms of contract. The New Zealand ombudsman initiated an investigation into the reasonableness of the standard telephone subscribers contract (see M Taggart *Corporatism, Privatisation and Public Law* (1990) Legal Research Foundation p 14).

[140] See evidence from Professor Roy Gregory to the select committee, referred to in the Third Report of the Select Committee on Public Administration (HC Paper 612 (1999–2000)) (Review of Public Sector Ombudsmen in England) para 11.

[141] Third Report of the Select Committee on Public Administration (HC Paper 612 (1999–2000)) (Review of Public Sector Ombudsmen in England) para 11.

[142] See, for example, the interview with the Parliamentary Ombudsman in Public Service Magazine ('It's all in a name' May 2002 24–26), where he admits that

Processing Complaints

When a complaint is received in the ombudsman's office from a member of Parliament, it is subjected to four initial questions[143]. First, it is checked to see whether it concerns a body and a matter within the ombudsman's jurisdiction. The mandatory provisions of the Act require that the complaint has to concern administrative actions by or on behalf of the departments listed in Sch 2 of the Act, but that the action is not excluded by Sch 3. Complaints can only be made by, or on behalf of, an aggrieved person who is resident or present in the UK, or the complaint must relate to an action taken while he or she was present in this country[144]. If the body complained against or the subject matter is outside the ombudsman's jurisdiction, the matter cannot be considered further. The ombudsman does receive significant numbers of complaints which are outside jurisdiction, including both those excluded by Sch 3 and those where the body complained against is not one which the ombudsman can investigate. In 2001–02, out of a total of 1988 cases concluded, 109 were rejected at this stage, on the basis that they were clearly outside jurisdiction. Where complaints cannot be investigated, the ombudsman writes to the complainant explaining why this is not possible.

Those complaints not rejected as being clearly outside jurisdiction are then considered further to see if there is evidence of administrative failure, and whether that failure caused personal injustice which has not been rectified. In addition, the complaint is examined to see if it is likely that the ombudsman's intervention will secure a worthwhile remedy. The ombudsman also generally expects the matter to have been put to the authority concerned, to give it an opportunity to provide redress. The complaint will not be taken any further if there is no evidence of

---

the lack of the power to conduct own-initiative investigations limits the scope of his work. However, a contrary view is expressed in the same article by Walter Merricks, the Chief Ombudsman at the Financial Ombudsman Service, who does not believe such a power fits very well with an ombudsman's role as an independent complaints handler (p 24).

[143]   See Parliamentary Ombudsman Annual Report 2001–2002 (HC Paper 897 (2001–02)) p 13.

[144]   Parliamentary Commissioner Act 1967, s 6(2). This provision covers situations of temporary visits, and also covers those who are in the country illegally. Indeed, a number of complaints about the action of immigration officers rests on this assumption, and they have been investigated. As we saw earlier, there are also specific provisions in relation to consular activities abroad.

maladministration resulting in un-remedied injustice, or there is no likelihood of a worthwhile remedy. In 2001–02, 812 cases were concluded at this stage, the majority of them because there was no prima facie evidence of maladministration. Other reasons for not pursuing the complaint at this stage include the fact that there is a right of appeal to a tribunal. Also if the complaint is not about administrative actions or it is time-barred it will be rejected. As indicated previously, in all cases, the ombudsman has an overall discretion whether or not to investigate.

Not all the cases remaining after this process result in a statutory investigation and formal report. Instead, in many of these, the complaints can be settled quickly and efficiently by making enquiries of the departments concerned. In many cases, these enquiries lead to an appropriate outcome for the complainant. Sometimes the result of these enquiries is that the complaint is taken no further because, for example, it becomes apparent that no injustice has been suffered, or no worthwhile outcome is likely. In 2001–02, 781 complaints were resolved following enquiries of the department, which represented 39% of all the cases concluded without a statutory investigation. In 44% of these cases, there was a positive outcome for the complainant.

In the remaining cases, a statutory investigation is initiated. When this happens, a statement of complaint is issued to the body concerned[145], and a copy is sent to the member who has referred the complaint. Even these cases do not necessarily result in a statutory report. In 2001–02, there were 91 cases where the investigation process was initiated, but was terminated either because an appropriate outcome was achieved, or no worthwhile remedy could be achieved. Where cases are resolved without the issue of a statutory report, a brief account of the agreed resolution is sent to the member who referred the case and the body complained against. In only a minority of complaints to the ombudsman is a statutory report issued. For example, in 2001–02, there were 195 statutory reports, which represent 10% of the total cases concluded in that year.

Where there is a full investigative process, this normally involves the ombudsman's staff in an examination of departmental files, interviews of

---

[145] Section 7(1) of the Parliamentary Commissioner Act 1967 provides that the principal officer of the department complained against must have an opportunity to comment upon any allegation contained in a complaint accepted for investigation.

officers involved in the case, and interviews of complainants. These latter interviews are usually conducted in the complainant's home, and sometimes in the presence of their member of Parliament, or other advisor. There is no opportunity to cross-examine, and any inconsistencies in the evidence cannot be tested as they could in a court. In many cases, the ombudsman can only note the inconsistencies, without passing any judgment. The ombudsman has expressed concern that poor record management has sometimes made it difficult to conduct satisfactory investigations or enquiries. Where this is the case, the ombudsman errs on the side of the complainant, so that if he or she 'puts forward a plausible account with some supporting evidence' the onus is then on the department to refute it. The department cannot rely on the lack of evidence because of its own inability to produce records[146].

When the investigation is complete, the ombudsman prepares a report and conclusions, and, if appropriate, recommendations as to the remedy. A draft is sent to the department, where it is checked for accuracy, and, where there is a finding of maladministration and injustice, to see if the department is prepared to grant the remedy suggested[147]. The final report is then sent to the referring member, and the body against whom the complaint was made.

Working Methods

The conduct of formal investigations, involving as it does the sending of investigators to departments to examine files, and if necessary interview officials, is very time consuming. It has been described as being of a 'Rolls-Royce' standard, involving a high level review, with each such investigation coming to the attention of the permanent secretary in the department. It is a method of working that has been very much influenced by the office of the Comptroller and Auditor General. Most other

[146]   See Parliamentary Ombudsman Annual Report 2000–2001 (HC Paper 5 (2001–02)) p 8.

[147]   In *R v Parliamentary Comr for Administration, ex p Dyer* [1994] 1 All ER 375, the court decided that this practice did not breach the rules of natural justice. The court said that fairness did not demand that the complainant be shown the draft report in the same way as the department. This was because it was the department that was being investigated and which was likely to face public criticism.

ombudsmen systems throughout the world employ a less vigorous method of investigation, and investigation staff will only call for files in the more difficult cases, and will rarely interview the civil servants concerned.

The Parliamentary Ombudsman system has attracted criticism in the past[148] because it was felt that this very thorough method of investigation was unnecessary for the more routine or simple type of case. Often, in these cases, a telephone inquiry can produce a change in the decision and immediate redress for a complainant. It has also been suggested that a less thorough investigation in some cases would not necessarily impair the ombudsman's effectiveness as an administrative critic[149]. However, the emphasis in the legislation is very much focussed on this very thorough method of investigation and report. This did influence the approach of the office, and to a large extent restricted the ability of the ombudsman to deal with complaints as appropriate, depending on their type and complexity. Notwithstanding the constraints of the legislative requirements, the ombudsman's office is now adopting a more flexible approach for routine and simpler cases. This clearly has to be done within the legislative framework, but it does conform with one of the ombudsman's stated purposes, which is to 'consider complaints, and where appropriate investigate them, with a view to impartial and speedy resolution'[150].

This flexible approach is evident in the recent changes to the organisation of the office, designed to make the process of complaint handling more efficient[151]. Before these changes, the functions of the office were divided into screening and investigation processes for complaints. Screening involved the appraisal of new complaints, in order to decide whether to conduct an investigation. Those complaints passing the screening process were then dealt with by the section dealing with investigations. In 2000–01 this process was replaced by integrated case-handling[152]. Complaints

---

148 See for example Justice *Our Fettered Ombudsman* (1977) JUSTICE.

149 See R Gregory and J Pearson 'The Parliamentary Ombudsman after twenty-five years: problems and solutions' (1992) 70 Public Administration 469.

150 Parliamentary and Health Service Ombudsman Business Plan 2002, para 1.

151 See the Parliamentary Ombudsman Annual Report 2000–2001 (HC Paper 5 (2001–02)) p 5. The improvements in working practices were introduced in April 2000.

152 On 1 April 2000, there were five integrated case-handling directorates, each covering particular departments and agencies. This number was reduced to four in September 2000, and by the end of the year to three (see Parliamentary

are now initially scrutinised to ensure that they are within jurisdiction. Provided that they are, they are dealt with by caseworkers, who see each case through to a conclusion. The conclusion may be a detailed investigation resulting in a statutory report. Equally, the complaint may be resolved by making enquiries of the body concerned. Investigations are only taken as far as is necessary to reach a fair and soundly based resolution. As a result of these changes, in 2000–01 18% of the total cases concluded were resolved with a positive outcome for the complainant without the need for a formal report. These changes represent a move towards a less time-consuming and cumbersome process, with the objective of obtaining a fair resolution of a complaint. The objective is not the preparation of a detailed report, unless that is an appropriate way of resolving the matter.

Remedies

Only where injustice has been found as a consequence of maladministration is a complainant entitled to a remedy. The remedies include apologies, compensation, and review of procedures. In common with other public sector ombudsmen world-wide, the Parliamentary Ombudsman has no power to order compensation or other action to remedy the injustice. The ombudsman's power is limited to recommendations about the appropriate action that a department should take. It is then for the department to respond in whatever way it deems necessary. The ombudsman needs to ensure that as far as possible the remedies are accepted and implemented by the bodies to which they are addressed. Solutions need to be negotiated where they are not readily forthcoming. If the recommendation is not followed, the lack of legal enforceability means that the complainant is left without a remedy. Despite this, there are no proposals for change. This is because judicial enforcement is seen as unnecessary, and also counter-productive.

It is considered unnecessary because the lack of judicial enforcement of remedies has not really been a problem for the Parliamentary Ombudsman. Sometimes obtaining a remedy may involve lengthy discussions with departments, and in rare cases, the Select Committee on Public

---

Ombudsman Annual Report 2000–01 (HC Paper 5 (2001–02)) p 15). This will be reduced to two towards the end of 2002, and will thus create a flatter management structure (see Parliamentary and Health Service Ombudsman Business Plan 2002 para 3.24).

Administration may have to question a department's reluctance to implement the recommendations[153]. However, in general, departments do tend to comply with recommendations. This is partly due to the existence of the select committee, backed up by the authority of Parliament, together with political considerations. Where a remedy is not forthcoming, the Parliamentary Ombudsman has the power to make a special report to Parliament, although this power has rarely been used[154].

Another argument against judicial enforcement is that it may be counter-productive. One of the strengths of the ombudsman system is that departments remain fully responsible. The ombudsman relies on departmental co-operation, both in carrying out investigations, and in providing appropriate remedies. To have judicial enforcement may lead to departments demanding a right of appeal, and could lead to a more confrontational approach. It would certainly alter the essential aspect of the office, which is co-operation. This co-operation is seen to be the key to the ombudsman's success, which enforcement through the courts may jeopardise[155]. This has been a consistent view of commentators and ombudsmen, and, as indicated, conforms to the recognised practice for ombudsmen's systems worldwide.

Although it is for the department to provide a remedy, the ombudsman often takes the initiative, indicating what would be considered suitable in the circumstances. However, the focus of the 1967 Act was on investigation and report, and not on redress. Indeed, the 1965 White Paper envisaged a largely passive role for the ombudsman in this respect, restricting the role to informing the sponsoring member of Parliament where a department had

---

[153] See Parliamentary and Health Service Ombudsman Business Plan 2002, para 3.21.

[154] The Parliamentary Commissioner Act 1967, s 10(3) empowers the ombudsman to lay a special report before each House of Parliament, where he considers that an injustice consequent on maladministration has not been, or will not be, remedied. The first occasion of this was in the 1970s, where there was a refusal to meet late claims for compensation after the upgrading of a road in Bexley (HC Paper 598 (1977–78)). Another was the Channel Tunnel Rail Link case (HC Paper 193 (1994–95)). Both of these cases raised issues of policy and public expenditure 'which one might well argue were for Parliament alone to settle' (see M Buckley 'Remedies, Redress and "Calling into Account": Some Myths about the Parliamentary Commissioner for Administration' (1998) Denning Law Journal 29–47, p 44).

[155] Justice *Administrative Justice: Some Necessary Reforms* (1988) Clarendon Press p 104.

rectified the matter. If the department had not acted to the ombudsman's satisfaction, the matter could be reported to Parliament[156]. It was only during the later stages of the passing of the legislation that the ombudsman's role in recommending an appropriate remedy was discussed[157]. Even then, it was felt that it was not appropriate for the ombudsman to concern himself with assessing compensation. Successive ombudsmen have had to develop this particular role in recommending compensation and other appropriate remedies.

Recommendations for compensation are not given in all cases where there has been a finding of injustice as a consequence of maladministration. This remedy is usually reserved for cases where the complainant has suffered financial loss through the maladministration. This would occur, for example, where loss has been incurred through reliance on incorrect advice from an official, or where money had been improperly withheld. Sometimes, a new decision or a review of procedures may be more appropriate. However, even where no financial loss has been incurred, the ombudsman can make a recommendation for compensation for distress and for the cost and inconvenience of pursuing the complaint. These 'consolatory' payments typically range from about £50 to £200. They can be larger, where the ombudsman considers that there has been 'gross inconvenience', awards of £400 sometimes being recommended in such cases[158].

Where financial loss has been sustained as a result of maladministration, the ombudsman's aim in recommending compensation is to restore complainants to the position they would have been in had the maladministration not occurred[159]. Some of these recommendations can involve large sums of money. For example, where complaints concern arrears of benefit, the awards can amount to thousands of pounds. There is often an additional sum added in respect of interest on the amount owed. In one case, where the Benefits Agency had made errors in the complainant's entitlement to industrial injuries disablement benefit, the complainant was awarded £19,526, plus £4,463 interest[160]. In a case where

[156]   The Parliamentary Commissioner for Administration (Cm 2767, 1965) para 11.
[157]   See Standing Committee Debates, Standing Committee B, Official Report, cols 302–305 (15 November 1966).
[158]   Case No C 1127/00.
[159]   Parliamentary Ombudsman Annual Report 1998–99 (HC Paper 572 (1998–99)) para 4.2.
[160]   Case No C 797/00.

the Valuation Office Agency had made an error in setting the rateable value of business premises, the recommendation was that the agency meet the difference in the rates bill for the period of the lease[161]. Compensation payments made by departments are ex gratia.

Where an investigation reveals that other citizens may be similarly affected by the maladministration, there is an expectation that the recommendations for compensation will also be applied to them. For example, in one case the Department for Social Security was recommended to compensate a complainant for the late payment of Severe Disability Premium. It then identified and reviewed more than 400 similar cases[162]. In a case involving the Ministry of Agriculture, Fisheries and Food and the Food Standards Agency, there were complaints about delays in making payments under the Arable Area Payments Scheme[163]. The investigations revealed that there had been unreasonable delay in meeting a statutory deadline for payments to farmers who had fully complied with the scheme rules and made timely claims. This was maladministration, and the remedy recommended was payment to reflect the interest on the amount between the deadline for payment and the dates when payments were made. In addition, the department agreed to review all cases where claimants had received their 1995 Arable Area Payments Scheme payment after the deadline and compensate those farmers in a similar position. Up to 31 March 2001, the department had made payments totalling £548,736 in 2,869 cases[164]. These cases are examples of the way the ombudsman system provides a generalised benefit as a result of individual case investigations.

The ombudsman's role in recommending appropriate remedies is also illustrated by the investigations into complaints about incomplete and inaccurate guidance about changes in the State Earnings Related Pension

---

[161] Case No C 722/00.

[162] See M Buckley 'The Parliamentary Ombudsman' (1998) 68 Adviser 6–8, p 7.

[163] One of these cases was the subject of a special report to Parliament under the provisions of the Parliamentary Commissioner Act 1967, s 10(4) (see Seventh Report of the Parliamentary Commissioner for Administration (HC Paper 635 (1999–2000)) (Investigation into delays in making payments under Arable Area Payments Scheme)).

[164] Parliamentary Ombudsman Annual Report 2000–01 (HC Paper 5 (2000–2001)) p 41.

Scheme (SERPS)[165]. As a result of the ombudsman's investigation, the Department for Social Security established a protected rights scheme for those who could demonstrate that they had been misled. Under this scheme, anyone widowed or reaching state pension age before 6 October 2002 would be exempt from the reduction of SERPS inheritance rights to a maximum 50% entitlement. The reduction would apply only to those who were 10 or more years from state pension age. For those within 10 years of state pension age, the reduction would be phased in. The department had consulted the ombudsman as this redress scheme had been developed, and the ombudsman was satisfied that it provided 'a global solution to the problem of making good the effects of past maladministration'[166].

Remedies: Some Causes Célèbres

Even in cases where the department has not accepted the ombudsman's conclusions and recommendations, there have been some spectacular successes in obtaining remedies. An early success, during the 1960s, was the Sachsenhausen case, which is often regarded as the case which established the ombudsman as an institution[167]. This case[168] arose as a result of complaints about the refusal of the Foreign Office to pay compensation to a number of former servicemen. The servicemen claimed to have been victims of Nazi persecution, by virtue of their detention in

---

[165]   See Third Report from the Select Committee on Public Administration (HC Paper 305 (1999–2000)) (State Earnings Related Pension Scheme (SERPS) Inheritance Provision); Fifth Report from the Select Committee on Public Administration (HC Paper 433 (1999–2000)) (Administrative Failure Inheritance SERPS); Government response to the Fifth Report from the Select Committee on Public Administration on Inheritance SERPS (HC Paper 264 (2000–01)); Second Report from the Select Committee on Public Administration (HC Paper 271 (2000–01)) (SERPS Inheritance Provision: Redress for Maladministration, Vol 2).

[166]   Parliamentary Ombudsman Annual Report 2000–01 (HC 5 Paper (2001–2002)) p 9.

[167]   M Buckley 'Remedies, redress and "Calling to Account": Some Myths about the Parliamentary Commissioner for Administration' (1998) Denning Law Journal 29–47, p 44.

[168]   For details see F Stacey *The British Ombudsman* (1971) Clarendon Press pp 248–258. See also R Gregory and P Hutchesson *The Parliamentary Ombudsman. A Study in the Control of Administrative Action* (1975) George Allen and Unwin pp 416–506.

Sachsenhausen concentration camp during the 1935–45 war[169]. The complainants' case was taken up by several members of Parliament, but to no avail. In June 1967, the case was submitted to the Parliamentary Ombudsman for investigation. The ombudsman, reporting in December 1967, found injustice as a consequence of maladministration by the department. This was on the grounds that the department had taken into account irrelevant information when reaching its decision, and had failed to take into account all the relevant information. The Foreign Secretary dismissed the findings of maladministration and disagreed with the ombudsman's conclusions and criticisms. Despite this, the Foreign Secretary reversed the decisions of the department, and awarded compensation to the complainants.

In the 1970s, the Parliamentary Ombudsman was not so successful with his *cause célèbre*. This concerned the case involving the collapse of the Court Line travel business in 1974. A number of members of Parliament received complaints from individuals, who felt that the Department of Industry was partly to blame for the losses they sustained at the collapse. The Parliamentary Ombudsman investigated, his investigation becoming the subject of a special report[170], in which it was concluded that the government could not be absolved from all responsibility for the losses. The ombudsman criticised ministerial statements made some two months before the collapse, concluding that they were likely to have left the public with a misleading impression. It was concluded that the government gave a misleading guarantee of the soundness of Court Line, and thereby misled people into investing money in a company that failed. The government rejected the ombudsman's conclusions, considering the issue a matter of political judgment, and departmental action was defended in Parliament. The government therefore did not feel it was appropriate to accept any financial responsibility for the losses caused by the collapse, and no remedy was forthcoming for the complainants.

The ombudsman's spectacular case in the 1980s was *Barlow Clowes*. This was important not just because it resulted in the 'most impressive'[171]

---

[169] The Foreign Office disputed the servicemen's claim that the conditions in which they were held were equivalent to those in the main Sachsenhausen camp.

[170] Fifth Report of the Parliamentary Commissioner for Administration (HC Paper 498 (1974–5)) (Court Line).

[171] See R Gregory and G Drewry 'Barlow Clowes and the Ombudsman' (1991) PL 192–214 and 408–442, p 420.

compensation ever paid, but also because of the scale of the inquiry[172]. It was described by the ombudsman at the time as 'the most complex, wide-ranging and onerous investigation' that the office had ever undertaken[173]. Others have called it 'a *deluxe* investigation in a class of its own'[174]. The case involved complaints from investors in the Barlow Clowes Investment Group who suffered financial losses after its collapse in 1988. The complainants' case was that these financial losses were incurred as a result of maladministration in the way that the Department of Trade and Industry had regulated the Barlow Clowes Investment Group. These regulatory matters related to the powers of the department to issue licences[175].

The Parliamentary Ombudsman reported in 1989. He accepted that he could not question the decision as to the granting or revoking of licences, as this would be to question the merits of a decision. However, he could question the processes by which the decision was reached, and it was here that maladministration was found. Five areas where there had been significant maladministration by the department, which had contributed substantially to the investors' losses, were identified. In particular, the department could have monitored more closely the activities of Barlow Clowes, and could have withdrawn the licence. The government disagreed with the ombudsman's findings, arguing that the department's actions had been of a reasonably acceptable standard, and that no financial regulator could, or should, guarantee the safety of investors' funds. The government also believed that the ombudsman should not be investigating cases where the complainants had no direct relationship with the relevant government department. Despite this, the government agreed to make substantial ex gratia payments to all investors who had suffered loss as a result of the collapse of Barlow Clowes, in what has been described as 'the most substantial financial remedy ever to result from an investigation'[176].

[172]   Complaints were taken up by 159 members of Parliament. It took 13 months to conduct the investigation and resulted in a 120,000 word report (see R Gregory and G Drewry 'Barlow Clowes and the Ombudsman' (1991) p 192).

[173]   Sir Anthony Barrowclough, in his Annual Report 1988 (HC Paper 301 (1988–89)) para 62.

[174]   R Gregory and G Drewry 'Barlow Clowes and the Ombudsman' (1991) p 439.

[175]   The Prevention of Fraud (Investments) Act 1958 makes it an offence for anyone to carry on the business of dealing in securities without a licence. The Department of Trade and Industry has the power to issue licences to businesses dealing with securities, together with some monitoring functions over those to whom it issues a licence.

[176]   Third Report from the Select Committee on the Parliamentary Commissioner for Administration (HC Paper 353 (1990–91)) (Report of the Parliamentary Commissioner for Administration for 1990) paras 7, 64.

The largest single investigation of the 1990s concerned the Channel tunnel rail link[177]. This was an investigation into complaints against the Department of Transport about planning blight to properties caused by its handling of the proposed rail link between 1990 and 1994. The ombudsman's remit did not permit an investigation of the policy of the department. However, the ombudsman found that the effect of the policy had been to keep the project alive when it could not be funded, thus causing uncertainty and blight. This was maladministration. He recommended that those affected to an extreme and exceptional degree by the generalised blight from June 1990 to April 1994 be granted financial redress. A special report was laid before Parliament, as the department was unwilling to consider making any such ex gratia payments[178]. The government did not accept that there had been maladministration, nor would it admit to any fault liability. Nevertheless, 'out of respect' for the ombudsman and the select committee, it conceded that it was willing to consider a compensation scheme[179]. This decision was confirmed by the succeeding Labour government in 1997, and the payment for redress was increased from £5,000 to £10,000. Details of the compensation scheme were publicised widely in the areas that had been affected.

If every decade brings a spectacular case, it will be interesting to see what the present decade brings. Already complaints are being referred to the ombudsman about the alleged failure by the regulatory authorities to exercise adequate supervision over the affairs of Equitable Life. This follows difficulties in connection with funding for certain types of insurance policy. The ombudsman deferred the decision on whether to investigate complaints until two inquiries into the matter had reported[180]. This was criticised in Parliament and the media, but the ombudsman has defended the decision. He considers it 'plainly inefficient, and potentially unfair', to

177   See Parliamentary Ombudsman Annual Report 1995 (HC Paper 296 (1995–96)) p 3.
178   Report of the Parliamentary Commissioner for Administration (HC Paper 193 (1994–95)) (Channel Tunnel Rail Link and Blight: Investigation of Complaints against the Department of Transport). This was laid before Parliament by virtue of the Parliamentary Commissioner Act 1967, s 10(3) as the injustice caused by the maladministration had not been, nor would not be, remedied.
179   See Fifth Special Report from the Select Committee on the Parliamentary Commissioner for Administration (HC Paper 819 (1994–95)) (The Channel Tunnel Rail Link and Blight: Investigation of Complaints against the Department of Transport).
180   The Financial Services Authority set up the Baird Inquiry and the government set up the Penrose Inquiry.

have two simultaneous but separate investigations covering much the same ground and taking evidence from much the same sources'[181]. However, the ombudsman considers that the situation is unsatisfactory and he has drawn it to the attention of the select committee[182].

Complaints Statistics

When the office was first established, it was anticipated that it would attract between 6,000–7,000 complaints a year[183]. Despite the steady increase in the numbers of complaints over the past ten years, the office is still a long way short of this estimate. From 1967 to 1991, the average number of complaints referred by members of Parliament each year was 803[184]. In 1992, there were 945 complaints referred. By 1996, the figure had more than doubled, and 1,933 new cases were received. This fell to 1,459 the following year. Since then there has been a steady increase, so that in 2001–02 there were 2,139 new cases, with an average number of new cases a year over the past five years of 1,687. The increase over the past 10 years may be partly explained by an increasing general public awareness of the role and usefulness of ombudsmen, coupled with increased publicity when the ombudsman intervenes in a particular noteworthy case. It may also be largely due to increased expectations on the part of the public[185]. Table 4.1 shows the workload of the office for the past 10 years.

---

[181]   Parliamentary Ombudsman Annual Report 2001–02 (HC Paper 897 (2001–02)) p 7.

[182]   Parliamentary Ombudsman Annual Report 2001–02 (HC Paper 897 (2001–02)) p 7.

[183]   F Stacey *Ombudsmen Compared* (1978) Clarendon Press p 129.

[184]   R Gregory and J Pearson 'The Parliamentary Ombudsman after twenty-five years: problems and solutions' (1992) 70 Public Administration 469, p 471.

[185]   Despite the increase, these are still small numbers. By contrast, many ombudsmen worldwide, serving far smaller populations, receive and investigate far more cases. For example, in the 1980s, in Denmark the ombudsman received more than 2,000 complaints from a population of about five million. In Sweden the ombudsman received about 4,000 cases each year from a population of about eight million. These figures are not a reflection of higher staffing levels in the ombudsmen's offices. The ratio of staff to cases investigated is about 1:10 for the Parliamentary Ombudsman, compared to 1:60 in Denmark, 1:85 in Sweden, and 1:80 in New Zealand (see W Gwyn 'The Ombudsman in Britain: a qualified success in government reform' (1982) 60 Public Administration 177, p 181).

Table 4.1

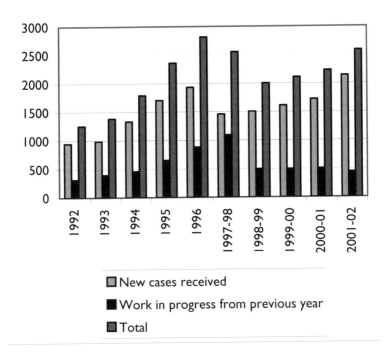

(Source: The Parliamentary Ombudsman Annual Reports)

As indicated earlier, and in common with many other ombudsman schemes, only a minority of cases result in a formal investigation followed by the publication of an official report. In the case of the Parliamentary Ombudsman, the percentage of complaints resolved in this way over the past 10 years has varied between 15% and 24%, the average being 20%. As discussed above, some cases are rejected outright as clearly outside jurisdiction. These are small in number, averaging 10% of all the complaints received over the last 10 years. In fact, this proportion has steadily decreased, and in 2001–02, the percentage was 5%. This small number of outright rejections should perhaps not be surprising, given that complaints are filtered through members of Parliament to the ombudsman. It may indeed be a cause for concern that members are submitting cases to the ombudsman which are clearly outside jurisdiction. For the remaining unsuccessful complaints, these are generally rejected after further examination of the papers. The reasons for this include the fact that there is a possibility of appeal to a tribunal, there is no evidence of maladministration, or no worthwhile outcome is likely.

Changes in working practices, outlined above, have allowed for another outcome to be revealed in the statistics. During the past five years, 1,667 cases have been resolved by making enquiries of the departments, without the need for formal investigations. In 978 of these, the result was a positive outcome for the complainant. In 2000–01, another procedure was introduced whereby formal investigations were concluded by the ombudsman without the issue of a formal report, where it appeared reasonable to do so. This occurred in 99 cases that year, and was the result of either an appropriate outcome being achieved, or the fact that no remedy was available. In 2001–02, 91 cases were resolved in this way. Tables 4.2 and 4.3 give the outcomes of cases for the past 10 years.

TABLE 4.2: OUTCOMES OF CONCLUDED CASES 1992 TO 1996

Year	Clearly outside jurisdiction	Concluded on the basis of the papers	Statutory investigation report issued	Total
1992	129	532	190	851
1993	138	577	208	923
1994	168	702	226	1096
1995	149	1077	245	1471
1996	159	1254	260	1673

(Source: The Parliamentary Ombudsman, *Annual Report 2001-02*, HC897, at p 16)

TABLE 4.3: OUTCOMES OF CONCLUDED CASES 1997-98 TO 2001-02

Year	1	2	3	4	5	6	Total
97-98	134	1431		110		376	2051
98-99	125	916		90		372	1503
99-00	139	1018		121		313	1591
00-01	99	777	252	313	99	247	1787
01-02	109	812	437	344	91	195	1988

Key:
1 = Clearly outside jurisdiction
2 = Concluded on the basis of the papers
3 = Resolved without positive outcome by enquiry of department
4 = Resolved with positive outcome by enquiry of department
5 = Investigation concluded other than by statutory report
6 = Statutory investigation report issued

(Source: The Parliamentary Ombudsman, *Annual Report 2001-02*, HC897, at p 16)

Of course, these statistics cannot tell the whole story. They do not, for example, indicate whether the outcome was a satisfactory one for the complainant. The 2000–01 annual report reveals that 313 cases (18% of the total cases concluded) were resolved with a positive outcome for the complainant, by making enquiries of the body concerned. In total 659 complaints (37% of the total) resulted in a positive outcome for complainants after intervention by the office[186]. The number of completed statutory investigations has fallen in the past two years because other means of resolving complaints are increasingly being used, a trend that is likely to continue.

The time taken to deal with complaints at all stages of the process has greatly improved in recent years. The office has a target of identifying all cases that are clearly out of jurisdiction, and notifying the referring member of this within two weeks[187]. In 2000–01, this target was achieved in 94% of

---

[186] Source: The Parliamentary Ombudsman Annual Report 2000–01 (HC Paper 5 (2001–02)) p 5.

[187] The time from which the targets are measured is the date of receipt of the member's letter referring to the complaint. If the letter does not provide sufficient information for a decision to be reached on the appropriate action to be taken, the time is measured from the date when sufficient evidence is provided by the complainant (Parliamentary and Health Service Ombudsman Business Plan 2002 para 3.6).

cases. In 2001–02, all cases in this category met the target[188]. Where complaints are not clearly out of jurisdiction, the office aims to achieve an appropriate outcome, or initiate the statutory investigation process within six weeks of receiving the complaint. The target here is 60%, and in 2001–02, this target was achieved in 68% of cases. In 2000–01, there were 55 cases that took longer than 13 weeks to reach this stage, but this had reduced to nine in 2001–02[189].

Where the statutory process is initiated, the aim is to resolve cases where no report is needed within six months of receiving sufficient information to enable a statement of complaint to be issued. In 2000–01, the target of 50% of cases falling within this timescale was achieved. Where the result is a statutory report, the aim is to complete nearly all cases within 11 months of receipt of the appropriate information, with only a handful going beyond 12 months. By 31 March 2001, the ombudsman's office had only 10 cases that were over 12 months old. By the end of March 2002, there was only one such case[190]. New investigations are now typically being completed in 9–10 months[191].

Types of Complaints

The department against which most complaints are recorded has always been the Department of Social Security[192], followed by the Inland Revenue. Their combined share of the total complaints has consistently accounted for over 40% of all complaints. In 2000–01, this rose to over 50%. That these departments attract the most complaints is not surprising, as the services they offer bring them into direct contact with the public[193]. They

[188]   Parliamentary Ombudsman Annual Report 2001–02 (HC Paper 897 (2001–02)) p 17.
[189]   Parliamentary and Health Service Ombudsman, Business Plan 2002 para 3.8; Parliamentary Ombudsman Annual Report 2001–02 (HC Paper 897 (2001–02)) p 17.
[190]   Parliamentary and Health Service Ombudsman, Business Plan 2002 para 3.12.
[191]   The Parliamentary Ombudsman Annual Report 2000–01 (HC Paper 5 (2001–02)) p 15.
[192]   There was a reorganisation of departments in June 2001. The Department for Work and Pensions now deals with benefits and child support, which were formerly dealt with by the Department of Social Security.
[193]   A previous Parliamentary Ombudsman observed that the high volume of complaints against the Department of Social Security 'is an indicator not . . . of their maladministration so much as of their day-to-day contact with the public'

are therefore more likely to be the subject of a complaint than those like the Treasury, which do not have such contact, and where there is no direct and immediate personal impact. In June 2001, following departmental reorganisation at Whitehall, benefits and child support became the responsibility of the Department for Work and Pensions. In 2001–02 this department accounted for 53% of the total number of investigation reports, 94% of which were concerned with the Benefits Agency and the Child Support Agency, which represented 50% of the total reports issued[194].

There are always large numbers of complaints related to the administration of social security benefits, the Benefits Agency accounting for 22% of all complaints received, and 49% of the complaints received by the Department for Work and Pensions. These complaints include such matters as the incorrect stoppage of benefit and the mishandling of benefit claims. Misleading or inadequate advice is a common cause for complaints against the Benefits Agency, as is unreasonable delay in processing claims. The way the department conducts fraud investigations is often the subject of complaints. The Child Support Agency is another body which generates large numbers of complaints. Many of these concern failures and delay in enforcement against non-resident parents who are reluctant to comply with maintenance awards.

The numbers of complaints relating to the Inland Revenue account for between 10% and 19% of all complaints in any year. As with the Department of Social Security, this has to be set in the context of the transactions conducted by the department. For example, there are 30 million-plus taxpayers and over one million companies with which the Inland Revenue is concerned. Typical complaints include delays, mishandling and inefficiency in dealing with fees and expenses. The department is often accused of giving wrong advice to taxpayers and making errors in valuations. Another type of complaint is that the department has breached confidentiality about a taxpayer's affairs to the taxpayer's employer. In 2001–02, 10% of complaints to the ombudsman concerned the Inland Revenue. These 206 complaints represented a slight decrease on the

---

(First Report from the Select Committee on the Parliamentary Commissioner for Administration (HC Paper 129 (1990–91)) (Report of the Parliamentary Commissioner for Administration for 1989) para 24). The department deals with some 20 million claims per year for a variety of benefits and allowances.

194 Parliamentary Ombudsman Annual Report 2001–02 (HC Paper 897 (2001–02)) p 21.

previous year when the figure was 214. In 2000–01, a number of complaints were a result of the National Insurance Contributions Office's new computer system, which had caused late payments. There were also complaints about the Revenue's operation of self-assessment, including allegations that the Revenue had been overzealous or had made mistakes in tax investigations and enquiries.

The Home Office accounts for about 5% of all complaints. Cases include delays and mishandling in relation to immigration matters and passport applications. In 2001–02, there was a considerable increase in the number of complaints against the Immigration and Nationality Directorate of the Home Office, 92 as against 64 in the previous year. As in previous years, delay was a common theme, particularly in dealing with applications for asylum and for leave to remain as a spouse. One significant outcome during the year was an ex gratia payment of £1,000 in an asylum case. The asylum application had been unreasonably delayed for over three years and the payment was to reflect the complainant's loss of entitlement to full-rate income support during this time. This was the first time that the directorate had recognised the effect of delay on entitlement to benefit[195].

Publicity

Lack of awareness about the existence and role of the ombudsman presents a major barrier to access. The Parliamentary Ombudsman has never received a large number of complaints. In 1978 it was conceded that the office was, by international comparisons 'by far the least used, in terms of population, of any of the Ombudsmen'[196]. In the 1980s, concern was expressed about the 'comparatively small number of people' seeking the help of the ombudsman, and greater publicity was urged for the office[197]. Complaints

---

[195]   Parliamentary Ombudsman Annual Report 2001–02 (HC Paper 897 (2001–02)) p 42.

[196]   F Stacey *Ombudsmen Compared* (1978) Clarendon Press p 170. The number of cases investigated is also small compared to other countries. For example, in 1974, in the UK with a population of 55 million, only 252 cases were investigated. Sweden, with a population of eight million, had 2,368 cases investigated in the same year. New Zealand, with a population of three million, had 414 investigated cases (see Justice *Our Fettered Ombudsman* (1977) JUSTICE p 4).

[197]   Justice *Administrative Justice: Some Necessary Reforms* (1988) Clarendon Press p 84.

have risen dramatically since then, but have never reached anything like the 5,000 to 6,000 anticipated when the office was established. When there have been sudden increases in the number of complaints, this is often following publicity after a particular noteworthy case. The filter on access does present problems in relation to publicity, as it prevents the ombudsman having a direct relationship with the public.

The 1967 Act requires little in the way of publicity, only requiring the ombudsman to make an annual report to Parliament on the performance of his or her functions. The ombudsman also has the power to lay before each House of Parliament other reports when he or she sees fit to do so[198]. Reports made by the ombudsman to Parliament are rarely debated in full, and they do not occupy a high priority on the legislative timetable. Indeed, this lack of priority for ombudsman matters can be seen in the lack of progress in implementing the proposals of the Cabinet Office review[199], which have wide support from interested parties, including the select committee[200].

Surveys have revealed little awareness of the Parliamentary Ombudsman. In 1995, 46% of respondents to a survey had heard of the office[201]. In 1996, a survey by the Consumers Association revealed only 34% awareness among the general population, with the higher socio-economic groups displaying more awareness. Thus, social classes ABC1 had 44% awareness, compared with 24% of those in social classes C2DE[202]. In 1997, another survey showed that only 14% of the public were aware of the existence of the Parliamentary Ombudsman, a figure that rose to 23%, after some prompting[203].

The ombudsman has made a number of attempts to improve the public awareness and accessibility of the office. A new leaflet was issued in

---

[198] Parliamentary Commissioner Act 1967, s 10(4).
[199] *Review of the Public Sector Ombudsman in England* (2000) Cabinet Office.
[200] See Parliamentary Ombudsman Annual Report 2000–01 (HC Paper 5 (2001–02)) pp 10–11.
[201] Research Study conducted for the Commission for Local Administration in England by MORI in 1995.
[202] Consumers Association *Ombudsmen* (1997) Consumers Association pp 15–17.
[203] Press Release from the Parliamentary Ombudsman, 17 July 1997 (see R Gregory and P Giddings 'The United Kingdom Parliamentary Ombudsman Scheme' in R Gregory and P Giddings (eds) *Righting Wrongs: The Ombudsman in Six Continents* (2000) IOS Press p 23).

January 1997, and all members of Parliament were sent a copy after the General Election in that year. The ombudsman holds seminars for MPs and their staff, to inform them of current developments in the work of the office, and to encourage them to refer complaints. There is also an annual consultation meeting with representatives of advisory and consumer organisations[204]. The present and past ombudsmen have also contributed articles to professional journals about the work of the office. More recently, a website[205] has been established, which not only provides information about the work of the office, but also offers advice to complainants about making complaints. Of course, potential complainants have to be advised that complaints must be referred by a member of Parliament, but the website has a network link for finding the appropriate MP.

In addition to the annual report, the Parliamentary Ombudsman also now produces six-monthly digests of cases investigated[206]. These contain brief details and anonymised summaries of all cases that result in formal reports, together with full reports on selected cases. In this way, all reports are brought to the attention of the public, providing a comprehensive overview of the type of work undertaken by the ombudsman. Not only do these digests provide the results of investigations in a convenient form, but they also provide a source of information for improving practice.

There is no doubt that publicity and awareness are important to the functioning of the office, and the efforts in this area are commendable. It is perhaps worth noting the practice in other jurisdictions. In France, the Mediateur has a popular brochure, and has regional visits and meetings. The Danish ombudsman meets the press every week, and distributes 200,000 copies of a brochure[207], describing the work of the office, to citizens. The Commonwealth ombudsman in Australia has advertised the existence of the office on milk bottle tops, by an arrangement with the milk suppliers. The Austrian ombudsman had a prime time television slot advertising the

---

[204]   Parliamentary Ombudsman Annual Report 2001–02 (HC Paper 897 (2001–02)) p 10.

[205]   The address is: http://www.ombudsman.org.uk.

[206]   Justice had suggested that it would be a good idea to have a digest of cases. At the time, information about these cases was scattered throughout the annual reports, the quarterly selected cases reports, and unpublished reports (*Administrative Justice: Some Necessary Reforms* (1988) Clarendon Press p 104).

[207]   The Parliamentary Ombudsman has distributed leaflets to public libraries and Citizens Advice Bureaux.

function of the office and explaining cases which had been recently resolved.

The issue of publicity cannot be divorced from the issue of direct access to the ombudsman. More publicity could lead to frustration, if members of Parliament are unwilling to forward the cases to the ombudsman. More publicity and outreach work in the wider community becomes more useful where complainants are able to refer their cases directly.

Improving Administration

The Parliamentary Ombudsman was established to supplement the work of members of Parliament in investigating complaints from members of the public about injustice caused by maladministration. As we have seen, the role is to investigate complaints from aggrieved citizens and recommend a remedy where the complaint is justified. In this, the Parliamentary Ombudsman is following the normally accepted role for an ombudsman, which is 'primarily a client-orientated office, designed to secure individual justice in the administrative state'[208]. The report by Justice in 1961[209] had taken a narrow, grievance-redressing view of the ombudsman's function, and had never considered that one of the objectives of the office might also be that of identifying and eradicating administrative inefficiency[210]. Despite this, it has become accepted that part of the ombudsman's role is to encourage public officials to maintain acceptable standards of good administration, a role that is in accordance with other ombudsmen in the world community[211].

---

[208] K Friedman 'Realisation of ombudsman recommendations' (1988) Fourth International Ombudsman Conference Papers p 105.

[209] Justice *The Citizen and the Administration: the Redress of Grievances* (1961) Stevens.

[210] R Rawlings 'Parliamentary redress of grievances' in C Harlow (ed) *Public Law and Politics* (1986) Sweet and Maxwell p 124.

[211] See, for example, research conducted in the 1980s, which found that 41 out of the 43 ombudsmen canvassed claimed to wish to improve administrative practice. The same number also included proposals for improving legislation and administrative rules in the catalogue of their functions (W Haller 'The place of the ombudsman in the world community' (1988) Fourth International Ombudsman Conference Papers pp 35–36).

In addition to providing appropriate redress for individuals, the Parliamentary Ombudsman does aim to promote improvements in the services provided by public bodies. The present ombudsman is quite clear that while the primary objective of the office is 'to obtain a remedy for those who have suffered injustice', working 'to ensure good public administration' is another important aim[212]. His predecessor was in agreement, seeing his task as 'primarily' to investigate an individual complaint and provide redress where justified, but also recommending improvements in systems 'in order to minimise the risk of the same mistake being repeated'[213]. The first Parliamentary Ombudsman noted that the effect of his existence encouraged departments to maintain standards[214].

How effective have the ombudsmen been in promoting good administrative practice? It has been claimed that ombudsman investigations in 1994 led to administrative improvements in 46 cases, with similar improvements in 76 cases in 1995[215]. More recently, there is evidence in the annual reports of changes in practice as a result of investigations. For example, in one case involving the Benefits Agency, a complainant was given inaccurate advice about the effect on child benefit entitlement of a proposed visit abroad. The complainant received an extra-statutory payment of £3,153 for lost entitlement. In addition, the agency agreed to produce a clearer leaflet setting out the entitlement for those going abroad, in order that similar mistakes would not be repeated[216]. Complaints against the Child Support Agency revealed that unrealistic expectations were being created about the amount of maintenance likely to be received by parents with care. This was as a result of the practice of the agency of imposing high interim assessments in order to encourage non-resident parents to provide sufficient accurate information. The agency often did not explain the purpose of this interim assessment and complainants were distressed when their expectations were later not fulfilled. As a result of the ombudsman's

---

[212] M Buckley 'The Parliamentary Ombudsman' (1998) 68 Adviser 6–8, p 7.

[213] See Sir William Reid's evidence to the Select Committee on the Parliamentary Commissioner for Administration (HC Paper 751 (1993–94)) (Report of the Parliamentary Commissioner for Administration for 1992, together with the proceedings relating to the reports and minutes of evidence) para 24.

[214] Sir Edmund Compton 'The Administrative Performance of Government' (1970) Public Administration 48.

[215] See R Gregory and P Giddings 'The United Kingdom Ombudsman Scheme' in R Gregory and P Giddings (eds) *Righting Wrongs: The Ombudsman in Six Continents* (2000) IOS Press p 34.

[216] Case No C 584/01.

investigations, the wording of the letter has been changed, in order to give parents a clearer understanding of what they can expect to receive[217].

How far should the Parliamentary Ombudsman go in developing the role in relation to good administrative practice? In 1988, Justice floated the idea of establishing a code of principles of good administration, but the ombudsman at the time was opposed to a code, fearing that such principles may become a cause of undesirable bureaucratic rigidity[218]. The next holder of the office was not opposed to such codes, but felt that it was not his role to draw these up, and that this should be left to departments[219]. This seems to be an unnecessarily conservative view[220]. Indeed, Justice considered that the best person to draw up codes of principles of good administration would be the Parliamentary Ombudsman[221]. The ombudsman in the Republic of Ireland has produced a short guide on best practice[222], and the Local Government Ombudsmen in England have produced a series of good practice guides.

Some have argued that the Parliamentary Ombudsman should concentrate more on audit and improvement of performance, rather than resolving individual complaints[223]. The ombudsman's role in scrutinising the administrative process is seen to be the more important objective of the office, with the individual complaint being primarily a mechanism for drawing attention to more general administrative deficiencies[224]. This has never been the approach of the ombudsmen themselves, who have consistently emphasised the grievance resolution aspect of the office. They do not want a purely administrative audit role, which involves concentrating

---

[217] See Parliamentary Ombudsman Annual Report 2000–01 (HC Paper 5 (2000–01)) p 28.

[218] Justice *Administrative Justice: Some Necessary Reforms* (1988) Clarendon Press p 20. The ombudsman at the time was Sir Cecil Clothier.

[219] This was Sir William Reid, Parliamentary Ombudsman from 1989–1997.

[220] It is not a view adopted by the Local Government Ombudsmen in England, who have been very proactive in developing codes of good administrative practice.

[221] Justice *Administrative Justice: Some Necessary Reforms* (1988) Clarendon Press p 23.

[222] *Public Bodies and the Citizen: The Ombudsman's Guide to Standards of Best Practice for Public Servants.*

[223] C Harlow and R Rawlings *Law and Administration* (2nd edn, 1997) Butterworths pp 427–432.

[224] C Harlow 'Ombudsmen in search of a role' (1978) 41 MLR 446. Harlow is more concerned with quality, rather than quantity, and admits that the ombudsman's procedure is not appropriate for handling large numbers of cases.

on a restricted number of large cases. The ombudsman believes that a reasonably large number of cases is necessary, in order to obtain an overview of how the administrative process is working. The Cabinet Office review did not challenge this view, making it clear that the ombudsman should retain the 'core role of handling complaints'[225]. While this is clearly important, the administrative audit function of the office must not be sacrificed. The Parliamentary Ombudsman is uniquely placed to provide independent assessment and criticism of the operation of the administration, a role that should be clearly articulated in any reformed system.

Access to Official Information

Part of the Parliamentary Ombudsman's function is to police the code of practice on Access to Government Information[226]. Those who feel that they have been denied access to government information can complain to the ombudsman, who reaches a decision as to whether the code has been breached. In reaching decisions, the ombudsman has to decide whether or not the relevant exemptions for withholding information exist, and assess whether or not the department has the information that is requested. The code is voluntary, and the ombudsman cannot compel departments to follow the recommendations. This aspect of the ombudsman's work has never formed a large part of the workload. For example, in 2001–02, there were 34 complaints that information had been wrongly withheld under the code, which was a slight reduction on previous years. The ombudsman dealt with many enquiries about information issues during the course of 2001–02, and commented on the information element of 79 maladministration cases. There were 20 statutory investigation reports issued in the year, and for the first time, a special report was published on the results of an investigation under the code.

The ombudsman notes that 2001–02 proved to be a 'frustrating year' in terms of policing the code. For the first time since the code came into

---

[225]   *Review of the Public Sector Ombudsmen in England* (2000) Cabinet Office para 7.30.

[226]   This extension to the remit has been said to be based on the proposition 'that failure to adhere to the official codes constituted evidence of maladministration' (P Giddings 'The Parliamentary Ombudsman: a successful alternative?' in D Oliver and G Drewry (eds) *The Law and Parliament* (1998) Butterworths p 136).

operation in 1994, a department refused to accept a recommendation that information should be released. The investigation[227] concerned a request to the Home Office for information about the number of times ministers in the department had made a declaration of interest under the Ministerial Code of Conduct. The Home Office refused to provide the information, relying on two exemptions in the code. The ombudsman found that the exemptions did not apply and recommended that the information be released. The Home Office's refusal to do so not only undermines the code, but also the ombudsman's 'independent role in investigating complaints' under it[228]. The ombudsman is also concerned about what appears to be a 'hardening of attitudes in departments', and the citing of exemptions at very late stages in the investigations. This calls into question the 'authority and standing' of the office[229].

There are also other concerns in relation to this aspect of the ombudsman's remit. Departments are increasingly delaying responding to the ombudsman's requests. Departments are allowed three weeks to respond to the initial statement of complaint, and three weeks to respond to the draft report. During 2001–02, there have been delays at both these stages of the process. In one case, concerning a request for information about the Hinduja brother's passport application[230], some nine months elapsed before the papers were eventually made available. In the case concerning the Home Office, the response to the ombudsman's draft report was not received until seven months had elapsed. Such delays are clearly unacceptable. There is also evidence that some departments are making it difficult for the ombudsman to conduct investigations. It also appears that the resistance to releasing information is because of 'embarrassment or political inconvenience' rather than because there is a case under the code[231].

---

[227] Case No A28/01. A special report was issued on this case (see Fourth Report of the Parliamentary Commissioner for Administration (HC Paper 353 (2001–02)) (Access to Official Information – Declarations Made Under the Ministerial Code of Conduct)). See also Parliamentary Ombudsman Annual Report 2001–02 (HC Paper 897 (2001–02)) pp 8, 45.

[228] Parliamentary Ombudsman Annual Report 2001–02 (HC Paper 897 (2001–02)) p 45.

[229] Parliamentary Ombudsman Annual Report 2001–02 (HC Paper 897 (2001–02)) p 9.

[230] Case No A33/01. See Parliamentary Ombudsman Annual Report 2001–02 (HC Paper 897 (2001–02)) p 46.

[231] Parliamentary Ombudsman Annual Report 2001–02 (HC Paper 897 (2001–02)) p 46.

There have however been a number of successes by the ombudsman, and investigations have resulted in a wide variety of previously withheld information being released. Some departments have made their internal departmental guidance available to the public, which marks a step forward in changing the culture of secrecy. There is a growing familiarity with the requirements of the code within central government departments.

The jurisdiction of the ombudsman in this area will be changed, as a result of the Freedom of Information Act 2000. Under the Act, there will be a statutory right to information held by public bodies, and the right will be extended to cover documents, rather than information, including Cabinet papers and documents predating the legislation. The legislation will be enforced by the Information Commissioner, and thus the ombudsman's role in relation to access to information will cease. These changes are not due to take place however until 2005[232], and the Parliamentary Ombudsman will continue to deal with complaints about the refusal of access to information at least until that date.

The provision of a statutory right to information is a welcome development, albeit that it will be some years before the Act will be implemented. The new proposals do however present some causes for concern. First, they will result in the creation of another public sector complaints body, which may be a source of confusion for complainants. There are no plans to bring the Information Commissioner within the proposed new integrated ombudsman system in England, although some kind of associate status is envisaged[233]. Although access to information complaints constitute a small part of the work of the office, many of the complaints investigated by the ombudsman in relation to maladministration have a freedom of information element. Arrangements will need to be made in the new system for dealing with complaints which raise matters that are within both jurisdictions.

Conclusions

The Parliamentary Ombudsman was originally established as an adjunct to Parliament, to assist members of Parliament in dealing with complaints

---

[232]   In November 2001, the Government announced that it would not bring these provisions into effect until January 2005.

[233]   *Review of the Public Sector Ombudsmen in England* (2000) Cabinet Office para 7.4.

from constituents. Most assessments are that it works well within its limited frame of reference. This was a conclusion from an early evaluation, but its restricted scope drew unfavourable comparisons with similar institutions in other countries[234]. A later evaluation, while concluding that the introduction of the ombudsman had 'improved the position of the citizen' in relation to the administration, nevertheless expressed concern about the lack of visibility and accessibility of office, and the fact that it was underutilised[235]. Evaluations of the office after its first quarter of a century in existence pronounced it a qualified success. To its credit, the office has been responsible for improvements in administrative practice and policy. It has brought redress to hundreds of complainants, and it has managed to do this without damaging civil service morale or significantly increasing departmental workloads. There was however a sense that it had been less effective than other ombudsman systems[236]. There was also a feeling that the office had not reached its full potential. It received few complaints and conducted very few investigations. The general conclusion was that it was 'capable of better things'[237].

What could it do better? One of the problems is accessibility. The system is not well known and attracts few complaints in comparison to other systems throughout the world. The problem of publicity is being tackled, but efforts in this direction are hampered by the fact that there is no direct access. The MP filter is no longer acceptable. It provides a barrier to access, without providing the necessary 'filtering' which would ensure that only complaints within jurisdiction reached the ombudsman. The restriction on own-initiative investigations also seems hard to justify. As for the jurisdictional restrictions, there seems to be no justification in principle why the ombudsman should not be able to investigate all the administrative actions of public bodies. The discretionary powers are wide enough to ensure that matters more appropriately dealt with by the courts or tribunals would not be investigated by the ombudsman. Similarly, all public bodies should be within the jurisdiction of the ombudsman, and mechanisms must be found to ensure that new public bodies are brought within remit, without the present unwieldy system of naming each individual body.

---

[234] Justice *Our Fettered Ombudsman* (1977) JUSTICE p 1.
[235] Justice *Administrative Justice: Some Necessary Reforms* (1988) Clarendon Press p 84.
[236] See R Gregory and J Pearson 'The Parliamentary Ombudsman after twenty-five years: problems and solutions' (1992) 60 Public Administration 469 p 471.
[237] See G Drewry and C Harlow 'A Cutting Edge? The Parliamentary Commissioner and MPs' (1990) 53 MLR 745.

On the credit side, the ombudsman's office scores highly on many of the criteria for judging ombudsman schemes. The holders of the office of the Parliamentary Ombudsman have never seen their role as citizen's champions, and the impartiality and independence of the office have never been in doubt. The powers given to the office to conduct investigations are unrivalled, and successive ombudsmen have conducted thorough and authoritative investigations into a wide range of administrative areas. Some of these have had far reaching consequences. Despite the lack of judicial enforcement for the recommended remedies, the ombudsman has succeeded in obtaining redress for thousands of complainants, and has brought about improvements in administrative practices. The time taken to deal with complaints, once a serious cause for concern, is now being effectively tackled. The restriction of the remit to complaints of maladministration, once a source of much criticism, has not proved to be a stumbling block to the ombudsman's ability to investigate many aspects of administrative conduct. Indeed, it appears that the ombudsman has not been prevented from investigating matters which ombudsmen with wider remits can investigate.

The environment in which the ombudsman operates is now very different to that existing when the office was first established. It is to the credit of successive ombudsmen that the limited frame of reference of the office has not stifled the ability to develop the system to be more in keeping with this changed environment. Thus, the office now deals with more cases, much more quickly, than it has in the past. It has also devised new working practices so that cases are resolved at an appropriate level, rather than being subject to the statutory investigation procedure. It has to be admitted though that this has been done in spite of the legislative framework. The service 'could be so much better' without the 'restrictions and cumbersome methods of work' imposed by the 1967 Act[238].

Over its 35 years in existence, the functions of the office have evolved. The emphasis now is very much on individual complaints being resolved, and redress being obtained where appropriate. This is commendable, and especially so if this can be done more speedily and effectively. Does this emphasis represent a move away from administrative audit? The office does have the stated function of promoting improvements in public services,

---

[238] Parliamentary Ombudsman Annual Report 2001–02 (HC Paper 897 (2001–02)) p 10.

although there is no statutory requirement to do so. One of the undoubted strengths of the ombudsman remedy is the effect that individual decisions have on promoting principles of good administrative practice. This aspect of the role must be highlighted, so that the ombudsman can continue to play an effective role in improving the quality of public services.

Chapter 5

The Health Service Ombudsman

Although the Department of Health is within the remit of the Parliamentary Ombudsman, National Health Service hospitals are excluded from that scheme. In order to rectify this, separate statutory ombudsman schemes for the health service were established in 1973[1]. The legislation establishing the schemes provided for separate Health Service Ombudsmen for England, Wales and Scotland. In fact, from the beginning, these three separate roles were filled by one person, who was also the Parliamentary Ombudsman at the time. This practice has been followed ever since[2]. The original legislation was consolidated in 1977 and 1978[3], which in turn was consolidated into the Health Service Commissioners Act 1993, as amended by the Health Service Commissioners (Amendment) Acts in 1996 and 2000. The 1993 Act remedied some inconsistencies between the different schemes in England and Wales and Scotland.

The health care system in the UK has been exposed to radical changes over the past few years, a process that seems set to continue for some time to come. The National Health Service used to be 'a wholly state-funded organisation with a highly centralised structure where care was provided

---

[1] The National Health Service Reorganisation Act 1973 established an ombudsman scheme for the National Health Service in England and Wales. The corresponding legislation for Scotland is the National Health Service (Scotland) Act 1972. There is a separate scheme for Northern Ireland.

[2] This will now change, however, in relation to Scotland, as a result of the new arrangements now coming into force. This will be discussed in Chapter 7.

[3] The National Health Service Act 1977, Pt V, for England and Wales, and the National Health Service (Scotland) Act 1978, Pt VI for Scotland.

by state owned and managed providers'[4]. Now, power and authority is being devolved to primary care trusts and health service care is being provided by both the public and private sectors. Changes in the health care system are driven not only by ideas of new public management discussed previously, but also by developments in medical science and technology. All this has implications for the work of the Health Service Ombudsman. This chapter will deal with general matters affecting the Health Service Ombudsman schemes, while focussing on the scheme in England[5].

Background

When the Parliamentary Commissioner Bill was being debated in Parliament in 1966 and 1967, it was strongly criticised because National Health Service hospitals were excluded from jurisdiction[6]. There were attempts to amend this provision and, in fact, the government was defeated at committee stage on this, but the exclusionary provision was restored at report stage. Despite a promise to look again at this issue, the government resisted pressure in the House of Lords to reinstate the amendment which would have allowed the investigation of complaints about National Health Service hospitals by the Parliamentary Ombudsman.

One of the arguments for including hospitals in the Parliamentary Ombudsman's remit was the unsatisfactory state of the procedures for complaints which existed in hospitals at the time. Although administered by a central government department and regional health authorities, there was, at the time, no standard procedure or code of practice for dealing with complaints made by in-patients and out-patients of hospitals. Ministerial guidance had been issued in 1966[7] recommending a procedure for dealing with complaints not involving serious disciplinary charges against staff

---

4   See S Kerrison and A Pollack 'Complaints as Accountability: The Case of Health Care UK' (2001) PL 115–133, p 132.

5   Particular issues relating to Scotland, Wales and Northern Ireland will be referred to in Chapter 7.

6   This was one of the exclusions in Sch 3 of the Parliamentary Commissioner Act 1967. The basis for this exclusion was that hospitals were independent, localised and had their own procedures for dealing with complaints.

7   Memorandum HM (66) 15, 7 March 1966.

or court proceedings. The memorandum containing the guidance had been supplemented by a letter in the same year, drawing attention to the need for hospitals to ensure that investigations into complaints were independent. It also emphasised that no one connected with the substance of the complaint should be involved in the investigation.

There were a number of proposals to improve the position in relation to hospital complaints in the years following the passing of the Parliamentary Commissioner Act 1967. In July 1968, the select committee reported that, in its view, the ombudsman should be empowered to look at complaints about hospitals[8]. At the same time, the Minister of Health published a discussion document on the health service[9]. This document included a suggestion that the Parliamentary Ombudsman's jurisdiction should be extended to include hospitals or, alternatively that a separate Health Service Ombudsman should be appointed.

Many voluntary organisations were in favour of an ombudsman[10], but doctors' organisations were generally critical. However, about this time, there were a series of reports into allegations of ill-treatment of patients in psychiatric hospitals. One of these reports recommended that a 'Health Service Commissioner, given the widest possible powers, should be appointed urgently to meet public anxiety about the investigation of complaints in the health service'[11]. In February 1972, the government announced that it intended to set up Health Service Ombudsmen, and the proposals were implemented in legislation in 1972 and 1973, as outlined above. The Acts provide for three ombudsmen, but it was decided that these three roles should be filled by the Parliamentary Ombudsman. The reason for this was that the volume of complaints to the Parliamentary Ombudsman had not proved to be as great as expected. There was therefore spare capacity to take on these additional complaints. The Health Service Ombudsman scheme became operational on 1 October 1973.

---

[8] Second Report from the Select Committee on the Parliamentary Commissioner for Administration (HC Paper 350 (1967–68)) para 37.
[9] *The Administrative Structure of the Medical and Related Service in England and Wales* (1968) The Department of Health and Social Security.
[10] See B Robb *Sans Everything* (1967) Nelson.
[11] Report of the Farleigh Hospital Committee of Inquiry (Cm 4557, 1971) p 29.

The Scheme

The office of the Health Service Ombudsman was created by the National Health Services Reorganisation Act 1973, Pt III, which was amended by the National Health Service Act 1977, Pt V, and consolidated by the Health Service Commissioners Act 1993. Schedule 1 of the 1993 Act sets out the matters in relation to the appointment and remuneration of the ombudsman. Like the Parliamentary Ombudsman, the Health Service Ombudsman is appointed by the Crown, and holds office during good behaviour, retiring at the age of 65. He or she can be relieved of office by request, otherwise removal can only take place on addresses from both Houses of Parliament. As in the case of the Parliamentary Ombudsman, the salary of the Health Service Ombudsman is charged on the Consolidated Fund. Where a person holds both offices of Parliamentary and Health Service Ombudsmen there is only entitlement to the Parliamentary Ombudsman's salary.

The Health Service Ombudsman is empowered to investigate the bodies which are listed in the Health Service Commissioners Act 1993, s 2. These are in effect health authorities, National Health Service Trusts[12] and Primary Care Trusts[13]. Certain other bodies, for example, the Dental Practice Board and the Public Health Laboratory Service Board are also within the ombudsman's remit. In addition, the ombudsman's jurisdiction extends to individuals providing services under the National Health Service. These are general practitioners, dentists, pharmacists and opticians, collectively known as family health service practitioners. The ombudsman's remit covers complaints from members of the public who have been refused information under the Code of Practice on Openness in the National Health Service[14].

Jurisdiction

During the 1990s, the jurisdiction of the Health Service Ombudsman was subject to major changes. This has been so extensive that the scheme is scarcely recognisable as the original that emerged in 1973. That scheme

---

[12] These were created by the National Health Service and Community Care Act 1990.

[13] These were established under the Health Act 1999.

[14] These Codes came into operation in June 1995. They are non-statutory. There have been very few complaints or enquiries about access to information.

was modelled on the Parliamentary Ombudsman, but the changes to the Health Service Ombudsman's jurisdiction has meant that the scheme has 'increasingly diverged' from the Parliamentary Ombudsman model[15]. Not only do the bodies subject to jurisdiction include private organisations, and individuals who provide services on a contractual basis, but the remit of the Health Service Ombudsman extends beyond maladministration. The original legislation specifically provided for investigation of complaints about 'hardship' caused by failures in service, in addition to maladministration[16]. This may not in practice have resulted in a wider remit than the other public sector ombudsmen, because of the wide interpretation given to the meaning of maladministration[17]. However, as we shall see, the Health Service Ombudsman can now also investigate complaints about the clinical judgment of practitioners in the health service. This extension of remit has no parallel with the Parliamentary Ombudsman, whose remit remains confined to administrative acts, rather than the merits of decisions.

A further difference between the two schemes results from the Health Service Ombudsman's role in relation to the National Health Service as a whole. The Health Service Ombudsman is a 'special mandate' ombudsman, dealing with only one area of administration, the health service[18]. This means that the role of the ombudsman in relation to the National Health Service as a whole is unlike the role of the Parliamentary Ombudsman, whose remit extends to the whole of central government activity. In addition, as we shall see, the Health Service Ombudsman has a particular function at the apex of the internal complaints system for the health service. While the Parliamentary Ombudsman is at the apex of the system in the sense that that office is normally used as a last resort, the Health Service Ombudsman's position in relation to health service complaints has no parallel with the Parliamentary Ombudsman system.

---

15   S Kerrison and A Pollack 'Complaints as Accountability? The Case of Health Care UK' (2001) PL 115–133, p 120.
16   See National Health Service Reorganisation Act 1973, s 115, which is now the Health Service Commissioners Act 1993, s 3.
17   Both the Parliamentary and Local Government Ombudsmen have found that a failure of service or a failure to provide a service amounts to maladministration. Also, the Parliamentary and Local Government Ombudsmen regard 'hardship' as a possible injustice consequent on maladministration.
18   See P Giddings 'The United Kingdom Health Service Commissioner Schemes' in R Gregory and P Giddings (eds) *Righting Wrongs: The Ombudsman in Six Counties* (2000) IOS Press p 339.

In 1996, the ombudsman's jurisdiction was extended to include complaints about the services provided by family health service practitioners[19]. Before April 1996, complaints about family health service practitioners were dealt with through statutory arrangements which essentially considered whether a practitioner was in breach of the National Health Service terms of service[20]. The extended remit allows the ombudsman to investigate any action taken by the practitioner, if the ombudsman considers that it may have caused hardship or injustice. The ombudsman can also consider complaints against those no longer working for the institution where the complaint arose, providing that the complaint is brought within three years of the last day on which the person was a health service provider[21]. The 1996 Act also extended the ombudsman's remit to include complaints about non-National Health Service providers where they are providing National Health Service services or treating National Health Service patients[22].

Like the Parliamentary Ombudsman, the Health Service Ombudsman is excluded from investigating personnel matters. Thus, the Health Service Ombudsman cannot investigate complaints about actions taken in respect of appointments, removals, pay, discipline, superannuation or other personnel matters[23].

Contractual and other commercial matters are also generally excluded[24], for the same reasons as the parallel exclusion in relation to the Parliamentary

---

[19]   Health Service Commissioners (Amendment) Act 1996, s 1, which inserted s 2A into the Health Service Commissioners Act 1993. As indicated above, family health services practitioners are family doctors, dentists, pharmacists and opticians. They have independent contractor status within the health service, operating under a contract for services.

[20]   The ombudsman has confirmed that the new remit is not concerned with judging whether there has been a breach of the statutory terms of service (see Health Service Ombudsman, Investigations Completed April–September 1998 (HC Paper 3 (1998–99)) p 5). The responsibility for breach of these terms rests with health authorities, and will transfer to primary care trusts.

[21]   Health Service Commissioners (Amendment) Act 2000, s 1, which amends s 2 of the Health Service Commissioners Act 1993.

[22]   Health Service Commissioners (Amendment) Act 1996, s 1, which inserted s 2A into the Health Service Commissioners Act 1993. The independent health care sector includes both private and voluntary providers. They are within the ombudsman's remit where they are providing NHS services, or where they are providing an individual patient with services that are funded by the NHS.

[23]   Health Service Commissioners Act 1993, s 7.

[24]   Health Service Commissioners Act 1993, s 7(3A).

Ombudsman. This exclusion prevents the ombudsman investigating complaints about the arrangements made between the health service and family health service practitioners[25]. However, as indicated above, there are specific provisions to allow the ombudsman to investigate complaints about health services funded by the National Health Service in the independent sector. This includes, for example, residential care in the private sector funded by the National Health Service[26]. These provisions in relation to funded services ensure that users of the National Health Service continue to have access to the ombudsman if they are dissatisfied with the service they receive, irrespective of the body from whom they receive their care. The ombudsman also has jurisdiction over matters arising from contracts between one health service body and another, or between a health service body and a non-health service body for the provision of services to patients[27].

As is the case with the Parliamentary Ombudsman, the Health Services Ombudsman cannot investigate any administrative action where the complainant has a right of appeal to an administrative tribunal, or a court of law[28]. This is subject to the proviso that the ombudsman has a

[25] This clarifies the position in relation to complaints from medical practitioners about the health service bodies with which they have agreed to provide general medical services. The ombudsman used to investigate such complaints, but a case in 1990 cast doubt on the ombudsman's jurisdiction in this area. The case (*Roy v Kensington and Chelsea and Westminster Family Practitioner Committee* [1990] 1 Med LR 328) concerned a dispute between a general practitioner and a Family Health Service Authority about payments for services. The Court of Appeal concluded that this relationship was a contractual one. Although the House of Lords cast some doubt on the Court of Appeal's interpretation, it did not overrule the decision (see *Roy v Kensington and Chelsea and Westminster Family Practitioner Committee* [1992] 1 AC 624). On this basis, the Health Service Ombudsman accepted that these complaints were outside jurisdiction because they dealt with contractual matters.

[26] Health Service Commissioners Act 1993, s 7(2)(a). Under the National Health Service and Community Care Act 1990, health authorities are able to arrange for the delivery of community care to individual patients. There was some concern that the 'contractual' exclusion may prevent the ombudsman investigating complaints about such services. This provision ensures that users of the National Health Service, wherever they obtain their care, will continue to have access to the ombudsman if they are dissatisfied with the service they receive.

[27] Health Service Commissioners Act 1993, ss 7(2)(b) and 7(2)(c). This would include, for example, a complaint about a failure to provide a proper diet by a contracted-out service.

[28] Health Service Commissioners Act 1993, s 4.

discretionary power to investigate if, in the circumstances, it is not reasonable to expect the complainant to resort to these remedies. If it is clear that a complainant believes that negligence is involved, and is seeking compensation, the ombudsman will not usually investigate the matter, as it is more appropriate for the courts to determine[29]. If, however, the complainant is seeking an explanation or trying to discover what went wrong, and in fact wants an apology and reassurance that action is being taken to reduce the risk of a recurrence of the problem, the ombudsman will investigate. Most complainants to the ombudsman appear to have no desire to use the courts and probably would have little chance of compensation if they did[30]. In these cases, the courts are not the appropriate mechanism for those aggrieved by their health care or treatment.

The Health Service Ombudsman is prevented from investigating action that has been, or is, the subject of a special statutory inquiry set up under the National Health Service Act 1977, s 84[31]. This section provides for the Department of Health to set up an inquiry into any aspect of the National Health Service that the Secretary of State deems advisable. These are rare

---

[29]   When a complaint is made, it may not be clear whether a complainant is seeking compensation for negligence. Indeed, as complainants do not know the facts at this stage, they would have no evidence on which to base a negligence claim. There is nothing to prevent a complainant using the ombudsman's findings to pursue an action for negligence. However, there are difficulties with this. None of the ombudsman's papers can be subpoened by the complainant, so independent sources of evidence would have to be sought. Where the ombudsman uncovers information that appears to indicate a risk to the health and safety of patients, this can now be disclosed to the health service regulatory bodies.

[30]   The courts use the 'Bolam' and 'Bolitho' tests to determine clinical negligence. *Bolam v Friern Hospital Management Committee* [1957] 2 All ER 118, [1957] 1 WLR 582 established the legal standard of care in such cases, setting a minimum standard below which practitioners must not fall. The appropriate standard of care was the exercise of the ordinary skill of a competent person exercising that particular art. This test must now take into account the decision in *Bolitho v Hackney Health Authority* [1998] AC 232, which decided that the reasonableness of professional opinion may be questioned. In determining professional negligence, risks and benefits are to be balanced, and there must be a defensible conclusion reached by experts on the particular course of action taken by doctors if negligence liability is to be avoided. Not only may it be difficult to prove negligence, but the amount of damages awarded may be small. Many of the complaints investigated concern old people or infants. There can be no claim for loss of earnings in these cases. Equally, if a death is involved, there are no dependants to be compensated.

[31]   Health Service Commissioners Act 1993, s 4.

and would only occur where there were serious concerns or allegations giving rise to widespread public concern. However the decision to hold such an inquiry, and the inquiry itself, might be the subject of a complaint to the ombudsman against the actions of the Department of Health.

Clinical Decisions

Clinical decisions were originally excluded from the Health Service Ombudsman's scheme. This meant that any action taken as a result of a clinical judgment in the provision of diagnosis, care or treatment, including wrong diagnosis and treatment, could not be investigated, despite any harm which may have befallen the patient. It was a wide exclusion, covering doctors, nurses and the professions allied to medicine. Its inclusion in the original act was at the insistence of the British Medical Association. It had been the subject of much controversy, and it was felt that the effectiveness of the ombudsman was much reduced by this limitation. From the inception of the scheme, by far the largest category of complaints rejected concerned those relating to clinical judgment[32].

From April 1996, the ombudsman has been able to investigate complaints which call into question the exercise of clinical judgment[33]. In order to carry out this new function, the ombudsman has medical and nursing advisors on the staff and can also call upon the services of independent professional assessors. These are appointed and briefed with the help of the ombudsman's own professional advisers[34]. The extension of remit to clinical decisions brings into sharp focus the relationship between the ombudsman and the courts. Many complaints involving clinical judgment involve serious allegations about care and treatment, sometimes resulting in death. Some of the allegations could be remedied by actions in the courts on the grounds of medical negligence. These complaints should thus be rejected on the grounds that there is a right of legal action in the courts, unless the

---

[32] In 1975, about one-sixth of cases were rejected as being outside jurisdiction because they were complaints about the diagnosis or treatment of patients solely concerned with the exercise of clinical judgment by medical staff (HC 282 1976, para 4). Since that date, the numbers of rejections on this ground has fluctuated from 40% to 16% of all rejections.

[33] Section 3(7) of the Health Service Commissioners Act 1993, inserted by the Health Service Commissioner (Amendment) Act 1996, s 6(2).

[34] Independent assessors are drawn from the national list of advisers and assessors, held by the Secretary of State.

ombudsman is satisfied that it would not be reasonable for the complainant to resort to the courts. The ombudsman believes that to reject complaints on the theoretical basis that there is a legal remedy would negate the intention of Parliament in extending the ombudsman's powers to include clinical complaints[35]. In deciding whether to exercise the discretion to investigate, the ombudsman looks at the remedy that the complainant is seeking. As indicated above, if damages or financial compensation appear to be the primary aim of the complaint, then the ombudsman will not investigate.

The ombudsman has noted the concerns of the government and the health service professions about the rising volume and cost of litigation, coupled with the level of dissatisfaction with the courts among some litigants and legal practitioners in medical negligence cases. While accepting that the court system should be efficient and effective, and that deserving cases should obtain damages, the ombudsman notes that the courts are not always the appropriate mechanisms for those aggrieved by their health care or treatment. The ombudsman system can provide an alternative remedy to those who are not seeking financial redress, and indeed is in a unique position to do so[36]. The Department of Health is currently conducting a review of the system of compensation for clinical negligence[37].

Since the change in jurisdiction, the ombudsman's office has become increasingly involved in the investigation of clinical complaints. More than 80% of cases investigated concern clinical care, and as these often involve serious and complex matters, this has obvious repercussions for resources[38]. It also changes the focus of the office, which had previously been concerned with administrative failures in the health service[39]. Concern has been expressed that this reduces the ombudsman's ability to

---

[35]   Health Service Ombudsman Annual Report 1997–98 (HC Paper 811 (1997–98)) p 13.

[36]   Health Service Ombudsman, Annual Report 1997–98 (HC Paper 811 (1997–98)) p 13.

[37]   See Health Service Ombudsman for England Annual Report 2001–02 (HC Paper 887 (2001–02)) p 3.

[38]   Health Service Ombudsman, Annual Report 2000–01 (HC Paper 3 (2000–01)) p 17.

[39]   Health Service Ombudsman, Annual Report 1997–98 (HC Paper 811 (1997–98)) p 5.

investigate the executive[40]. There are also concerns as to whether the ombudsman remedy, based as it is on 'procedures of political and administrative accountability' is really appropriate for dealing with complaints about clinical judgment[41]. However, it has to be admitted that in the past it was often difficult to draw a clear line between clinical judgment and administrative matters[42]. The effectiveness of the Health Service Ombudsman was in the past reduced by this limitation[43].

Maladministration and Injustice

The Health Service Ombudsman has a wider remit than the Parliamentary Ombudsman. As indicated above, rather than being confined to allegations of maladministration, the ombudsman can also investigate failures in a service provided by a health service body and failures to provide a service which it was a function of the body to provide[44]. In addition, the complainant can allege to have suffered not only injustice, but also hardship as a result of this failure or as a result of maladministration. Whether this wider remit has any practical consequences is unclear. Under the other public sector ombudsmen schemes, the concept of maladministration has proved to be so flexible that it can encompass a failure of service or failure to provide a service. Equally, 'hardship' can be regarded as a possible injustice consequent on maladministration[45]. The concept of maladministration has already been discussed in detail in Chapter 2, and the issues connected with it apply equally to the Health Service Ombudsman. Maladministration covers such matters as not following proper procedures or agreed policies, failing to have proper procedures, giving wrong information or inadequate

---

[40]   S Kerrison and A Pollock 'Complaints as Accountability? The Case of Health Care UK' (2001) PL 115–133, p 125.

[41]   P Giddings 'The Health Service Ombudsman after twenty-five years' (1999) PL 201–210, p 205.

[42]   See M Seneviratne *Ombudsmen in the Public Sector* (1994) Open University Press pp 62–63. By way of example, if a psychiatric patient commits suicide, and a relative complains that the patient was inadequately supervised, is this a matter of clinical judgment or maladministration?

[43]   For example, the ombudsman could not investigate decisions not to resuscitate elderly patients, as this was seen as resting on clinical judgment.

[44]   Health Service Commissioners Act 1993, s 3.

[45]   See 'A Commission for Public Administration in England', a note by the Local Government Ombudsmen for England and the Parliamentary and Health Service Ombudsman. Annex A in the *Review of the Public Sector Ombudsmen in England* (2000) Cabinet Office pp 81–82.

explanations of care, or not dealing promptly or thoroughly with the original complaint.

Where complaints relate to failures of service, the ombudsman can test the allegations against the published service standards in the Patient's Charter[46]. Criticisms for alleged 'failures' of service may present difficulties where the main problem relates to the adequacy of resources. This is a difficult area, as funding of the National Health Service has generated much controversy in recent years. The level of funding is relevant when discussing alleged service failure, but to what extent should resource issues be taken into account? Delays may not necessarily be maladministration if they result from financial constraints and the need to assess priorities between competing demands for resources. Delay in itself may not therefore be a sufficient cause for criticism in relation to failures of service. To merit criticism, it must reasonably be attributed to maladministration and not to resource problems beyond the control of the health service body. The ombudsman takes into account the shortage of resources and the stress under which many staff work. In one case, he found unacceptable delay in the attention the patient received from an anaesthetist, but did not criticise staff for giving priority to patients with more urgent needs[47].

A different view is taken where the resource problems are within the control of the authority. This can be illustrated by a case example. The complaint involved allegations of neglect of duty. The ombudsman found that problems with the physical environment in the hospital were compounded by inadequate staffing levels on the ward. Nursing numbers were not only below establishment, but were not at the right levels of seniority. The hospital claimed that this was due to recruiting and financial problems. The ombudsman concluded that the staff shortages were within the control of management, particularly as they related to planned leave of absence. It was a management responsibility to plan for eventualities such as study leave, annual leave, maternity leave and staff sickness. There was a marked discrepancy between the general shortage of staff at the hospital, and the

---

46   See P Giddings 'The United Kingdom Health Service Commissioner Schemes' in R Gregory and P Giddings (eds) *Righting Wrongs: The Ombudsman in Six Continents* (2000) IOS Press p 345.

47   Health Service Ombudsman, *Investigations Completed April–September 1998* (HC Paper 3 (1998–99)) pp 5–6. See also P Giddings 'The United Kingdom Health Service Commissioner Schemes' in R Gregory and P Giddings (eds) *Righting Wrongs: The Ombudsman in Six Continents* (2000) p 346.

particularly acute shortage on the complainant's ward. This could not be accounted for by reference to recruitment and financial problems[48].

Procedures and Powers

As with the other public sector ombudsmen, there is no provision for the Health Service Ombudsman to conduct own-initiative investigations. Complaints can only be investigated where they are referred by an individual or body of persons who claim to have suffered injustice or hardship[49]. The complaint has to be made by the person aggrieved, unless the complainant has died or is for any reason unable to act for him or herself. In these cases, the complaint may be made by the personal representative or by a member of the family, or by some body or individual suitable to act as a representative[50]. 'Suitable' is not defined in the Act, but the ombudsman takes a generous view of this, and few problems have been caused by this requirement. A complainant acting through an agent, for example, a doctor, member of Parliament or local councillor, is treated as making the complaint him or herself.

In the normal course of events, complaints are received from patients or would-be patients, although they can be made by consumer groups. Community Health Councils cannot make complaints about services, but they can assist or write on a complainants behalf. There is provision for health service bodies to refer complaints to the ombudsman for investigation[51]. Health service bodies can use this procedure where it is obvious that the complainant will not be satisfied unless there is an independent investigation. This procedure may also be used where, for example, a serious complaint is made against senior members of the authority, a factor that makes it desirable to have a completely independent inquiry. This procedure is rarely used.

---

[48] Third Report from the Select Committee on the Parliamentary Commissioner for Administration (HC Paper 44 (1991–92)) (Reports of the Health Service Commissioner for 1990–91 together with proceedings of the Committee relating the report, minutes of evidence and appendices) para 18.

[49] Health Service Commissioners Act 1993, s 8.

[50] Health Service Commissioners Act 1993, s 9.

[51] Health Service Commissioners Act 1993, s 10. In these cases, the complaint must be properly made to the authority, and must be referred to the ombudsman within 12 months of its reception.

Unlike the Parliamentary Ombudsman scheme, there is no requirement for complaints to be filtered through a member of Parliament. However, complaints will only be accepted after they have completed the National Health Service internal complaints procedure. There is no residence requirement for complainants to the Health Service Ombudsman, but there is a time bar. The complaint must be made, in writing, within a year from the date when the complainant first had notice of the matters alleged in the complaint[52]. The ombudsman has discretion to investigate complaints beyond this time limit, if it is considered reasonable to do so[53]. It may be reasonable to waive the time requirement where the delay is caused by the illness of the complainant, or because other remedies have been pursued without success. There are obvious difficulties with investigating complaints relating to events in the distant past.

The legislation gives the ombudsman a great deal of freedom to determine the procedure to be followed in receiving and investigating complaints. All matters in connection with the initiation, continuance or discontinuance of an investigation are for the discretion of the ombudsman, as are questions of whether a complaint is duly made out[54]. Before commencing an investigation, the ombudsman must allow the health service body concerned the opportunity to comment upon the allegations. An exception to this is where the complaint is made by a member of staff of the hospital or health authority complained about on behalf of a person unable to complain for him or herself. In this case, before accepting the complaint, the ombudsman has to be satisfied that there is no one more appropriate to take up the complaint. This exception is important in relation to 'whistleblowers', who express concerns about the safety, health or well-being of patients, in order that they may be afforded some protection from victimisation[55].

---

[52]   Health Service Commissioners Act 1993, s 9.

[53]   Health Service Commissioners Act 1993, s 9(4).

[54]   The Health Service Commissioners Act 1993, s 3 provides that the ombudsman 'may' investigate.

[55]   They are also afforded some protection against victimisation by virtue of the Employment Rights Act 1996, Pt IVA (this was inserted by the Public Interest (Disclosure) Act 1998, s 1). This protects individuals who make disclosures in the public interest and allows them to bring an action in the event of victimisation following that disclosure. This provision protects staff who may express concern about the health, safety or well-being of patients. It ensures that staff are able to exercise freedom of speech on issues of patient and client care, and are not penalised for speaking out in good faith.

An investigation must be held in private, and the ombudsman has discretion to allow representation, not only for complainants, but also for staff involved in the investigation. Like the Parliamentary Ombudsman, the Health Service Ombudsman has wide powers in relation to the obtaining of information, the production of documents, and the taking of evidence from witnesses[56]. Obstructions of the ombudsman in the performance of these functions will be treated as if they were a contempt of court[57]. The ombudsman has the power to pay any expenses incurred in connection with an investigation.

The New National Health Service Complaints Procedure

As indicated above, before a complaint can be made to the ombudsman, the internal health service procedure must be invoked and normally exhausted[58]. This requirement was introduced when the new National Health Service complaints procedure was established in April 1996. The Health Service Ombudsman is at the final stage of this new scheme[59], a

---

[56] See *Hession v Health Service Comr for Wales* [2001] EWHC Admin 619, which clarified the Health Service Ombudsman's power to question witnesses. Hession was a retired consultant psychiatrist. A patient in his care had committed two murders on the second night after being discharged from a psychiatric unit. The ombudsman investigated a complaint against the hospital trust from the parents of the victims. A witness summons was served on Dr Hession, to answer questions relevant to the complaint that the patient was inappropriately discharged. Dr Hession sought judicial review, claiming that the ombudsman did not have power to investigate, and that answering questions would breach patient confidentiality. The judge confirmed that the ombudsman had the same powers of the court in this matter. The doctor's duty to give evidence overrode the duty of confidentiality to the patient. The court said that the legislation clearly allowed for confidential matters to be investigated, and the fact that the investigation was in private afforded protection to the party whose confidence may be invaded. It was confirmed that the ombudsman had the power to conduct investigations as he saw fit, and thus the court could not limit the scope of the questions which may be put to Dr Hession. The judge was confident that the ombudsman, having much more information about the case, was best placed to decide which questions were relevant and necessary.

[57] Health Service Commissioners Act 1993, ss 11–13.

[58] Health Service Commissioners Act 1993, s 4(5).

[59] *Acting on Complaints: the Government's proposals in response to 'Being Heard' the report of a review committee on NHS complaints procedures* (1995) Department of Health p 3.

role which allows the ombudsman to assess the operation of the complaint handling process at local level. The Health Service Ombudsman is thus at the apex of the complaints pyramid for National Health Service complaints, and the complaints process acts as a filtering mechanism, so that only complaints that remain unresolved find their way to the ombudsman. In 2000–01, over half the complaints made to the ombudsman were rejected because local action had not been exhausted[60].

The new procedure is based on the findings of the Wilson Report[61], which reviewed the previous procedure, established in 1985[62]. The Wilson Report proposed a three-stage process for dealing with complaints in the health service. The first stage would be internal, practice-based and informal, and would be concerned with providing an apology or explanation. For complaints unresolved at this stage, stage two would involve a panel of at least three people, including a lay chair and lay majority who would report to the statutory health service body. The final stage would involve the referral of unresolved complaints to the Health Service Ombudsman, whose jurisdiction would cover all complaints and procedures. The government was largely in agreement with these proposals, with the additional element, that if a stage-two panel was not established, the complainant could refer the complaint directly to the ombudsman[63].

The new system provides a unified procedure for dealing with complaints. The procedure encourages the resolution of complaints at local level, and thus all complaints must first be considered through 'local resolution'. In the case of National Health Service trusts, authorities or boards, the final response to written complaints must be by way of a letter from the chief executive. In the case of family health services, all practitioners are required to have a practice-based procedure for dealing with complaints. Such complaints are concluded by a letter from the practice concerned.

---

[60]   Health Service Ombudsman Annual Report 2000–01 (HC Paper 3 (2000–01)) p 22.

[61]   *Being Heard* (1994) The report of a review committee on NHS complaints procedures (The Wilson Report) Department of Health.

[62]   The Hospital Complaints Procedure Act 1985 obliged health authorities to establish complaints procedures for hospital patients. There were different procedures for clinical and non-clinical complaints.

[63]   *Acting on Complaints: the Government's proposals in response to 'Being Heard', the report of a review committee on NHS complaints procedures* (1995) Department of Health.

If complainants are not satisfied by this final letter, they can ask for an independent review of the complaint by an independent review panel. These panels consist of a lay chair, and the majority of members must be independent of the service provider that is the subject of the complaint. The request to convene a panel is made to a 'convenor', who is usually a non-executive director of the National Health Service body concerned. The role of the convenor is central to the new procedure. When convenors receive requests, they must decide, after taking appropriate advice, whether to set up an independent review panel. Alternatively, they may decide to refer the complaint back for further attempts at local resolution, or decide that nothing further can be done to resolve the complaint. If the convenor decides not to set up a panel, as full an explanation as possible has to be given to the complainant of why this decision has been made. In these cases, convenors are also required to tell complainants of their right to complain to the Health Service Ombudsman about that decision[64].

The national guidance on the role of convenors requires them to act impartially. They must also seek advice from a lay person drawn from lists of such people who are considered suitable to chair independent panels. Where there are clinical issues, they must also seek appropriate professional advice from someone who has not been involved in the complaint. The purpose of this is to advise the convenor whether the clinical aspects of the case have been fully and fairly assessed at the local resolution stage of the procedure. It is not the role of convenors or their clinical advisors to investigate or pass judgment on the quality or adequacy of the clinical care of the patient. Nor are convenors to re-investigate the complaint, and thus compromise their independence.

Where there is a refusal to convene a panel, complainants can take the case to the ombudsman. Equally, complainants can complain to the ombudsman if not satisfied with the outcome of the review panel's determination. The ombudsman has no power to recommend that convenors convene a panel. That decision is properly within the discretion of the convenor, acting on behalf of the National Health Service body concerned. However, if there is some evidence of maladministration in the decision-making process, the ombudsman can invite the body to consider their decision afresh, in the light of the ombudsman's findings. Unless the

---

[64]   In 2000–01, 82% of investigable complaints concerned cases where the convenor had refused to grant an independent review (Health Service Ombudsman Annual Report 2000–01 (HC Paper 3 (2000–01)) p 24).

ombudsman makes such a recommendation, the convenor normally cannot change the decision whether or not to convene a panel. In the absence of the ombudsman's recommendation, a convenor can only review the decision about convening a panel in the exceptional cases where wholly fresh evidence is brought forward and the nature of the complaint is changed.

Complaints Handling under the New Procedure

There have been a number of complaints to the ombudsman about the operation of the new complaints procedure, especially about stage two of the process. The ombudsman has warned that 'elementary errors' in managing stage two of the procedure 'can undermine the whole process'[65]. The ombudsman has taken the view that failure to act in accordance with the procedure can be regarded as maladministration causing injustice. In the first few years of its operation, there were a number of concerns about the process. One area was in relation to clinical issues. Despite the fact that the convenor is required to obtain appropriate clinical advice where there are clinical issues, there were a number of complaints where such advice was not sought. Even where advice was sought, in some cases it was obtained from those who had been involved in the complaint or whose impartiality might be doubted. If there is some doubt about whether appropriate clinical advice has been sought, the ombudsman will almost always investigate. If it is clear, even before an investigation, that there has not been appropriate clinical advice, the ombudsman will advise the National Health Service body to have the decision reconsidered[66].

The ombudsman has emphasised that the convenor's role is not to investigate or attempt to resolve the complaint. The role is to obtain enough understanding of the details and circumstances in order to make a recommendation about the next stage of the process. The purpose of obtaining clinical advice is to decide whether the complainant has had a full and satisfactory response on clinical issues at the local resolution stage. It is not to reassess the clinical aspects of the complaint, but to assess the adequacy of the response to these clinical aspects. Convenors are not

65   Health Service Ombudsman for England Annual Report 2001–02 (HC Paper 887 (2001–02)) p 12.
66   Health Service Ombudsman Annual Report 1996–97 (HC Paper 41 (1997–98)) p 74.

supposed to investigate the complaint, but to consider whether the local response was adequate, whether it needed further local resolution, or whether there should be an independent review. Any more than this, and there is the danger that convenors will not be acting impartially or distancing themselves enough from those involved in the earlier stages of the complaint. The role of the adviser is to help the convenor reach a decision, and not to pre-empt the role of an independent panel and their assessors. The ombudsman has noted that convenors and clinical advisers often misunderstand the purpose of clinical advice at this stage. While understanding that the distinction can be difficult to make in practice, the ombudsman confirms that it is crucial to the convening process.

Convenors are required to provide adequate reasons for their decisions not to convene panels. The national guidelines require as full an explanation as possible to be given to complainants. This will enable them to understand the decision, and will enable them to articulate the basis of their dissatisfaction if they wish to complain to the ombudsman. The ombudsman has said that he considers the absence of adequate reasons addressing specific concerns as prima facie evidence of maladministration[67].

Some conveners are not providing adequate explanations about why there was a decision not to refer the case to an independent review. Other problems concern delay in the convening process, failures to explain time limits, and failures by the convenors to explain to complainants their right to refer the matter to the ombudsman. In one complaint, concerning dental treatment, the ombudsman was critical of the fact that an examination by an independent dental adviser was made conditional on the agreement of the dentist complained about[68].

The ombudsman has also received complaints about the operation of the independent review panels themselves. There is no detailed national guidance on the conduct of these panels, a factor which, the ombudsman notes, may have reflected a wish by the National Health Service executives to keep the panels informal and user-friendly[69]. The complaints received

---

[67] Health Service Ombudsman Annual Report 1996–97 (HC Paper 41 (1997–98)) p 75.

[68] See Health Service Ombudsman for England Annual Report 2001–02 (HC Paper 887 (2001–02)) p 12.

[69] Health Service Ombudsman Annual Report 1996–97 (HC Paper 41 (1997–98)) p 77.

by the ombudsman reveal considerable variability in the conduct of panels and in the style and structure of reports. The ombudsman notes that panels need to follow the basic requirements of natural justice and fairness. The ombudsman has criticised panels for failing to identify and take evidence from key witnesses and from the parties to the complaint. Panels have also been guilty of taking clinical evidence in the absence of clinical assessors.

Other problems with the operation of appeal panels include failures to observe the statutory directions about what to include in the reports. These directions require that reports must include the finding of facts relevant to the complaint. They must also contain the opinion of the panel on the complaint having regard to the findings of fact, and the reasons for the panel's opinion. Reports of assessors must also be included in the report, together with the reasons for any disagreement by the panel with any matter included in the report of the assessors. The ombudsman has emphasised that the functions of the independent review panels are to consider complaints according to the terms of reference decided by convenors. They are to investigate the facts impartially and to report their findings in writing with appropriate suggestions and comments.

The changes to the complaints system in 1996 clearly placed the Health Service Ombudsman at the apex of a more integrated National Health Service complaints system. The ombudsman now has a role in monitoring standards for complaint handling across the health service as a whole. This role, it has been argued, should bring a 'much-needed coherence' to the complaints process in the health service, which is an 'important part of the service's relationship with its patients and public'[70]. This overview has enabled the ombudsman to advise that the procedure is 'unduly complicated and time-consuming'[71]. There is widespread dissatisfaction with the second tier of the process, and the work of the review panels varies widely in quality. Moreover, members of the review panels are not accepted as independent. The ombudsman notes that it is essential that the procedure has a component that is accepted by the parties as 'independent,

---

[70] P Giddings 'The Health Service Ombudsman after twenty-five years' (1999) PL 201–210, p 209.

[71] Health Service Ombudsman for England Annual Report 2001–02 (HC Paper 887 (2001–02)) p 3. The ombudsman is at the third tier of the process, which can result in reports sometimes being completed four or five years after the event giving rise to the complaint.

impartial and authoritative'[72]. There is presently a review of the complaint handling system. The ombudsman has advocated that in any new system there should be stricter time limits for local resolution, and 'fast-tracking' to the ombudsman of suitable cases where local resolution is ineffective[73].

Working Methods

When a complaint (or enquiry) is made to the ombudsman's office, it is checked to see if it is within jurisdiction, whether it could be dealt with another way, and whether an investigation would be an appropriate outcome. This screening process reveals that a large proportion of complaints are non-investigable for various reasons. In 2001–02, 68% of complaints were in the non-investigable category. The largest single reason for this was that the complaints were premature, that is, the local complaints procedure had not been exhausted. Almost 73% of non-investigable cases came within this category, and they represented half of all the complaints dealt with during the year. The remaining cases that were non-investigable were outside jurisdiction, or were closed, withdrawn, no action was required, or the enquiry was answered[74].

A formal investigation is conducted for only a proportion of investigable complaints, although that proportion has increased. In 1999–2000, investigations were conducted in 19% of investigable cases. In 2000–01, the proportion was 28%, and in 2001–02, it was 23%. This represents 8% of all complaints dealt with during the year. A larger proportion of cases are being investigated partly because of the nature of the complaints, and partly because of a change in the criteria for accepting them for investigation. Previously, one of the criteria for acceptance was whether the complainant had provided prima facie evidence of maladministration or failure of service. Now that the vast majority of complaints are concerned with clinical judgment, this criteria is very difficult to meet, particularly as many cases involve serious and complex issues. The ombudsman now has

---

[72] Health Service Ombudsman for England Annual Report 2001–02 (HC Paper 887 (2001–02)) p 4.

[73] Health Service Ombudsman for England Annual Report 2001–02 (HC Paper 887 (2001–02)) p 3.

[74] Health Service Ombudsman for England Annual Report 2001–02 (HC Paper 887 (2001–02)) p 27.

to commence an investigation, in order to be sure that matters needing investigation are not overlooked[75].

In the majority of investigable cases, no further action is taken for a variety of reasons. These include cases where it is considered that the complaints have been adequately dealt with. There are also cases where it is considered that further action would be unlikely to achieve any added benefit for the complainant. Sometimes a formal investigation is not undertaken because there is no evidence that there had been un-remedied injustice or hardship. Conclusions on these cases are only reached after scrutiny of the relevant papers and the appropriate professional advice in clinical cases. Complainants are given a full explanation of the decision[76]. In a small number of investigable cases, direct action is taken for the benefit of complainants without the need for a formal investigation. In 2001–02, there were 40 such cases. In 26 of these, the ombudsman's staff wrote to the relevant health body with advice for improvement in future complaint handling. For the rest, the health service bodies agreed to take further action to resolve the complaint[77].

When a complaint has been received and accepted, investigators usually go to the authority concerned, examine the files and interview the relevant staff. Investigators invariably interview the complainant, often in his or her home. The extension of jurisdiction to include clinical complaints has resulted in new procedures for the ombudsman's office. In these cases, independent professional assessment of the issues has to be obtained in order to assist the ombudsman in reaching a decision. The ombudsman's normal practice is to appoint two assessors where the complaint is concerned with the clinical judgment of one professional discipline or speciality. If the case involves different disciplines or specialities, only one assessor from each discipline is normally appointed, so that the investigation does not become too complicated.

---

[75]   Health Service Ombudsman Annual Report 2000–01 (HC Paper 3 (2000–01)) p 17.

[76]   Health Service Ombudsman, Annual Report 2000–01 (HC Paper 3 (2000–01)) pp 23–34. Where the ombudsman decides not to conduct an investigation, the Health Service Commissioners Act 1993, s 14 provides that a statement of reasons be sent to the complainant and any member of Parliament who assisted in the making of the complaint.

[77]   Health Service Ombudsman for England Annual Report 2001–02 (HC Paper 887 (2001–02)) p 2.

The external assessors are appointed on a case by case basis, and they act in an individual and not a representative capacity. Assessors are not expected to say what they would have done in the circumstances, or what was the best possible action. They are to use their knowledge and experience to give advice, having regard to what was reasonable or responsible in the circumstances. In addition, they must take into account all the relevant professional guidance on standards and good practice that, in their view, a professional working in the capacity in question could be expected to take into account. The ombudsman believes that this independent professional advice is a critical element in clinical judgment cases, although the decision whether to uphold the complaint rests with the ombudsman.

When a formal investigation is completed, a draft report is sent in confidence to the body investigated[78]. The final report is sent to the complainant and the health service body concerned. In addition, a copy is sent to anyone who was the subject of allegations in the complaint[79].

The increase in the numbers of complaints, and the thoroughness of the process for dealing with them, means that this is not a speedy process. The time taken to complete investigations is a source of concern, and performance targets have been set for various stages of the complaint handling process. In 2001–02, the office replied to more than 80% of correspondence received within the target of 18 days. Reports of 255 investigations were completed in 2001–02, representing a 10% increase on the previous year. Unfortunately, the time taken to complete an investigation rose to 63 weeks on average, which is significantly above the 49 weeks target. Not surprisingly perhaps, clinical investigations take longer, averaging 65 weeks, compared to 54 weeks for non-clinical investigations. The number of cases which are over nine and 12 months old is falling[80]. The ombudsman recently completed stage one of a review

---

[78]   The draft is sent to the health service body, in order that it can comment on the facts, their interpretation and the recommended remedy. Occasionally, parts of the report may be shown to the complainant, where there may be a dispute about the facts or some other aspect of the report that may be challenged. Complainants are not shown the draft findings or draft recommendations.

[79]   Health Service Commissioners Act 1993, s 14.

[80]   At the end of March 2002, there were 63 cases over nine months old, including 36 which were over 12 months old. The figures for the previous year were 87 and 46 respectively (Health Service Ombudsman for England Annual Report 2001–02 (HC Paper 887 (2001–02)) pp 28–29).

of working methods, designed to make the process more responsive, accessible, transparent and speedier[81].

Remedies

In common with the other public sector ombudsmen, when a complaint is made, the Health Service Ombudsman can only recommend a remedy. There is no power of enforcement. If it appears that the injustice or hardship will not be remedied, the ombudsman can make a special report[82]. The legislation does not focus on remedies, simply allowing the ombudsman to investigate and report on the outcome of the investigation[83]. Unlike the other ombudsmen, the Health Service Ombudsman does not generally recommend any financial redress[84]. If the complainant is seeking compensation and damages, this is more appropriately dealt with by the courts, as it usually involves allegations of negligence. The ombudsman will not therefore accept the case for investigation.

On rare occasions, the ombudsman does believe that reimbursement for financial loss is appropriate[85]. This occurs where there has been an identifiable financial loss or costs as a direct result of maladministration. In these cases, the health service body is invited or recommended to make an ex-gratia payment. The sums involved are usually modest. They are to reimburse for lost property, for example, clothing or jewellery. In one case[86], a hospital failed to safeguard a ring belonging to the complainant's mother

---

[81] See Health Service Ombudsman Annual Report 2000–01 (HC Paper 3 (2000–01)) p 17.

[82] Health Service Commissioner Act 1993, s 14(3). Originally, this report was to be made to the Secretary of State, who was required to lay a copy of it before each House of Parliament. Since 1996, the ombudsman now lays special reports before Parliament.

[83] Health Service Commissioner Act 1993, s 14.

[84] The ombudsman has noted that, although there does not appear to be any reason why financial redress should not be paid under the National Health Service complaints procedure, few payments have been made. Indeed, any suggestion that a complainant may be seeking a money award is seen as a sign that legal action is intended, and therefore the complaint is excluded from the procedure. The ombudsman has suggested that the Department of Health review this matter.

[85] In 1999–2000, reimbursement was recommended in only four cases, two of which concerned the cost of dental treatment (see Health Service Ombudsman Annual Report 1999–2000 (HC Paper 542 (1999–2000)) para 4.6).

[86] Case No E 40/96–97.

after it was removed before an operation. The proper procedures had not been followed, and the hospital was recommended to make an ex gratia payment. Sometimes there will be a recommendation for payment to cover the cost of travelling to and from hospital for treatment.

Where complaints relate to services for which a charge is made, for example dental services, the ombudsman may recommend a refund of the National Health Service fee paid. The ombudsman may also recommend payment to compensate for the additional cost of treatment incurred as a result of maladministration. In one case[87], a hospital was recommended to reimburse the cost of attending an initial assessment at a private clinic for anorexia treatment. The ombudsman found that proper consideration was not given to the complainant's request for an extra-contractual referral, and that adequate alternative treatment had not been offered. Very occasionally there will be a recommendation for payment for distress, although the Health Service Ombudsman has not been as ready to award consolatory payments as the other public sector ombudsmen[88]. Nor have there been payments to compensate for inconvenience, which the other ombudsmen often award[89].

---

[87] Case No E 308/95–96.

[88] There is a difficulty for health service bodies who may wish to make small consolatory payments to complainants. Current rules only allow payments where there is demonstrable financial loss, or if the ombudsman finds maladministration and recommends payment. The ombudsman raised this matter with the Secretary of State in connection with a complaint (Case No E 1458/98–99) about the actions of a health authority in placing noisy and disruptive clients in the adjoining house to the complainants. The ombudsman found that the hardship caused to the complainants was not a result of maladministration. However, he felt that the policy of not allowing small payments in recognition of the distress caused in such cases was not in keeping with a modern service provider. The Secretary of State is unwilling to consider any change to the rules, apparently on the grounds that it would divert funds from patient care. The ombudsman notes that taken to its logical conclusion, this argument would prevent compensation for clinical negligence. It is also worthy of note that central and local government are much readier to make consolatory payments (see Health Service Ombudsman Annual Report 2000–01 (HC Paper 3 (2000–01)) pp 28–29).

[89] The ombudsman has noted that the NHS compares unfavourably with both central and local government in its extreme reluctance to offer financial redress for the consequences of unsatisfactory service, including distress and inconvenience. There are current discussions taking place about reforming the NHS complaints procedure. The ombudsman advises that there should be the development of a code of practice for the NHS which would lay down guidelines for NHS organisations regarding redress, including financial redress where appropriate for justified complaints (see Health Service Ombudsman for England Annual Report 2001–02 (HC Paper 887 (2001–02)) p 3).

Although financial remedies are rare, and usually involve a small amount of money, payment of these sums has not been without problems. In 1989, on Treasury advice, the Department of Health revised its instructions to health authorities so that all cases involving a recommendation of compensation had to be referred to the department. The reason for this was that it was felt unreasonable to expect health authorities to make informed judgments about whether a case would create an awkward precedent. Despite the fact that this would result in delay, the department was concerned that payments may set precedents which could have ramifications for the entire public service. The select committee thought that to insist on all payments being subject to scrutiny by the Department of Health was excessively bureaucratic. It recommended that the department press for the restoration of the discretion for health authorities to pay small sums of money[90]. In 1990, health service bodies were given the discretion to make financial awards, up to a limit of £5,000[91].

In the majority of cases, the recommended remedy for a complainant is an apology[92] from the health service body. This is in many cases entirely appropriate as many complainants are seeking explanations for what went wrong, or an assurance that nothing did go wrong. An investigation that uncovers the facts may afford the direct benefit they require. All ombudsmen are concerned with providing generalised benefits as well as resolving individual grievances. This is especially true for the Health Service Ombudsman. Great importance is placed on the contribution made by the office to the quality of service which the National Health Service provides. Although the remedying of individual grievances is important, of equal importance are the changes made to the system to ensure that higher standards of service are provided. The remedies proposed by the

---

[90]   Second Report from the Select Committee on the Parliamentary Commissioner for Administration (HC Paper 433 (1988–89)) (Report of the Health Service Commissioner for 1987–88) para 7.

[91]   Second Report from the Select Committee on the Parliamentary Commissioner for Administration (HC Paper 441 (1989–90)) (Report of the Health Service Commissioner for 1989) para 52. The discretion does not apply where compensation is recommended when there is no cash loss, but these kinds of cases are even rarer.

[92]   The apology is conveyed through the ombudsman, rather than being made directly by the health service body (see Health Service Ombudsman Annual Report 1983–84 (HC Paper 537 (1983–84)) para 129). Sometimes, in addition, the health service body is invited by the ombudsman to convey an apology directly.

ombudsman will almost certainly seek to prevent a repetition of similar maladministration or failures in the future.

The ombudsman has identified a particular area where an adequate remedy may not be forthcoming[93]. This is in relation to the independent review process. It is not legally possible for a second independent review panel to be set up to rehear a complaint, except where the panel's actions or constitution are so flawed that it would be a nullity. If the ombudsman finds problems with the actions of the independent review panel, there is a lack of an effective remedy. This problem has been drawn to the attention of the Health Department, and the suggestion has been made that the rules be amended to allow that a second panel be set up, if the ombudsman recommends it[94].

Although there is no power to impose a remedy, the recommendations are almost invariably accepted by the health authority concerned. Those investigated are given three months to notify the ombudsman of the specific action taken to implement the ombudsman's recommendations. There is no right of appeal. In most cases, a satisfactory reply is received. The matter is pursued until the ombudsman is satisfied that every recommendation has been acted upon. It is rare for health authorities to persist in a refusal to accept the ombudsman's findings or proposed solutions. If this does happen, the health authority concerned can be brought to the attention of the select committee by the ombudsman. The select committee can then require the health authority to appear before them to give an explanation and answer questions.

This sanction may not be as effective in the case of recalcitrant practitioners, as it is for health authorities. Where individual practitioners do not agree with the ombudsman's findings, and refuse to apologise to a complainant, for example, the possibility of intervention by the select committee may hold no particular threat. For these cases, the ombudsman has discussed the possibility of using publicity as a sanction[95]. At present, health service bodies, but not individuals, are named in investigation reports. It has been suggested that it would be consistent if reports into complaints about family

---

[93] See Health Service Ombudsman Annual Report 1997–98 (HC Paper 811 (97–98)) p 18.

[94] So far, no action has been taken in relation to this.

[95] See Health Service Ombudsman Annual Report 1998–99 (HC Paper 498 (98–99)) para 2.9.

health service practitioners named the practice concerned. The ombudsman's view is that, because of the personal nature of the relationship between family practitioners and patients, it is only appropriate to name the health authority area in which the practice is situated. However, the right to identify the practice or practitioner is not ruled out where there are serious cases or repeat complaints. The publicity sanction may also be used where practitioners will not accept the ombudsman's recommendations, or where they remove patients from their lists for no other reason than that the patient has made a complaint.

Complaints Statistics

The numbers of complaints dealt with by the Health Service Ombudsman has increased dramatically since the office was established. In the first year of operation, the ombudsman received 361 complaints, a figure which rose steadily in each decade. The average number of complaints each year in the 1970s was 700, and in the 1980s, 800[96]. In 1995/96, there were just under 1,800 complaints, and since then complaints have always exceeded 2,000 per year. The figures for the number of complaints received over the last five years are shown in Table 5.1.

TABLE 5.1 NUMBER OF COMPLAINTS

2001/02	2660
2000/01	2595
1999/00	2526
1998/99	2869
1997/98	2660

(Source: Health Service Ombudsman Annual Reports)

Although there has been a marked increase in the number of complaints received in recent years, a striking feature of these figures is that overall

---

[96]   P Giddings 'The United Kingdom Health Service Commissioner Schemes' in R Gregory and P Giddings (eds) Giddings *Righting Wrongs: The Ombudsman in Six Continents* (2000) IOS Press p 346.

the number of complaints is small, when set against some 7.5 million admissions to hospitals, and 50 million outpatients treated per year.

Only a small proportion of these complaints results in a final report. Despite the increase in the number of complaints, the number of results reports issued each year has remained between 100 and 255[97]. The proportion of cases accepted for investigation reached a low ebb in 1997–98, when it represented only 4% of complaints received. This increased to 5.5% the following year. Concern was expressed by consumer groups about this small proportion[98]. The ombudsman's response was that a large number of complaints had to be referred back because they had not been pursued through the National Health Service complaints procedure. There were also a number of complaints that were outside the ombudsman's jurisdiction. If these complaints were discounted, action was taken in over 20% of investigable complaints. This figure includes cases which were not formally investigated, but where the body complained about agreed to take further internal action in response to the complaint[99].

As already indicated above, the proportion of investigable complaints accepted for investigation increased over the last two years. This significant increase resulted from the large number of complaints about clinical judgment. Because of the nature of these complaints, it is very difficult for complainants to provide prima facie evidence of maladministration or failure of service. This used to be one of the criteria adopted by the ombudsman for accepting a case for investigation. The ombudsman feels that this is too difficult a test to meet in clinical cases, and is now prepared to commence investigations where the complainant cannot provide this evidence. Many of the complaints that are investigable have already been considered by the independent review panel under the NHS complaints procedures. In these cases, the ombudsman has to decide whether an investigation would be likely to 'add value'. It is unlikely that the ombudsman would conduct an investigation where there is no evidence that the panel's investigation is unsound. To conduct an investigation in such circumstances 'would

---

[97]   The exception is 1989/90, when only 89 reports were issued.

[98]   See Health Service Ombudsman Annual Report 1998–99 (HC Paper 498 (1998–99)) p 6.

[99]   Health Service Ombudsman Annual Report 1998–99 (HC Paper 498 (1998–99)) p 6.

raise false hopes for complainants' and would be 'wasteful of public funds'[100].

Each case report contains more than one grievance. Over the last 10 years, the average number of grievances investigated each year has been 408. The average number of grievances found to be justified over this period was 260, representing an average of 64% of justified grievances[101]. The high number of justified grievances is probably partly a result of detecting the cases which are not viable, and thus not pursuing them further.

Clinical complaints now account for the largest single category of complaints, followed by complaint handling and communication. Other areas, for example, delays in appointments and removals from general practitioner lists are also areas which have been the subject of the ombudsman's investigation. There have been complaints about the deputising service operated by general practitioners, consent to treatment, confidentiality, personal records and patients' property. Some of these issues will be discussed below.

Removal from General Practitioner Lists

The extension of the ombudsman's remit to the actions of family practitioners has made it possible for complaints about the removal of patients from the lists of general practitioners to be investigated. The terms of service for National Health Service care by general practitioners, as set out by statute, allows the practitioner to request the removal of a patient from his or her list at any time. There is no requirement to give reasons to the patient or the health authority concerned. Soon after the extension of remit, the ombudsman received a number of complaints in this area. The ombudsman's view is that, notwithstanding the statute, general practitioners, as providers of public services, implicitly accept an obligation to adhere to certain standards. This means that they should try to make a success of the doctor-patient relationship, and if this is not possible, they

---

[100] Health Service Ombudsman for England Annual Report 2001–02 (HC Paper 887 (2001–02)) p 1.
[101] See Health Service Ombudsman Annual Report 2000–2001 (HC Paper 3 (2000–01)) p 27.

should explain their reasons to the patient[102]. Even though there is no formal requirement to give reasons, the ombudsman maintains that general practitioners should exercise the right to remove patients in a considered and responsible way[103].

The ombudsman accepts that there are occasions when removal from the list is an appropriate cause of action, for example, where patients are abusive or violent. Nevertheless, it is a drastic action, which can have serious consequences for the patient, and the lack of explanation only adds to the distress. The ombudsman's approach is to consider whether the actions of the practitioner were fair, reasonable, consistent with what a body of his or her peers might have done in the circumstances, and in line with the standards demanded of public servants[104]. The ombudsman feels that some general practitioners are too hasty in removing patients, and that a preferable approach would be to consult colleagues or discuss the problem with the patient. The ombudsman has also expressed concern that some practitioners are too ready to believe that a complaint is evidence that the doctor-patient relationship has broken down. This could inhibit complaints, because of the fear that the outcome would be removal from the list[105]. The ombudsman has expressed concern about the rising number of justified complaints about removals from lists. These account for the largest number of complaints about family practitioner services. In 2001–02, nine such cases were investigated, eight of which were upheld in full or in part. The ombudsman is concerned that in these cases, no warning is given to patients, and sometimes the actions of general practitioners is hasty and ill-judged[106].

---

[102] See Health Service Ombudsman Annual Report 1997–98 (HC Paper 811 (1997–98)) p 10. This view is in line with the advice to GPs from their professional bodies, where it is suggested that patients should normally be given reasons for removal from the list.

[103] Health Service Ombudsman for England Annual Report 2001–02 (HC Paper 887 (2001–02)) p 20.

[104] Health Service Ombudsman Annual Report 1998–99 (HC Paper 498 (1998–99)) p 9.

[105] Health Service Ombudsman Annual Report 1997–98 (HC Paper 811 (1997–98)) p 11.

[106] Health Service Ombudsman for England Annual Report 2001–02 (HC Paper 887 (2001–02)) pp 18–20.

Communications

The ombudsman has noted problems about poor communications, which have been a feature of complaints over the years. Failure in communication amongst staff, or between staff and patients or relatives is a recurring theme. Indeed, the select committee has seen fit to comment on this, recognising that the 'problems that arise through a breakdown in communications are manifold'[107]. Poor communications, involving a failure to listen to relatives and friends, can put patients' lives at risk. One example[108] of this is where nursing staff ignored relatives' concerns about an elderly patient, which resulted in the patient being given inappropriate treatment for his condition.

In other cases, poor communication is the cause of needless distress, where patients and relatives are not made fully aware of the seriousness of the patient's condition. One case[109] concerned the death of a baby born prematurely. The baby's mother complained that staff had not communicated with her about the seriousness of her baby's condition. The ombudsman was critical of the informal methods of passing information between clinical staff and parents. He found that there was no opportunity for the parents to discuss their questions with medical staff. The lack of communication had left the parents unprepared for the baby's sudden decline and death. In another case[110], poor communication resulted in the daughter of an elderly man agreeing to his discharge to accommodation that proved to be unsuitable.

Publicity

In common with other public sector ombudsmen, there is concern that insufficient numbers of people know of the existence of the Health Service Ombudsman. The legislation requires little in terms of publicity. The

---

[107]   Fourth Report from the Select Committee on the Parliamentary Commissioner for Administration (HC Paper 368 (1990–91)) para 28.

[108]   Case No 2343/99–00. See Health Service Ombudsman Annual Report 2000–01 (HC Paper 3 (2000–01)) p 8.

[109]   Case No E 1095/98–99. See Health Service Ombudsman Annual Report 2000–01 (HC Paper 3 (2000–01)) p 8.

[110]   Case No E 1641/99–00. See Health Service Ombudsman Annual Report 2000–01 (HC Paper 3 (2000–01)) p 8.

requirement is to send copies of final reports to the parties concerned, but these do not have to be made public. The ombudsman makes annual reports to Parliament, and there is also a power for the ombudsman to make special reports where injustice has not been, or will not be remedied, or otherwise as is thought fit. In general, the ombudsman's reports receive little media coverage. Media interest is likely to occur when there is select committee involvement, which is usual in the most serious complaints.

In addition to the annual reports, three times a year[111] the ombudsman publishes details of all the cases investigated. Some of the more significant cases appear in the form of a short report, with the remainder appearing as summaries of the matters investigated and the ombudsman's findings. There is also a companion volume published which contains the full text version of reports that are of particular interest, or complexity, or both. These published volumes of completed investigations name the health service bodies against whom complaints are made, but maintain the anonymity of complainants and individual members of staff. In the case of complaints against general practitioners, the ombudsman names the health authority in which the practice is situated, while maintaining the anonymity of the individual practitioner and practice[112].

At one time, the ombudsman's publications were circulated to health service bodies by the Department of Health. This is no longer the case, a matter about which the ombudsman has expressed some concern[113]. Without this process, there is a danger that those who could learn lessons from the reports may not have ready access to them. In order to alleviate this problem, the ombudsman has started to publish occasional newsletters in order to raise awareness. There is also co-operation between the Department of Health and the ombudsman's office, which enable chief executives and others within the health service to be alerted when the reports are published[114]. This process is aided by direct links between the health service bodies and ombudsman's websites.

[111] It used to be twice a year, the change occurring in 2000–01.
[112] The ombudsman does, however, reserve the right to name individuals and practices if the circumstances warrant it. This may occur, for example, if there are particular serious failures, or where there are repeat offenders.
[113] Health Service Ombudsman Annual Report 1999–2000 (HC Paper 542 (1999–2000) para 1.16.
[114] Health Service Ombudsman Annual Report 2000–01 (HC Paper 3 (2000–01)) p 4.

If there is concern that service deliverers may not be sufficiently well informed about the ombudsman, there is even more concern about public awareness. Successive ombudsmen have made efforts to publicise their work and make the office more approachable. In 1996 a revised information leaflet was issued. This was produced in several languages and formats to assist those with learning and visual difficulties. The leaflets are widely distributed, and a special booklet has also been sent to all family health service practitioners explaining the ombudsman's role. The ombudsman's office has an informative website[115], and the ombudsman uses various opportunities to explain the work of the office in the media, including professional journals.

The Citizen's Charter initiative provided an opportunity to publicise the work of the ombudsman. Patient's Charters, established under the original Citizen's Charter initiative, contained references to the role of the Health Service Ombudsman. However, while this initiative should have contributed to a greater awareness of the ombudsman, there was evidence that local charters did not always refer to the office[116]. Research for the Wilson Committee[117] found ignorance and confusion about procedures for complaining about the health service. Where the charter programme ought to help is in giving, both locally and nationally, clear benchmarks based on the charter standards to inform patients whether or not they have a right to complain. In addition, as the ombudsman is at the apex of the National Health Service complaints procedure, complainants ought to become aware of the ombudsman as soon as they start to use this procedure. Whether they will be able to negotiate their way through the procedure to reach the ombudsman eventually is of course another matter.

Improving Administration

As a 'special mandate' ombudsman[118], the Health Service Ombudsman occupies an important position in relation to the delivery of health services,

---

[115]   The address is www.ombudsman.org.uk.

[116]   See *Being Heard* The report of a review committee on NHS complaints procedures (The Wilson Report) (1994) Department of Health.

[117]   *Being Heard* (1994).

[118]   As indicated above, this refers to the fact that the Health Service Ombudsman deals with only one area of the administration, that is, the health service (see R Gregory and P Giddings 'The Ombudsman Institution: Growth and Development'

and to improving administrative performance. This role has been made more pertinent by the establishment of the ombudsman at the apex of the internal complaints system for the health service. This role in the complaints system affords a unique opportunity to comment on good practice, both in relation to the handling of complaints and in relation to other administrative and clinical shortcomings.

The ombudsman's annual and other reports provide numerous examples of cases where systems were deficient. As a result, improvements have been recommended and systems changed. Cases have also highlighted situations where law or practice needs to be remedied, with some success. For example, a recent complaint revealed confusion about who was responsible for responding to a complaint about deputising services. It was unclear whether responsibility lay with the commissioning doctor, the deputising doctor, or the deputising service. The ombudsman drew this to the attention of the Department of Health, and revised guidance is to be issued to general practitioners[119]. The extension of the ombudsman's remit to cover the actions of retired practitioners was a result of the ombudsman drawing attention to this loophole. The ombudsman has also published the results of investigations into complaints that have a more general application. One such report concerned issues in relation to long-term care[120], which the ombudsman published to 'illustrate the issues involved and how mistakes can be avoided'[121].

The most common remedy recommended by the Health Service Ombudsman is a review of procedures. Indeed, the particular advantage of the ombudsman is that individual cases can result in generalised benefits because of these changes in practice. To give some examples, as a result of the ombudsman's investigations procedures for prescribing have been reviewed with the aim of avoiding errors, as have arrangements for referring patients between specialties. In relation to hospital wards, there have been changes to discharge procedures, and procedures for maintaining the

---

in R Gregory and P Giddings (eds) *Righting Wrongs: The Ombudsman in Six Continents* (2000) IOS Press pp 8–9).

[119] Health Service Ombudsman Annual Report 2000–01 (HC Paper 3 (2000–01)) p 2.

[120] Fifth Report of the Health Service Commissioner (HC Paper 504 (1995–96)) (investigation of complaints into long term NHS care).

[121] P Giddings 'The Health Service Ombudsman after twenty-five years' (1999) PL 200–210, p 204.

supervision of patients during ward handover. Laundry arrangements have been reviewed to prevent the loss of personal clothing. Other improvements in practice have been recommended to promote better communications with patients, relatives and carers. Protocols have been introduced in one hospital trust for managing the care of patients coming into accident and emergency departments with severe abdominal pain. This resulted from a complaint after a person died six days after been discharged from an accident and emergency department. The ombudsman was critical of several aspects of the patient's care, in which the hospital failed to diagnose peritonitis as a result of a perforated duodenal ulcer[122].

The ombudsman has also been able to comment on and suggest improvements to the complaints procedure. The procedure is governed by statutory directions and detailed guidance, to which the ombudsman can refer when dealing with complaints about its operation. Investigations into the operation of the procedure is not concerned simply with compliance with the guidance, but also whether it has been fair, and not caused injustice or hardship to citizens. The ombudsman has reminded review panels of the procedures they must follow when investigating complaints. The ombudsman has made a formal response to the Department of Health's review of the complaints procedure, raising issues about access and redress[123]. The Health Service Ombudsman's work is important for the part it can play in relation to improving standards[124]. However, as has been noted, it is very difficult to judge the impact of the ombudsman on the health service's administrative performance. There have been so many changes, reorganisations and reforms to the health services, that 'it is not possible to isolate the effect of just one process'[125]. The ombudsman is, however, very much part of the network to improve standards of practice in the health service.

---

[122]   Health Service Ombudsman for England Annual Report 2001–02 (HC Paper 887 (2001–02)) p 7.
[123]   See Health Service Ombudsman for England Annual Report 2001–02 (HC Paper 887 (2001–02)) p 3.
[124]   There are a number of bodies concerned with regulating, monitoring and improving the National Health Service, including the National Institute for Clinical Excellence and the Commission for Health Improvement.
[125]   P Giddings 'The Health Service Ombudsman after twenty-five years' (1999) PL 200–210, p 204.

Conclusion

The Health Service Ombudsman scheme was established to rectify the omission of the health service from the Parliamentary Ombudsman's scheme. Although modelled on the Parliamentary Ombudsman, it always had important differences. It was established to investigate one particular service sector, and its remit extended beyond maladministration and injustice. Since the mid-1990s, changes in remit have caused the two schemes to diverge more fundamentally. Unlike the other public sector ombudsmen, the Health Service Ombudsman can investigate decisions in relation to clinical judgment. The remit also extends to individual contractors in the health service, and the function of the ombudsman in relation to the internal health service complaints procedures has no direct parallel with the other public sector ombudsmen schemes.

Assessments of the effectiveness of the office are generally favourable. There is no doubt about its independence and impartiality. Its accountability mechanisms, by means of reports and the select committee, are unquestioned. It offers a free service to complainants, and has adequate powers to perform its investigative function. It is directly accessible, although lack of awareness and the requirement to use internal procedures do present hurdles to its availability. The restricted jurisdiction, which in the past attracted criticism, has now been rectified. The remedies recommended are almost invariably followed, and the scheme has brought about improvements in administrative practice within the health service. The fact that the Wilson Committee[126] gave the scheme strong endorsement 'can be considered a substantial vote of confidence' in its effectiveness[127].

Problems with the scheme include accessibility. There is a lack of awareness about the office and its function[128]. In addition, the internal procedures may be so time-consuming and confusing that complainants are exhausted by the process, before they exhaust it. There is also the problem of delay in the ombudsman's office, a problem that may be exacerbated by the

---

[126] *Being Heard* (1994) Department of Health.

[127] P Giddings 'The United Kingdom Health Service Commissioner Schemes' in R Gregory and P Giddings (eds) *Righting Wrongs: The Ombudsman in Six Continents* (2000) IOS Press p 353.

[128] This problem is not confined to the Health Service Ombudsman; other public sector ombudsman schemes exhibit the same difficulties.

increasing number of complaints about clinical matters, which are invariably complex, and thus resource intensive. There may also be issues about compliance in relation to practitioners, over whom the ombudsman has little influence.

The extended remit, although rectifying earlier criticisms of the office, does create another set of problems. The work of the Health Services Ombudsman's office is now mainly concerned with complaints about clinical care and treatment, rather than administrative matters. Ombudsmen have traditionally provided a mechanism for holding the administration to account, by providing remedies for administrative failures. This aspect of the Health Service Ombudsman's role is becoming increasingly sidelined, as the number of investigations into administrative actions is reduced. This change of role is further emphasised by the ombudsman's ability to investigate the actions of family practitioners, who are self-regulated professionals not administrators. It has been suggested that the effect of the changes may be to change the ombudsman into a conciliation service that is 'mainly concerned with mediating between NHS practitioners and their patients'[129].

The changes to the role and function of the Health Service Ombudsman over the years is testament to the adaptability of the ombudsman concept. There is no doubt that the Health Service Ombudsman is fulfilling a need, by providing remedies for shortcomings in the health service. The ombudsman is also helping to raise standards of practice and procedure. The extended remit into clinical matters provides redress in cases where there is no question of negligence or where negligence would be difficult to prove. The advantage of the ombudsman remedy in these cases is that it provides answers and explanations for complainants. In many cases that is all they require. Whether this takes the ombudsman into areas which are not appropriate is a question for debate. Perhaps at this stage the last word should be left to the ombudsman. Noting that the office now deals predominantly with complaints about clinical care and treatment, the ombudsman has commented: 'That is, after all, what is of most concern to those who use the NHS'[130].

---

[129]   S Kerrison and A Pollack 'Complaints as Accountability? The Case of Health Care UK' (2001) *Public Law* 115–133, p 127.

[130]   Health Service Ombudsman for England Annual Report 2001–02 (HC Paper 887 (2001–02)) p 1.

Chapter 6

The Local Government Ombudsman

There are a total of six Local Government Ombudsmen in the UK: three for England, and one each for Wales, Scotland[1] and Northern Ireland. The Local Government Act 1974 provided for the establishment of a body of ombudsmen known as the Commission for Local Administration in England, and a body of two or more ombudsmen known as the Commission for Local Administration in Wales. Arrangements for Scotland and Northern Ireland were provided for by the Local Government (Scotland) Act 1975 and the Commissioner for Complaints (Northern Ireland) Act 1969, respectively. This chapter will focus on the position in England. Chapter 7 will discuss the particular features of the other three systems.

Background

The exclusion of local authorities from the Parliamentary Ombudsman's jurisdiction was widely criticised at the time that office was established. It was not long however before Justice, which had played a major part in preparing the ground for the Parliamentary Ombudsman, considered whether the concept should be extended to local government. In a report published in 1969, Justice concluded that an 'Ombudsman-like institution' was needed to carry out for local government similar functions to those carried out in relation to central government by the Parliamentary Ombudsman[2], that is, to investigate complaints of maladministration by

---

[1]   As we shall see in ch 7, there is now an integrated ombudsman scheme for Scotland.
[2]   *The Citizen and his Council: Ombudsmen for Local Government?* (1969) Stevens para 18.

local authorities. The report recommended the appointment of one chief commissioner and five or six commissioners for local administration. The suggestion was that they would work from a central office, rather than being regionally based, in order to facilitate liaison between them and the Parliamentary Ombudsman.

The government of the day accepted the idea in principle[3] and the White Paper on reform of local government, published in 1970[4], contained proposals for the establishment of a system of local ombudsmen. The proposal was that 10 or more local ombudsmen be set up, based in different parts of the country, who would examine complaints of maladministration by local authorities. By analogy with the Parliamentary Ombudsman, and contrary to the recommendations of Justice, complaints would have to be channelled through local councillors, rather than be received directly from members of the public. These proposals fell with the Labour government, but the Conservative government took up the plan for a system of local ombudsmen. Their proposals included up to nine local ombudsmen for England, and one for Wales. The ombudsmen were to report to representative bodies of local authorities and water authorities, and they would be financed by local authorities. The Bill incorporating these provisions received the Royal Assent in February 1974, just before a general election.

The Scheme

The official title for the Local Government Ombudsmen in England is the Commission for Local Administration. It was established by the Local Government Act 1974, Pt III, which provided for a body of ombudsmen known as the Commission for Local Administration in England. The English Local Government Ombudsmen are appointed by the Queen on the recommendation of the Secretary of State[5]. The Act did not specify the number of ombudsmen to be appointed, but it did say that they should divide England into areas, and that one or more ombudsmen should be responsible for each area. The Commission deals with organisation, finance and accommodation, and one of the ombudsmen acts as chair. Each Local

---

3   787 HC Official Report cols 1501–1507 (1968–69).
4   Reform of Local Government in England (Cmnd 4276, 1970).
5   The Local Government Association is consulted before appointments are made.

Government Ombudsman has identical powers and each operates independently over their particular geographical area.

Although there had been talk of nine local ombudsmen, England was in fact divided into three areas, on a population basis, with one local ombudsman[6] for each area. The three ombudsmen are based in London, York and Coventry, and the boundaries of the three areas are changed periodically, in order to secure an equal spread of the workload[7]. The Parliamentary Ombudsman is an ex-officio member of the Commission, but takes no part in the investigations carried out by the Local Government Ombudsmen. This ex-officio membership enables the two offices to share experiences, to compare notes on how problems are tackled and to consider matters of mutual interest. The other three Local Government Ombudsmen from Wales, Scotland and Northern Ireland also attend meetings by invitation, thus ensuring that all seven of the statutory public sector ombudsmen meet together on a regular basis. The ombudsmen began to receive complaints on 1 April 1974.

Jurisdiction

In common with the other statutory ombudsmen, the Local Government Ombudsmen are empowered to investigate complaints of injustice arising out of maladministration. The bodies whose administrative actions are subject to investigation by the Local Government Ombudsmen are mainly local authorities, but jurisdiction also extends to other locally organised services, for example police authorities and fire authorities. The original

[6]   Unlike the Parliamentary Ombudsmen, who have been either civil servants or lawyers, the Local Government Ombudsmen have a variety of backgrounds. These include personnel management, the diplomatic service, academic lawyer, councillor, town clerk. They are not all from local government and some have been legally qualified.

[7]   Mr Tony Redmund deals with London boroughs north of the River Thames (including Richmond but excluding Harrow), and authorities in Essex, Kent, Suffolk, Surrey and East and West Suffolk. He is the Chair of the Commission. He replaced Sir Edward Osmotherly, who retired in 2001. Mrs Pat Thomas, based in York, deals with the West Midlands (except Coventry City), Cheshire, Derbyshire, Lincolnshire, Nottinghamshire, Shropshire, Staffordshire and the north of England, except the cities of York and Lancaster. Mr Jerry White, based in Coventry, deals with London boroughs south of the River Thames (except Richmond, but including Harrow), the cities of York, Lancaster and Coventry; the west, south west and most of central and eastern England.

list of bodies within jurisdiction[8] included water authorities, but this ceased when that service was privatised. Other bodies have been brought within jurisdiction as a result of legislative enactment[9]. This includes for example, school admission appeals panels in local authority or voluntary schools[10]. The Local Government Ombudsmen are therefore able to consider complaints about all types of local authority services, dealing with significant areas of local administration. In practice, the vast majority of investigations involve local councils. This factor resulted in the ombudsmen adopting the informal title of Local Government Ombudsmen in the early 1990s, as it would make explicit that their responsibilities were confined almost entirely to local government[11]. There is no power for ombudsmen to investigate the actions of parish and town councils[12].

The Local Government Ombudsman system was set up primarily as a method of handling individual grievances involving the provision of local services. The purpose of the office however, as set out in its annual reports[13], is twofold. Not only is it to provide investigation and resolution of grievances, but it also provides guidance intended to promote fair and

---

[8]   See Local Government Act 1974, s 25.

[9]   The Local Government Act 1974, s 25(2) provides for bodies established by Act of Parliament with power to levy rates or issues precepts to be brought within jurisdiction by Order in Council.

[10]   The relevant authorities now subject to the Local Government Ombudsman's jurisdiction are: district, borough, city or county councils (not town or parish councils); education appeal panels; school governing bodies in relation to admission matters only; school organisation committees; the Commission for New Towns (housing matters only); housing action trusts (but not housing associations); police authorities, including the National Intelligence Service and the National Crime Squad (but not individual police officers); fire authorities; joint boards of local authorities; national park authorities; the Greater London Authority; the London Transport User's Committee; the London Development Agency; English Partnerships (planning matters only); the Environment Agency (flood defence and land drainage matters only); the Norfolk and Suffolk Broads Authority.

[11]   Local Government Ombudsman Annual Report 1990–91 p 4.

[12]   Where parish councils carry out a function on behalf of a local authority, complaints can be investigated by the Local Government Ombudsmen. There is an arbitration service to deal with disputes within a parish council or between an individual organisation and the parish council. The Local Government Ombudsmen do not consider extension of jurisdiction in this area a high priority (see Report of the Financial Management and Policy Review of the Commission for Local Administration in England Stage II (1996) p 33).

[13]   See, for example, Local Government Ombudsman Annual Report 2000–01 p 1.

effective administration in local government. The great bulk of the work, however, centres around individual grievance handling, a primary concern being to secure the resolution of individual complaints.

Exclusions from Jurisdiction

In common with the Parliamentary Ombudsman, the Local Government Ombudsmen are not allowed to question the merits of decisions taken without maladministration by authorities in the exercise of their discretion[14]. In addition to this limitation, there are also some administrative actions which are outside the jurisdictional limits of the Local Government Ombudsmen. Thus, they are prevented from investigating 'general matters', that is, complaints about the action of an authority which affects 'all or most of the inhabitants of the area of the authority concerned'[15]. This prevents, for example, an investigation of a complaint concerning improper expenditure or other wrongful action on financial matters. It is for the Local Government Ombudsmen to decide whether a complaint comes within this exclusion[16].

The Local Government Ombudsmen, like other public sector ombudsmen, are prevented from investigating an administrative action where the person aggrieved has a right to take the matter to a tribunal or minister, or where there is a remedy in a court of law[17]. This prohibition is subject to the proviso that in these cases there is a discretionary power to investigate reviewable or appealable decisions if it is not considered reasonable for the complainant to resort to these remedies. If there is a specific statutory right to appeal, the ombudsmen are unlikely to accept the complaint. Even in these situations, they may consider complaints where complainants are unaware of their rights of review or appeal, and the authority has failed to advise them of it. Equally, where complainants are prevented by absence, illness or some other incapacity from resorting to appeal, and where there is no possibility of bringing an out-of-time appeal, the ombudsman are likely

---

[14] Local Government Act 1974, s 34(3).
[15] Local Government Act 1974, s 26(7).
[16] Occasionally, the ombudsmen receive complaints alleging that councils are wasting money, or setting too high a rate for council tax. These are rejected, by virtue of s 26(7), and these rejections have not been challenged.
[17] Local Government Act 1974, s 26(6).

to accept the complaint. However, where a right of appeal has been used, the ombudsmen have no jurisdiction to deal with a complaint[18].

Where the only remedy is in court, the Local Government Ombudsmen are much more prepared to exercise their discretion generously in favour of the complainant. Many of the matters which are a source of grievance for complainants may be pursued in the courts through judicial review proceedings. This possibility is not usually a bar to investigation by the ombudsmen. The Local Government Ombudsmen do not normally expect complainants to resort to this remedy, which may be costly, and for which there may be an uncertain outcome. The possibility of the remedy of judicial review will not therefore be a bar to the ombudsmen's acceptance of a complaint. A recent case illustrates this approach. The case[19] concerned a complaint about the council's handling of an application by a charity for a street collection permit. The application was refused. The licensing committee which dealt with the application was a quasi-judicial body, and it would have been possible to make an application for judicial review to have the decision quashed on the grounds that it was procedurally flawed. The ombudsman was clear that this was an appropriate case for investigation, as it was not considered reasonable to expect a charity to spend money donated for charitable purposes on court action. In addition, the cost of the action would not be proportionate to the amount of money likely to be raised through the street collection.

The ombudsman will also investigate complaints about housing repairs, for example, even though these matters concern failures to comply with contractual obligations. As such, they can be dealt with in the civil courts, but the ombudsmen do not normally consider it reasonable for complainants to risk incurring high costs to pursue civil actions[20]. On the other hand,

---

18   In *R v Comr for Local Administration, ex p Field* [1999] EWHC Admin 754, the applicant sought judicial review of the ombudsman's decision to refuse to investigate an allegation of maladministration in connection with the refusal of planning permission by a planning authority. The ombudsman claimed to have no discretion to investigate, as the applicant had already used the right to appeal to the minister, a decision that was endorsed by the court.

19   Report on an Investigation into Complaint No 99/B/04467 against Portsmouth City Council.

20   The approach of the ombudsmen in housing repair cases depends to a large extent on whether the repairs have actually been done. If they have not, the ombudsmen will usually conduct an investigation, with a view to ensuring that the repairs are carried out. If they have been done, and the complainant is seeking compensation, the ombudsmen will not normally investigate.

where complainants are clearly seeking compensation for negligence or other contractual matters, complaints will not normally be accepted. If the complaint is about the way the claim was handled, or there are high costs compared to the benefits to be gained, the ombudsmen may investigate.

In addition to the exclusions discussed above, there are a number of matters, listed in Sch 5 of the 1974 Act, that may not be investigated even though they are concerned with administrative action taken by the authorities within jurisdiction. For example, matters concerned with the internal affairs of schools, personnel matters, action taken in connection with the commencement and investigation of legal proceedings and commercial and contractual matters are expressly excluded. Each of these exclusions has been criticised, and there appears to be little justification for many of them. Despite the fact that there have been recommendations for the removal of some of them[21], and that the ombudsmen themselves believe that their role is sometimes unnecessarily and illogically restricted because of them, there are no plans to extend jurisdiction to these areas. It could be argued that the Local Government Ombudsmen should be able to investigate all local authority matters, except where there are positive justifications for not doing so. The Local Government Ombudsmen have consistently noted the need to remove many of the exclusions, with only limited success. There seems to be no justification for denying a remedy where injustice has arisen from maladministration relating to the administrative action of a local authority. All administrative actions should be within jurisdiction and open to investigation, unless an alternative remedy is available[22]. The exclusions can be a source of dissatisfaction and confusion for complainants and they may undermine confidence in the ombudsman system itself. They will be considered in turn.

Commercial and Contractual Matters

This exclusion[23] prevents the Local Government Ombudsmen from investigating actions taken by a local authority in connection with contractual matters or commercial transactions. Its inclusion in Sch 5

---

21 See Report of the Committee of Inquiry on the Conduct of Local Authority Business (Cm 9797, 1986) (The Widdicombe Report).

22 See, for example, Local Government Ombudsman Annual Report 1991–92 p 58.

23 Local Government Act 1974, Sch 5, para 3.

appears to be because there is a similar exclusion in the 1967 Act for the Parliamentary Ombudsman. The Schedule specifically excludes from jurisdiction transactions relating to the operation of harbour undertakings, the provision of entertainment, the provision and operation of industrial establishments, and the provision and operation of markets. However the exclusion does not cover transactions relating to the acquisition or disposal of land. This means that matters concerning tenancies, leaseholds and mortgages are within jurisdiction. For example, a complaint about the way a council decided to give or withhold a licence to assign a shop lease is within jurisdiction. The original legislation has been amended to allow transactions relating to the grant, renewal or revocation of licences for market stalls to be within jurisdiction[24]. This amendment was in response to concerns about unfairness in the allocation process[25].

This exclusion has been criticised. Soon after the establishment of the scheme, Justice argued that commercial and contractual matters should be within jurisdiction[26]. A major review of local government in the 1980s concluded that commercial and contractual matters with members of the public were not 'different in kind from cases involving other local authority dealings with the public'. It called for a review of the exclusion[27]. The government at the time was not convinced, arguing that ombudsmen are concerned with the 'interaction between the executive arm of Government and the general public'. Actions taken by public bodies in buying and selling services were 'fundamentally different', and there was therefore no case for providing protection through the Local Government Ombudsman, as there were other legal safeguards and remedies[28].

---

[24]   See the Local Government Administration (Matters Subject to Investigation) Order 1993, SI 1993/940, art 2. The amendment also allows the ombudsmen to investigate complaints about the provision of moorings, where these are not provided in connection with dock or harbour undertakings.

[25]   The Local Government Ombudsmen had at various times urged the government to include within jurisdiction the administration of market operations and the provision of moorings (see, for example, Local Government Ombudsman Annual Report 1991–92 p 58). The amendment is a recognition that market stall allocation is principally an administrative function, rather than a commercial transaction.

[26]   *The Local Ombudsman: a Review of the First Five Years* (1980) JUSTICE p 13.

[27]   The Widdicombe Report (Cm 9797, 1986) p 22.

[28]   The Conduct of Local Authority Business. The Government Response to the Report of the Widdicombe Committee (Cm 433, 1988) p 29.

Tendering matters are seen as contractual, and therefore outside jurisdiction. There is however a duty on public authorities to exclude from contracts any consideration of matters which are non-commercial[29]. Local authorities are thus prevented by law from discriminating against contractors on the basis of political or irrelevant considerations. Authorities must also give written reasons for decisions to exclude a contractor from an approved list, not to invite or accept tenders, or to terminate a contract[30].

Despite the exclusion, the Local Government Ombudsmen have investigated cases involving the use of unreasonable and misleading methods to select firms whose services a local council was to promote[31]. There have also been investigations into complaints about unreasonable delay in determining applications for hackney carriage licences[32] and public entertainment licences[33] resulting in loss of earnings. The exclusion has not prevented investigations about complaints concerning delays in registering private residential homes for the elderly, even though these homes are commercial enterprises[34]. The Local Government Ombudsmen

---

[29] Local Government Act 1988, s 17.

[30] Local Government Act 1988, s 20. Soon after the Act, its provisions were tested in the case of *R v London Borough of Enfield, ex p T F Unwin (Roydon) Ltd* (1989) 46 BLR 1. The case concerned a contractor who was suspended from Enfield's list of approved contractors, the only reasons being that there were 'inquiries into the conduct' of the borough's staff. The contractor started proceedings for judicial review seeking orders of: mandamus requiring reasons for the decision to suspend it from the lists of contractors; and certiorari to quash the decision. Enfield did not deny that it had failed to comply with the duty to give reasons, imposed by the statute. There were however 'substantial and serious allegations of offences or irregularities in the relationship' between it and the contractor, and while these allegations were being investigated by the police, the council said it was not possible to provide further details. The court accepted the dilemma of local authorities in cases such as these, and decided that the standard of fairness which a contractor was entitled to expect depended on all the circumstances. In this case, the fact that an investigation was underway did not deprive the contractor of the right to be told of the accusations and to be given a chance to answer before a decision was made. In the circumstances, it was held that Enfield was not justified in failing to give reasons for its decisions. Because of the prior relationship with the council, the contractor was entitled to a legitimate expectation of fair treatment.

[31] Reports No 87/C/205 and 87/C/706.

[32] Report No 86/C/0647/1100/1101.

[33] Report No 99/C/493.

[34] Reports No 88/C/1377 and 88/C/0776.

thus appear to take a more robust line in pursuing commercial matters than the Parliamentary Ombudsman[35].

Given that the ombudsmen do not investigate where there is a remedy in the courts, there seems to be little justification for the continuation of this exclusion. Matters for which there was a civil remedy in contract would be likely to be rejected by the ombudsmen on that ground. The ombudsmen have at various times called for this exclusion to be repealed. They are concerned that there are issues that fall within the statutory definition of commercial and contractual matters that are not capable of litigation because no contract exists[36]. The involvement of the ombudsmen would be confined to administrative aspects of commercial and contractual matters, which is entirely appropriate.

Personnel Matters

Like the Parliamentary Ombudsman, the Local Government Ombudsmen are prevented from investigating complaints about action taken in respect of appointments, removals, pay, discipline, superannuation and other personnel matters[37]. This exclusion does produce anomalies. For example, a delay in paying housing benefit can be investigated, but a delay in paying a local authority pension to an ex-employee or his or her family cannot[38]. Also, maladministration could be found if an application for council property was lost, but not if it were an application for a job with a local authority which was lost.

The reasoning behind the exclusion is that employment law should be uniform in the public and private sectors, and that personnel matters are really the concern of collective bargaining and industrial relations. The primary function of the Local Government Ombudsman is to provide support for the consumers of local government services rather than for those who are employed to provide them. However, the exclusion also

---

[35]   See P Birkinshaw *Grievances, Remedies and the State* (2nd edn, 1994) Sweet and Maxwell p 222.

[36]   See for example Report of the Financial Management and Policy Review of the Commission for Local Administration in England Stage II (1996) p 48.

[37]   Local Government Act 1974, Sch 5, para 4.

[38]   A complaint in relation to pensions could be dealt with by the Pensions Ombudsman.

relates to potential and ex-employees, who are not protected by collective bargaining procedures. In connection with potential staff and appointments procedures, there was some concern in the 1980s about 'political appointees'. There was a recommendation that a code of practice be drawn up to govern officer appointment procedures, breach of which would constitute prima facie maladministration, which would allow an applicant to complain to the Local Government Ombudsman[39]. The government was unwilling to extend jurisdiction into this area, but devised other methods to prevent 'politically biased or prejudiced' selection and appointment procedures[40].

In general, however, central government has always considered that personnel matters are essentially concerned with relations between employer and employee, and not with the relations between a public authority and the public. It has always resisted attempts to bring such matters within the remit of the Local Government Ombudsmen. The ombudsmen themselves have on occasions expressed the belief that personnel complaints from those not currently employed by the authority against which they wish to complain should be within jurisdiction[41]. They have not however pursued the matter and do not attach high priority to bringing personnel matters within jurisdiction[42].

Internal School and College Matters

The Local Government Ombudsmen are prevented from investigating actions by local authorities in the exercise of functions in relation to instruction within schools[43]. This is an extremely wide exclusion, which prevents investigation of most of the matters relating to the internal affairs of any school or other educational establishment run by a local authority. It excludes matters to do with conduct, curriculum, discipline, internal organisation and management. Education departments themselves do come within the Local Government Ombudsman's jurisdiction, as do school

---

[39]   The Conduct of Local Authority Business. The Government Response to the Report of the Widdicombe Committee (Cm 433, 1988) p 221.
[40]   Cm 433, 1988 p 30.
[41]   See Local Government Ombudsman Annual Report 1988–89 p 54.
[42]   Report of the Financial Management and Policy Review of the Commission for Local Administration in England Stage II (1996) p 49.
[43]   Local Government Act 1974, Sch 5, para 5.

organisation committees[44]. This means that matters concerning, for example, allocations, catchment areas, grants, and school buses are within jurisdiction. Once again, the exclusion produces anomalies. For example, there can be an investigation into the treatment of a child in a local authority home, but not in a local authority school. The Local Government Ombudsmen have expressed concern about this anomalous situation, particularly where child protection issues are concerned[45].

This exclusion has been the subject of some debate, and as long ago as 1980, Justice was critical and recommended that internal school matters should be brought within jurisdiction[46]. The Local Government Ombudsmen endorsed this view, claiming that internal school matters should be within their jurisdiction in the same way that complaints about matters internal to any other local authority establishment are within jurisdiction[47]. There appears to be no logical reason why any action of a local authority in the exercise of its administrative functions should be outside the Local Government Ombudsman's jurisdiction[48].

The government has steadfastly refused to extend jurisdiction to this area, on the grounds that the 'control and instruction of children within school' is a 'professional rather than an administrative function'[49]. There is also a view that internal school matters are more properly dealt with by head teachers with the support of school governors. In addition, the removal of the exclusion could add significantly to the ombudsmen's workload[50]. On the other hand, any extension of jurisdiction in this area would not involve the ombudsmen investigating professional judgments. Their remit would be confined to 'administrative' actions as in other local authority areas. It is worth noting that in Scotland, under its new ombudsman system[51],

---

44   See School Standards and Framework Act 1998.
45   See Local Government Ombudsman Annual Report 1999–2000 p 46.
46   Justice did recognise that implementation of this might not be feasible in the immediate future for reasons of cost and limited resources (*The Local Ombudsman: a Review of the First Five Years* (1980) JUSTICE para 43).
47   See Local Government Ombudsman Annual Report 1980–81 p 43.
48   See Local Government Ombudsman Annual Report 1988–89 p 54.
49   Cm 433, 1988 p 29.
50   Report of the Financial Management and Policy Review of the Commission for Local Administration in England Stage II (1996) pp 49–50.
51   This is discussed in Chapter 7.

internal organisation and management of schools will be within jurisdiction.[52]

The Local Government Ombudsmen have given as wide an interpretation as possible to this exclusion, and have investigated matters other than those which directly concern conduct, curriculum, internal organisation, management or discipline. For example, in one case, a child was suspended from school in circumstances where the Local Government Ombudsman said that he felt the child should have received help from an educational psychologist. The ombudsman criticised both the local authority and the school, notwithstanding the lack of jurisdiction to examine the conduct of the school[53]. In another case[54], there was a finding of maladministration because of the poor treatment of a pupil after an incident at a school. There has also been an investigation of a complaint about the council's delay in informing the parents of a child, who had had an accident in the school playground, of the results of the council's investigation into the matter[55].

Nevertheless, the ombudsmen are concerned that some of their investigations may be subject to challenge. The legislation refers to 'any action concerning' these excluded areas. If the ombudsmen investigate a complaint about the provision of special educational needs, for example, they may need to consider whether the provision in the school complies with the child's statement of special educational needs. The investigation may be challenged because it is 'action concerning' the giving of instruction. The ombudsmen have proposed that the words 'any action concerning' should be deleted from the legislation, in order to remove the possibility of challenge in these cases[56].

The Local Government Ombudsmen can investigate the actions of appeal committees established to hear appeals about admissions into schools[57],

---

52   Scottish Public Services Ombudsman Act 2002, Sch 4, para 9. The Scottish Public Services Ombudsman will not be able to investigate complaints about the giving of instruction, conduct, curriculum and discipline.

53   Case report 82/J/5509.

54   Case report 87/A/961.

55   Case report 90/B/306.

56   Local Government Ombudsman Annual Report 1999–2000 pp 45–46.

57   See Education Act 1980, s 7(7). For a description of the operation of these appeals, see M Seneviratne 'Ombudsman's Decisions' (1997) 19(3) JSWFL 329–337, pp 334–335.

including voluntary and foundation schools[58]. Indeed, many of the complaints to the Local Government Ombudsmen about education matters are concerned with the operation of such appeals. Although there have been a number of complaints against local education authorities in relation to these panels, the appeal panels of foundation schools now generate most of the complaints. These complaints reveal procedural flaws, lack of proper reasons for decisions, and questions about the independence of the clerks to the panels[59].

Court Proceedings

The Local Government Ombudsmen are prevented from investigating complaints about the commencement or conduct of civil or criminal proceedings before any court of law[60]. Local authorities have many powers where there is a criminal sanction attached, and thus a decision on whether to commence proceedings in such cases, or a failure to do so, could be construed as coming within this exclusion. For example, it could be argued that a complaint about the failure of a council to take action following an unauthorised cutting of trees is covered by this exclusion, as it is a criminal offence to lop trees in a conservation area unless the local authority is notified of the intention to do so.

Such an interpretation would lead to the exclusion of many, if not most, enforcement complaints. Indeed, there would be many matters excluded from jurisdiction because criminal proceedings are often possible, even if remotely. The Local Government Ombudsmen have not adopted such a rigid interpretation. They have taken the view that administrative actions taken before court proceedings are within jurisdiction, a view confirmed by the government[61]. Indeed, the Local Government Ombudsmen frequently investigate such matters. For example, a complaint that a local authority had failed to exercise its powers to deal with the unlawful eviction and harassment of a tenant in privately rented accommodation has been

---

[58]   See School Standards and Framework Act 1998. The Local Government Ombudsmen can also investigate the actions of exclusion appeals panels, but only for those schools within the jurisdiction of the local education authority.

[59]   See Local Government Ombudsman Annual Report 2000–01 p 17.

[60]   Local Government Act 1974, Sch 5, para 1.

[61]   Cm 433, 1988 p 29.

investigated[62]. Similarly, the ombudsmen will investigate the local authority's actions when they are deciding whether to serve an enforcement notice.

However, once proceedings have commenced, the ombudsmen are unable to investigate. This can cause difficulties, as illustrated by a case involving a nuisance neighbour. The complainant had complained for over 10 years about nuisance caused by her neighbour. The ombudsman found maladministration in the way the council had dealt with the problem over a three-year period. However, the ombudsman was prevented from examining the events after this period, because the council had commenced court proceedings against the neighbour. There was delay in bringing the case to trial, and the allegations were that this was due to faults by the council. During this time, the complainant had suffered many more incidents of nuisance from the neighbour, but the ombudsman had been unable to examine any additional injustice caused to the complainant[63]. It has been recommended that that the ombudsmen ought to be allowed to investigate complaints about the commencement of legal proceedings, while leaving the conduct of such proceedings outside jurisdiction[64].

The Local Government Ombudsmen are also prevented from investigating action taken by police authorities in connection with the investigation or prevention of crime[65].

Discretionary Powers

Even where complaints refer to matters which are within jurisdiction, and are against the bodies specified to be within remit, the Local Government Ombudsmen are not bound to accept cases for investigation. The ombudsmen have discretion whether or not to investigate, the legislation providing that they 'may' do so[66]. Moreover, it is for the ombudsmen to determine, at their discretion, whether to initiate, continue or discontinue

---

[62]   Report No 89/A/1581.

[63]   See Local Government Ombudsman Annual Report 1999–2000 p 46.

[64]   See Local Government Ombudsman Annual Report 1999–2000 p 46; Report of the Financial Management and Policy Review of the Commission for Local Administration in England Stage II (1996) p 47.

[65]   Local Government Act 1974, Sch 5, para 2.

[66]   Local Government Act 1974, s 26.

an investigation, and it is for them to decide whether complaints are duly made[67]. The courts are reluctant to interfere with a decision by the Local Government Ombudsman in the exercise of this discretion[68].

Complaints must be made in writing, and can be made directly to the ombudsman or to a local councillor. They must be made within 12 months of the complainant first having notice of the matters alleged in the complaint. Where the complaint is received after this time, the ombudsman has discretion to accept it, where it is considered 'reasonable' to do so[69].

The Local Government Ombudsmen have no discretion to undertake an investigation without a complaint. This is in line with the other public sector ombudsmen in the UK. Even if the local authority consents to an investigation, or requests one, the ombudsmen have no discretion to investigate without an aggrieved member of the public referring the matter. This prevents the ombudsmen investigating where, for example, they see a report in the media of child cruelty or abuse of the elderly where there is local authority involvement.

There have been recommendations that the ombudsmen be allowed to conduct investigations on their own initiative in certain circumstances. The suggestion is that this should occur where there was 'reason to suppose that injustice has occurred', provided that there was 'good ground for concern', and that the investigation was not used to conduct an inquiry into the general procedures of an authority rather than an individual case[70]. Justice has recommended that the Local Government Ombudsmen should have the power to make investigations without a complaint, provided that the local authority consents or the Secretary of State gives approval[71]. The Local Government Ombudsmen have suggested that their powers be extended to give them discretion to investigate without a complaint at the request of a local authority. In addition, they have recommended that they

67   Local Government Act 1974, s 26(10).
68   For example, in one case (*R v Comr for Local Administration in England, ex p Newman* (1987) unreported, CA), the court refused to interfere with a decision by the ombudsman not to investigate a complaint. The court did however note that this did not preclude the possibility of judicial review in extreme cases. As discussed in Chapter 2, the courts are now becoming more active in reviewing the ombudsmen.
69   Local Government Act 1974, s 26(4).
70   Cm 433, 1988 p 222.
71   *Administrative Justice: Some Necessary Reforms* (1988) Clarendon Press p 135.

be given the power to investigate where there is a suspicion that there may be maladministration and injustice, and where an impartial investigation would be in the public interest[72].

However, the ombudsmen are now of the view that such a wide discretion is undesirable, although they do see some merit in investigating at the request of a local authority[73]. There are no plans to make the necessary amendment to allow such investigations and, indeed, the Cabinet Office review was clear that such an extension was both unnecessary and undesirable[74].

Maladministration and Injustice

The Local Government Ombudsmen investigate complaints from members of the public who have 'sustained injustice in consequence of maladministration' in connection with action taken by a relevant authority[75]. As noted previously, maladministration is not defined by statute, but the Local Government Ombudsmen have given the concept a flexible and wide-ranging interpretation. The ombudsmen will find maladministration where there have been failures to follow procedures, failure to fulfil statutory duties, failure to keep proper records, and unreasonable delay. The Local Government Ombudsmen have issued a *Guide to Good Administrative Practice*[76], and they do expect local authorities to adhere to certain minimum standards. For example, poor record-keeping has been criticised, as has poor liaison between departments. The ombudsmen also regard the giving of reasons as a basic requirement in administration, failure of which will amount to maladministration.

There is also an expectation that all local authorities have internal complaints procedures. A failure to have one, or to rely on one which is incomplete or inadequate may lead to a finding of maladministration. There

---

[72]   See Report of the Financial Management and Policy Review of the Commission for Local Administration in England Stage II (1996) p 54.
[73]   Local Government Ombudsman Annual Report 1999–2000 p 48.
[74]   *Review of the Public Sector Ombudsmen in England* (2000) Cabinet Office p 48.
[75]   Local Government Act 1974, s 26.
[76]   This was issued in 1993. In 1992, the ombudsmen began to publish a series of guidance notes, setting out advice on good administrative practice in particular areas of activity.

have been criticisms of a council's failures to have a proper complaints procedure to deal with complaints made about the handling of an incident at a child's school. Councils are also expected to use the complaints procedures they have, and will be criticised where there has been no adherence to the procedure, or where complaints have not been properly investigated. Difficult issues arise where problems are caused by staffing and resource constraints. While sympathetic to the difficulties that councils have to face when their scarce resources are inadequate, they will not be allowed to excuse maladministration on these grounds. Indeed, it is difficult for the ombudsmen to find otherwise when there is a clear statutory duty and statutory timescale against which the actions of the council can be judged.

The maladministration must be found to cause injustice before any action is required from the council. This requirement emphasises the Local Government Ombudsman's primary role as being concerned with the individual complaint. There may be poor procedures and maladministration revealed during the course of the investigation, but without injustice, there is no requirement for the authority to do anything. However, if poor practices are unearthed in the investigation, with or without injustice being caused, there is an expectation that the authority will take action to rectify the shortcomings disclosed.

There have been a few reports issued by the Local Government Ombudsmen where there has been a finding of maladministration but no injustice. As with the other public sector ombudsmen, it is not necessary to show financial loss in order for there to be a finding of injustice, but there must be some prejudice to the complainant. This can include such matters as hurt feelings, and the denial of the opportunity to take part in a consultation exercise. Injustice can arise because complainants have had to live in unsuitable accommodation for longer than was necessary. A denial of payment or benefit because of unreasonable delay will be injustice, as will distress and anxiety. In one case, concerning maladministration in connection with the transfer arrangements from primary to secondary school, the fact that the transfer was not handled in accordance with the law was deemed to be injustice[77]. In another case, the injustice was the fact that the complainant had had to correspond with the council and pursue the matter over an unnecessarily long period[78].

[77]   Report No 99/A/3223.
[78]   Report No 87/B/1350.

Remedies

Where the Local Government Ombudsmen report a finding that injustice has been caused to the complainant in consequence of maladministration, the report includes a recommendation as to what action the authority should take to remedy this. The local authority has a duty to consider the report and notify the ombudsman of the action taken, or what action is proposed to be taken[79]. The action taken by local authorities falls into two broad categories. Firstly, there is actual redress for the complainant, by a reconsideration of the decision or compensation. Secondly, there could be a review of procedures by the authority to try to prevent similar maladministration occurring again.

When making recommendations for appropriate remedies, the ombudsmen try, as far as possible, to put complainants into the position they would have been in but for the fault. Although recognising that each case has to be considered on its own merits, in order to be fair and consistent, the ombudsmen aim to provide similar remedies for similar injustice. They have thus devised guidelines for remedies, the aim of which is to promote consistency in the remedies recommended[80]. The general principle used by the ombudsmen is that the remedy must be appropriate to the injustice. Where it is not possible to put the complainant in the position he or she would have been in but for the maladministration, financial compensation may be the only means of recompense.

Sometimes the recommendation is that the council take some specific action. This will usually be the case where the injustice arises from the failure to take action. For example, the ombudsmen might recommend that a statement of special educational needs is issued without delay. There might be a recommendation that the council perform the necessary assessment for entitlement to benefit, or make the necessary repairs to a council house. Sometimes there may be a recommendation to take action to ameliorate the effects of an injustice. An example of this is where a council is asked to provide specialist services to a child whose education has been adversely affected by the council's inaction. In one planning complaint the remedy involved making alterations to the highway.

---

[79] Local Government Act 1974, s 31.
[80] This is found in Remedies: Guidance on Good Practice 6 (1997).

Financial compensation is recommended where there has been financial loss, or where there is no other action which would provide an appropriate remedy, for example, where there has been undue delay. In one case, maladministration in relation to housing allocation resulted in a family being in unsatisfactory accommodation for a protracted period. It was recommended that, among other remedies, the complainant be paid £1,500 for this[81]. Financial compensation may also be appropriate where a complainant has incurred costs which would not have been necessary but for the maladministration. Clearly, where the complainant is owed money, for example, where a grant or housing benefit has not been paid, the remedy will involve payment of the money due, sometimes with the addition of interest.

Ombudsmen also have to consider the appropriate remedy where the complainant has suffered a loss of opportunity. This may happen, for example, where the complainant looses the right of appeal because the council failed to inform him or her of this right. Where it is reasonably certain that the outcome would have been beneficial to the complainant, the compensation will reflect this. In other cases, where the outcome is uncertain, only a small sum will be recommended. If, as is sometimes the case, it is reasonably certain that there would not have been a beneficial outcome for the complainant, there will be no finding of injustice, and therefore no remedy will be necessary. The ombudsmen may allow recovery of legal or other professional expenses incurred while pursuing the dispute with the council if this professional help is considered justifiable, but this will only occur in exceptional circumstances.

The Local Government Ombudsmen often recommend modest compensation of a few hundred pounds for 'distress' and 'inconvenience'. Sometimes these payments are not so modest. In one case, there was a recommendation for the payment of £1,000 for the 'protracted uncertainty' and 'consequent distress' caused over failures in the transfer arrangements to a secondary school. The child had missed the first week of secondary education, which the ombudsman considered was a disadvantage to her.[82] In another case, a council agreed to pay £1,000 to a complainant who had suffered stress and fear due to the failure to take effective action in response

---

[81]   Report No 99/B/3040.
[82]   Report No 99/A/3223.

to complaints about nuisance and violent and threatening action from a neighbour[83].

In addition, the ombudsmen always consider whether some financial remedy should be given for the 'time and trouble' taken by a complainant in making a complaint. For such a recommendation there would have to be something over and above the time and trouble routinely expected in pursuing a complaint. These payments are usually modest, being between £25 and £250. The ombudsmen expect, as a matter of course, that councils will make an apology where appropriate, and in some circumstances, an apology is the only remedy required. The ombudsmen may also recommend that the authority reviews its practices, procedures or policies. Where the council has already undertaken a review, or agreed to do so, that fact will be mentioned in the report.

Local authorities have statutory power to make compensation payments to redress grievances where it appears to them to be appropriate in the light of the contents of the ombudsman's report[84]. There is now also statutory authority for making such payments in the absence of an ombudsman's report, for example, where an authority believes that there is a justified complaint and compensation would be appropriate[85]. This removes any doubt about the legality of payments made when the ombudsman considers that a settlement without an investigation is appropriate. It also allows authorities to pay compensation under their own internal complaints procedures.

Compliance

The Local Government Ombudsmen can only make recommendations for appropriate remedies. They have no power to enforce them. Most local authorities comply with the recommendations, and provide the remedies

---

[83] Report No 98/A/5275.
[84] Local Government Act 1974, s 31(3).
[85] Local Government Act 2000. The ombudsmen had urged the government to introduce legislation, so that there could be no doubt about this (see Local Government Ombudsman Annual Report 1999–2000, p 47). The legislation gives a general power to pay compensation. Before this, some councils would make such payments, some would not, and some would only do so after referring the matter to the Secretary of State. This lack of statutory power hindered the ombudsmen's ability to effect local settlements.

sought by the ombudsmen. However, not all authorities are prepared to accept the ombudsman's decision. On average, over the years, about 6% of the recommendations of the Local Government Ombudsman have been without effect[86]. Around one-fifth of authorities, which have had an adverse report at one time or another, have been prepared to ignore the recommendations[87]. Over the last 10 years, there have been 2,800 reports of maladministration and injustice issued. Of these, 89 have resulted in an unsatisfactory outcome, and there are a further 76 which were awaiting settlement at the end of April 2001[88].

These figures could indicate that compliance is not a serious issue, as unsatisfactory outcomes represent only a small proportion of the ombudsmen's total caseload[89]. However, the very fact that there are authorities that do not comply may bring the system into disrepute. There is no parallel in this respect with other ombudsman systems, and the Parliamentary and Health Service Ombudsmen do not have this problem with enforcing their recommendations[90]. Where the authority is not prepared to comply, the sanction is for the ombudsmen to make a further report[91]. This report must be considered by the full council. If the ombudsman is still not satisfied with the response of the council after issuing the further report, councils can be obliged to publish a statement in a local newspaper. These statements state the details of any action recommended by the

---

[86]   See Report of the Financial Management and Policy Review of the Commission for Local Administration in England Stage II (1996) p 157.

[87]   See Third Report from the Select Committee on the Parliamentary Commissioner for Administration (HC Paper 448 (1985–86)) (Local Government Cases: Enforcement of Remedies) para 8.

[88]   Local Government Ombudsman Annual Report 2000–01 p 43.

[89]   It is estimated that unsatisfactory outcomes represent only a fraction of 1% of the ombudsmen's total caseload (see Report of the Financial Management and Policy Review of the Commission for Local Administration in England Stage II (1996) p 157).

[90]   The Parliamentary Ombudsman can make reports to Parliament, and both the Parliamentary and Health Service Ombudsmen are assisted by the Select Committee on Public Administration, which can call Permanent Secretaries and Chief Executives before it to justify their actions. The Local Government Ombudsmen report to many different local authorities, whose attitudes to critical reports can vary greatly.

[91]   The Local Government Act 1974, s 32, provides that where the authority does not notify within a reasonable time, or where the ombudsman is not satisfied with the action proposed, or no action is taken by the authority, the ombudsman must make a further report.

ombudsman, any supporting material the ombudsman may require, and, if the council wishes, a statement of its reasons for not complying with the recommendations. This puts councils under a greater obligation to state publicly why they do not intend to implement a remedy required by the Local Government Ombudsman. It is an attempt to make the fact of non-compliance a matter of public debate, while at the same time ensuring that proceedings remain voluntary.

There have been, at various times, discussions as to whether the Local Government Ombudsmen's recommendations should be enforceable in the courts, as a way of tackling the problem of compliance[92]. However, the prevailing view is that enforcement through the courts could create more problems than it solved. Enforcement could make local authorities defensive, and many may want procedures to become more judicial. Investigations could become more lengthy and costly, and authorities may object that there was no opportunity to test the facts by cross-examination. Another proposal, that offending authorities should be brought before the select committee[93], was felt to encroach upon the independence of local government[94]. There are currently no plans to introduce court enforcement, and, indeed, the ombudsmen themselves are not pressing for it[95]. They believe that such enforcement powers would change the relationship between themselves and councils, and that the system would become

---

[92] See for example the Widdicombe Report (Cm 9797, 1986) p 220; Justice *Administrative Justice: Some Necessary Reforms* (1988) Clarendon Press p 131; Third Report from the Select Committee on the Parliamentary Commissioner for Administration (HC Paper 448 (1985–86)) (Local Government Cases: Enforcement of Remedies).

[93] Third Report from the Select Committee on the Parliamentary Commissioner for Administration (HC Paper 448 (1985–86)) (Local Government Cases: Enforcement of Remedies) para 3. There was also discussion in the Stage II Report (Report of the Financial Management and Policy Review of the Commission for Local Administration in England (1996)) of the suggestion that the Select Committee on the Parliamentary Commissioner for Administration be enlarged to include the Local Government Ombudsmen. This was to increase the probability of the Local Government Ombudsmen's recommendations being given effect. The conclusion was that 'it would be inconsistent with the constitutional position of local authorities' (paras 9–10).

[94] Justice *Administrative Justice: Some Necessary Reforms* (1988) Clarendon Press p 126.

[95] A contrary view was expressed in 1988, where one commentator felt that there was an argument for judicial enforcement (M Jones 'The Local Ombudsman and Judicial Review' (1988) PL 608–622).

adversarial rather than investigative and co-operative. This would be detrimental to complainants[96].

Procedures and Powers

Complaints to the Local Government Ombudsmen can be made by any individual or body of persons, whether incorporated or not, except certain public bodies[97]. Complainants, therefore, can be companies, amenity societies, housing groups and partnerships, as well as individuals. Complaints must be made by the person aggrieved by the maladministration, but a representative can act where the person has died or is for some reason unable to act for him or herself. In these cases, the complaints would be made by the personal representative, member of the family, or any other suitable representative of the person aggrieved. There is no requirement that the complainant be a resident, council tax payer, or elector in the area of the local authority concerned. The complainant does not even have to be resident in the UK. The complaint has to be in writing, and this can be by letter, or complaint form. The complainant need not specify the actual maladministration, only the action of the local authority alleged to have constituted it[98].

When the Local Government Ombudsman scheme was established in 1974, complaints had to be made through a local councillor, although this requirement could be dispensed with if the councillor refused to refer the complaint. This requirement was extensively criticised[99]. The procedure mirrored the similar provision in relation to the Parliamentary Ombudsman, and it was based on the premise that councillors are the appropriate people to take up complaints on behalf of their constituents, and that the ombudsmen were there as an adjunct to the representative process. The analogy with members of Parliament was never really appropriate. Local councillors are in a different constitutional position than MPs, as councillors have executive authority and a much clearer relationship with the services

---

[96]   Report of the Financial Management and Policy Review of the Commission for Local Administration in England Stage II (1996) p 158.

[97]   Local Government Act 1967, s 27.

[98]   See *R v Local Comr for Administration, ex p Bradford Metropolitan City Council* [1979] QBD 287, [1979] 2 All ER 881.

[99]   See Justice *The Local Ombudsman: a Review of the First Five Years* (1980) JUSTICE.

for which they are responsible. The local councillor filter was removed in 1988[100], and now the vast majority of complaints are made directly.

The Local Government Ombudsmen have a range of powers at their disposal to ensure that they can conduct thorough investigations. They can require information and documents to be produced, and can compel the attendance and examination of witnesses[101]. Crown privilege is excluded in relation to enquiries of government departments, and the ombudsmen can compel the production of documents or the giving of evidence[102]. Any obstructions in this respect may cause the offender to be dealt with as if a contempt of the High Court had been committed. Information obtained by the ombudsmen is not to be disclosed except for the purposes of writing the report, or in connection with court proceedings for perjury, breach of the Official Secrets Acts, or obstructing the ombudsmen[103]. The ombudsmen are protected from actions for defamation[104], and have power to reimburse complainants and others for expenses[105].

Internal Complaints Procedures

Before the ombudsmen investigate complaints, they must be satisfied that the complaint has been brought to the notice of the authority concerned. The authority must have had a reasonable opportunity to investigate and

---

[100] Local Government Act 1988, s 29, Sch 3, para 5 amended the Local Government Act 1974, s 26(2).

[101] Local Government Act 1974, s 29.

[102] In one case, the Local Government Ombudsman requested documents from the council, in order to investigate a complaint from a couple about the council's failure to give them proper consideration in relation to the adoption of a second child. The council refused, and the ombudsman obtained a subpoena to compel production of the documents. The council applied for this to be set aside. In *Re Subpoena (Adoption: Comr for Local Administration)* [1996] 2 FLR 629, the court refused to set the subpoena aside. It was clear that Parliament had intended that the ombudsman had the right to investigate matters relating to adoption. In order to do this, access to the relevant documents was required, even though for reasons of confidentiality the contents could not be disclosed to the parties. Provided that the ombudsman demonstrated a bona fide need for access, and was prepared to observe the rules on confidentiality, disclosure would be ordered.

[103] Local Government Act 1974, s 31.

[104] Local Government Act 1974, s 32.

[105] Local Government Act 1974, s 28.

reply to the complaint[106]. Where councils have not had a reasonable opportunity to deal with complaints, they are 'premature' and are not accepted by the ombudsmen for investigation. They are referred to the councils concerned with a request that they should investigate them. If a complainant is not satisfied with the outcome of the council's investigation, the complainant can complain to the ombudsmen again.

This raises the question of what is a 'reasonable opportunity'. When the Local Government Ombudsman system was established in 1974, few councils had complaints systems. Although there is no statutory requirement for authorities to have authority-wide complaints procedures[107], there is now general agreement that each local authority should have effective complaints systems, and nearly all of them do[108]. The Local Government Ombudsmen are now at the apex of a complaints system which consists of internal and external review. They are the 'ultimate rung' on the complaints ladder, providing a final, independent mechanism for citizens' grievances. In these circumstances, what is a 'reasonable opportunity' now is different to what it was in the 1970s.

In 1997, the ombudsmen issued a consultation paper seeking views on whether it would be appropriate to require complainants to exhaust all their council's complaints systems before the ombudsmen would consider their complaint, unless there were exceptional circumstances. They also conducted a pilot study to enable an assessment to be made of the likely effects of such a requirement on complainants, local authorities and the ombudsmen themselves[109].

---

[106]   Local Government Act 1974, s 26(5).

[107]   As long ago as 1974, Redcliffe-Maud (*Report of the Committee on Local Government Rules of Conduct* (Cmnd 5636, 1974)) recommended the adoption by local authorities of clearly established, well publicised procedures for the reception and investigation of complaints by members of the public. In 1978, the Local Government Ombudsmen, in consultation with the Local Authority Associations, issued a Code of Practice for local authorities in relation to complaints. This was replaced in 1992 by a guidance note, *Devising a Complaints System*. There are statutory requirements for complaints procedures for social services and some education department functions.

[108]   According to the Audit Commission, 98% of councils do have complaints procedures. See Report of the Financial Management and Policy Review of the Commission for Local Administration in England Stage II (1996) p 146.

[109]   See Local Government Ombudsman Annual Report 1996–97. The pilot study was conducted between April 1998 and March 1999. About a quarter of local authorities in England took part.

The results of the pilot study convinced the ombudsmen that to introduce such a requirement would not be beneficial. It did not save investigative time when the complaint eventually came back to the ombudsmen, and it did not reduce the ombudsmen's costs. There was also a number of categories of complaint excluded from the referral back procedure. For example, where the complaints procedures were inadequate, and where complainants seemed particularly vulnerable and likely to be deterred from pursuing the complaint, they were not referred back. These exceptions are necessary in order to prevent hardship, and to avoid wasting resources. If there is a list of exceptions, there is the danger that complaints excluded may be as numerous as those dealt with under the new procedure. Another drawback of the requirement to exhaust internal procedures was that it increased dissatisfaction among complainants, which could result in a loss of confidence in the ombudsman system.

The ombudsmen therefore decided not to introduce a formal requirement to exhaust all the stages of councils' complaints procedures before a complaint is investigated[110]. However, unless there are exceptional circumstances, complaints to the ombudsmen will be referred to the council's chief executive if there is no evidence that the council has had an opportunity to consider and respond to the complaint. After a specified time, complainants can come back to the ombudsman, if they are not content with the council's response[111]. In practice, just less than a quarter of complaints are referred back to councils each year, because they are premature[112].

Working Methods

The investigation of complaints must be conducted in private, but other than this, the Local Government Ombudsmen have discretion on how to

---

[110]   Where there is a statutory complaints procedure, as in the case of social services, complainants are expected to use this procedure, only referring the complaint to the ombudsman where they do not achieve satisfaction.

[111]   See Local Government Ombudsman Annual Report 2000–01 pp 5–6. From 1 April 2001 to 31 March 2002, complainants could come back within 12 weeks. From that date, the time period is reduced to eight weeks.

[112]   In 2000–01, out of a total of 18,220 complaints, 4,333 (24%) were premature (Local Government Ombudsman Annual Report 2000–01 p 38). The figures for 1999–2000 were 16,759 and 3,708 (22%) respectively (Local Government Ombudsman Annual Report 1999–2000 p 38).

conduct the investigation[113]. The procedure for dealing with complaints involves an initial appraisal to see if the complaint is within jurisdiction and relates to an authority subject to the Local Government Ombudsmen's jurisdiction. Any complaints outside jurisdiction but perceived to be within the jurisdiction of the Parliamentary or Health Service Ombudsmen are forwarded to them. Complaints against other bodies are returned to the complainants with such advice as is necessary. If it is not clear what the complaint is about, further details are requested from the complainant. About half the complaints to the ombudsmen are premature, outside jurisdiction, or are not pursued as a result of the ombudsmen's discretion not to continue with them. This latter category includes situations where complainants wish to withdraw complaints, where they can no longer be contacted, or where the complainant decides to take court action.

If the complaint is within jurisdiction and there seems to be a prima facie case of maladministration and injustice, the local authority will be asked to comment on the allegations. It may be that this shows that the authority has acted reasonably, or that the injustice claimed would not justify the cost of investigation. If so, the complainant is informed of this by letter, and the complaint is taken no further. Sometimes a complainant is given an opportunity to respond to this letter before a final decision is made. The ombudsmen categorise these cases as 'no maladministration' without a report. The term is used where the ombudsmen have exercised their discretion to terminate an investigation of a complaint because there is no evidence of maladministration, or insufficient evidence to justify completing the investigation.

If a prima case is established, the ombudsman may invite the local authority to settle the case, making appropriate suggestions as to a remedy. If a complaint is resolved in this way, it is called a local settlement. The term is used to describe the situation where, during the course of an investigation, the council takes, or agrees to take, some action which the ombudsman considers a satisfactory response to the complaint. It could result from the council on its own initiative recognising that there was fault causing injustice, and proposing a remedy that the ombudsman considers satisfactory. It may be that the council accepts the ombudsman's suggestion that there was fault. Sometimes a council will settle, even though

---

[113]   Local Government Act 1974, s 28(2).

it does not consider it was at fault, and sometimes the council and the complainant agree on a satisfactory outcome[114].

The Local Government Ombudsmen believe that it is in the interests of complainants to achieve local settlements, rather than prolong investigations and issue formal reports. Their aim is to obtain redress for those who have suffered injustice as a result of maladministration, and they will only issue reports in these cases where it is in the public interest to do so. Some complaints are more susceptible to local settlement than others. Complaints concerning council house repairs and housing benefit are more likely to be settled locally, whereas planning complaints are fairly resistant to this outcome. Local settlements constitute a growing category of outcome for complainants, with very few complaints resulting in a formal investigation and the issuing of an investigation report. Formal investigations are reserved for those cases where there is prima facie evidence of maladministration, but where no local settlement has been achieved. Sometimes where there is a local settlement, a report will be issued if it is thought to be in the public interest.

Where cases are accepted for investigation, the normal procedure is for an investigator to visit the local authority concerned, examine files, and interview the relevant officers, the complainant, and anyone else involved in the case. After all the information has been obtained, a draft report is written, setting out the findings, but not the ombudsman's conclusions and recommendations. This is sent to both the authority and the complainant for comment. Its circulation to the parties is an attempt to obtain an agreed statement of the facts. The draft report may be amended in the light of the comments received, and the final report is then prepared.

A copy of the final report is sent to the complainant, the chief executive of the authority, and the referring councillor, if there is one. The ombudsman can make the following findings: maladministration and injustice;

---

[114] No formal report is issued in these cases, and the parties are informed by letter that the investigation is being discontinued. There was concern that this practice may not accord with the Local Government Act 1974, s 30(1), which provides that, when an investigation is conducted, a report on the investigation is to be issued. Counsel's advice on this is that the practice is within the law, as s 26(10) of the Act gives the ombudsmen discretion to initiate, continue or discontinue an investigation. The ombudsmen would like the 1974 Act to be amended to give express statutory recognition to the practice of discontinuing investigations by letter (see Local Government Ombudsmen Annual Report 1999–2000 p 49).

maladministration but no injustice; no maladministration. The report usually contains a recommendation as to an appropriate remedy, where there is a finding of maladministration and injustice. Copies of reports[115] are usually sent to local newspapers, and members of the public can take copies of the report, subject to a reasonable charge being made by the authority. There is no appeal against the findings of the Local Government Ombudsman, although the reports are subject to judicial review[116].

The thoroughness of the Local Government Ombudsman's investigation procedure has been noted in the past[117]. There are few criticisms of the working practices, and in common with the other ombudsman systems in the UK the procedure is thorough and rarely restricted to an examination of the documents, except in the most straightforward of cases. Evaluations of working practices are favourable[118]. The recent Cabinet Office review was impressed by the flexibility of approach of the Local Government Ombudsmen, and their use of informal resolution where appropriate[119]. The organisation is cost effective, with £467 being the average cost per complaint in 2000-01, a reduction on the previous year when it was £509. Indeed, the average cost of complaints at today's prices have decreased remarkably over the past decade[120]. It has been noted that the annual cost of the service is a fraction of the cost of resolving a similar number of complaints through legal processes[121].

One of the negative aspects about the procedure is the time taken to resolve complaints, and one of the goals of the organisation is to reduce the time

---

[115]   These are anonymised, except for the name of the authority.

[116]   See *R v Local Comr for Administration, ex p Eastleigh Borough Council* [1988] 3 All ER 151. In *R v Local Comr for Administration, ex p Croydon* [1989] 1 All ER 1033, the High Court granted a declaration that the Local Government Ombudsman's finding of maladministration was unjustified.

[117]   See F Stacey *Ombudsmen Compared* (1978) Clarendon Press p 221; W Gwyn 'The Ombudsman in Britain: a qualified success in government reform' (1982) 60 Public Administration 77; N Lewis, M Seneviratne and S Cracknell *Complaints Procedures in Local Government* (1986) University of Sheffield p 60.

[118]   See Local Government Ombudsman Annual Report 1989–90 p 9, reporting on the review of working practice conducted by Coopers and Lybrand in 1989. See also Report of the Financial Management and Policy Review of the Commission for Local Administration in England Stage II (1996).

[119]   *Review of the Public Sector Ombudsmen in England* (2000) Cabinet Office pp 46, 52, 55.

[120]   Local Government Ombudsman Annual Report 2000–01 pp 28–29.

[121]   Report of the Financial Management and Policy Review of the Commission for Local Administration in England Stage II (1996) p 61.

taken to decide cases. The ombudsmen have managed to reduce the numbers of complaints that take more than 12 months to decide, which is commendable given the year on year increase in the numbers of complaints being referred to the ombudsmen. At the end of April 2000, there were only 200 such complaints, compared to over 800 in 1995. This number increased to 364 in 2001, an increase that was mainly accounted for by the huge increase in complaints about housing benefit received in the London office[122]. Around 80% of complaints are determined within six months, and around half within three months.

The ombudsmen commission consumer surveys periodically in order to test consumer satisfaction with the service. The latest one, in 1999, found an improvement in satisfaction since the 1994 survey. Altogether, 61% of respondents were satisfied with the time taken to deal with the complaint. Over half (58%) felt that they had been kept well informed of the progress of the investigation of their complaint. Half were satisfied with the way their complaint was dealt with. In relation to the ombudsmen's staff, 70% of respondents found them helpful and 66% found them efficient[123]. Research in 1986 found that local authority officers were generally satisfied with the thoroughness, fairness and impartiality of the ombudsman's procedures[124]. A survey in 1995 of local authorities found very high levels of satisfaction with the ombudsman in terms of fairness, staff attitudes and clarity[125].

Cases Investigated

In every year since its inception, the number of complaints to the Local Government Ombudsman has increased. Although there has been a dramatic increase in recent years, it should be noted that, as with the Parliamentary Ombudsman, the number of complaints is negligible when compared with the number of decisions taken daily by administrators. The vast majority of complaints considered are not investigated to the point of issuing a full report, as Table 6.1 indicates. As indicated above, some are rejected initially because they are outside jurisdiction, or because there is no prima facie case of maladministration. Some are concluded after initial enquiries have

---

[122] Local Government Ombudsman Annual Report 2000–01 pp 26–27.
[123] Local Government Ombudsman Annual Report 1999–00 p 8.
[124] N Lewis, M Seneviratne and S Cracknell *Complaints Procedures in Local Government* (1986) University of Sheffield p 55.
[125] Local Government Ombudsman Annual Report 1999–2000 p 8.

been made. In the majority of cases, this is because the evidence shows no injustice or maladministration. In other cases there is a local settlement. The numbers of complaints proceeding to a final report have decreased over the years, reflecting the ombudsmen's emphasis on achieving informal local settlements where possible and appropriate.

TABLE 6.1   NUMBER OF COMPLAINTS AND OUTCOMES 1996-97 TO 2000-01

	96-97	97-98	98-99	99-00	00-01
Total Number of Complaints	**15,406**	**15,262**	**15,653**	**16,759**	**18,220**
Outside Jurisdiction	1763 (11%)	1879 (12%)	1873 (12%)	1965 (12%)	2176 (12%)
Premature Complaints	3038 (20%)	3058 (20%)	4070 (26%)	3708 (22%)	4333 (24%)
Discretion not to pursue	585 (4%)	907 (6%)	1891 (12%)	2451 (15%)	2760 (15%)
No maladministration (no report issued)	7190 (47%)	6529 (43%)	5109 (33%)	5516 (33%)	4963 (27%)
Local settlement (no report issued)	2417 (16%)	2414 (16%)	2251 (14%)	2786 (17%)	3727 (20%)
Local settlement (report issued)	47 (<1%)	24 (<1%)	42 (<1%)	53 (<1%)	60 (<1%)
Issued reports (number of complaints on which reports were issued)	366 (2%)	451 (3%)	417 (3%)	280 (2%)	201 (1%)

(Source: Local Government Ombudsman Annual Reports)

Although only a small number of complaints result in a final report, many councils settle complaints satisfactorily after a complaint to the ombudsman. For example, in 2000–01, 3,787 complaints were resolved by local settlements, which represents 32% of all complaints determined, excluding premature complaints and those outside jurisdiction[126]. In many of these cases there may have been a finding of maladministration if the authority had not averted the need for it by admitting some fault and doing enough to remedy it to the satisfaction of the ombudsman. It is probably more accurate, therefore, to say that in about 25% of cases, the complainants' efforts in registering their complaints produced a satisfactory result.

Every year the subject which attracts the most complaints is housing, typically accounting for between 37% and 41% of complaints. In 2000–01, 45% of complaints were about housing matters, around half of them concerned with housing benefit[127]. Other categories of complaint against housing departments include, perhaps not surprisingly, council house repairs, with allegations of failures and delays. Other significant categories are housing transfers, neighbour nuisance, general housing management issues and homelessness. Not surprisingly, these complaints are mainly against inner city authorities, particularly London boroughs. It is certainly the London boroughs which have accounted for the huge increase in housing benefit complaints in recent years.

Planning matters are the next biggest category of complaint. These used to account for around 30% of complaints each year, but now typically 17% to 20%, a reduction reflecting the very large numbers of housing complaints referred to ombudsmen. These complaints tend to be more common in the more rural authorities. Almost half of these are concerned with neighbour amenity, with allegations of failures to consult about, or take proper account of objections to, proposed developments. Other complaints include allegations about incorrect or unclear advice about the need for planning permission, and failures to enforce planning conditions. Planning complaints often account for between 30% and 40% of issued reports. This large proportion is indicative of the fact that planning complaints are often very difficult to resolve by local settlement.

---

[126]   Local Government Ombudsman Annual Report 2000–01 p 22.
[127]   Local Government Ombudsman Annual Report 2000–01 p 25.

Education departments generate between 6% and 9% of all complaints. Many of these complaints concern the conduct of school admission appeals committees and the appeal process. There is a code of guidance for these committees, and in many of the cases investigated, this guidance has not been followed. Most of these types of complaints relate to foundation schools, which are not within the control of local education authorities. Another common area of complaint is in relation to special educational needs, where councils have either delayed issuing statements, or have not provided education in accordance with an issued statement.

Social services departments in the past used to generate very few complaints, accounting for between 3% and 4%. This has steadily increased, and in the last two years, they accounted for between 6% and 7%[128]. Many of these complaints are about failures or delay in relation to aids and adaptations for the physically handicapped. Some relate to failures to deal properly with children in care, including failures to give proper advice about access to such children. Maladministration has also been found in some of these cases, where there has been a failure to have adequate arrangements for dealing with complaints.

Publicity

The Local Government Ombudsmen do have greater scope for publicising their work than the Parliamentary Ombudsman. Reports of the Local Government Ombudsmen are sent to the complainant, to the member who referred it, if applicable, and to the authority concerned[129]. An investigation report identifies the authority concerned, but maintains anonymity for the complainant and other individuals[130]. The authority is obliged to advertise

---

[128]   This increase may be attributed in part to the ombudsman's initiative in writing to voluntary organisations in 1988 reminding them that they could act on a complainant's behalf (see Local Government Ombudsman Annual Report 1989–90 p 11). Another reason was the requirement under the Children Act 1989 and the Community Care Act 1990 for social services departments to establish complaints procedures which refer to the role of the Local Government Ombudsman (see Local Government Ombudsman Annual Report 1991–92 p 31).

[129]   Local Government Act 1974, s 30(1).

[130]   There was provision in the Local Government Act 1974 (s 3A, which was inserted by the Local Government and Housing Act 1989, s 32(1)(b)) for individual councillors to be named in a report. This was where the action constituting maladministration was taken with the involvement of a councillor, and the

a report and make it available for public inspection for a period of three weeks. Every investigation report is therefore a matter of public record, although there are provisions to direct councils not to publicise where the ombudsmen consider non-publication to be in the public interest[131]. The local press and sometimes the national press publicise Local Government reports, although they do tend to concentrate on those reports which are critical of the council concerned. There is, not surprisingly, more media interest when the local authority refuses to do what the ombudsmen recommends, than when there is a successful outcome.

Despite these mechanisms for publicising their work, the Local Government Ombudsmen, in common with the other public sector ombudsmen, are concerned about lack of awareness among members of the public. In 1995, a survey showed that only 47% of respondents had heard of the Local Government Ombudsmen[132]. Respondents in the lower socio-economic groups had less awareness. In 1996, a survey by the Consumers' Association found that 41% of respondents had no awareness of any of the public sector ombudsmen, a figure that rose to 51% in lower socio-economic groups. A similar result was found in 1997, when a survey for

---

councillor's conduct constituted a breach of the National Code of Conduct. This code primarily covers non-pecuniary interests. There are statutory obligations in relation to pecuniary interests, breach of which are criminal offences. Authorities may also have standing orders in relation to members' interests. The ombudsmen's powers in this respect will change as a result of the Local Government Act 2000. Section 57 of the Act establishes the Standards Board for England, which will investigate complaints about breaches by councillors of their authorities' code of conduct. Authorities are to adopt their individual codes in accordance with the Act. The Standards Board for England has nine members and a budget of £7 million. The Local Government Ombudsman's budget for 2000–01 was just over £8.5 million. This suggests that the Government anticipates a considerable workload for the Standards Board, although in the past, findings of breaches of the National Code have been relatively infrequent. (For a discussion of the Local Government Ombudsman's role in dealing with breaches of the code, see C Crawford 'Reviewing the Local Ombudsmen' (1999) 22 JLGL 34–39.) The Local Government Ombudsman and the Standards Board for England are establishing protocols to ensure that complaints are dealt with appropriately, and that complainants are clear about the relative remits of the two bodies.

[131] Local Government Act, s 30(7). There is however no power for the ombudsmen to direct that a report should not be disclosed by a councillor, complainant or anyone else.

[132] This was a survey by MORI, commissioned by the Local Government Ombudsmen (see Local Government Ombudsmen Annual Report 1998–99).

the Citizen's Charter Unit revealed that less than half the population was aware of the Local Government or Parliamentary Ombudsmen[133].

As a result of these findings, the Local Government Ombudsmen have worked hard to improve public awareness, both of ombudsman schemes in general and of their own scheme in particular. In addition to publishing annual reports, and individual reports[134], they also publish guidance notes on good administrative practice, and annual digests of cases. They publish a complaints leaflet, which is frequently revised, and available in different languages and formats. They have a website[135], through which they have improved access to the service by means of online enquiry forms and complaints forms. Complainants can make their complaint electronically, and there can be communication by email. The Local Government Ombudsmen have regular meetings with a wide range of voluntary bodies and those who advise complainants. They travel widely to publicise their work, taking up opportunities for interviews in the media when possible. They also publicise their work in local authorities, taking part in relevant seminars and workshops on complaints systems. Complainants are asked how they found out about the ombudsman service, with a view to improving publicity in appropriate areas.

Accountability

Unlike the Parliamentary and Health Service Ombudsmen, the Local Government Ombudsmen do not report to Parliament, and there is no Parliamentary select committee to oversee their work. When the Local Government Ombudsman scheme was first established, it reported to the 'Representative Body'. This consisted of members from local authority associations[136], and it was set up[137] to receive and comment upon the ombudsman's annual reports and individual reports. It also reviewed the

---

[133]   This was conducted by MORI in 1997 (see *Review of the Public Sector Ombudsmen in England* (2000) Cabinet Office p 20).

[134]   They circulate these to a wide range of interested organisations and individuals.

[135]   The website address is: www.open.gov.uk/lgo.

[136]   These were the Association of County Councils, the Association of District Councils and the Association of Metropolitan Authorities. There was also a representative from the water authorities.

[137]   The Local Government Act 1974, s 24, provided for the establishment of such a body, to consist of bodies appearing to the Secretary of State to represent local authorities.

budget of the estimated expenditure of the office, which the ombudsmen prepared[138].

The Representative Body was abolished on 1 April 1990[139] having been widely criticised, mainly because it was felt to be inappropriate that a body representing the interests of those investigated should play such a major role in deciding the budget[140]. It had never been particularly supportive of the ombudsmen, and it had certainly never occupied a similar role in relation to the Local Government Ombudsmen as that taken by the select committee in relation to the Parliamentary Ombudsman. Its demise was said to be 'no sad loss'[141]. Now, the Local Government Ombudsmen submit their annual report to the local authority associations for their comments, but they themselves arrange for the publication of the report. The ombudsmen also have regular meetings with the local authority associations, to discuss the business plan, and the draft of the annual report.

---

[138] At the time, funds were provided by local authorities, by means of a levy. The Representative Body could make comments to the ombudsmen, and ultimately to the Secretary of State, if the ombudsmen insisted on proceeding with a budget estimate that the Representative Body regarded as excessive. Since 1989, funding has been provided directly from the Revenue Support Grant (see Local Government Planning and Land Act 1980, s 56(9)).

[139] Local Government and Housing Act 1989, s 25.

[140] Widdicombe was critical of the fact that a body which represented those who are the subject of investigation should play a major part in deciding the budget of the investigators. It had recommended a review of the position of the Representative Body because of this, and also because of its opposition to reform (Cm 9797, 1986 p 223). Lewis had argued that an 'immediate reconstruction of its role and function is perhaps the most urgent reform required in the local ombudsman field' (N Lewis 'The Case for Change in the Ombudsman Service' (1979) Municipal and Public Services Journal 597, p 597). In 1980, Justice recommended its abolition, and thought that it would assist the Local Government Ombudsmen if a new body were established which was more impartial, and would thus have more impact (see *The Local Ombudsman: a review of the First Five Years* (1980) p 28). There was a recommendation in 1986 that it be replaced with a body which included a substantial representation of consumer interests (see N Lewis, M Seneviratne and S Cracknell *Complaints Procedures in Local Government* (1986) University of Sheffield p 41). Birkinshaw noted the unsupportive nature of the Representative Body (P Birkinshaw *Grievances, Remedies and the State* (1st edn, 1985) Sweet and Maxwell p 143).

[141] P Birkinshaw *Grievances, Remedies and the State* (2nd edn, 1994) Sweet and Maxwell p 223.

Every three years, the ombudsmen are required to review the operation of the scheme[142]. This was last done in 1999, the results of which are reported in the 1999–2000 annual report. The ombudsmen consult a wide range of bodies in conducting these reviews.

Valuable though the select committee has been in supporting the work of the Parliamentary and Health Service Ombudsmen, there have never been any plans to increase the remit of the select committee to include the Local Government Ombudsman. Indeed, there has always been considerable constitutional hesitation in bringing aspects of local government directly under the supervision of Parliament in this way. The Cabinet Office review of the public sector ombudsmen proposes that the new integrated ombudsman scheme will be accountable to Parliament[143]. The review does not refer to the role of the Select Committee on Public Administration in the new system. However, the ombudsmen themselves have suggested that the new scheme should be answerable to the select committee for the general conduct of its activities. It would, however, have no role in the investigation of individual complaints[144].

Good Administrative Practice

The Local Government Ombudsmen have two purposes. In addition to investigating and resolving complaints, they also offer guidance which is intended to promote fair and effective administration in local government. It is in this latter role that the Local Government Ombudsmen have been most effective. Indeed, their success here has been recognised by government, which noted in 1988 that the service had 'proved a positive force for good' not only in redressing individual grievances, but also 'by providing a spur to more responsive, efficient and fairer local administration'[145]. The valuable function they performed in this area was

---

[142]   Local Government Act 1974, s 23(12), as amended by the Local Government Act 1988, Sch 3.

[143]   *Review of the Public Sector Ombudsmen in England* (2000) Cabinet Office para 5.17.

[144]   *Review of the Public Sector Ombudsmen in England* (2000) Cabinet Office p 83.

[145]   The Conduct of Local Authority Business. The Government Response to the Report of the Widdicombe Committee (Cm 433, 1988) paras 6, 18.

given statutory recognition in 1989, and now the ombudsmen have legislative authority to provide advice and guidance on good administrative practice[146]. They also provide individual authorities and other bodies with 'large amounts' of ad hoc advice when requested[147]. A number of guidance notes on good practice have been produced over the years, including some on complaints systems, council house repairs, disposal of land and remedies. They also publish annual digests of selected cases, which are chosen to illustrate points of particular interest of general application. These cases indicate good administrative practice and the way the ombudsmen reach their decisions.

From this evidence, it can certainly be argued that the Local Government Ombudsmen are most effective when they go beyond the individual complaint. They sometimes conduct investigations into groups of cases, where similar complaints against an authority appear to indicate some systemic defect. Recent examples of this include the investigations into complaints about the administration of housing benefit. These have mainly been in relation to some London boroughs, but there have also been systemic problems outside London. As a result of these investigations, the ombudsman has met with councils to discuss changes in their systems, with a view to achieving major and lasting improvements[148]. Complaints from residents of private nursing homes, whose care has been purchased by local authorities, have raised issues about the appropriate responsibilities of councils in these situations. While the ombudsmen have noted that such complaints raise issues relating to statutory responsibilities that only the courts can decide, they consider that councils should ensure that the service is properly provided. They have raised the issue with the Permanent Secretary at the Department of Health, in order that appropriate guidance may be issued to social services authorities[149]. The ombudsmen's work in dealing with complaints about education appeal panels has also highlighted a number of problems with their operation. In addition to suggesting improvements for appeal panels in their reports, they were also

---

[146] Local Government Act 1974, s 12A, inserted by the Local Government and Housing Act 1989, s 22.
[147] Local Government Ombudsman Annual Report 2000–01 p 28.
[148] See Local Government Ombudsman Annual Report 1999–2000 pp 10–11 and Annual Report 2000–01 p 3.
[149] See Local Government Ombudsman Annual Report 1999–2000 p 21.

able to give evidence about their operation to the Leggatt review of tribunals[150] suggesting improvements[151].

There are other examples where investigations have had wide reaching implications for administrative procedures and practice, and for changes in the law. For example, in planning procedures, the ombudsmen were influential in establishing the practice of 'neighbour notification' as part of the publicity element of planning applications. This practice is now widespread. In the field of education, the publicity following adverse reports against education authorities illegally charging for school trips led to a change in the law in this area.

Conclusions

The Local Government Ombudsman system has probably been the most successful of the public sector ombudsmen in terms of its accessibility and visibility. It has dealt with a rising volume of complaints, and has been responsible for redressing grievances for thousands of citizens. It has also proved to be impressive in improving procedures within local authorities. In terms of the standard criteria for assessment of ombudsman schemes, it scores highly. There is no doubt about the independence and impartiality of the office. It publishes annual reports about its work, and all investigation reports are published. Although no longer having the Representative Body to report to, it consults widely with local authorities and consumer and other interest groups about its work.

It has been directly accessible since 1989, and it has improved accessibility by means of its website, and its work with consumer and advisory bodies. Although complainants are expected to have raised their grievance with the authority before referring their complaint to the ombudsmen, there is no formal requirement for internal complaints procedures to have been exhausted. The service is free to complainants, and cost effective in terms of dispute resolution procedures. It has adequate powers to conduct investigations. Moreover, the legislation establishing the scheme allows more flexibility than that of the Parliamentary Ombudsman. The Local Government Ombudsmen have thus been able to be more imaginative in

---

[150]   Review of Tribunals: Consultation Paper (2000). See also Tribunals for Users: One System, One Service (2001).
[151]   See Local Government Ombudsman Annual Report 2000–01 p 5.

finding solutions to complaints, and have been able to offer more local resolution where appropriate.

The high regard in which the system is held was evidenced by the general outcry when there was a recommendation in 1995 that the Local Government Ombudsman was no longer necessary[152]. The proposal was that a new complaints system be established, under which local authorities would be statutorily obliged to operate their own local complaints systems. The role of a body like the ombudsmen would be limited to the validation and monitoring of each local authority's system. Concern was expressed that this proposal would not be in the interests of complainants, and that there was a need for a wholly independent body to investigate complaints of maladministration[153]. The government distanced itself from this proposal, and it was quietly forgotten. There can be no doubt of the need for an independent system, and the Local Government Ombudsmen have shown themselves to be effective in this role. Indeed, the Cabinet Office review was sufficiently impressed by the Local Government Ombudsmen's organisation, practices and procedures, that it considered many aspects of that system appropriate to be used in the model for the new integrated ombudsman scheme[154].

---

[152] See the report of Sir Geoffrey Chipperfield *Review of the Commission for Local Administration: Stage One* (1995), which commenced in July 1995, and reported in November 1995. The review was part of the Department of the Environment's programme of finance, management and policy reviews.

[153] See Local Government Ombudsman Annual Report 1994–95; The Public Law Project *Review of the Local Government Ombudsman* Volume 1 (1996) Report of Seminar Proceedings.

[154] *Review of the Public Sector Ombudsmen in England* (2000) Cabinet Office pp 46, 52, 55.

Chapter 7

Devolution

This chapter will examine particular features of the ombudsman arrangements in Northern Ireland, Scotland and Wales. These arrangements are different in several ways to those in England, and they are also different to each other. What they have in common is that the United Kingdom Parliamentary Ombudsman remains responsible for dealing with some complaints in each of the jurisdictions. These are complaints about 'reserved matters', that is, those matters that remain the responsibility of the UK Parliament at Westminster. These include foreign affairs, defence, and taxation. Thus, the United Kingdom Parliamentary Ombudsman continues to deal with complaints about the inland revenue and customs and excise[1].

Northern Ireland

The Northern Ireland Ombudsman is the popular name for two offices. It includes both the Assembly Ombudsman for Northern Ireland[2], and the Northern Ireland Commissioner for Complaints[3]. The former, originally established as the Northern Ireland Parliamentary Commissioner for Administration, deals with complaints relating to the actions of the Northern

[1] At present, the United Kingdom Parliamentary Ombudsman also deals with complaints about Freedom of Information.
[2] This office, formerly known as the Northern Ireland Parliamentary Commissioner for Administration, was established in 1969, by the Parliamentary Commissioner Act (Northern Ireland) 1969.
[3] This office was also established in 1969 by the Commissioner for Complaints (Northern Ireland) Act 1969.

Ireland Assembly. The latter is concerned with local councils, local boards and the health service. When the two offices were first established in 1969, the United Kingdom Parliamentary Ombudsman held the former post. A separate appointment was made for the post of Commissioner for Complaints[4]. However, in 1972, when the United Kingdom Parliamentary Ombudsman retired, the post of Northern Ireland Parliamentary Ombudsman was filled by the existing Northern Ireland Commissioner for Complaints. Since then, the two Northern Ireland Ombudsmen offices have always been held by the same person. As a result, although operating under two pieces of legislation, the office does function as one system. There are however proposals to review the legislation under which the office operates, and it may be that in the future, the two offices will be integrated in one piece of legislation[5].

Background

The introduction of the two ombudsmen in 1969 in Northern Ireland has to be set within the context of the political and social system there. Northern Ireland has had a 'complex and turbulent' history, which has 'focussed substantially' on religious differences between the Roman Catholic minority and the Protestant majority[6]. The creation of the ombudsmen was partly a response to the unrest among the minority Roman Catholic population. There were 'repeated complaints of discrimination and persecution' against Roman Catholics by both local and central government, both of which were dominated by the protestant Unionist Party[7]. There was a feeling that the Roman Catholic minority 'were not receiving a fair deal'[8], and the establishment of the ombudsmen was in part a measure to contribute towards solving the problem of community relations.

---

[4]   This was Mr J M Benn, who was formerly the Permanent Secretary of the Northern Ireland Ministry of Education.

[5]   The Northern Ireland Assembly has resolved that a review of the two offices be conducted.

[6]   G Drewry 'The Northern Ireland Parliamentary Ombudsman' in R Gregory and P Giddings (eds) *Righting Wrongs: The Ombudsman in Six Continents* (2000) IOS Press p 285.

[7]   H J Elcock 'Opportunity for Ombudsman: the Northern Ireland Commissioner for Complaints' (1972) Public Administration 87–93, p 87.

[8]   K P Poole 'The Northern Ireland Commissioner for Complaints' (1972) PL 131–148, p 131.

In 1969, when the Northern Ireland Parliamentary Ombudsman was established, there was a separate, semi-independent Parliament in Northern Ireland, with the Executive exercising powers devolved from Westminster[9]. The Parliamentary Commissioner Act (Northern Ireland) 1969 established an ombudsman on much the same lines as that for the UK Parliament, to investigate complaints of maladministration in relation to the Stormont Government. At various points since 1969, the Northern Ireland Parliament has been abolished, there has been direct rule from Westminster, and there have been various 'power sharing' Northern Ireland Assemblies. Throughout this period, the Northern Ireland Parliamentary Ombudsman has continued in existence, dealing with complaints relating to the central administrative departments of Northern Ireland. In 1996, the title was changed to the Assembly Ombudsman for Northern Ireland, to reflect the new title of the devolved legislative arrangements[10].

In May 1969, during the passage of the Bill establishing the Northern Ireland Parliamentary Ombudsmen, it was announced that a system would be established to deal with complaints against those public bodies which were outside the field of central government. In December that year, the Northern Ireland Commissioner for Complaints system came into operation. This office was to investigate such bodies as the Electricity Board, the Fire Authority, and the Hospital Board, as well as local authorities[11]. Northern Ireland was therefore the first country within the UK to have a local government ombudsman. As indicated above, both offices have been held by the same person since 1972, and the ombudsman is known as the Northern Ireland Ombudsman. The legislation establishing the two offices is similar[12] and the ombudsman's staff deal with complaints across the two jurisdictions. The ensuing discussion will therefore deal with the two offices together.

---

[9]   These were devolved under the Government of Ireland Act 1920. See generally G Drewry 'The Northern Ireland Parliamentary Ombudsman' in R Gregory and P Giddings (eds) *Righting Wrongs: The Ombudsman in Six Continents* (2000) IOS Press.

[10]   Ombudsman (NI) Order 1996, SI 1996/1298 (NI 8). There is provision for the title to revert to the Northern Ireland Parliamentary Ombudsman, if there were a return to direct rule.

[11]   See generally H J Elcock 'Opportunity for Ombudsman: the Northern Ireland Commissioner for Complaints' (1972) Public Administration 87–93.

[12]   There are some important differences, in relation to access and remedies, which will be discussed later.

The Schemes

The Northern Ireland Ombudsman deals with complaints from those who claim to have suffered injustice as a result of maladministration by government departments and public bodies in Northern Ireland. These bodies include all district councils, education and library boards, health and social services boards and trusts, as well as government departments and their agencies[13]. Like the other public sector ombudsmen in the UK, the Northern Ireland Ombudsman's remit is confined to maladministration. As in those systems, the concept of maladministration is not defined in the legislation, but it is clear that the ombudsman cannot question the merits of decisions taken without maladministration. Matters in connection with maladministration have been discussed in previous chapters, and it is not proposed to repeat them here. In the forthcoming review of the Northern Ireland Ombudsman, mentioned above, the issue of maladministration may be examined, in order to determine whether this is the appropriate remit, or whether, for example, the ombudsman should be able to look at a broader concept such as 'fairness'.

The ombudsman for both schemes is appointed by the Queen, on the recommendation of the First and Deputy First Ministers of the Assembly. As indicated above, the two posts are held by the same person, and it is publicly advertised, and is subject to a selection process. The ombudsman holds office during good behaviour, retires at 65, and can only be removed by the Assembly. The office is staffed by civil servants on secondment from various departments and their agencies. The ombudsman's salary is charged directly to the Consolidated Fund and the operational costs of the office are included in the Northern Ireland Estimates, which are approved by the Assembly[14].

Jurisdiction

The Assembly Ombudsman deals with government departments and their agencies, as well as the cross border bodies established after the Belfast

---

[13]   Bodies within jurisdiction are listed in the Commissioner for Complaints (Northern Ireland) Act 1969, Sch 1 and the Parliamentary Commissioner Act (NI) 1969, Sch 1.

[14]   The present office holder is Mr T Frawley. The number of staff in post at the end of March 2002 was 19. The budget for both offices for 2001–02 was £955,000.

Agreement[15]. The Commissioner for Complaints' jurisdiction includes the Northern Ireland Housing Executive, the Education and Library Boards, health and social services authorities and local councils[16]. The Commissioner for Complaints also deals with health service complaints, including those relating to professional judgment. The jurisdiction of the Northern Ireland Ombudsman is thus similar to the combined jurisdictions of the Parliamentary, Health[17] and Local Government Ombudsmen in England, except for reserved matters[18].

One area of activity not within the ombudsman's remit is housing associations. This is not unlike the situation in England, where the Local Government Ombudsmen do not have jurisdiction over housing associations[19]. However, unlike in England, there is no independent statutory ombudsman for such complaints[20]. This may become a serious omission in the future with the change in emphasis in the work of the Housing Executive in Northern Ireland. Rather than being a direct provider of housing, the Housing Executive is now becoming a funding body and policy maker. If housing associations are to be the major providers of social housing in Northern Ireland in the future, tenants of these bodies will need to be provided with an independent grievance mechanism. The forthcoming review will need to address this issue.

[15] See The Belfast Agreement: an agreement reached at the multi-party talks on Northern Ireland (Cm 3883, 1998). These new bodies, which include such matters as tourism and lighthouses, were established under the North/South Co-operation (Implementation Bodies) (NI) Order 1999, SI 1999/859. The Northern Ireland Ombudsman has joint jurisdiction over these bodies with the Ombudsman in the Republic of Ireland.

[16] Unlike mainland Britain, local councils in Northern Ireland do not deal with housing, education or social services. Planning matters are dealt with by the Assembly.

[17] The Commissioner for Complaints (Amendment Order) 1997 brought professional judgment for health service professionals within remit. Before this, the remit was confined to health authorities' administrative functions.

[18] The United Kingdom Parliamentary Ombudsman also deals with the administrative actions of the Northern Ireland Office, the court service and humans rights commission in Northern Ireland.

[19] In England, these were renamed 'social landlords' by the Housing Act 1966.

[20] In England there is an Independent Housing Ombudsman, established by the Housing Act 1996, who deals with complaints against social landlords. For a discussion of the Independent Housing Ombudsman and the jurisdiction of the Local Government Ombudsmen in relation to social housing, see M Seneviratne 'Ombudsmen and Social Housing' (2002) 24(3) JSWFL (forthcoming).

The jurisdiction of the Assembly Ombudsman is set out in the Parliamentary Commissioner Act (Northern Ireland) 1969. This was a replication of the Act setting up the Parliamentary Ombudsman at Westminster[21], but with the jurisdiction being restricted to the Northern Ireland Government at Stormont. It even included a member filter, with complaints having to be referred by members of the Northern Ireland Parliament. The legislation setting up the Commissioner for Complaints follows that of the Assembly Ombudsman, with some important differences. First, there is no member filter. Second, contractual and commercial matters are within jurisdiction. Finally, there is the possibility of court enforcement of the Commissioner for Complaints' report.

Unlike the public sector ombudsman schemes in mainland Britain, the Northern Ireland Ombudsman can investigate complaints about personnel matters. It has been suggested that employment matters are expressly included because one of the principal reasons for establishing the ombudsman was the prevention of discrimination in employment[22]. Jurisdiction over personnel matters was thus considered to be in response to the 'special sensitivity' that exists in Northern Ireland about religious discrimination[23]. Complaints about personnel issues are a significant part of the ombudsman's workload. For example, in 2001–02, 18% of the complaints to the Assembly Ombudsman concerned employment issues, and they accounted for 17% of the issued reports[24]. These complaints concerned unsuccessful applications for employment, failures to be invited for job interviews, failures to be shortlisted, handling of grievance procedures and the handling of promotion boards. None of them alleged discrimination on religious grounds.

Since the ombudsman's office was established there have been other developments in relation to discrimination in employment. There is now

---

[21]   The Parliamentary Commissioner Act 1967.

[22]   K P Poole 'The Northern Ireland Commissioner for Complaints' (1972) PL 131–148, p 147.

[23]   G Drewry 'The Northern Ireland Parliamentary Ombudsman' in R Gregory and P Giddings (eds) *Righting Wrongs: The Ombudsman in Six Continents* (2000) IOS Press p 290.

[24]   There were 46 such complaints out of a total of 250, and four reports out of a total of 23 (see, Northern Ireland Ombudsman Annual Report 2001–02 (NIA 89/01) pp 16, 22). There are no figures for the number of such complaints to the Commissioner for Complaints. However, there were 52 investigation reports in that year, 12 of which concerned employment matters (p 57).

Fair Employment legislation, and an Equality Commission, which cover employment practices in both the public and private sectors. Complainants can therefore have recourse to these other bodies rather than the ombudsman. It could be argued that public service staff are privileged over employees in the private sector, in having an extra body to deal with complaints about employment issues. It may well be that jurisdiction in this area has outlived the purpose for which it was created. Even if the ombudsman were to retain jurisdiction for potential employees, in terms of the appointment process, there is a case for excluding from remit personnel issues of those in employment. Their complaints could be dealt with through established industrial relations mechanisms.

As indicated above, the Commissioner for Complaints also has jurisdiction over the handling of local government contracts. This is unlike the other public sector ombudsmen in the UK, where contractual and commercial arrangements are specifically excluded. It is also unlike the Assembly Ombudsman, who has no jurisdiction over Assembly contracting arrangements. The ombudsman interprets this aspect of jurisdiction narrowly. If the complaint is about the operation of the contract itself, it is felt more appropriate that the matter be dealt with by the courts or by arbitration. Tendering however is seen as an administrative function, and complaints about this aspect of contracting will be investigated. The ombudsman does not investigate the 'merits' of tendering arrangements, which means that there will not be an examination of the terms of the award. There can however be an investigation into such matters as allegations that a late tender was accepted, or that information was not disclosed to a tenderer.

A recent case illustrates this aspect of jurisdiction, in which Belfast City Council was found guilty of maladministration in its handling of a tendering process[25]. The investigation revealed that there had been serious mishandling of the process, with the contract being awarded to the wrong tenderer. Moreover, the council had failed to meet its statutory obligation to publish the results of the tendering exercise, which had deprived tenderers of their right to be informed promptly of the outcome of the tendering process. The investigation revealed that, had the process been properly conducted, the complainant would have been awarded the contract. The ombudsman recommended that the council pay £50,000 to

[25]   Case No CC69/98.

the complainant, representing the assessed loss suffered by not being awarded the contract. The council also agreed to take steps to rectify the serious shortcomings in its tendering procedures, so that future tenders would be carried out in a manner that accorded with equity and accepted good practice[26].

As with the other public sector ombudsmen, the Northern Ireland Ombudsman will not accept complaints where the complainant has a right of appeal to a court or tribunal. The ombudsman has discretion in these cases to accept complaints for investigation where it would not be reasonable to expect the complainant to use these remedies, or where the remedy granted by the tribunal could reasonably be considered to be inadequate[27]. The ombudsman exercises this discretion in a similar way to the other public sector ombudsmen. As with the other UK ombudsmen, there is no provision for the ombudsman to investigate on his own initiative. While the advantage of having such a power is recognised, it is argued that it could result in the ombudsman being subject to undesirable pressure from the media and members in the Assembly to conduct investigations.

Remedies

The ombudsman has the usual range of remedies at his disposal. These include the requirement for verbal and written apologies, compensation payments, rectifying the action where possible and recommendations to improve procedures. Where monetary compensation is recommended, the aim is to try to put complainants back to the position they would have been in if nothing had gone wrong. They tend in general to be modest, the view being that if substantial awards are sought, the complainants should go to court for damages. However, there have been some large awards, particularly in the case of complaints about the awards of grants. In these cases, the ombudsman has awarded payments of many thousands of pounds, and even in one case £150,000. In 2001–02, in all 10 cases that were settled following a report by the Assembly Ombudsman, compensation was paid. Payments ranged from £2,000 to £300[28]. For the Commissioner for Complaints, all but two of the 16 settlements achieved in cases upheld

---

[26]   Northern Ireland Ombudsman Annual Report 2000–01 (NIA 83/00) p 117.
[27]   Commissioner for Complaints (Northern Ireland) Act 1969, s 5(3); Parliamentary Commissioner Act (Northern Ireland) Act 1969, s 5(2).
[28]   Northern Ireland Ombudsman Annual Report 2001–02 (NIA 89/01) p 22.

involved some monetary element. The amounts ranged from £84, to reimburse the cost of materials, to £5,000. This latter payment was a consolatory award for serious shortcomings in an appointment process[29].

The remedies awarded are similar across the two jurisdictions. However, the powers in relation to compliance are different. The recommendations of the Commissioner for Complaints, but not the Assembly Ombudsman, can be enforced in the county court. The Commissioner for Complaints Act (NI) 1969, s 7 allows the complainant to apply to the county court to have the ombudsman's report upheld and a suitable remedy given[30]. The court can award damages to compensate for any expense incurred in relation to the maladministration and for the loss of opportunity of acquiring a benefit as a result of the maladministration. The court can also issue injunctions. The complainant has six months from the issue of the report to make the application, and the ombudsman's report is accepted as evidence of the facts, 'unless the contrary is proved'[31]. Both the public body and the complainant have a right of appeal to the High Court from the county court decision.

It is not clear why court enforcement was seen as appropriate in the case of the Commissioner for Complaints, particularly as it runs counter to the accepted methods used by ombudsmen. Ombudsmen in the public sector worldwide make recommendations only, using informal methods to persuade public bodies to accept their recommendations. There are no indications in the Parliamentary debates on the legislation why this method of enforcement was seen to be appropriate. It is however suggested that the power was introduced to enable the office to be more effective in its remit of combating discrimination[32]. The power has seldom been used. Since the inception of the scheme, there have only been about 30 cases where there has been recourse to the county court, which represents about 6% of findings of maladministration.

---

[29] Northern Ireland Ombudsman Annual Report 2001–02 (NIA 89/01) p 57.

[30] The way the legislation is framed, the complainant can take the report to the county court for damages, even if the ombudsman does not recommend compensation. Moreover, the legislation does not say that the county court is to be used only where the public body refuses to accept the ombudsman's recommendation.

[31] Commissioner for Complaints Act (NI) 1969, s 7(8).

[32] C White 'Enforcing the Decisions of Ombudsmen – the Northern Ireland Local Government Ombudsman's Experience' (1994) 45(4) Northern Ireland Legal Quarterly 395–402, p 397.

The last time enforcement proceedings were taken was in the mid-eighties. The case involved a complaint against Craigavon Borough Council, which was found to have wrongly refused to lease land to the Gaelic Athletics Association, to allow it to develop sporting facilities[33]. The council refused to pay compensation to the Association, which had been recommended by the ombudsman. The complainants therefore sought enforcement in the county court, where damages of £107,763 were awarded. The council appealed to the High Court[34], which reduced the damages to £100,064, and made the stipulation that the club should make a payment to acquire the lease. The final twist to this story occurred when the Local Government Auditor surcharged the councillors involved in the decision[35]. Perhaps it is not surprising that there has been no necessity for county court enforcement since this case.

The ombudsman has another remedy not given to the other public sector ombudsmen. Where the ombudsman concludes that a public body is likely to continue in a course of bad administrative conduct which gives rise to injustice, he may ask the Attorney-General to apply to the High Court for mandatory injunction or other relief [36]. This power has never been used.

Court enforcement gives an edge to the work of the office, but it does raise the question of whether it is any longer necessary or appropriate. It was never extended to the work of the Assembly Ombudsman, and it will be interesting to see, when the offices are reviewed, which practice will be adopted for any integrated system that emerges.

Procedures and Powers

The Northern Ireland Ombudsman has the same range of powers as the other public sector ombudsmen in the UK to ensure that there can be full and thorough investigations of complaints. These include powers in relation to the taking of evidence, obstruction and contempt. There is

---

[33] Case No CC573/79.
[34] Such an appeal is allowed by virtue of the Commissioner for Complaints Act (NI) 1969, s 7(4). This is the only time it has been used.
[35] The councillors who were surcharged had acted against the administrative and legal advice of their chief officers. They were ineligible to sit as councillors for five years.
[36] Commissioner for Complaints Act (NI) 1969, s 7(5).

absolute privilege for the ombudsman's reports. Only the person aggrieved can make a complaint, this definition including an association. Complaints must be in writing, but the ombudsman has discretion to take incompletely formulated complaints. Unlike the legislation for the other public sector ombudsmen, the Commissioner for Complaints has a duty, explicit in the Act, to try to effect a settlement, in addition to the duty to report after an investigation[37].

The ombudsman does not publish individual investigation reports, but submits an annual report to the Assembly. The annual report is very detailed, giving statistical information about complaints for both offices. There is separate statistical information about health service matters. Although individual reports are not published, synopses of them are given in the annual reports. The ombudsman is also presently considering publishing quarterly abstracts of the investigation reports. There is provision for special reports to be made to the Assembly, but this is for Assembly Ombudsman matters only. Although the ombudsman does not publish investigation reports personally, complainants and public bodies are free to give what publicity they wish to the report.

The accountability mechanisms of the Northern Ireland Ombudsman are complicated by the fact that originally the Northern Ireland Parliamentary Ombudsman was seen as an adjunct to the Northern Ireland Parliament. When this ceased to exist, and there was direct rule, the office became accountable to the Westminster Parliament, through the select committee. There is no select committee in the Assembly to whom the ombudsman reports. The annual report is laid before the Assembly, and the Speaker receives it, and charges individual chairs of the various standing committees of the Assembly to take note of issues in their particular areas. These standing committees shadow the work of each department.

As indicated above, complaints about the Assembly are filtered through an Assembly member. The barrier this may present to access has been alleviated by the practice of accepting complaints directly, and referring them to appropriate members inviting them to sponsor. The Commissioner for Complaints had direct access from the inception of the office. Even with direct access, lack of knowledge about the office may be a barrier to access. In 2000–01, a survey revealed that only 45% of those surveyed

---

[37] Commissioner for Complaints Act (NI) 1969, s 7.

had heard of the ombudsman[38]. The ombudsman is trying to raise the visibility of the office. To this end, he and his staff give talks to the staff of public bodies and interested citizens. The ombudsman is particularly concerned to raise awareness with the 108 Assembly members who can sponsor complaints. As is the case with the other ombudsmen, the Northern Ireland Ombudsman has a website[39] in order to assist with publicity.

Working Methods

The ombudsman's working practices emphasise the settlement aspects of the role. The same procedure is followed whether the complaint relates to Assembly matters, health matters or local government matters. When a complaint is made, there is an initial sifting to see if it is within jurisdiction, both in terms of the matter complained about and the body against whom the complaint has been made. It is also checked to see if it has been raised with the body concerned, is within the statutory time limits, and has been referred by a member of the Assembly, where necessary. There must also be sufficient information supplied concerning the complaint.

Where these requirements are not met, a letter is sent to the complainant[40] explaining why the complaint cannot be dealt with. The letter may suggest an appropriate course of action, for example, what further details are required. If the matter is not one that can be dealt with by the ombudsman, there will be a suggestion as to the mechanism that can be used for the complaint. Where the complaint satisfies all the requirements, it progresses to the next stage of the procedure. The target for the issue of a reply to this initial stage is five working days. For the Assembly Ombudsman, the average time taken in 2001–02 was 1.2 weeks, for the Commissioner for Complaints it was 1.3 weeks and for health service complaints it was 1.4 weeks[41].

---

[38]   The ombudsman arranged for this public awareness survey, as part of the Northern Ireland Social Omnibus Survey (see Northern Ireland Ombudsman Annual Report 2000–01 (NIA 83/00) p 8).
[39]   The address is: www.ni-ombudsman.org.uk.
[40]   A letter is sent to the member of the Assembly where there has been a referral.
[41]   Northern Ireland Ombudsman Annual Report 2001–02 (NIA 89/01) pp 22, 57 and 105.

The next stage involves a preliminary investigation of the complaint, to ascertain whether there is any evidence of maladministration and, if so, how this has caused injustice. This involves informal telephone calls to the body concerned, and sometimes a written request for information. In the case of health service complaints, it may also be necessary to seek independent professional advice. Once all the information has been gathered, a decision is taken as to the appropriate course of action. There are three possible outcomes. Where there is no evidence of maladministration, the complainant will be informed that the complaint is not suitable for investigation, stating the reasons why. If there is evidence of maladministration, but it is found that this has not caused the complainant a substantive personal injustice, an investigation report will be issued, explaining why the case is not considered to warrant further investigation. This report may contain criticism of the body concerned. If there is evidence of maladministration which appears to have caused substantive personal injustice to the complainant, the ombudsman will commence an in-depth investigation. The target for this stage of the process is 13 weeks. The average time taken for this stage by the Assembly Ombudsman was 14.5 weeks, for the Commissioner for Complaints it was 13.6 weeks, and for health service complaints it was 16.1 weeks[42].

Not all cases that reach stage three of the process will result in a full, formal investigation. If, at the beginning of this stage, the maladministration and injustice can be readily identified, an early resolution to the complaint will be sought where appropriate. In these cases, the ombudsman writes to the chief officer of the body concerned, outlining the maladministration and suggesting a remedy. If this is accepted, the case is resolved. If not, a full formal investigation will be undertaken. A full investigation will also be conducted where the complaint is not considered suitable for early resolution. The full investigation is conducted by means of interviews with the complainant and relevant officials, as well as an examination of the relevant documents. In the case of health service complaints, professional advice may be obtained from independent clinical assessors[43].

---

[42] Northern Ireland Ombudsman Annual Report 2001–02 (NIA 89/01) pp 22, 57 and 105.

[43] In clinical judgment cases, the ombudsman seeks to establish if the actions complained of are based on a reasonable and responsible exercise of clinical judgment. There is also a need to establish whether the standard of care was what a patient should reasonably expect to receive.

When the investigation is concluded, the ombudsman prepares a draft report, containing the facts of the case and the likely findings. The case will then be reviewed with the complainant, and the body concerned will be given an opportunity to comment on the accuracy of the facts, the likely findings and the redress, if any, that the ombudsman proposes to recommend. After comments on the draft have been received, the final report is issued. This is sent to the complainant, the member of the Assembly, where appropriate, and to the body concerned. The target is to complete cases involving a full investigation within 12 months of receiving the complaint.

Complaints Statistics

With a population of 1.6 million people, the Northern Ireland Ombudsman operates on a much smaller scale than in mainland Britain. In the first year of the office, 33 complaints were received. Over the last five years they have averaged over 600 a year in the combined offices, although, unlike other ombudsmen systems, in the four years before 2001–02, the numbers showed an annual decrease[44]. During 2001–02, the ombudsman's office dealt with 2,379 telephone calls, and there were 84 personal callers[45]. There were also 660 complaints received, made up as follows: 250 (38%) for the Assembly Ombudsman; 107 (16%) about health and social services; 303 (46%) for other Commissioner for Complaints matters.

In 2001–02, the Assembly Ombudsman received 250 written complaints, relating to government departments and their agencies, 176 of which related to agencies. Even though these have to be sponsored by a member of the Legislative Assembly[46], the majority (143) were submitted directly. The Department of the Environment attracted the most complaints[47]. The majority of these[48] related to planning matters, this being a departmental function in Northern Ireland. The types of issues raised are not unlike those dealt with by the English Local Government Ombudsmen in planning areas. They concern grievances about the granting of planning permission from

---

[44]   Northern Ireland Ombudsman *Facing the Future* at p 5.
[45]   Northern Ireland Ombudsman Annual Report 2001–02 (NIA 89/01) p 10.
[46]   Ombudsman (Northern Ireland) Order 1996, SI 1996/1298 (NI 8).
[47]   There was a total of 83 complaints.
[48]   There were 74 complaints about planning matters.

neighbours concerned about the effects of it on their property. There were also complaints about failures to proceed with enforcement actions and the handling of objections to planning applications. The Department for Social Development had 56 complaints, 41 of which related to benefits. As with the United Kingdom Parliamentary Ombudsman, many of these relate to the Child Support Agency, and concern mishandling of applications for child maintenance support. Other complaints concerned benefit problems about the mishandling of claims for incapacity benefit, and delays in processing appeals. During 2001–02, 109 cases were cleared at the initial sift and 91 were cleared without an in-depth investigation. Six cases were settled, and a full report was issued in 23 cases. Of the issued reports, six concerned planning complaints and four concerned benefits matters. Altogether, 10 cases were fully upheld and four were partially upheld.

As Northern Ireland Commissioner for Complaints, the ombudsman received 303 complaints in 2001–02[49]. As in previous years, it was the Northern Ireland Housing Executive that attracted the most complaints[50]. These mainly concerned repairs, allocations and grants. Investigation reports were issued for 52 cases and 18 cases were settled without a report. Of the 52 investigation reports issued, 32 concerned housing and 12 were about personnel matters. Altogether, 16 cases were fully upheld, and settlements were achieved in all of these. The types of issues addressed in complaints about education included the processing of maintenance applications, school transport, and statements of special educational needs. Personnel complaints raised issues about unsuccessful job applications, failures to be short-listed or re-graded and irregularities in disciplinary proceedings. The reports on housing complaints reveal a variety of matters including refusals of grants for disabled facilities and delays in the process. There were also complaints about renovation grants, procedures for dealing with noise nuisance, delays in being re-housed and tenancy successions.

Health service complaints are part of the Commissioner for Complaints' functions. However, there is a separate section in the annual report dealing with health and social services complaints. In 2001–02, there were 107 such complaints, the largest service group complained about being hospital medical and dental staff, followed by social work staff and general

---

[49]   Northern Ireland Ombudsman Annual Report 2001–02 (NIA 89/01) p 52.
[50]   There were 125 of these, representing 41% of all complaints.

practitioners[51]. The cases investigated covered similar issues to those investigated by the Health Service Ombudsman in England. For example, they were concerned with aspects of diagnosis, treatment and care, rejections of applications for independent reviews, removals from doctor's lists, and complaints handling. Altogether, 45 of these cases were resolved without detailed investigation and two cases were settled. There were 39 cases which were referred to the body concerned to deal with under the Health Service Complaints Procedure. There were 52 cases accepted for investigation, and six full reports were issued. In two of these cases, the complaints were fully upheld, and the recommended awards were an apology for one and an apology together with a consolatory payment of £1,000 for the other.

Conclusion

The offices which comprise the Northern Ireland Ombudsman, although legally two offices, effectively operate as an integrated service. As such, it deals with the entire range of services provided by local and regional government, including the health service, in Northern Ireland[52]. The remit and powers of the office are similar to those of the other public sector ombudsmen in the UK, and it thus scores highly in terms of impartiality, independence and accountability. Access for part of the work is filtered through Assembly members, but this requirement does not appear to have caused many problems for complainants. Barriers to access because of lack of visibility of the office is of concern, in the same way that it concerns ombudsmen on the mainland.

Features of the system which tend to attract comment are in relation to the extended jurisdiction for employment and contractual complaints, matters that are expressly excluded from the jurisdiction of the ombudsmen elsewhere in the UK. In relation to the former, there are arguments for its removal from remit, given the other legislative provisions about discrimination in employment. The latter has been restricted to complaints

---

[51]   The numbers were 31, 26 and 13 respectively (see Northern Ireland Ombudsman Annual Report 2001–02 (NIA 89/01) p 103).

[52]   As previously noted, the United Kingdom Parliamentary Ombudsman deals with complaints about matters reserved for the Westminster Parliament.

about the tendering process, arguably administrative functions which the Local Government Ombudsmen in England have sometimes investigated. Another area of interest is the power of enforcement through the county court. This model of enforcement is occasionally seen to provide the solution for recalcitrant local authorities in England, which refuse to follow the Local Government Ombudsman's recommendations. The existence of this power does not appear to have caused the Northern Ireland Ombudsman many problems, but as it has not been used for nearly 20 years, it is difficult to assess its advantages and disadvantages.

An interesting feature of the office is that, although established largely to deal with political and religious discrimination, the cases investigated are not in the main concerned with these aspects of service provision. They tend to be concerned with the normal mistakes and incompetence in any administrative system. Another important feature of the Northern Ireland Ombudsman is the fact that it operates as an integrated service. It has not therefore suffered the problems in relation to jurisdictional issues that have beset the ombudsmen in England. Any future review should regularise this position, as there can be no justification for two separate local and regional ombudsman systems within such a small jurisdiction.

Scotland

The ombudsman system in Scotland is undergoing a fundamental transformation, a process precipitated by devolution. Before devolution, Scotland had three separate ombudsmen systems, a situation like that in England and Wales. Complaints relating to local government were dealt with by the Commissioner for Local Administration in Scotland[53]. Complaints about central government, including the Scottish Office, were within the province of the Parliamentary Commissioner for Administration. A separate ombudsman for health service complaints was also established for Scotland[54]. In fact, this latter role was filled by the Parliamentary Ombudsman, who was also Health Service Ombudsman for England and Wales.

[53] This was established by the Local Government (Scotland) Act 1975, Pt II.
[54] National Health Service (Scotland) Act 1972.

Devolution

As a result of devolution, complaints about devolved matters are now a matter for the Scottish Parliament, which is required to make provision for the investigation of complaints about maladministration in relation to these matters[55]. When responsibilities were transferred to the new Scottish Parliament and Executive on 1 July 1999, transitional arrangements provided for the creation of a new office of Scottish Parliamentary Commissioner for Administration. The function of this ombudsman was to deal with complaints about devolved matters in Scotland, which were previously within the jurisdiction of the Parliamentary Commissioner for Administration. The post was held by the present United Kingdom Parliamentary Ombudsman, who reported to the Scottish Parliament. The Health Service Ombudsman for Scotland continued as before, except that the reporting arrangements were changed, so that the report was made to the Scottish Parliament. The United Kingdom Parliamentary Ombudsman is still responsible for complaints about 'reserved' matters, those matters which have not been devolved to the Scottish Parliament. These include national taxation and social security matters. The jurisdiction of the Local Government Ombudsman in Scotland was unchanged as a result of devolution.

The Scotland Act 1998 made specific requirements of the Scottish Parliament to provide for complaints of maladministration in relation to the actions of the executive and administration. In order to fulfil this obligation, the Scottish Executive began a consultation exercise in October 2000, with a view to proposing the necessary legislation[56]. In addition to these specific requirements, there is a more general power enabling the Scottish Parliament to make provision for investigating complaints about action by the administration and other authorities acting in the devolved areas. The Scottish Executive therefore decided not to focus on the arrangements for

---

[55]   Scotland Act 1998, s 91. Transitional arrangements were made (Scotland Act (Transitory and Transitional Provision) (Complaints of Maladministration) Order 1999, SI 1999/1351) for the investigation of such complaints until the Scottish Parliament made the necessary provisions.

[56]   *Modernising the Complaints System* (2000). The consultation document was distributed widely to around 800 organisations and individuals, and elicited 86 responses. Questionnaires were also sent by the Scottish Parliamentary, Health Service and Local Government Ombudsmen, on behalf of the Executive, to 650 recent complainants, asking for information and comments on the outcome and handling of complaints. Altogether, 220 completed questionnaires were returned.

the Scottish Executive in isolation. Instead, the consultation exercise was expanded to consider the arrangements for other public services in Scotland, particularly the Health Service Ombudsman and the Local Government Ombudsman[57]. Another consultation document was issued in July 2001, incorporating the responses to the earlier consultation and setting out the Executive's proposals[58]. These proposals formed the basis for the Bill, which was introduced in the 2001–02 session of the Scottish Parliament. The Scottish Public Services Ombudsman Act 2002 was passed in April, and its implementation is now taking place. In June 2002, the Scottish Parliament approved the nomination of the new ombudsman and three deputy ombudsmen[59]. This recommendation will now go to the Queen for formal appointment.

Before examining the new system in Scotland, a brief summary of the system it replaces will be given.

The Post-devolution System

As indicated above, the system after devolution consisted of three separate schemes, plus the addition of the new Scottish Parliamentary Ombudsman, who dealt with complaints about devolved matters. The United Kingdom Parliamentary Ombudsman's jurisdiction still extends to Scotland in relation to reserved matters. The Scottish Parliamentary Ombudsman, under the transitional arrangements[60], was appointed by the Queen, and had power

---

[57]   *Modernising the Complaints System* proposed integrating the present ombudsmen into one system, because it was felt that a one-stop shop would provide a simpler and more effective means for members of the public to make complaints. Other proposals within the document suggested ways of making it easier to complain to the new ombudsman, and publicising the functions of the office. There were also proposals for reinforcing the ombudsman's independence from the authorities subject to investigation and making his or her activities more transparent.

[58]   *A Modern Complaints System: Consultation on Proposals for Public Sector Ombudsmen in Scotland* (2001). For a discussion of this document see M Seneviratne '"Joining up" the Scottish Ombudsmen' (2002) 24(1) JSWFL 89–98; J McFadden 'The Public Sector Ombudsman System in Scotland' (2001) Scottish Constitutional and Administrative Law and Practice 16–20.

[59]   On 27 June, the Scottish Parliament approved the nomination of Professor Alice Brown as the Scottish Public Services Ombudsman. It also agreed the nomination of three Deputy Ombudsmen: Eric Drake, Carolyn Hirst and the Reverend Lewis Shand Smith. They are expected to take up their posts in the near future.

[60]   Scotland Act 1998 (Transitory and Transitional Provisions) (Complaints of Maladministration) Order 1999, SI 1999/1351 (the 'Order').

to investigate complaints of alleged maladministration causing injustice, in the same way that the United Kingdom Parliamentary Ombudsman has. The Scottish Parliamentary Ombudsman could investigate the administrative actions of members of the Scottish Executive, any other office holder in the Scottish Administration, and a number of Scottish and cross-border public authorities[61]. Complaints had to be referred by a member of the Scottish Parliament.

The procedure adopted by the Scottish Parliamentary Ombudsman was similar to that adopted by the United Kingdom Parliamentary Ombudsman. Once a complaint was appropriately referred, it was checked to see if it was within jurisdiction. It had to involve administrative actions, and those actions had to cause injustice to the complainant. The ombudsman also needed to be convinced that an investigation would be likely to achieve a remedy or other worthwhile outcome for the complainant. If these conditions were satisfied, the ombudsman would try to seek a resolution for the complaint, which might or might not involve a formal investigation. The investigation might consist of enquiries of the body complained about, and an informal resolution of the matter. The more complex or obdurate cases may have required formal investigation. Redress consisted of apologies, explanations, rectifying the problem, or financial compensation. The main difference in approach of the Scottish Parliamentary Ombudsman was that he has been more ready to embark on formal investigations of complaints[62].

In 2001–02, the Scottish Parliamentary Ombudsman received 67 new complaints, compared to 60 in the previous year. There were 79 cases concluded during the year, of which 11 were formal investigation reports. Altogether, 68 cases were concluded without a formal investigation, 30% of which were resolved by enquiries of the body concerned. In 32% of the cases not accepted for formal investigation, there was no prima facie evidence of maladministration[63]. As in the previous year, most complaints concerned the Scottish Executive Environment and Rural Affairs Department[64]. Many of these complaints related to agricultural subsidies and there were also complaints arising from the outbreak of foot and mouth

---

[61]   These are listed in the schedules to the 'Order'.
[62]   See Scottish Parliamentary Ombudsman Annual Report 1999–2000 para 2.2.
[63]   Scottish Parliamentary Ombudsman and Health Service Ombudsman for Scotland Annual Report 2001–02 (SP Paper 595 (Session 1 2002)) p 7.
[64]   There were 14 new cases opened, and 7 remaining from the previous year.

disease in 2001. The next largest category of complaint concerned the Scottish Legal Aid Board[65]. Altogether, 92% of cases that were clearly out of jurisdiction were decided within two weeks. Of those cases not clearly out of jurisdiction, 60% were resolved or a statement of complaint was issued within six weeks. The average investigation time was 70 weeks[66].

Scotland always had a separate Health Service Ombudsman, although the office had always been held by the person who was also Health Service Ombudsman for England and Wales. After devolution, the jurisdiction, remit and working practices remained the same. The only difference was that the Scottish Health Service Ombudsman reported to the Scottish Parliament[67]. In 2001–02, the Health Service Ombudsman for Scotland received 225 complaints against National Health Service bodies and practitioners in Scotland. Of these, 27 were accepted for formal investigation, and of the 25 investigation reports issued, 76% related to complaints about clinical matters[68]. The methods of working are similar to those adopted by the Health Service Ombudsman for England. The complaints received reveal the same kinds of issues as in England.

The Local Government Ombudsman system in Scotland came into existence on 1 January 1976[69]. The reasons for its establishment were the same as those advanced for the introduction of Local Government Ombudsmen in England[70]. It had much in common with the English scheme, with similar jurisdiction, remit, procedures and powers. As in England, there was no

---

[65]   There were eight complaints.
[66]   Scottish Parliamentary Ombudsman and Health Service Ombudsman for Scotland Annual Report 2001–02 (SP Paper 595 (Session 1 2002)) pp 8–11.
[67]   Before devolution, the Health Service Ombudsman published one annual report, which dealt with England, Wales and Scotland. Since 1999–2000, separate annual reports are prepared for each jurisdiction.
[68]   Scottish Parliamentary Ombudsman and Health Service Ombudsman for Scotland Annual Report 2001–02 (SP Paper 595 (Session 1 2002)) p 2.
[69]   It was established by the Local Government (Scotland) Act 1975, Pt II. This was subsequently amended by the Local Government (Miscellaneous Provisions) (Scotland) Acts 1981 and 1985.
[70]   See Justice *The Citizen and his Council: Ombudsmen for Local Government?* (1969) Stevens. When Justice examined whether the ombudsman concept should be extended to local government, it only considered England and Wales. However, it noted that there was 'no reason why' there should not be a similar local government ombudsman scheme in Scotland (at para 34). See J G Logie and P Q Watchman *The Local Ombudsman* (1990) T & T Clark pp 13–15, and generally for an evaluation of the Local Government Ombudsman in Scotland.

longer a member filter on complaints[71]. Not surprisingly, given the size of the population in Scotland, it was a much smaller office than in England, with one ombudsman, who was employed on a part-time basis[72], assisted by full-time staff. It also received a much smaller number of complaints[73].

As in England, the legislation under which the Local Government Ombudsman operated emphasised investigation and report. The holders of the post in Scotland have consistently indicated that this approach to complaint-handling was too elaborate, and they always encouraged local resolution of complaints where possible[74]. This led to a decline in the numbers of cases formally investigated. In 2000–01, there were only nine formal investigations, the lowest since the office was established. On the other hand, there was a significant increase in the number of local settlements, which reached 210 in that year[75]. Although all ombudsmen will try to achieve local settlements, and will try to achieve co-operation with the bodies they are investigating, negotiation and co-operation seemed to be a particular feature of the Scottish Local Government Ombudsman's office. Local authorities very rarely refused to accept the ombudsman's recommendations, and in the last eight years, there was only one further report issued[76].

The ombudsman dealt with similar types of cases and complaints as the Local Government Ombudsmen in England. Complaints about revenues, particularly the administration of benefits, were common, as were planning complaints, where councils were often caught between developers and affected neighbours. Complaints about education and social work also featured significantly. As indicated above, the emphasis was on settlement, and the ombudsman only used the statutory power to conduct formal investigations where the issues were complex or where the initial

[71]   This was abolished in 1988.
[72]   The part-time nature of the post was flexible, averaging around two and a half days each week. The ombudsman was assisted by a full-time deputy. The last deputy has recently retired, and was not replaced, in view of the imminent changes to the entire public sector ombudsman system in Scotland.
[73]   The total number of complaints received by the office each year was around 900. In 2000–01 it was 964; in 1999–2000 it was 961; in 1998–99, it was 934. Only a very small number of these were accepted for full investigation: 9 in 2000–01; 17 in 1999–2000; 11 in 1998–99.
[74]   See Local Government Ombudsman for Scotland Annual Report 2000–01 pp 5–7.
[75]   Local Government Ombudsman for Scotland Annual Report 2000–01 p 8.
[76]   Local Government Ombudsman for Scotland Annual Report 2000–01 p 6.

action had only revealed a limited picture of the events. Formal investigations were conducted where there were public policy considerations or where it was felt that the whole of local government might benefit from the investigation of an issue.

Since devolution, then, there were four separate ombudsman systems operating in Scotland. The possibilities for overlap and confusion were clearly apparent. Moreover, the existing legislation, with its emphasis on investigation and report, had restricted the ability of the various ombudsmen to achieve negotiated informal solutions where appropriate. It is therefore not surprising that the Scottish Executive decided to introduce a completely new system. The proposals for the new system will now be examined.

A New Integrated System

The new system will provide an integrated service, combining the offices of the Scottish Parliamentary Ombudsman, the Health Service Ombudsman for Scotland, the Local Government Ombudsman and the Housing Association Ombudsman for Scotland. The Scottish Public Services Ombudsman Act 2002 provides for the appointment of one ombudsman[77], to be known as the Scottish Public Services Ombudsman, who is appointed by the Queen on the nomination of the Scottish Parliament[78]. There is provision for the appointment of up to three deputy ombudsmen at any one time, who are appointed in the same way. Unlike the previous system, the ombudsman and deputies are fixed-term appointments, with the possibility of renewal, and they may be full- or part-time[79]. The office is

---

[77] A collegiate model, like that proposed for England, was never a sustainable option for a country of five million people.

[78] Scottish Public Services Ombudsman Act 2002, s 1. The formal title of 'ombudsman' was chosen in preference to 'commissioner', as it was felt that 'ombudsman' was the most widely understood and used name throughout the world for the office envisaged. As indicated above, recommendations for appointments have now been made.

[79] Schedule 1 of the Act provides that these offices are for a period of up to five years, to be determined by the Parliamentary corporation. They can be re-appointed for a second term, but re-appointment for a third term will only be possible if 'by reason of special circumstances, such reappointment is desirable in the public interest' (Scottish Public Services Ombudsman Act 2002, Sch 1, para 4(2)).

financed by the Scottish Parliament, which will pay all expenses and the salaries and allowances of the ombudsman, deputies and staff[80].

It is not difficult to see the reasons for deciding upon an integrated service. Anticipated advantages include simpler procedures and greater accessibility for complainants. One office is likely to achieve a higher profile, and there will be associated benefits in terms of efficiency and effectiveness. The consultation documents did discuss two possible models for the new office: a college system[81] or a system involving one ombudsman supported by deputies. The college model was rejected on the basis that it would not result in simpler procedures, greater efficiency or effectiveness. The Act is not prescriptive in relation to the appointment of deputies, except in relation to the maximum number. This leaves scope for the office to be divided in whatever ways are appropriate, depending on variations in workload and business priorities at any given time. It may be that deputies will specialise in particular types of complaints, or particular regions[82].

Jurisdiction

The bodies subject to investigation are specified in Pts 1 and 2 of Sch 2 of the Act[83]. Part 1 includes the Scottish Parliament and Scottish Administrations, health service bodies and individuals providing health

---

[80]   The levy that is now paid by local authorities to fund the Local Government Ombudsman will be discontinued, and there will be an equivalent reduction in the revenue support grant to take account of this.

[81]   In a college model, there are separate ombudsman appointments, with the ombudsmen sharing the same premises, support staff and other resources. They are responsible for their own sphere of activity.

[82]   The appointment of deputies will enable the office to preserve and develop specialised expertise. For example, a deputy may be responsible for local government complaints. The consultation document did envisage that the initial allocation of responsibilities to the deputies would be in accordance with the following three functions: the Scottish Parliament (with the addition of the External Complaints Adjudicators for Scottish Enterprise and Highlands and Islands Enterprise); health (with the addition of the complaint-handling functions of the Mental Welfare Commission); and local government (with the addition of the Housing Association Ombudsman for Scotland). There is, of course, no need for the new body to be bound by this suggestion, nor for the initial allocations to remain for any fixed period of time.

[83]   Scottish Public Services Ombudsman Act 2002, s 3.

services, local government bodies[84], and registered social landlords.[85] The list of bodies and individuals in Pt 1 cannot be amended by Order in Council, and thus will need primary legislation for any changes. Part 2 of the schedule contains a list of over 70 Scottish public authorities and cross-border public authorities, including, for example, the Parole Board for Scotland, Scottish Enterprise and the National Consumer Council. This list can be amended by Order in Council, so that entries can be modified or removed. Additions can be made to it, provided the bodies proposed to be added are public bodies, or are exercising functions of a public nature[86].

These provisions ensure that the combined scheme will cover the entire remit of the three existing schemes[87]. The consultation document noted that it was important that the bodies subject to the new ombudsman's jurisdiction were clearly identifiable, and that therefore how they were specified in the legislation was crucial. There is no automatic presumption that a public authority is within jurisdiction, and thus bodies are only within jurisdiction if specifically listed[88]. The reason for this approach is to avoid any doubt or confusion about jurisdiction. The provision for amendment to one of the lists by subordinate legislation should allow a relatively easy way to add new bodies, as necessary.

As well as ensuring that the entire remits of the existing schemes are covered, the new ombudsman service has some significant additions to its jurisdiction. First, registered social landlords are within jurisdiction. This is an interesting addition as these bodies do not strictly operate in the public sector, and are not established by statute. They are presently within the jurisdiction of the Housing Association Ombudsman, whose remit is thus integrated into the new ombudsman scheme. The reason for their

---

[84]   This includes local authorities and also joint boards, and National Park authorities.

[85]   These were formerly known as housing associations. The reasons for their inclusion in the new scheme is discussed below.

[86]   The list in Part 1 thus consists of those bodies that can be described generically. Bodies listed in Part 2 are more difficult to describe generically, and are therefore individually listed.

[87]   There are some additions, which are discussed below.

[88]   One of the options discussed in the consultation document was that the legislation would specify those bodies that are not within jurisdiction, rather than listing the authorities that are. This would create an assumption that public bodies were within jurisdiction, unless specifically excluded. An advantage of this approach is that it would remove the need for regular amendments to the legislation as authorities are created and dissolved.

inclusion within the new scheme is that social landlords share many of the same characteristics as public sector landlords. In addition, the issues which concern housing association tenants are very similar to those which concern public sector tenants. There are also plans in Scotland to establish New Housing Partnerships, which may result in local authority tenants becoming tenants of social landlords. It was therefore felt appropriate that the new scheme should cover this increasingly large area of social housing, rather than have a separate ombudsman system for this area.

Another addition in the new system is the complaint handling function of the Mental Welfare Commission[89]. This body had jurisdiction in connection with the investigation of complaints concerning mental health cases. There had been a recommendation that such complaints should be within the remit of the Health Service Ombudsman[90], a recommendation that was accepted by the Scottish Executive. It was therefore logical that the Mental Welfare Commission's function of investigating the handling of complaints relating to mental health should transfer to the new Public Services Ombudsman, along with the other responsibilities of the Health Service Ombudsman[91]. Scottish Enterprise and the Highlands and Islands

---

[89] It is estimated that this will result in a 50% increase in the number of complaints normally received by the Health Service Ombudsman. In addition, the Scottish Executive Health Department is considering changes to the NHS complaints procedure in Scotland. One option proposed is to remove the existing second stage of the procedure. If local settlement does not achieve satisfaction, complainants would go directly to the ombudsman. This again would considerably increase the workload (see Scottish Parliamentary Ombudsman and Health Service Ombudsman for Scotland Annual Report 2001–02 (SP Paper 595 (Session 1 2002)) p 4).

[90] This was a recommendation from the Millan Committee, which reported in January 2001 (*New Direction – Report on the Review of the Mental Health (Scotland) Act 1984*). That Committee examined the role and powers of the Mental Welfare Commission, and considered the relationship between it and the Health Service Ombudsman. It recommended that the investigation of the handling of complaints by National Health Service bodies under the National Health Service complaints procedure concerning people with mental disorders should be the responsibility of the Health Service Ombudsman. It also recommended that where the Health Service Ombudsman or the Local Government Ombudsman deal with complaints, which include issues concerning the provision of care for a person with a mental disorder, there should be a requirement to consult with the Mental Welfare Commission. The Commission should then offer such advice and support as it deems appropriate.

[91] The new ombudsman will be required to consult the Mental Welfare Commission in dealing with such complaints.

Enterprise are also within jurisdiction, even though they were not covered by the existing schemes[92].

A number of bodies are not within jurisdiction. These include, for example, nationalised industries, on the grounds that they are commercial organisations, with their own internal complaints procedures and which, furthermore, are subject to company law. Advisory non-departmental public bodies are not within jurisdiction, as their role is solely to provide advice to ministers and does not involve providing a service to the public. Water authorities, which are subject to investigation by the Water Industry Commissioner, are not within jurisdiction. Similarly the Scottish Agricultural and Biological Research Institutes are not listed in the bodies subject to investigation on the grounds that they were established as limited companies and do not provide a service directly to the public. Those authorities which deal only with matters reserved to Westminster fall within the jurisdiction of the United Kingdom Parliamentary Ombudsman, and are therefore not within the ambit of the new scheme.

At present, the Scottish Parliamentary Ombudsman and the Health Service Ombudsman have functions in relation to investigating complaints about access to information. This role will be discontinued under the new system, becoming instead part of the functions of the new Scottish Information Commissioner.

Exclusions from Jurisdiction

The new ombudsman is responsible primarily for the investigation of complaints of injustice resulting from maladministration and failures of service[93]. Once again, maladministration is not defined in the legislation, although the consultation document did suggest that the ombudsman might produce guidance on matters which are covered by the term. This guidance could form part of the publicity material produced by the ombudsman. The ombudsman cannot question the merits of decisions taken without maladministration[94]. The consultation document made it clear that

---

[92] These bodies had external adjudicators for dealing with complaints. These complaints bodies will now be wound up.

[93] The ombudsman will also be dealing with the additional matters that are currently investigated by the specialist ombudsmen.

[94] Scottish Public Services Ombudsman Act 2002, s 7(1). This provision does not apply to cases of clinical judgment (se s 7(2)).

it would not be constitutionally appropriate for an appointed official to question decisions of elected representatives.

Schedule 4 of the Act lists a number of matters that the ombudsman cannot investigate. These include actions taken by the Scottish Executive or police authorities in connection with the investigation or prevention of crime or for security matters[95]. The commencement or conduct of court proceedings are also excluded, although administrative matters in relation to courts and tribunals can be investigated. The new ombudsman has no role to play in relation to staff appointments or other personnel matters, as these are specifically excluded[96]. Similarly, the exclusion in relation to contractual and commercial transactions follows the existing legislation[97].

The new ombudsman has jurisdiction to investigate complaints about maladministration in the internal organisation or management of schools under local authority control. This is entirely appropriate, as the internal organisation of schools involves significant administrative activity, with scope for maladministration leading to injustice. Of course, the ombudsman will not be able to question professional judgments about education. Although the ombudsman will not be able to investigate action concerning the giving of instruction and conduct, curriculum and discipline in schools, administrative matters within schools will be matters for investigation. This is a significant extension of jurisdiction.

Procedures and Powers

It was recognised in the review of the existing system by the Scottish Executive[98] that integrating existing ombudsman systems could be problematic if it resulted in any reduction in the remit and powers of the individual schemes. All the existing schemes were empowered to investigate allegations of maladministration causing injustice, but some of the existing ombudsmen had additional powers. For example, the Health Service Ombudsman has the power to investigate concerns about poor

---

[95]   Scottish Public Services Ombudsman Act 2002, Sch 4, para 1.
[96]   Scottish Public Services Ombudsman Act 2002, Sch 4, para 7.
[97]   Scottish Public Services Ombudsman Act 2002, Sch 4, para 6. There is specific reference in the paragraph to health service contracts, which are not excluded.
[98]   A Modern Complaints System: Consultation on Proposals for Public Sector Ombudsmen in Scotland (2001).

service by a health service body. There can also be an investigation into the failure of a health service body to purchase or provide a service that it was their function to provide. The care and treatment provided by a doctor, nurse or other trained professional can be investigated, as can general practitioners, and dentists, pharmacists or opticians providing a National Health Service locally. There was a commitment therefore that the existing powers would be retained in any new system.

The new system extends jurisdiction by not restricting the new Public Services Ombudsman to maladministration. The ombudsman can now investigate actions in the exercise of administrative functions, and any service failure[99]. This is defined as meaning 'any failure in a service provided by the authority' and 'any failure of the authority to provide a service which it was a function of the authority to provide'[100]. However, as was noted in earlier chapters, the concept of maladministration has proved to be remarkably flexible, and it is possible that service failures provide evidence of maladministration. Nevertheless, it is interesting to see this area of service delivery being expressly included within the new ombudsman's remit. There is still power to investigate clinical matters in relation to the health service. There is also power to investigate any action taken by or on behalf of a social landlord[101].

The new Act specifically provides for the ombudsman to deal with complaints in the most appropriate matter. The emphasis is no longer on investigation and report. The ombudsman can 'take such action' as may be necessary in reaching a decision, and the action may 'in particular, include action with a view to resolving' matters[102]. This recognises the important function of seeking informal or local solutions to problems, instead of carrying out full investigations.

Existing access arrangements are extended, so that complaints to the new ombudsman can be made directly, without the necessity for referral by a

---

[99]   Scottish Public Services Ombudsman Act 2002, s 5(1). The reference to service failure does not apply to family health service providers, or registered social landlords.

[100]   Scottish Public Services Ombudsman Act 2002, s 5(1A).

[101]   The Housing Association Ombudsman for Scotland scheme had the power to investigate complaints against landlords relating to matters other than injustice caused by maladministraton, if satisfied that it is in the public interest to do so. This latter provision ensures that this useful power is retained.

[102]   Scottish Public Services Ombudsman Act 2002, s 2(4) and s 2(5).

member of the Scottish Executive. Complaints can be made by the 'person aggrieved', or a person 'authorised in writing' to act for the person aggrieved[103]. Members of the Scottish Parliament can still refer complaints, if authorised by complainants to do so. There is also provision for complaints to be made by personal representatives, where the aggrieved person has died or is unable for any reason to act for him or herself [104]. It is still normally necessary to make complaints in writing[105]. However, the ombudsman is given discretion to accept oral complaints in special circumstances[106].

Complaints have to be made within 12 months of the time when the matter complained about first came to the attention of the aggrieved person, but there is discretion to accept beyond this time if appropriate[107]. Complaints can be made about retired health service providers within three years of their retirement[108]. The new ombudsman has the same powers in relation to gathering evidence as the existing ombudsmen, and the same provisions as to confidentiality. The investigation must be conducted in private, and the ombudsman must give those subject to complaint an opportunity to comment on the allegations[109]. In other respects however it is for the ombudsman to establish appropriate procedures for investigating complaints[110].

The primary focus of the new scheme continues to be the investigation of individual complaints. There is no provision for the ombudsman to initiate investigations, as it is felt that this could be a distraction from this role. There was also a feeling that to allow such investigations may trespass on

---

[103] Scottish Public Services Ombudsman Act 2002, s 9(1).
[104] Scottish Public Services Ombudsman Act 2002, s 9(3).
[105] They can also be made electronically (Scottish Public Services Ombudsman Act 2002, s 10(3)).
[106] Scottish Public Services Ombudsman Act 2002, s 10(3). This may include, for example, where a complainant has problems with reading and writing, or where there is exceptional urgency. In practice, it would be expected that the ombudsman's staff would write out the terms of the complaint on behalf of the aggrieved person and then ensure that this was agreed before any further action were taken.
[107] Scottish Public Services Ombudsman Act 2002, s 10(1).
[108] Scottish Public Services Ombudsman Act 2002, s 10(2). The Health Service Commissioners (Amendment) Act 2000 makes a similar provision for England and Wales.
[109] Scottish Public Services Ombudsman Act 2002, s 12(1) and s 12(2).
[110] Scottish Public Services Ombudsman Act 2002, s 12(3).

internal audit arrangements. Authorities may make complaints to the ombudsman, provided they are authorised in writing to do so by a person aggrieved[111].

In accordance with standard practice, there is no power to enforce the recommendations of the ombudsman or to impose sanctions. The decisions of the ombudsman remain as recommendations to the authorities concerned. The ombudsman has discretion to lay before the Scottish Parliament a special report on any case of unremedied injustice and copy it to Scottish Ministers. It would be for the Scottish Ministers or Scottish Parliament to take whatever action they considered necessary in these cases. There is no right of appeal against the ombudsman's decision, as this is not considered necessary or appropriate because the ombudsman is not making enforceable decisions. The ombudsman is therefore the ultimate point in the complaints process.

Reports and Accountability

The arrangements for providing reports on the results of investigations are similar to those of the existing ombudsmen, although more extensive. Thus, the report of an investigation must be sent to the complainant or their authorised representative, any member of the Scottish Parliament or local councillor who assisted with the complaint, the authority or person investigated and Scottish Ministers. A copy must also be placed in the Scottish Parliament Information Centre. The authorities which are the subject of reports must make arrangements for publicising the reports[112]. Reports will not identify individuals, unless, taking into account the public interest, the ombudsman considers it necessary to do so. Special reports may be laid before the Scottish Parliament and copied to the Scottish Minsters where any injustice or hardship as a result of maladministration has been found and it has not nor will not be remedied. The ombudsman may also advertise the report and make copies available for inspection or purchase. This is a less prescriptive approach than at present, and it has the advantage of allowing publicity when appropriate, in order to encourage compliance.

---

[111]   Scottish Public Services Ombudsman Act 2002, s 9(1) and s 9(2).
[112]   Scottish Public Services Ombudsman Act 2002, s 15.

The ombudsman has to lay an annual report before the Scottish Parliament, and may lay other reports before the Parliament as is thought fit[113]. The ombudsman will submit annual accounts to the Auditor General for Scotland for auditing[114].

Conclusion

The new scheme in Scotland provides an integrated service, which is more than an amalgamation of the existing schemes. The title of the new office is 'Public Services Ombudsman', and additional public service and quasi-public service providers have been brought within remit. It is explicitly indicated that jurisdiction is to include failures of service as well as maladministration. While not being prescriptive about the procedures to be adopted by the ombudsman, the new scheme is designed to be open, accountable and easily accessible. It accords with the recognised criteria for ombudsman schemes, being accessible, accountable and independent, with adequate powers of investigation. Because it is integrated, it addresses the issues of confusion, overlap and inefficiencies associated with having three separate schemes. The implementation of the legislation will be watched closely, and it may provide lessons for other proposals for integrated schemes in the rest of the UK.

Wales

Before devolution, Wales had three ombudsmen. Complaints relating to local government were dealt with by the Commissioner for Local Administration in Wales[115]. Complaints about central government were dealt with by the Parliamentary Ombudsman, as in the rest of Great Britain.

---

[113]   Scottish Public Services Ombudsman Act 2002, s 17. There is also provision for the Scottish Parliament to give the ombudsman directions as to the form and content of the annual report. This may include, for example, details of complaints received and completed during the year and the outcomes. It may also include the numbers and subjects of the complaints, the authority complained against, and the time taken to deal with complaints. The ombudsman may also be directed to indicate any issues arising from the complaints which are considered to contain lessons for Scottish public authorities generally, or which may require action by the Parliament.

[114]   This office is now known as Audit Scotland.

[115]   This was established in the Local Government Act 1974.

There was also a separate ombudsman for health service complaints in Wales[116], although this latter role was actually performed by the Health Service Ombudsman for England and Scotland, who was also the Parliamentary Ombudsman. After devolution[117], Wales is in a similar position to that existing in Scotland before the implementation of the Scottish Public Services Ombudsman Act. It now has four separate ombudsman systems. In addition to the three ombudsmen just noted, a Welsh Administration Ombudsman was created to investigate complaints about the National Assembly for Wales.

The Local Government Ombudsman for Wales was established by the same legislation that established the English Local Government Ombudsmen, and the powers, procedures and jurisdiction are exactly the same[118]. The Local Government Ombudsman for Wales also has powers in relation to the investigation of allegations that members of local authorities in Wales have failed to comply with the authority's code of conduct[119]. After devolution, the Local Government Ombudsman's jurisdiction remains as

[116] The National Health Service Reorganisation Act 1973 created separate health service ombudsmen for England and Wales. That Act was amended by the National Health Service Act 1977, Pt V and consolidated in the Health Service Commissioners Act 1993, as amended by the Health Service Commissioners (Amendment) Acts in 1996 and 2000.

[117] The Government of Wales Act 1998 provided for the establishment of the National Assembly for Wales. Its law-making powers are limited, with power to make delegated but not primary legislation. It exercises many of the functions formerly exercised by the Secretary of State for Wales.

[118] Of course, that office is much smaller, receiving about 1,000 complaints a year about local authorities in Wales. About half of the complaints are rejected because they are not concerned with maladministration, or there is no evidence of injustice. One-fifth of the complaints are normally settled satisfactorily once the ombudsman becomes involved, or they are withdrawn. The ability of local authorities to settle complaints has been facilitated by the Local Government Act 2000, which provides a power for authorities to pay compensation to complainants without the need for an ombudsman's report or the consent of the Assembly to make such payments. Fewer than 5% of complaints require the issue of a formal investigation report (Local Government Ombudsman for Wales Annual Report 2000–01 p 1). Compliance with the ombudsman's reports has not been a problem, and there have been no further reports issued during the last four years.

[119] See the Local Government Act 2000, Pt III. Each authority has to adopt a code of conduct for its members. Anyone will be able to make an allegation that a member has breached the code. As a result of the investigation, the ombudsman may decide to refer the outcome of the investigation to the authority's Monitoring Officer for consideration by the Standards Committee. The matter

before. The United Kingdom Parliamentary Ombudsman's remit now covers matters not devolved to the Welsh Assembly[120]. The Health Service Ombudsman for Wales' jurisdiction continues as before, except that the Health Service Ombudsman publishes a separate report for Wales, and reports this to the Welsh Assembly.

The Welsh Administration Ombudsman

The Welsh Administration Ombudsman investigates complaints about maladministration by the Welsh Assembly and certain other public bodies[121]. Investigations can only relate to administrative matters, and there is no power to investigate the merits of decisions taken without maladministration[122]. There are the usual exclusions to jurisdiction, including commercial and contractual matters and personnel issues. The powers and procedures are similar to that adopted by the Parliamentary Ombudsman, and indeed, the present Parliamentary Ombudsman holds the position of the Welsh Administration Ombudsman. Complaints must be brought within 12 months of the complainant becoming aware of the matters complained about. Complaints must be made by the person aggrieved, but there is no requirement for these to be referred by a member of the Welsh Assembly. In addition to there being direct access, the public bodies subject to jurisdiction can refer complaints on behalf of complainants.

---

can also be referred to the President of the Adjudication Panel for Wales for adjudication by a tribunal. It is for the Standards Committee or case tribunal to decide whether or not there has been a breach of the code of conduct, and if so, what penalty should be imposed.

[120]   These include national taxation and social security matters.

[121]   In addition to the National Assembly for Wales, these bodies are: the Arts Council of Wales; the Countryside Council of Wales; the Office of Chief Inspectors of Schools in Wales; the Sports Council for Wales; the Wales Tourist Board; the Welsh Development Agency; the Welsh Language Board. The following bodies are also included in so far as they relate to Welsh matters: the Environment Agency; the Forestry Commissioners; Urban Development Corporations.

[122]   The Welsh Administration Ombudsman also deals with complaints about access to official information, under the National Assembly for Wales' Code of Practice on Public Access to Information (2001). Where an authority within the ombudsman's jurisdiction does not respond appropriately to a request for information, there can be a complaint to the ombudsman, who will investigate and, if the complaint is upheld, recommend a remedy. A detailed report on the investigation will be provided.

After an investigation, a report is sent to the complainant, any Assembly member who assisted the complainant, and the First Secretary to the Assembly. Where a complaint is upheld, and maladministration and injustice found, the ombudsman will make recommendations as to an appropriate remedy. These remedies are the same as for the Parliamentary Ombudsman, including apologies, improvements in procedures and compensation. If the ombudsman is not satisfied with the action taken or proposed by the public body concerned to remedy the injustice, a further report is prepared. This is laid before the Assembly with a proposal by the First Minister that the recommendations be approved.

Since devolution, there have been very few complaints about the devolved bodies[123]. This can be explained partly by the fact that taxation and social security are reserved matters, and these are areas which generate large numbers of complaints. In addition, it seems that the Welsh Assembly has been very ready to settle cases early if they might be referred to the Welsh Administration Ombudsman[124].

Review of the Ombudsman System in Wales

Like the other parts of the UK, the arrangements for the ombudsman service in Wales is in need of review. This is not just a result of devolution, although the creation of another ombudsman in Wales has focussed attention on a system where a multiplicity of ombudsmen can cause confusion, duplication, and inefficiencies. In addition, the legislation establishing the ombudsmen is now outdated, being enacted for a time when there were few applications for judicial review and few complaints institutions in the public sector. The legislation is also very prescriptive, and thus restricting of the ombudsmen's attempts to provide appropriate remedies.

In August 1998, the Advisory Group to the Welsh Assembly recommended to the (then) Secretary of State for Wales that the posts of Welsh Administration Ombudsman, Health Service Ombudsman for Wales and the Local Government Ombudsman for Wales should be combined. In March 2001, the Secretary of State for Wales and the First Minister of the Welsh Assembly announced that there was to be a joint review of the public

[123]   These have been fewer than 60 each year.
[124]   See British and Irish Ombudsman Association Conference Report 24–25 May 2001 p 20.

sector ombudsman services in Wales. To date, there has been very little progress with this, although the consultation process is due to begin in the near future. It would be very surprising if that review did not conclude, as in England and Scotland, that an integrated system was required. It cannot be in anyone's interest to have four separate ombudsmen for such a small population. One issue to bear in mind however is that any proposals to change the system which involves primary legislation will have to be implemented by the Westminster Parliament. The Welsh Assembly's law-making powers are limited to the making of delegated legislation. It could be some time therefore before any change is forthcoming.

Conclusion

This chapter has presented a brief discussion of the particular features of the ombudsman arrangements in Northern Ireland, Scotland and Wales, in so far as they are different from the position in England. The present arrangements and the future reviews are leading to a system where each country will have an integrated ombudsman service for all matters not reserved for the Westminster Parliament. Thus, health, local government and devolved matters will come within an integrated ombudsman service. This should simplify matters. Most issues will be dealt with by the devolved ombudsmen, with the Parliamentary Ombudsman providing a service for Westminster matters.

Chapter 8

The police service

In all the areas of the UK, there are specialised mechanisms for dealing with complaints in relation to the police service. In some other countries, by contrast, the national ombudsman investigates such complaints[1]. It has been noted that the function of an ombudsman is 'to investigate complaints from citizens that they have been treated by the public authorities in an unfair or arbitrary manner'[2]. The police, in the nature of their work, are likely to occasion many complaints of this type, and therefore one would 'most expect to find provision'[3] for an ombudsman for the police service. This is not the case in most of the UK. The Home Office, which is responsible for policing, is within the remit of the Parliamentary Ombudsman. However, the Parliamentary Ombudsman has no power to investigate the actions of the police[4]. The administrative activities of police authorities[5] are within the remit of the Local Government Ombudsmen, but again, there is no power to investigate complaints about the conduct of police officers.

---

[1] This is the case in Sweden, Finland, Denmark, New Zealand and Norway, for example (see F Stacey *The British Ombudsman* (1971) Clarendon Press p 334).
[2] F Stacey *The British Ombudsman* p 334.
[3] F Stacey *The British Ombudsman* p 334.
[4] The Parliamentary Ombudsman could investigate complaints that the Home Secretary had failed to adhere to the statutory machinery for setting up an inquiry into examining a compliant against the police, for example, or failed to exercise some of his other general powers of surveillance of police forces.
[5] The major responsibilities of police authorities are oversight of, and setting the budget for, the local police force.

The mechanisms for dealing with complaints about police conduct have grown up independently of the ombudsman systems established for public services in central and local government. This chapter will provide a brief overview of the systems for dealing with complaints against the police in the UK, but will first deal with some general issues about such complaints.

Police Complaints

Mechanisms of accountability are essential in any public service, but for the police service they have an additional dimension. Because of their role in the criminal justice system, the police are in a unique position. In order to carry out their law enforcing function, police officers have a range of powers and equipment denied to ordinary citizens. They have the power to arrest, to deprive citizens of liberty, to question and detain. They have the ability to impose upon personal and community freedom in a way that no other body of persons can. Their coercive powers are considerable and the way they exercise these powers involves a significant amount of discretion. Given this, some external control over how the power is exercised is vitally important. Police officers must be called to account for the way they perform their job, just like any other public servant. Moreover, the police must be accountable in order that there is public confidence in the service. This public confidence in the police is essential in a democratic society.

There is a tripartite system for controlling the police in the UK, consisting of the Home Secretary[6], local police authorities and chief constables. Individual police constables are subject to the criminal law, and can of course be prosecuted for crimes they may commit in the course of carrying out their duties[7]. As with other public services, individuals can also pursue civil claims for damages against the police, for example, for personal injury caused by a police officer[8]. There is also the possibility of individuals

---

[6]   In the case of Scotland, this is Scottish Ministers.

[7]   This includes the common law offence of misfeasance in a public office.

[8]   This emerged in the 1980s as an important alternative remedy for complaints about police conduct (see G Smith 'Police Complaints and Criminal Prosecutions' (2001) 64(3) MLR 372–392). Often, the motive for suing is not financial, but is rather to bring facts to light or to make the police accountable. Apparently, success in the civil courts in actions for damages is higher than pursuing a remedy through the complaints or criminal process (see S Ward 'Is it a Fair Cop?' (2002) 99(4) Law Society Gazette 20–21, p 21).

pursuing remedies under the Human Rights Act, as the police service is a public authority and must therefore act in conformity with human rights legislation. However, it is the mechanisms for dealing with complaints about the conduct of the police that are an important part of the process of democratic policing, and it is these mechanisms that are the focus of this chapter. These mechanisms must be robust enough to command the confidence of the public. Satisfaction with the complaints process is important in achieving public support for the police[9].

Internationally, the mechanisms for dealing with complaints against the police can take a number of forms. There could be complete self-regulation, where the police conduct and regulate investigation into complaints with no external input or oversight. At the other extreme, complaints against the police could be dealt with by a body entirely independent of the police, which has complete responsibility for the investigation of all complaints against the police. Within this range, there are hybrid systems with varying degrees of internal and external investigation and civilian oversight, supervision and audit of the complaint handling function. In some of these hybrid systems, the oversight function comes into play after an investigation has been conducted internally by the police. In this kind of system, the police investigate and determine complaints. The function of the oversight body is to review this process in order to examine whether the process was fair, impartial and thorough, and the sanction imposed appropriate. In other types of systems, the external element provides a supervisory function, which may involve independent assessors accompanying police officers as they investigate allegations. Some systems allow independent investigation for serious complaints, involving death or serious injury, for example. All of these models can focus on individual cases only, or they can also provide more general oversight of policies and procedures within police forces.

Since the late 1950s, the need for a more effective system for dealing with complaints against the police has been a 'live issue' in Britain[10]. At that time, the mechanism for dealing with police complaints was self-regulation,

---

9   See generally A Goldsmith and C Lewis (eds) *Civilian Oversight of Policing: Governance, Democracy and Human Rights* (2000) Hart; G Smith 'Police Complaints and Criminal Prosecutions' (2001) 64(3) MLR 372–392.

10 M Maguire 'Complaints against the Police: The British Experience' in A J Goldsmith (ed) *Complaints Against the Police: the Trend to External Review* (1991) Clarendon Press p 177.

with the police investigating themselves. In 1962, the Royal Commission on the Police raised the issue as to whether the police should be responsible for investigating complaints against their colleagues[11]. Since then there has been the introduction of more external oversight of police complaints in the UK. As elsewhere in the world, it has been noted that the police have had a 'disproportionate and negative influence' on the powers given to these external bodies'[12]. The introduction of varying degrees of civilian oversight has not stopped the 'growing momentum for independent investigation'[13] of police complaints. Nor has it prevented the complaints process serving a 'predominantly managerial function' and leaving the needs of complainants to be 'woefully neglected'[14].

England and Wales

The system in England and Wales is in the process of transformation, with proposals to abolish the existing Police Complaints Authority and replace it with an Independent Police Complaints Commission[15]. In this section, there will be a brief history of the police complaints system in England and Wales, an evaluation of the work of the Police Complaints Authority, and an overview of the proposals for reform.

The Police Complaints Board

The Police Complaints Board was the first attempt in England and Wales at establishing civilian oversight of police complaints. It was established

---

[11]   Royal Commission on the Police, Final Report (Cmnd 1728, 1962). There was a minority report filed by three members of the commission, which recommended a police ombudsman or commissioner of rights to oversee police investigations, with similar powers to those eventually granted to the Police Complaints Authority.

[12]   C Lewis 'Entrenching Civilian Oversight' in A Goldsmith and C Lewis (eds) *Civilian Oversight of Policing: Governance, Democracy and Human Rights* (2000) Hart p 20.

[13]   G Smith 'Police Complaints and Criminal Prosecutions' (2001) 64(3) MLR 372–392, p 372.

[14]   G Smith 'Police Complaints and Criminal Prosecutions' (2001) 64(3) MLR 372–392, p 391.

[15]   These proposals are in Pt II of the Police Reform Bill, which is, at the time of writing, proceeding through Parliament.

in 1976, following the emergence in the late 1950s and early 1960s of police behaviour as a political issue[16]. During this time, there was mounting evidence that the police protected their own, and there was mistrust of the internal investigations conducted by the police[17]. The Police Act 1964 established a procedure whereby the investigation of complaints was conducted by a senior officer from a different force. Such was the dissatisfaction with this system that in July 1969, 160 Members of Parliament signed a motion asking for the Police Act to be amended, in order to introduce an independent element into the process. In the same month, it was reported that the Home Secretary was considering establishing a system for investigating complaints against the police similar to that of the proposed Health Service Ombudsman[18].

Later that year, the National Council for Civil Liberties published a pamphlet advocating independent regional tribunals, with legally qualified chairs, to hear complaints from members of the public against the police[19]. Also in 1969, Justice set up a special committee to make recommendations on investigations of complaints against the police. This recommended that complaints should continue to be investigated by the police, but complaints should be examined by an independent investigator, where the complainant was not satisfied. The independent investigator would report to the chief constable concerned. The police officer complained against would, at this stage, have a right of appeal to a central review tribunal consisting of a legally qualified chair and two senior officers from another force[20].

The Police Complaints Board had limited powers[21]. It exercised limited review power in terms of complaints, and it relied solely upon investigations

---

16   See P Hain 'Introduction' in P Hain, D Humphrey and B Rose-Smith (eds) *Policing the Police*. Volume I. *The Complaints System: Police Powers and Terrorism Legislation* (1979) John Calder.

17   See C Lewis *Complaints Against the Police: The Politics of Reform* (1999) Hawkins Press pp 29–30.

18   *The Guardian* 23 July 1969, reported that Elystan Morgan, a Parliamentary Secretary at the Home Office, had told the Parliamentary Labour Party Home Office group this on the previous day.

19   M Jones *The Police and the Citizen* (1969) National Council for Civil Liberties.

20   Justice Recommendations Submitted to the Police Advisory Boards' Joint Working Party on the Investigation of Complaints (1970) pp 4–5, 7.

21   The Police Act 1976 provided for three-person tribunals to hear complaints against the police where the case had not been referred to the Director of Public Prosecutions. Almost immediately after its establishment, the Police Complaints

by the police. It proved to be ineffective and the public lost confidence in its ability to perform its oversight function[22]. This loss of confidence was partly a result of the greater social awareness among the middle classes, during the 1970s and 1980s, about the injustices perpetrated upon minority groups by the state in general and its coercive arm, the police[23]. The Brixton riots in 1981 and the subsequent inquiry into them by Lord Scarman in 1982 eventually led to its demise[24]. The Scarman inquiry report included recommendations for a radical reform of the system for handling complaints against the police, in order to restore public confidence in it[25]. Two models were posed. In the first, there would be independent investigation for all complaints against the police. In the second, there would be lay supervision for serious complaints. It was the second model that was adopted to replace the Police Complaints Board.

The Police Complaints Authority

The Police Complaints Authority was established under the Police and Criminal Evidence Act 1984, to replace the Police Complaints Board. Its statutory functions were defined in Part IX of that Act. This was replaced by the Police Act 1996, Pt IV which became effective from 1 April 1999. The Police Complaints Authority is a body independent of the police service. It presently consists of 19 members, including the chair and deputy chair[26],

---

Board recognised the difficulty with investigating complaints of serious assault, which relied on the word of the complainant against police officers. In its annual and triennial reports, the board questioned whether more independent investigations were required for such complaints.

22   C Lewis *Complaints Against the Police: The Politics of Reform* (1999) Hawkins Press p 66.

23   C Lewis *Complaints Against the Police: The Politics of Reform* p 53.

24   C Lewis *Complaints Against the Police: The Politics of Reform* p 43.

25   There had also been an inquiry in the late 1970s into policing, chaired by Lord Plowden (The establishment of an independent element in the investigation of complaints against the police: report of a Working Party appointed by the Home Secretary (1981) Home Office). Although events were overtaken by the 1981 inner city disturbances, and Scarman's concerns with declining confidence in the police, it was the recommendations of the Plowden report which were developed to create the Police Complaints Authority (the author is grateful to G Smith, email communication of 20 June 2001, for this information).

26   The present chair is Sir Alistair Graham, who succeeded Peter Moorhouse. His appointment is initially for a three-year term. There were 19 members at the end of March 2002.

appointed[27] after the positions have been advertised in the national press. They are fixed-term appointments, for a period of three years, renewable for a further term. In addition, there are around 60 staff, many of whom are seconded from government departments for a minimum of three years, although some are recruited directly. The members are the governing body of the authority, and they set the policy. They each have their individual caseload. The authority deals with around 17,000 complaints a year, with a 'modest budget'[28].

The Police Complaints Authority has a supervisory function in relation to complaints about police conduct. The police remain responsible for conducting investigations into complaints, but the authority has powers to supervise these investigations. It performs its supervisory function where the complaints allege serious misconduct and incidents of public concern. It is required to supervise any complaint involving death or serious injury, and in other cases, it has discretion whether or not to supervise the investigation. The authority also reviews the outcome of each investigation undertaken by the police, whether supervised by it or not, and it can decide whether misconduct action should be taken against any officer. In addition, police forces can refer for supervision any situation not involving a complaint that raises grave or exceptional issues. This will normally happen in cases involving shooting incidents, deaths in police custody and serious corruption. The aim of the supervisory process is to ensure that the investigation by the police is thorough, impartial and effective.

The Complaints Process

The Police Complaints Authority cannot receive complaints from members of the public directly. Where complaints are made directly[29], these have to

---

27 The Police Act 1996, Sch 5 provides for the chair to be appointed by the Queen and all other members by the Home Secretary.

28 The budget for 2001–2002 was £4.4 million, and was an increase on the 2000–01 budget which was £3.4 million. The chair of the authority noted that it has been 'under-resourced for many years' (see Police Complaints Authority Annual Report 2000–01 p 3). The increase in the budget allowed for the appointment of five new members, five additional case workers and a head of research (see Annual Report and Accounts of the Independent Police Complaints Authority 2001–02 (HC Paper 1008) p 3).

29 Every year, more than 2,000 complainants do complain directly to the Police Complaints Authority. In 2001–02, the number was 2,678 (Annual Report and

be forwarded to the police force concerned. Before there can be an investigation of a complaint it has to be recorded by the force of the police officer about whom the allegation is made. Complaints by, or on behalf of, members of the public must relate to the conduct of a serving officer in the police force. They cannot be accepted if they relate to the direction or control of the police force. Where complaints are recorded by the police, there are three courses of action available. Less serious complaints, that is, those where neither a criminal nor disciplinary offence is alleged, can be resolved informally. [30] About 35% of complaints are resolved in this way[31], without any Police Complaints Authority involvement. Other complaints are investigated by the police, some of which are supervised by the Police Complaints Authority.

There has to be supervision by the Police Complaints Authority where there is an allegation that an officer has, or may have, caused death or serious injury. Complaints about alleged actual bodily harm, corruption or a serious arrestable offence must be referred to the Police Complaints Authority, and these are supervised at its discretion. Forces can voluntarily refer any other complaint for supervision. The Police Complaints Authority can call in any recorded complaint for a supervised investigation. In 2001–02, there were 937[32] referrals of cases requiring or inviting the authority to supervise the investigations, and the authority agreed to supervise 622[33]. These included 162 non-complaint matters voluntarily referred by police forces, which included road traffic incidents, deaths in police care or

---

Accounts of the Independent Police Complaints Authority 2001–02 (HC Paper 1008) p 10).

[30] The procedure for dealing with less serious complaints informally was introduced by the Police and Criminal Evidence Act 1984, Pt IX.

[31] In 2000–01, outcomes were achieved on 31,034 complaints. Of these, 10,553 (34%) were informally resolved. A further 34% were withdrawn or not proceeded with. The remaining 9,842 were investigated by the police. Of these, 91% were not substantiated (Home Office Statistical Bulletin *Police Complaints and Discipline* (2001) 21/01 pp 10–11).

[32] Of these 937, 355 (38%) were complaints about death or serious injury; 223 (24%) alleged actual bodily harm; 18 (2%) involved corruption; and 27 (3%) were about serious arrestable offences. There were 72 voluntary referrals, and in seven cases referral was required by the authority. There were 177 (19%) referrals of non-complaint matters (Annual Report and Accounts of the Independent Police Complaints Authority 2001–02 (HC Paper 1008) p 13).

[33] Annual Report and Accounts of the Independent Police Complaints Authority 2001–02 (HC Paper 1008) p 13.

custody, and firearms incidents[34]. Of the 622 cases accepted for investigation, 317 (51%) involved allegations of death or serious injury. There were 46 cases involving complaints about actual bodily harm, and 14 involving serious arrestable offences and eight involving corruption. The authority supervised the investigation of 53 cases referred voluntarily, and six cases that were called in by the authority.

Supervision of an investigation[35] involves a number of statutory responsibilities. These include approval of the appointment of the investigating officer and of the terms of reference for the investigation. The authority can require an investigating officer to be appointed from another police force and can impose any requirements deemed necessary for the proper conduct of the investigation. Supervision involves meetings with the investigating officer, the constant monitoring of progress and intervention when necessary. It may involve being called out in the middle of the night to attend the scene when there has been a death in custody to ensure that all the time-sensitive actions have been taken. In the case of a death, the member of the authority may attend the post mortem. In serious or sensitive cases, the supervising member of the authority may meet with bereaved relatives and local community representatives to explain the process and to provide reassurance about the integrity of the investigation. Moreover, the statutory responsibilities of the supervising member include the final approval of the investigation[36].

All formal investigations, whether supervised or not, are reviewed by the Police Complaints Authority to ensure that they are thoroughly investigated

---

[34] There were 50 supervised investigations into road traffic incidents, in which 44 members of the public died and 22 were seriously injured. They formed the largest category of non-complaint referrals. There were 36 referrals for deaths in care or custody, and 18 other incidents causing death (Annual Report and Accounts of the Independent Police Complaints Authority 2001–02 (HC Paper 1008) pp 3, 32).

[35] Supervision of an investigation is undertaken by a member of the authority. There are 13 authority members (none of whom work full-time) and 12.5 caseworkers responsible for supervised investigations. Only about one in eight cases are supervised by the Police Complaints Authority (Annual Report and Accounts of the Independent Police Complaints Authority 2001–02 (HC Paper 1008) p 20).

[36] When a police investigation is complete, the Police Complaints Authority issues a formal statement indicating whether it is satisfied with the quality of it, and specifying any areas of concern if it is not.

and that the conclusions and actions from the investigation are appropriate[37]. Final reports of all police investigations are sent to the Deputy or Assistant Chief Constable of the force concerned. This officer considers whether the report indicates that the officer complained about may have committed an offence. If this is the case, the report is sent to the Crown Prosecution Service, which decides whether or not to prosecute[38]. If there is a prosecution, even in the case of an acquittal, the police officer can also, in exceptional circumstances, be charged with a breach of the code of conduct on the same facts. The Police Complaints Authority must be informed whether there are to be misconduct charges, and if not, the reasons for this.

After the internal police decisions, the Police Complaints Authority reviews the whole case, and decides whether to accept the recommendation of the police force. The reviewing member of the authority can seek further information or investigation, if not satisfied with the quality or adequacy of the investigation. The member can also raise concerns with senior police office managers if the general standard of investigations is unsatisfactory, or if the investigating officers appear biased or prejudiced in their approach. If there is a disagreement between the force and the Police Complaints Authority, the authority has the power to recommend, and if necessary direct, that misconduct charges are brought. At the end of the process, the Police Complaints Authority member responsible for supervising the case writes to the complainant setting out the outcome of the case. Where there is to be no misconduct hearing, the reasons for the authority's decision is given. In 2001–02, the authority reviewed 7,148 cases and finalised 7,554 cases[39]. Two-thirds of caseworker resources and half the member resources are devoted to these misconduct reviews. In addition, the Police Complaints Authority reports annually to Her Majesty's Inspectorate of Constabulary on the performance of complaints investigation departments.

---

[37]   This misconduct review is completed only after the Crown Prosecution Service has considered whether to bring criminal proceedings.

[38]   Prior consent of the Director of Public Prosecutions is needed before there can be a prosecution of a police officer.

[39]   Annual Report and Accounts of the Independent Police Complaints Authority 2001–02 (HC Paper 1008) p 20.

Problems with the Police Complaints Authority

Although the Police Complaints Authority is an improvement on its predecessor, the Police Complaints Board[40], criticisms of it have resulted in proposals for major changes in the system[41]. One of the principal problems is in relation to independence[42]. Although the authority itself is independent of the police, the complaints system as a whole does not provide sufficient perceived and actual independence. The Police Complaints Authority's ability to perform an effective service is limited by its remit, which prevents an independent investigation of allegations of police misconduct. Even the most serious cases are investigated by police officers, the remit of the authority being confined to supervision of the investigation by an independent Police Complaints Authority member. Furthermore, for the majority of complaints, there is no supervision[43]. The system of the police investigating the police 'will never convince complainants or the public at large that grievances are investigated thoroughly and independently'[44]. There is very low public confidence in the system[45], which seems to pay little attention to the needs of complainants.

[40] It was an elaboration of the Police Complaints Board rather than a new system (see D Carter 'Complaints Against the Police' (1985) (March) Legal Action pp 37–39).

[41] See 'Foreward' by the Chair in Annual Report and Accounts of the Police Complaints Authority 1999–2000. See also KPMG *Feasibility of an Independent System for Investigating Complaints against the Police* (2000), which concluded that both the Police Complaints Board and Police Complaints Authority had failed to offer a solution to widely held concerns about the complaints system in England and Wales.

[42] In *Sultan Khan v UK* (2000) 8 BHRC 310, it was found that the police complaints process did not meet the requisite standards of independence to constitute sufficient protection against the abuse of authority.

[43] P Birkinshaw *Grievances, Remedies and the State* (2nd edn, 1994) Sweet and Maxwell p 237.

[44] M Cunneen and J Harrison 'Framework for a New System' (2001) Legal Action (August) 6–8, p 6. They also note that there are 'grave concerns about the lack of independence' in the system.

[45] As long ago as 1991, a study found that the vast majority of complainants were in favour of investigations being conducted by an independent body (see M Maguire 'Complaints Against the Police: the British Experience' in A Goldsmith (ed) *Complaints Against the Police: the Trend to External Review* (1991) Clarendon Press). This was an empirical study that looked at the complaint handling of three police forces and a selection of 100 Police Complaints Authority cases. There were also interviews with 100 complainants. The overwhelming majority (90%) of complainants felt that an investigation should not be done by the police (see M Maguire and C Corbett *A Study of the Police Complaints System* (1991) HMSO).

Even the name of the authority is problematic. It gives the impression that it is an agency of the police, rather than an independent oversight body[46]. Also, the fact that it is the Police Complaints Authority that writes to a complainant with the outcome of the police investigation reinforces the view that the authority is the agent of the police. Public perception of its role is not assisted by the fact that the authority is often the bearer of bad news, for example that no misconduct was found as a result of an investigation. The authority is often blamed for problems in the system. Because it is the body that communicates with complainants, it is often held responsible for delays, even though the authority may only be able to influence a part of it. For example, investigations into serious complaints can take between one and two years to complete. The Police Complaints Authority is responsible for only a part of this process, but may be held responsible by the complainant for the entire timescale.

There are also problems with access to the system. There is no direct access for complainants to the Police Complaints Authority. Complaints can only be referred to the authority where they are recorded by the police force concerned. Where a police force refuses to record a complaint, the Police Complaints Authority cannot assist complainants. There is no right of appeal to the Police Complaints Authority, and no right of redress for complainants in these circumstances. The Police Complaints Authority has no role in misconduct hearings, which are presided over by senior police officers with no independent input. Nor is it permitted to give information to the complainant if an officer is found guilty after such a hearing. Its limited resources make effective communication with complainants difficult. Moreover, there is no provision for compensation for complainants as a result of the complaints process. Compensation can only be obtained by pursuing an action for damages in the civil courts. Indeed, often people do not bother with the police complaints procedure, as success in the civil courts is higher than in the complaint or criminal process[47]. The steady increase in the number of successful damages claims is 'in stark contrast to the relatively few complaints substantiated and the infrequency of criminal or disciplinary proceedings'[48].

---

[46]   The authority has now started to refer to itself as the 'independent Police Complaints Authority'.

[47]   See S Ward 'Is it a Fair Cop?' (2002) 99(4) The Law Society Gazette 20–21, p 21.

[48]   G Smith 'Police Complaints and Criminal Prosecutions' (2001) 64(3) MLR 372–392, p 391.

The Independent Police Complaints Commission

Proposals to establish a new system for dealing with police complaints are contained in the Police Reform Bill, presently before Parliament. Part 2 of the Bill provides for the creation of an Independent Police Complaints Commission[49]. The Government had announced its intention in June 2001 to introduce legislation to establish a new complaints system[50], following a number of suggestions for reform. These included proposals from the Police Complaints Authority itself[51] and Liberty[52]. The report on the Stephen Lawrence Inquiry[53] had also called upon the Home Secretary to consider the steps that should be taken to ensure that serious complaints against police officers were independently investigated. In response, the Home Office appointed management consultants to examine the process of investigation into police complaints[54], and the Home Office published its proposals for reform in 2000[55]. All the proposals suggested a system with more actual and perceived independence.

The Bill provides for the abolition of the Police Complaints Authority, and its replacement by a body to be called the Independent Police Complaints Commission. The chair of the new Commission will be appointed by the Queen, for a period not exceeding five years, but with the possibility for re-appointment for a second term. There is provision for the appointment

[49] Part 2 of the Bill contains 18 clauses relating to the new body, which will have the status of a non-departmental public body.

[50] See White Paper *Policing a New Century: A Blueprint for Reform* Cm 5326, 2001.

[51] The Police Complaints Authority submitted detailed recommendations to the House of Commons Home Affairs Committee in 1997. The committee accepted most of the recommendations and subsequently recommended that there should be more independent investigation of complaints (First Report from the Home Affairs Select Committee (HC Paper 258 (1997–98)) (Police Complaints and Disciplinary Procedures)).

[52] J Harrison and M Cunneen *An Independent Police Complaints Commission* (2000) Liberty.

[53] *The Stephen Lawrence Inquiry: Report of an Inquiry* by Sir William Macpherson of Cluny; advised by Tom Cook, John Sentamu, Richard Stone (Cm 4262, 1999).

[54] KPMG *Feasibility of an Independent System for Investigating Complaints against the Police* (2000). The remit of the study was to establish whether and in what way the investigation into police complaints should be changed. It was also to determine whether openness and transparency were more significant factors than independent investigations in terms of public confidence in the process.

[55] *Complaints Against the Police – Framework for a New System* (2000) Home Office.

of at least ten additional members of the new Commission, to be appointed by the Home Secretary, for the same period[56]. The change of name will reinforce the independence of the new body from the police, and hopefully result in a change in public perception of its role. In addition, there is provision for the police to communicate directly with complainants, which should avoid the problem of the new commission being seen as the agent of the police. The commission will have a similar structure to the present Police Complaints Authority, and will be concerned, as now, with investigating complaints in relation to the conduct of police officers. It will have no remit to investigate complaints in relation to the direction and control of the police service.

Under the new system, complaints will be lodged by the victim, as now, but there is also provision for complaints to be made by those adversely affected by the conduct complained about, and by members of the public who witness it. There is provision for complaints to be made by third parties, on behalf of complainants. In addition, it will be possible for complaints to be made directly to the commission, as well as to the police service concerned[57]. There will be a right of appeal to the Independent Police Complaints Commission if the police refuse to record a complaint[58]. One of the problems with the present system is the lack of information given to complainants about the progress of their complaint. Under the new system, there will be a duty to keep the complainant informed on progress and outcome[59]. Complainants will have a right of appeal to the commission, where they are dissatisfied with the process completed by the police. The commission will then decide whether an independent investigation is needed.

There will be four procedures available for dealing with complaints. As now, the police will be able to conduct their own investigations, and there is provision for investigations to be conducted under the supervision of the new commission. There is also a new power for the police to conduct investigations under the management of the commission. More importantly, the commission will be able to conduct its own investigations, and to this

---

[56]   Police Reform Bill, clause 8.
[57]   Police Reform Bill, clause 11. Complaints will also be able to be lodged at Citizens Advice Bureaux or with members of Parliament.
[58]   Police Reform Bill, Sch 3.
[59]   Police Reform Bill, clause 19.

end, it will have its own team of investigators[60]. Police officers are required to co-operate with investigations, and chief police officers are responsible for obtaining and preserving evidence in cases involving officers under their direction and control. As now, the commission will be responsible for complaints involving death or serious injury. There is also the power to investigate or supervise where no complaint has been made. It is for the commission to decide which procedure will be used in any particular case[61].

There is also provision for complaints to be resolved informally. This will be renamed 'local resolution'. The new local resolution procedure will allow a police force to apply to the commission for authority to use local resolution rather than carry out a formal investigation. This will occur where there are no prospects of obtaining the necessary evidence to substantiate a complaint. The use of local resolution will be approved where complaints, if proved, would not lead to criminal proceedings or a disciplinary outcome of a fine or more serious sanction[62]. The use of local resolution will address the problem of the length of time taken to complete the complaints process. The intention is to extend its use as much as possible to complaints which, if proved, would result in minor disciplinary sanctions. It is also envisaged that other techniques, such as mediation and restorative justice, will be used as a means of resolving complaints quickly and effectively at local level.

There is no doubt that the new system will mean fundamental changes for investigating complaints against the police. For the first time, there is the possibility of a body independent of the police conducting its own investigations into police conduct. Not only does this allow for the genuine, independent investigation of serious complaints, but it should also improve public confidence in the system. It will assist in making the police service fully accountable.

---

[60] Police Reform Bill, Sch 2, Pt 3, para 14(4). The commission will be able to make arrangements with police forces for officers to be seconded to the commission to act as investigators. The commission will also be able to employ its own specially trained civilian investigators. The report by Liberty recommends that no more than a quarter of the staff in the new organisation should be seconded or former police officers (J Harrison and M Cunneen *An Independent Police Complaints Commission* (2000)).

[61] This will depend on the seriousness of the case and public interest requirements.

[62] Annual Report and Accounts of the Independent Police Complaints Authority 2001–02 (HC Paper 1008) pp 6–7.

There are however some criticisms. It has been argued that the Home Secretary's dual policing and complaints responsibilities may compromise the independence of the commission[63]. There are also concerns that the commission will have no power to prosecute officers in respect of criminal charges, that function remaining with the Crown Prosecution Service[64]. One concern is that, because of the structural relationship between the Crown Prosecution Service and the police, there may be problems in fulfilling this role impartially[65]. However, the main problem is in relation to the resourcing of the new body. Unless it is adequately resourced[66], the commission will be restricted in the number of complaints that it can investigate. Unless there is a statutory requirement to investigate, lack of resources will oblige it to allow the police to conduct investigations. There may therefore be few complaints that are independently investigated, and thus the new powers could be 'illusory and ineffective'[67]. This would result in the new system substantially replicating the current position, which would not achieve the public confidence required.

---

[63]   See G Smith 'The Police Complaints Commission: Independent From Whom?' (2002) 47 Criminal Justice Matters 40–41.

[64]   The new commission will however have power to present cases against police officers at misconduct hearings, where the commission has directed a police force to bring disciplinary charges.

[65]   M Cunneen and J Harrison 'Framework for a New System' (2001) Legal Action 6–8, p 7. See also the Butler Inquiry (The Inquiry into Crown Prosecution Service Decision-making in Relation to Deaths in Custody and Related Matters (1999)). This was conducted following a number of high profile deaths in custody where there was no prosecution. The inquiry recommended changes, involving a review by the Treasury counsel, with the aim of improving confidence in the Crown Prosecution Service's role. *R v DPP, ex p Manning* [2001] QB 330, was the first case in which the new procedure was used. There had been an initial decision by the Crown Prosecution Service not to prosecute, which was found to be 'unsustainable in law' by the Divisional Court. It was referred back to the Crown Prosecution Service, but the Director of Public Prosecutions still decided not to prosecute.

[66]   It has been estimated that the cost of the new system will be in the region of £14 million a year, compared with the Police Complaints Authority's present budget of £4.4 million. The Police Ombudsman for Northern Ireland has a budget in excess of £5 million.

[67]   M Cunneen and J Harrison 'Framework for a New System' (2001) Legal Action 6–8, p 8. See also South Africa, which has a system similar to Northern Ireland, but which can only investigate deaths in custody (of which there are many) because of a lack of resources.

Scotland

Scotland too is in the process of changing its system for investigating complaints against the police[68]. As in England and Wales, responsibility for the police in Scotland follows a tripartite model, consisting of the police authority[69], chief constable, and Scottish ministers. There is no equivalent body to the Police Complaints Authority in Scotland, and complaints are dealt with primarily by police forces. There is some general oversight of the complaints process provided by Her Majesty's Inspectorate of Constabulary[70] and police authorities. Both these bodies scrutinise the complaints process. Some police authorities have sub-committees that examine complaints files at random. The inspectorate examines complaints handling procedures as part of its annual inspection process. The Scottish Executive is currently consulting on proposals to reform the existing arrangements. This section will provide an outline of the existing system, and describe the options for reform.

The Present System

Complaints alleging criminal conduct on the part of police officers are investigated on behalf of the Lord Advocate by the Regional Procurator Fiscal for the force area in which the officer serves. Complaints alleging misconduct are investigated by the officer's force either at local level or by the Deputy Chief Constable. If upheld, complaints can result in penalties ranging from warnings to dismissal from the service. For both criminal and conduct complaints, the Regional Procurator Fiscal or police force can request the appointment of investigating officers from another force in

---

[68] The process is still at the consultation stage (see *Complaints Against the Police: A Consultation Paper* (2001) Scottish Executive).

[69] As in England and Wales, police authorities are responsible for setting the budget and making senior appointments in the police service. They also deal with complaints against chief officers. They have to be kept informed of the manner in which the chief constable deals with complaints against officers.

[70] This is a statutory body, established by the Police (Scotland) Act 1967, ss 33, 40 and 40A (as amended). It is independent of police forces, police authorities and the Scottish Executive. Its formal powers are restricted to the efficient management and effective performance of police forces in Scotland. The inspectorate visits and enquires into any matter concerning or relating to the operation of police forces. It submits annual reports to Scottish ministers on police forces, and has a duty to keep informed on how complaints by the public are dealt with within police forces.

order to carry out the investigation. Police authorities are responsible for dealing with complaints against chief officers.

Where members of the public are dissatisfied with the handling of a complaint against the police they can ask Her Majesty's Inspectorate of Constabulary to review their complaint[71]. Following the review, the Inspectorate will report their findings to the complainant and send a copy to the chief constable and constable against whom the complaint was made. The inspectorate cannot compel the chief constable to change the decision. The only power is to direct the chief constable to reconsider the complaint and take into account any further evidence which may have become available. Where a chief constable is directed to re-examine a complaint, Scottish Ministers and the police authority are advised of this. There are around 40 requests from dissatisfied complainants to the inspectorate each year.

In 2000, the inspectorate conducted a review of the procedure for dealing with complaints against the police. The report[72] concluded that the overwhelming majority of complaints against police officers were investigated with thoroughness, impartiality and integrity. It did however note that there were significant differences in the way forces recorded and investigated complaints. It felt that there was a need to emphasise the role of the Crown and Procurator Fiscal service in respect of the independent investigation of criminal allegations against police officers. One of the findings of the report was that some complainants found it difficult to register complaints, and that there was too much mystery surrounding the complaints process.

The system for dealing with criminal allegations is independent of the police. However, where there are complaints that do not allege criminal conduct, the police are left to investigate the matter themselves. The only independent element in this process is provided in the review of the systems, provided by the police authorities and the inspectorate. There is no independent element in the investigation process itself.

---

[71]   Police (Scotland) Act 1967, s 40A.
[72]   HM Inspectorate of Constabulary *A Fair Cop? Investigation of Complaints against the Police in Scotland* (2000).

Proposals for Reform

The proposals for reform are designed to enhance the independence of the system. There are no proposals to make any changes to the process of investigation for criminal allegations. These will continue to be dealt with by the Regional Procurator Fiscal, as before. In relation to non-criminal complaints, it has been decided that a new body should be established for these, leaving the police authorities and inspectorate their efficiency and management roles in so far as they conduct a general review of the handling of complaints[73].

Two models for the new body are suggested. The first, called an 'ombudsman', would have a wider role than the Inspectorate, but it would be essentially supervisory[74]. Thus, the ombudsman would have the power to order that a new investigation be conducted, and would oversee any new investigations. The ombudsman would also be able to conduct random sampling of the complaints systems.

The second model involves the establishment of a new independent Police Complaints Body with responsibility for handling all complaints at first instance[75]. Complaints could be made directly or referred to it. Within this model, there are various options. The new body could decide that there was a prima facie case for investigation, and then either refer the case to the police to deal with, or undertake a supervisory role in connection with the police investigation. In the second option proposed, less serious complaints could be referred to the police to deal with, with the independent body supervising the investigation of more serious cases, and criminal allegations being referred to the Regional Procurator Fiscal. Any findings in relation to misconduct would be referred to the police authority to deal with. The third option is for the new body to supervise investigations into all complaints. Finally, the most radical option is for the body to undertake its own investigations into serious or all complaints. This would involve the new body employing its own investigation staff.

---

[73] *Complaints against the Police in Scotland: A Consultation Paper* (2001) Scottish Executive paras 41, 43.

[74] *Complaints against the Police in Scotland: A Consultation Paper* (2001) para 47.

[75] *Complaints against the Police in Scotland: A Consultation Paper* (2001) Scottish Executive para 48.

The consultation document makes no recommendation as to a preferred model, but seeks views on which model would provide the best balance between independent examination of complaints against the police and speedy and efficient investigation. Whatever the outcome of the review, primary legislation will be required to effect the necessary change.

Northern Ireland

In Northern Ireland, the model adopted for dealing with complaints involves a completely independent system of investigation. Described as 'probably the most advanced model of police oversight in the world'[76], it represents a major change in the process of dealing with complaints, and for the accountability of the police service. The office, created under the Police Act (Northern Ireland) 1998, Pt VII, followed the proposals of the review of the police complaints system in Northern Ireland[77]. The previous system, the Independent Commission for Police Complaints was similar to the Police Complaints Authority. Under that system, which was established in 1988, officers of the Royal Ulster Constabulary investigated complaints against fellow officers under the direction of the Independent Commission for Police Complaints. The review recommended that the Independent Commissioner for Police Complaints for Northern Ireland be replaced by a Police Ombudsman. The new office was established in October 2000[78].

---

[76]   N O'Loan 'The Police Ombudsman for Northern Ireland – An Introduction' (2000) 14 (August) The Ombudsman 7. In Queensland and New South Wales in Australia, New Zealand and South Africa there are similar institutions to that in Northern Ireland, but none is equal in terms of its independence and statutory powers. The Republic of Ireland has announced plans to create a similar system (see N O'Loan, 'Police Ombudsman for Northern Ireland' 2002 (Spring) 8(2) Visiting Times pp 10–13, p 13).

[77]   The review (*A Police Ombudsman for Northern Ireland?* (1997) HMSO Belfast) was conducted by Dr Maurice Hayes, who was the former Northern Ireland Ombudsman. The Patten report (*A New Beginning: Policing in Northern Ireland* (1999) HMSO) saw the Police Ombudsman as providing the key to the effectiveness of the new policing arrangements in Northern Ireland.

[78]   For a discussion of the background to the setting up of the office, see M O'Rawe and L Moore 'Accountability and Police Complaints in Northern Ireland: Leaving the Past Behind?' in A Goldsmith and C Lewis (eds) *Civilian Oversight of Policing: Governance, Democracy and Human Rights* (2000) Hart.

The creation of the new system has to be set in context. Northern Ireland is a 'small but sadly troubled region within the United Kingdom'[79]. In Northern Ireland, there is a population of 1.5 million people, and a police force of 13,000, which is armed. During the past 30 years, there has been a total of 3,300 deaths, 302 of which were police officers, and 43,244 people have been injured, of which 9,320 were police officers. The population is deeply split, on religious grounds, in its perception of and support for the police. The work of the office has also to be seen within the context of the changes to the policing arrangements as a result of the peace process in 1998[80].

The Police Ombudsman for Northern Ireland

The Police Ombudsman[81] is appointed for a fixed term of seven years and is accountable to the Secretary of State, and thence to Parliament. The ombudsman's role is to ensure the efficiency, effectiveness and independence of the police complaints system and to secure the confidence of the public and members of the police force in the system. The remit of the office is to investigate, informally resolve, or seek mediation of a complaint. The ombudsman can carry out inquiries and monitors trends and patterns in complaints. The office has a budget in excess of £5 million a year[82], and a staff of 104[83]. When the office was established, it was

[79] I Topping 'The Police Complaints System in Northern Ireland' in A J Goldsmith (ed) *Complaints Against the Police: the Trend to External Review* (1991) Clarendon Press p 233.

[80] This resulted in changes to the Royal Ulster Constabulary, which was renamed the Police Service of Northern Ireland (see *A New Beginning: Policing in Northern Ireland* (1999) HMSO).

[81] The first Police Ombudsman is Mrs Nuala O'Loan. She was a law lecturer and former chair of the Northern Ireland Electricity Consumers' Council. She has served in the past as the convenor for complaints for the Northern Ireland Health and Social Services, and has been a member of the General Consumer Council for Northern Ireland.

[82] It is estimated that it would cost £80 million a year to reproduce the Northern Ireland model in England and Wales.

[83] This is soon to be increased to 120. Staff are employed to deal with all the processing and investigation of complaints, and to carry out extensive research and analysis. The investigators have been recruited from all over the world, including a senior police complaints officer from South Africa, a detective chief inspector from Hong Kong, and a scene-of-crimes officer and a senior investigator from New South Wales. There are also staff members with experience in fraud

estimated that there would be 3,000 complaints a year. In the first six months, it received 2,643 complaints. In the first 12 months, it received 4,696 allegations from 3,733 complainants. The office receives complaints from any member of the public, and operates a service 24 hours a day, seven days a week.

The ombudsman primarily deals with complaints about the Police Service of Northern Ireland[84], but jurisdiction also covers the Belfast Harbour Police, Larne Harbour Police, Belfast International Airport Police and Ministry of Defence Police. The office investigates complaints about the conduct of police officers, and these are considered on the basis of whether the officer has complied with the Police Code of Conduct. The office handles the whole range of complaints, from allegations of police incivility to allegations involving very serious criminal offences. The ombudsman cannot investigate conduct that has already led to criminal or disciplinary action, unless there is new evidence that was not available at the time of the original investigation. Matters to do with the direction and control of the police are also outside the remit[85], and actions of off-duty police officers cannot be investigated, unless the fact of being a police officer is relevant to the complaint. The ombudsman has a wide range of powers, including accessing and seizing any documentation or property.

The ombudsman is also required to supply statistical information on complaints. There is a duty to monitor trends and patterns in complaints, and the power to make recommendations for improving practice. The ombudsman also has the power to publish special reports[86].

---

investigation. The office also has staff seconded from the Metropolitan Police Service, and from other police services in England and abroad.

[84]   This used to be the Royal Ulster Constabulary.

[85]   These complaints must be analysed and referred to the police. Although not allowed to deal with complaints about policy, the ombudsman can comment in general terms on policy.

[86]   The Police (Northern Ireland) Act 1998, s 62 allows this. The report into the Omagh bombing was conducted under this power (see A Statement by the Police Ombudsman for Northern Ireland on her investigation of matters relating to the Omagh bombing on 15 August 1998 (2001)). There has also been a report into the use of baton rounds, where seven investigation reports were reviewed. It was found that the discharge of baton rounds was fully justified and proportionate, as were the authorisation and directions given (see *Baton Rounds Report* (2002) Research Report 1/2002).

The Complaints Process

The ombudsman's office is the first port of call for any complaint against the police, and provides a 'one-stop' service. It is free to complainants. Complaints can be made by or on behalf of members of the public. If an individual is afraid or reluctant to complain, the Police Ombudsman can still conduct an investigation. As well as written, email, fax and telephone contact, the office is open to personal callers and referrals are accepted from solicitors. The ombudsman's staff will, in certain circumstances, visit complainants at home or attend at an agreed venue. The police are also under an obligation to refer complaints to the ombudsman. The ombudsman can investigate in the absence of a complaint if she believes that an officer may be in breach of the law or may have acted in a way that is inconsistent with the disciplinary code[87]. There is a requirement for the ombudsman to investigate cases of death or serious injury.

Complaints must be made within one year of the incident complained about, although there is discretion to accept complaints out of time. If the complaint is about the police service in general, it will be referred to the chief constable. Complaints may be resolved informally where appropriate. In these situations, the matter will be referred to the police to deal with, provided the complainant agrees. Informal resolution provides a flexible and simple procedure for minor complaints, that is, where the conduct, if proved, would not justify criminal proceedings. Normally, a local senior police officer conducts the informal resolution, after which the related papers are forwarded to the ombudsman. These are then examined to ensure that all the elements of the complaint have been dealt with, the process has been properly handled, and the matter been dealt with to the satisfaction of the parties involved. The types of cases which are resolved informally include allegations of failure of duty and incivility.

---

[87] The power to conduct own-initiative investigations is found in the Police Act 1998, s 55(6). The ombudsman has conducted an investigation on her own-initiative where there appeared to be an excessive use of force. The case involved a high speed chase of a stolen vehicle. An officer fired a revolver in the direction of the vehicle, but the vehicle continued undeterred. The car and the passenger were not captured and it did not appear that anyone was injured. There was no complaint, but the ombudsman investigated because she was concerned with the proportionality and necessity of the police actions, and the level of danger to other members of the public.

If the complaint is not suitable for informal resolution, there will be an investigation, conducted by staff in the ombudsman's office. Each investigator has the same powers as a police officer for the purpose of conducting an investigation. Investigators can obtain search warrants, secure evidence, seize property[88] and make arrests[89]. The police can be compelled to supply material to the investigators, and they are under a duty to preserve crime scenes and to facilitate the work of the office. It is a criminal offence to restrict, impede or obstruct the ombudsman's investigation. About one-quarter of complaints are investigated.

After an investigation, if there is evidence of a criminal or disciplinary offence by a police officer, there can be a recommendation about appropriate criminal prosecution or disciplinary action. The Police Ombudsman has the power to direct the chief constable to bring disciplinary proceedings against officers of, or below the rank of, chief superintendent. If the officer complained about is an assistant chief constable, a deputy chief constable or the chief constable, the ombudsman can recommend that the police authority bring disciplinary proceedings. There can be a recommendation for compensation, and this does not affect other legal rights a complainant may have[90]. If the ombudsman rejects the complaint, reasons are given for this decision. The Police Ombudsman's decision is final. If however new information becomes available that the complainant could not reasonably have known about, the ombudsman may start a new investigation.

Evaluation

For the first time, there is a system for the independent investigation of complaints against the police. This is a high profile and accessible office[91],

---

[88]   For example, boots, batons, log books and vehicles have been seized.

[89]   These arrest and detention powers are governed by the Police and Criminal Evidence Order (NI) 1989, SI 1989/1341 (NI 12), as amended. The office has not made many arrests. As a matter of policy, arrests are not normally made at the officer's home, as the ombudsman does not want to expose families to trauma. Arrests are not normally made in front of colleagues either. The ombudsman works in co-operation with the Police Service of Northern Ireland to ensure where possible that arrests are made with maximum privacy (see N O'Loan 'Police Ombudsman for Northern Ireland' (2002) 8(2) Visiting Times 10–13, p 12).

[90]   So far, there have been no recommendations for compensation.

[91]   Before the office began to receive complaints, there was a wide-ranging consultation process, to establish what people wanted from the office, and how

and in the short time since its inception it has demonstrated its ability to conduct robust investigations. It also appears to have been given sufficient resources to enable it to carry out its remit effectively[92], as without proper funding, there can be no effective accountability, no matter what power an office is given[93]. There is a growing confidence in the office, even within the police force.

Conclusion

The police are providing a public service, and like other public services, they should be accountable. There are various mechanisms of accountability for the police, but, in order to ensure public confidence in policing, it is essential to have satisfactory processes for dealing with

---

to make it accessible. There was also a major campaign to make the public aware of the work of the new ombudsman. The ombudsman has pursued a robust media relations campaign. Leaflets and posters about how office works have been sent to police stations, libraries, solicitors offices, and Citizens Advice Bureaux. The office has a website (www.policeombudsman.org). The ombudsman visited more than 40 organisations across Northern Ireland in the first six months of her appointment. In a survey conducted in October 2000, 57% of respondents had heard of the office, and of this 81% knew the office was independent of the police. A follow-up survey in March 2001 revealed that public awareness had raised to 65%, with 83% knowing that the office is independent. 61% of those who were aware of the office knew that they could complain directly.

[92]   Contrast this with the position in South Africa, where the South African Independent Complaints Directorate has similar powers to the Police Ombudsman. In South Africa, the complaints body has the power of control over all matters of police complaint. However, it has a small budget and is understaffed. South Africa has 125,000 police officers, and the Independent Complaints Directorate has only 125 staff. There are over 800 deaths in police custody in South Africa each year, so not surprisingly, all its resources will be concentrated on these (see N O'Loan 'Police Ombudsman for Northern Ireland' (2002) 8(2) Visiting Times 10–13, p 11). For a discussion of the South African system, see B Manby 'The South African Independent Complaints Directorate' in A Goldsmith and C Lewis (eds) *Civilian Oversight of Policing: Governance, Democracy and Human Rights* (2000) Hart Publishing. Manby notes that 'perhaps the most serious problem' facing the complaints directorate is its 'lack of resources when faced with the size of its mandate' (p 218).

[93]   The ombudsman claims that despite a budget in excess of £5 million, it is cost effective. The money spent on the office represents 1% of the policing budget, and the office saves the Government money in the long term, if unresolved police malpractice leads to riots.

complaints. The public has a deep suspicion of the way complaints against the police are handled, and thus the complaints system must be seen to be independent and fair if it is to command public confidence. It also needs the capacity to resolve minor complaints quickly and effectively. There should be openness in relation to the findings of the investigation, and it needs to be accessible to complainants.

It is no longer considered acceptable for police complaints to be dealt with entirely by the police themselves. Systems for investigating police complaints in the UK have varying degrees of external involvement and oversight. The Northern Ireland model is probably the most advanced, with the Police Ombudsman being responsible for the processing and conduct of independent investigations. The proposals envisaged for England and Wales are moving towards more external oversight, but they have not followed the Northern Ireland model[94]. Time will tell whether this proves to be more satisfactory than the Police Complaints Authority that it is to replace. It is yet unclear what system Scotland will adopt, although the proposals envisage more external oversight than there is at present.

In all three systems, the existing and proposed models operate independently of the other systems for the independent investigation of complaints about local and central government services. There is thus a specialist system for the police service, and there are no calls for integration into the mainstream ombudsman system. This is perhaps not surprising, given that the focus of police complaints systems is the conduct of individual officers, rather than the more general administrative processes investigated by the other public sector ombudsmen. Notwithstanding this, the mechanisms should still conform to recognised criteria of ombudsman systems, particularly in relation to independence and access. The three systems for investigating police complaints operating in the UK will make interesting areas for study and comparison over the next few years.

---

[94]　Various reasons have been put forward for this. It is true that Northern Ireland has very different problems to England and Wales, and that maybe such a radical reform is not necessary. There is also the view that the police should take responsibility for complaints and use them as a management tool. On the other hand, the Police Ombudsman does refer minor complaints to the police for informal resolution, and complaints statistics are published for the police, so that they can be used for management purposes. Another problem with replicating the Northern Ireland system in England and Wales is the cost, as it is estimated that this would be £80 million to reproduce the same system.

Chapter 9

Conclusions

The world has witnessed the rapid growth of ombudsman systems in the last 40 years, with a proliferation of such schemes, not only in the public sector, but also for private sector organisations. Ombudsmen schemes trace their origins to the Swedish ombudsman introduced in the nineteenth century. However, they are not direct transplants, and throughout the world they have developed into new territories and have been adapted to a wide variety of systems and cultures[1]. Indeed, one of the great strengths of ombudsmen is their remarkable adaptability for a wide range of political and constitutional contexts. It is for this reason that it has been said that ombudsmen 'cannot be bought off the peg' but 'must be made to measure'[2].

The growth of ombudsman schemes in the public sector was partly due to a recognition that the systems of control of public bodies were not adequate to deal with the increasingly complex post-war governments. Certainly, since the 1939–1945 war, there have been movements towards both the protection of human rights and the protection of citizens against public bureaucracies. It was the latter that was of concern in the UK, where it was claimed that the 'procedure for securing . . . personal freedom [was] efficient', but that the procedure for 'preventing the abuse of power' was

---

[1]   P Giddings 'The Future of the Ombudsman' in R Gregory and P Giddings (eds) *Righting Wrongs: The Ombudsman in Six Continents* (2000) IOS Press p 459.

[2]   See G E Caiden 'The Institution of Ombudsman' in G E Caiden (ed) *International Handbook of the Ombudsman: Evolution and Present Function* (1983) Greenwood Press p 13, quoting S A de Smith, the Constitutional Commissioner for Mauritius.

not[3]. More recently, the proliferation of schemes is a reflection of the increase in consumerism, and the fact that people are now prepared to challenge the decisions of public bodies.

The purpose of this book has been to describe and evaluate the work of the public sector ombudsmen in the UK, setting their work within the context of other mechanisms of administrative justice. As we have seen, the ombudsman system in the UK consists of a number of separate offices, some with general central or local government remits, and others with specialist functions for the health service and police. These schemes are very different from their Scandinavian forebears. They are also different to each other, but they have all been very much influenced by the Parliamentary Commissioner Act 1967, which established the Parliamentary Ombudsman. Thus, the remit of each scheme has generally been restricted to maladministration, and the emphasis of their work has been on investigation and report.

From its inception, the Parliamentary Ombudsman arrangements in this country were subject to a great deal of adverse publicity. It is true that some of this was because people were mistaken about the extent of the ombudsman's powers in other countries, and therefore had unrealistic expectations of the institution. However, there were also criticisms in relation to access, to the narrow jurisdiction, and to the fact that the institution had a civil service orientation. Although criticisms still existed in the early 1990s, some 25 years after the establishment of the Parliamentary Ombudsman's office, there was some evidence that the office was being 'praised, in moderation, even by journalists, lawyers and academics'[4]. Since that time, the ombudsman system as a whole has been transformed. This has been partly a result of devolution. It is also a reflection of the changing context in which the ombudsmen operate, which has resulted in changes in the working practices of the ombudsmen, so that they are now focusing primarily on resolving complaints.

Previous chapters have examined each ombudsman system in turn, highlighting their strengths and weaknesses. In this final chapter it is proposed to draw these conclusions together, and to examine the strengths

---

[3]   A Denning *Freedom under the Law* (1949) Stevens p 126.
[4]   R Gregory and J Pearson 'The Parliamentary Ombudsman after twenty-five years: Problems and Solutions' (1992) 70 Public Administration 469–498 p 471.

and weaknesses of the system overall and some general issues affecting them all. As has been noted, changes are already taking place in the system as a result of devolution. More changes are due to take place as a result of proposals to integrate schemes, a process which is seen as necessary given the changes in the delivery of public services. These changes present an opportunity to build upon the successful features of the ombudsman system, and at the same time eliminate some of the problems.

Evaluation: BIOA Criteria

As we have seen, the proliferation of ombudsman schemes, particularly in the private sector in the 1980s, focussed attention on the characteristics that ombudsmen were to display before they could be deemed worthy of the title[5]. This concern led to the establishment of the BIOA, a self-regulatory organisation[6], operating on a voluntary basis with a small secretariat and minimum funding[7]. As previously discussed, the association has developed a set of criteria which an ombudsman scheme must satisfy in order to be deemed worthy of the name 'ombudsman'. Those schemes that satisfy the criteria can be full voting members of the association. The core role of an ombudsman, according to the BIOA criteria is 'to investigate and resolve, determine or make recommendations with regard to

[5]   It is not just in the private sector where there has been an inappropriate use of the ombudsman model. In February 2001, the Home Secretary proposed that a Victims Ombudsman be established, with the power to investigate complaints of sub-standard treatment, to seek redress and to act as a champion of victims' interests (see *Criminal Justice System — the Way Ahead*). This proposal was part of a package of statutory rights for victims, where the ombudsman would be the arbiter of last resort, should the complainant remain unhappy with the agency's response. This proposal was criticised as inappropriate, as the UK Ombudsmen do not act as 'champions'. It is worthy of note that the 'champion' of children's rights and interests in Wales is known as the Children's Commissioner, even though in some countries such offices are known as Children's Ombudsman (see R S Bearup and V J Palusci 'Improving Child Welfare through a Children's Ombudsman' (1999) 23(5) Child Abuse and Neglect 449–457; K Hollingsworth and G Douglas 'Creating a children's champion for Wales? The Care Standards Act 2000 (Part V) and the Children's Commissioner for Wales Act 2001' (2001) 65 (1) MLR 58–68; M Seneviratne 'Ombudsmen for Children' (2001) 23(2) Journal of Social Welfare and Family Law 217–225).

[6]   N O'Brien has referred to it as a 'conversational forum' ('Justice by any other name' (2001) The Ombudsman 7–8, p 7).

[7]   The funding is derived from the member's subscriptions. For more details see R James *Private Ombudsmen and Public Law* (1997) Dartmouth pp 223–241.

complaints'. Within this core role, ombudsmen schemes must have four key criteria: independence from those over whom there is a power of investigation; effectiveness; fairness and public accountability[8].

The BIOA sets out detailed requirements for each of these criteria which should be achieved by the ombudsmen in the longer term. In relation to 'independence', it is expected, for example, that the jurisdiction, powers and method of appointment of ombudsmen are matters of public knowledge. Those appointing the ombudsman should be independent of the bodies subject to jurisdiction. Appointments should be for a minimum of three years, which may be renewable, or until a specified retirement age. Appointments should not be subject to premature termination, other than for incapacity or misconduct. Independence must also be assured by the fact that it is for the ombudsman to decide whether a complaint is within jurisdiction. In addition, the office must be adequately staffed and funded so that complaints can be effectively and expeditiously investigated and resolved.

As we have seen, the public sector ombudsmen in the UK are generally Crown appointments, and this is seen as a mark of their independence. All posts are publicly advertised, and are subject to formal selection procedures. Most are permanent appointments until retirement, although some are for fixed terms. There are issues of independence in relation to the members of the Police Complaints Authority, who are appointed by the Home Secretary, but this has not prevented the authority being granted full voting membership of the BIOA[9]. Although no doubt all the ombudsmen would welcome more funding, they appear to have experienced few problems in securing adequate budgets for their work. In addition to the BIOA criteria, the public sector ombudsmen have made it clear that they are independent, in the sense that they are not consumer champions, but are impartial investigators into complaints.

Ombudsmen need to be effective. This can be achieved in a number of ways. They must, for example, be accessible to complainants and have sufficient powers to enable them to perform their tasks. The BIOA criteria

---

[8]   These criteria can be found on the BIOA website: www.bioa.org.uk/BIOA-New/criteria.htm.

[9]   This point has, however, prevented the Prisons and Probation Ombudsman being accepted as a full voting member, as the appointment is by the Home Secretary, who has responsibility for the prisons and probation service.

indicate that in order to be accessible, there should be adequate publicity for ombudsmen schemes by those subject to complaint. In addition, those subject to complaint should be required to have proper internal complaints procedures. The ombudsman's procedures should be straightforward for complainants to understand and use, and complainants should not be charged for using the system. In addition, the system should be directly accessible 'unless otherwise specified by or under statute'. This latter provision ensures that the Parliamentary Ombudsman system complies with the criteria, even though the system can only be accessed by members of Parliament. All the ombudsmen discussed in this book are acutely conscious of the need to publicise their offices, and have made efforts to increase the awareness of their offices among the public and other relevant organisations. Equally, although the systems have normally to be accessed in writing, efforts are made to assist where this causes difficulties, and arrangements have also been made for electronic access.

The powers of the public sector ombudsmen are extensive. The ombudsmen can investigate any complaint duly made, and have the right to obtain the information they require. Not only can they examine documents, but they can also conduct interviews with relevant parties. They give reasons for their decisions, and act fairly to all the parties concerned. Some of the ombudsmen only allow the public body complained against to see and comment upon the findings in the draft report, but others allow both sides to see the draft. All the public sector ombudsmen make recommendations, and have no power to enforce these in the courts[10]. This is in accordance with international norms for ombudsmen. The recommendations are normally complied with. Where there has been concern is in relation to local government, but even there, non-compliance is not a major issue. Where there is non-compliance, the ombudsmen can publicise this fact.

All the public sector ombudsmen are established by statute. Their work is subject to public scrutiny by means of annual reports, which they all publish, and which contain detailed statistical information about complaints received, their outcomes, and general issues affecting the office. In addition, ombudsmen publish anonymised summaries of investigation reports. The Parliamentary and Health Service Ombudsmen can report on investigations to Parliament, and the work of both offices is overseen by a select committee.

---

[10] The exception is the Northern Ireland Ombudsman, but this power has not been used since the 1980s.

The Local Government Ombudsman has no body with general oversight of its work, but all investigation reports are published. The Local Government Ombudsman also conducts regular reviews of the work of the office, which are published.

The Effectiveness of the Ombudsmen

The above criteria have been used to assess the effectiveness of each ombudsman scheme. Some general points about the effectiveness of the system as a whole will now be made. As noted, in order to be effective, ombudsmen need to have wide powers of investigation, and in this respect, the public sector ombudsmen score highly. Not only does the legislation give them extensive powers to enable them to acquire all the necessary information, but their working practices have meant that the thoroughness of their investigations cannot be faulted. Where their effectiveness can be criticised is in relation to jurisdictional coverage. Without wishing to repeat the discussions of the preceding chapters, many of the statutory exclusions of jurisdiction cannot be justified, and there have been numerous calls for their abolition, and an extension of the ombudsmen's remits. Indeed the general principle should be that the broadest possible jurisdiction should be encouraged, except where a clear case for exclusion exists. This would mean that all administrative action would be subject to scrutiny, in the absence of clear reasons for exclusion.

As well as removing many of the statutory exclusions, the bar on the ombudsmen conducting investigations on their own initiative should also be re-examined. The UK ombudsmen are out of line with most other systems in being unable to conduct an investigation without an individual complaint. Such a power is not likely to be extensively used, in particular because of resource constraints. It would however allow the ombudsmen to investigate where, for example, they had reason to believe that a particular section of a department or authority was not dealing properly with its business. The Cabinet Office review rejected the idea of own-initiative investigations out of hand, claiming that such investigations are 'inconsistent with impartiality'[11]. The present ombudsmen are not pressing for this power, but the select committee is of the view that there may be a

---

[11]   *Review of the Public Sector Ombudsmen in England* (2000) Cabinet Office para 6.15.

case for these investigations 'in certain circumstances'[12]. The power to conduct own-initiative investigations would enhance the effectiveness of the ombudsmen, and serious consideration should be given to this in any future reform.

All the public sector ombudsmen receive relatively few complaints, and investigate very few cases. The Local Government Ombudsmen receive the most complaints, and numbers for the others are gradually increasing. The small percentage of cases investigated is not necessarily a problem, as other methods are available for the resolution of complaints. Now more cases are being satisfactorily resolved without a formal report, as the emphasis of the ombudsmen is increasingly on resolution rather than investigation. However, there is no doubt that the ombudsmen could be more extensively used. In this respect, the efforts to increase public awareness and improve access to the schemes is commendable, especially as it is evident that it is vulnerable members of society in particular who lack knowledge about the schemes. The member filter for the Parliamentary Ombudsman is a barrier to access, and it does restrict the ability of the ombudsman to engage in outreach work with members of the public. The Cabinet Office review's conclusion that the filter should be abolished[13] is not before time, and there can be few who would disagree with this conclusion.

Ombudsmen should be able to ensure that adequate remedies are available where maladministration is found. The public sector ombudsmen in the UK can only recommend a remedy, and they do not make legally binding decisions. This, in itself, does not mean that they cannot provide an adequate remedy, and is in line with the powers of other ombudsmen worldwide[14]. One of the strengths of the ombudsman system is the fact that they are able to recommend a wide range of remedies. They do recommend financial redress, but they are also able to recommend that decisions be reconsidered, and that faulty procedures be rectified.

---

[12] *Third Report of the Select Committee on Public Administration* (HC Paper 612 (1999–2000)) (Review of Public Sector Ombudsmen in England) para 11.

[13] *Review of the Public Sector Ombudsmen in England* (2000) Cabinet Office para 3.52.

[14] The Parliamentary and Health Service Ombudsmen generally have no problem in persuading departments and authorities to give the remedy recommended. The Local Government Ombudsmen have experienced problems over the years by authorities who have refused to follow the recommendations.

Moreover, ombudsmen are able to recommend financial redress in cases where the courts would have no power to award damages.

A major problem with all the ombudsmen schemes is the time taken to deal with complaints. All the ombudsmen are concerned about delay, and all have set targets in an attempt to alleviate the problems. Delay is inevitable where complaints are subject to formal investigations, which of necessity have to be thorough and extensive. All the schemes were designed in such a way that investigation and report was the appropriate outcome for complaints within jurisdiction. Now, despite the intentions of the original legislation, the schemes are becoming more 'resolution' focussed, working as far as possible to produce appropriate results for complainants without using formal investigative machinery where this is not required. Their working practices have thus been tailored to meet individual cases, so that informal settlements and mediation are now becoming common mechanisms for resolving complaints. This accords with the 'modern purpose' of ombudsmen which, it is claimed, is to 'resolve disputes fairly by whatever means are appropriate'[15]. This approach has the advantage of improving the time taken to resolve complaints, while allowing for formal investigation where necessary.

The Ombudsman's Role

The primary role of all the public sector ombudsmen is to provide remedies for injustice caused as a result of maladministration. The concepts of maladministration and injustice have been explored in the preceding chapters. As that discussion revealed, maladministration is not defined in any of the legislation, and it has been left to the ombudsmen to develop the concept over the years. One issue of central concern is whether the concepts of maladministration and injustice are too restrictive. Among all the ombudsmen in developed countries, it is only in the UK that the ombudsmen are confined to investigating cases of maladministration. Ombudsmen in other countries have powers to either look at unreasonable action by public authorities, or report on failures in public services.

Over the years, there have been criticisms that the remit is too restrictive. However, the concept of maladministration has proved to be remarkably

---

[15]   E B C Osmotherly 'Modernising the Ombudsman Service' (2000) JLGL 41–43, p 41.

flexible, and successive ombudsmen have interpreted its meaning liberally. It is interesting nevertheless that the Health Service Ombudsman is not restricted to maladministration. From its inception that office has always been able to investigate complaints about failures of service. The new public services ombudsman system in Scotland also has a remit which includes service failure as well as maladministration. It is unclear whether the specific reference to 'service failure' in fact extends the remit beyond maladministration, as it is possible that such failure does provide evidence of maladministration. The Health Service Ombudsman can investigate matters of clinical judgment in the health service, but there is no express power for the other ombudsmen to investigate the judgment of other professionals in the public sector.

Therefore, it would seem that confining the ombudsmen to complaints of maladministration does not present a significant limitation on their ability to redress grievances. Nonetheless, there are still arguments for change in this area. Reference to the word 'maladministration' may, for example, deter complainants. Ombudsmen in the private sector are not limited to complaints about maladministration, but can take into account what is fair and reasonable in all the circumstances. The Cabinet Office review[16] did not discuss whether the remit of the ombudsmen should be extended beyond maladministration, and the select committee, when examining the review, did not discuss it either[17]. Despite this omission, the limitations of the term are 'long overdue for examination'[18]. There should certainly be some discussion about whether widening the remit to include notions of fairness and reasonableness would make the public sector ombudsmen more effective.

Although the primary role of the ombudsmen is dispute resolution, their work is not confined to this. They are also concerned with improving administrative practice. Ombudsmen therefore have two roles: grievance redress and fostering good practice. The two functions of ombudsmen are not in conflict, but are complementary. By investigating individual cases, ombudsmen may highlight more generalised weaknesses in the system. Uncovering these weaknesses is of advantage to consumers of public

---

[16] *Review of the Public Sector Ombudsmen in England* (2000) Cabinet Office.

[17] *Third Report of the Select Committee on Public Administration* (HC Paper 612 (1999–2000)) (Review of Public Sector Ombudsmen in England).

[18] D Lewis and R James 'Joined-up Justice: Review of the Public Sector Ombudsman in England' (2000) 4 International Ombudsman Yearbook 109–140, p 116.

services in general, as it ought to result in systems improvement. Complaints can be used to provide feedback to public bodies about their performance. This feedback can relate to improvements in the way complaints are dealt with internally, which may result in fewer cases being referred to the ombudsman. It can also relate to improvements in other procedures and practices where the complaints reveal failures in the system. Ombudsmen thus perform a quality control function and provide general oversight of the administration.

The ability to reveal systemic faults is one of the advantages of the ombudsman system. Individual cases have limited significance, but taken as a whole, the ombudsmen's decisions 'help to propagate principles of good administrative practice'[19]. The Local Government Ombudsmen have been particularly pro-active in this respect, producing a series of good practice guides based on their investigations of complaints. The ombudsmen are thus ideally placed to seek out systemic causes of injustice in a way that courts and tribunals are ill-equipped to do[20]. Ombudsmen can therefore assist in raising standards in public services, and thus improve the position for citizens in general.

Ombudsmen and Alternative Remedies

The ombudsmen in the UK were established to investigate citizen complaints and provide redress for grievances. On one level, therefore, ombudsmen are an alternative dispute-resolution mechanism. As such they provide a real alternative to the traditional justice system, given their wide powers of investigation, access to documents, and independence. The courts, the traditional institution for dispute resolution, are not designed to review the facts or decide on the correct administrative decision. While tribunals are usually ideal at reviewing decisions, neither they nor the courts are equipped to investigate the manner in which the decision has been reached and find if there has been maladministration. Ombudsmen were designed to fill this gap. Thus, the ombudsmen as originally conceived in the UK were not intended to present an alternative dispute resolution

---

[19]   G Drewry 'The Ombudsman: Parochial Stopgap or Global Panacea?' in P Leyland and T Woods (eds) *Administrative Law Facing the Future: Old Constraints and New Horizons* (1997) Blackstone Press p 83.

[20]   N Lewis *The Classical Ombudsmen* (1992) University of Sheffield.

mechanism to the courts or tribunals. They were established to deal with grievances where no other remedy was available.

As we have seen, the Parliamentary Ombudsman was originally established as an adjunct to Parliament, and thus part of the political and administrative regimes. The work of the office was to supplement the work of members of Parliament in investigating complaints about government departments. The ombudsman's remit was limited to providing remedies for maladministration, rather than to adjudicate legal claims or appeals against the merits of discretionary decisions. This established the ombudsmen as a system for providing additional remedies, rather than as an alternative mechanism for pursuing legal rights. The grievances they investigate generally have no cause of action in court, except perhaps judicial review. The powers granted to the ombudsmen thus allow them to address administrative problems that the courts and tribunals cannot effectively solve.

To reinforce this distinction, the ombudsmen are precluded from investigating complaints where there are legal remedies or other appeal mechanisms. They do however have discretion to investigate where it would not be reasonable for a complainant to use these remedies. The ombudsmen, as we have seen, do not normally investigate where a complainant is able to take the case to a tribunal or to use a statutory appeal procedure. If a complainant is seeking damages for a contractual or negligence matter, the ombudsmen do not accept the complaint. The situation is different, however, where the only legal remedy available to complainants is judicial review. The ombudsmen will usually accept these cases for investigation.

The expansion of judicial review was probably not foreseen when the ombudsmen's offices were established in the 1970s and 1980s. Now, concepts of maladministration and illegality are coming closer, and a grievance may sometimes be pursued by means of both the ombudsman remedy and the court. Some see this overlapping and parallel jurisdiction as problematic, as it may result in a dual set of values being applied to the same problem[21]. This would be unfortunate, as 'broadly consonant norms'

---

[21]   C Crawford 'Complaints, Codes and Ombudsmen in Local Government' (1988) PL 246–267, p 263; C Crawford 'Rule of Law, Lawyers or Ombudsmen?' (2001) 4(4) JLGL 73–79, p 74.

are needed rather than 'two separate hierarchies of conflicting norms'[22]. On the other hand, others see the parallel jurisdictions as a benefit for consumers, as it provides some choice of redress mechanism[23]. Certainly, the dividing line between the courts and the ombudsmen, which was once clearly distinct, is now becoming more contentious[24]. There is now a need for debate about how the relationship between the courts and ombudsmen should develop, in order to ensure that citizens use the appropriate mechanisms for resolving their disputes, particularly as both systems are concerned with 'the proper regulation of government's treatment of the citizen'[25].

The Complaints Pyramid

Another issue to be addressed is the relationship of ombudsmen to other internal complaints mechanisms operated by public bodies. In well-established ombudsman systems, the ombudsman is at the top of a pyramid of grievance-handling machinery, the last port of call when other complaint-handling procedures have been exhausted. As we saw in Chapter 3, the citizen's charter programme has been particularly influential in the area of consumer rights and complaints systems in public services. This has led to a change of culture, to more effective internal procedures, and a recognition that complaints can be used for managerial purposes to improve service delivery. Ombudsmen systems are now one among many schemes for handling complaints.

---

[22]   A W Bradley 'The Ombudsman and the Protection of Citizens' Rights: A British Perspective' in G E Caiden (ed) *International Handbook of the Ombudsman: Evolution and Present Function* (1983) Greenwood Press p 107.

[23]   D Lewis and R James 'Joined-up Justice: Review of the Public Sector Ombudsman in England' (2000) 4 International Ombudsman Yearbook 109–140, p 129.

[24]   See R Nobles 'Keeping the Ombudsmen in the Place – The Courts and the Pensions Ombudsman' (2001) Public Law 380–402, for a discussion of the strained relationship between the courts and the Pensions Ombudsman. See also J Farrand 'An Academic Ombudsman' (2001) 9(1) Journal of Financial Regulation and Compliance 11–29.

[25]   A W Bradley 'The Ombudsman and the Protection of Citizens' Rights: A British Perspective' in G E Caiden (ed) *International Handbook of the Ombudsman: Evolution and Present Function* (1983) Greenwood Press p 107.

In some areas of the public sector, this has resulted in the creation of an intermediate layer of complaint handling, with the establishment of adjudicators funded by the relevant department or organisation, but operating independently of them. The growth of these systems for internal and external reviews calls into question the appropriate function of ombudsmen. Where there is an adjudicator scheme, should the ombudsman be focussing on quality assurance for these schemes? Should there be a requirement that the internal scheme be exhausted before a complaint can be referred to the ombudsmen? In the health service, the Health Service Ombudsman can only be approached when the National Health Service complaints procedure has failed to give satisfaction. By contrast, the Local Government Ombudsmen provide an opportunity for councils to resolve complaints referred to them, but there is no formal requirement for the internal procedures to be exhausted.

Within central government, the adjudicator schemes currently operate as duplicate systems with the Parliamentary Ombudsman. These schemes will not accept complaints that have been through the Parliamentary Ombudsman system, but the Parliamentary Ombudsman does accept complaints from those dissatisfied with the adjudicator process. There is evidence that the adjudicator schemes are providing remedies for numerous complainants, but there appears to be no resulting reduction in the numbers of complaints to the Parliamentary Ombudsman. It may be appropriate for these external mechanisms to resolve routine complaints, leaving the more complex or resistant ones for the Parliamentary Ombudsman. There are problems with this approach however, not least the length of time it could take before there was a final resolution of the case. This can be a source of dissatisfaction for complainants, which has consequences for the credibility of the system as a whole. In addition, the ombudsman is concerned that insufficient cases may come through to his office for there to be an adequate assessment of the functioning of the administration. A reasonable number of cases is required in order to conduct a meaningful audit.

The Cabinet Office review favoured the proliferation of independent complaints examiners in the public sector, but recommended that information about the relative remits of these and the ombudsman should be available for complainants. There seems however to be little merit in having parallel systems, not least because it could result in confusion for complainants.

Oversight of Ombudsmen

All the public sector ombudsmen schemes are subject to judicial review. As we have seen, the courts have been generally reluctant to interfere with the ombudsmen's exercise of their discretionary powers, although there are signs of more judicial activism in this area. At one time, judicial review cases concerned public bodies, usually local authorities, challenging jurisdictional aspects of the ombudsman's role, or taking issue with the ombudsman's findings. Now, the applicants in judicial review cases are mainly complainants, who are objecting to the ombudsman's refusal to take on their case, or challenging the ombudsman's findings. While it is accepted that the ombudsmen, as public bodies, should not be beyond the jurisdiction of the courts, the increase in the number of applications for review is of concern. Not only is it resource intensive for the ombudsmen, but too much judicial intervention could destroy the basis of the ombudsman system, that is, its informality, flexibility and accessibility[26].

There is no general body charged with oversight of the work of the public sector ombudsmen. The Parliamentary and Health Service Ombudsmen report to the Select Committee on Public Administration, which has been very supportive of their work, but there is no similar body for the Local Government Ombudsmen. No government department has overall responsibility for their work, in the way, for instance, that the Lord Chancellor's Department has responsibility for the court system or the Council on Tribunals oversees the operation of administrative tribunals. It was concern about the lack of regulation that led to the establishment of the BIOA in 1993. However, this is a voluntary self-regulatory body, which has no power to regulate schemes. What it has done is to act as a focal point for ombudsmen, and to raise awareness among the public about ombudsmen schemes. There is now a dedicated resource in the Cabinet Office for ombudsman issues[27].

---

[26]   See N O'Brien, who notes that the 'essence of ombudsman activity . . . lies in its fluidity, its refusal to be ensnared by traditional judicial forms and precedent' ('Justice by any other name' (2001) The Ombudsman 7–8, p 7).

[27]   This location seems to be because the Cabinet Office deals with the charter programme, and is co-ordinating best practice for handling complaints. The Central Secretariat of the Cabinet Office, working closely with the Lord Chancellor's Department, now provides a focal point within government for ombudsman schemes.

An Integrated Ombudsman System

As we have seen, the ombudsman system at present in the UK consists of a number of separate schemes. This is unlike the normal arrangements for ombudsman's systems around the world. The usual model is for the national ombudsman to have jurisdiction over a wide range of public services, including central and local government and the police. As has been indicated, the recent Cabinet Office review has proposed that the public sector ombudsmen in England be joined-up to form an integrated service[28]. Various aspects of the review's recommendations have been discussed in the preceding chapters where appropriate. This section will describe in more detail the proposals to integrate the ombudsmen in England.

Similar projects to integrate schemes are taking place in the rest of the UK. In Scotland, integration has already occurred. In Northern Ireland, the system operates as an integrated ombudsman scheme, although it is in fact two separate offices operating under two separate pieces of legislation. There is to be a review of the legislation, which will no doubt result in an integrated scheme. Wales has yet to conduct its review of the ombudsman system, but when it does, it is likely to result in a single ombudsman system. This move towards integration is mirrored in the private sector, where a number of ombudsman schemes have been incorporated into one single Financial Ombudsman Service.

It is hardly surprising that there are proposals to integrate the public sector schemes. When the three separate schemes were established in the UK, it was on the basis that publicly provided services would be the discrete responsibility of central or local government or the National Health Service. This assumption is no longer valid, as services may now be provided by a combination of authorities. There are complaints which now cross the jurisdictional boundaries of the three ombudsman systems. This is especially so in the area of health and social services, but similar problems can arise in other areas. For example, complaints about nursing care purchased by a local authority in a private nursing home may involve both the Local Government and Health Service Ombudsmen. Similarly, a complaint about delay by a local authority in issuing a statement of a child's special educational needs may also concern fault by a local health authority which has delayed in providing reports for the child's assessments. Claims

[28] *Review of the Public Sector Ombudsmen in England* (2000) Cabinet Office.

for housing benefit may be delayed, or otherwise subject to maladministration, due to faults on the part of either, or both, a local authority and the Department of Social Security. Thus, the existing boundaries between the work of the three ombudsmen no longer reflect service delivery in the public sector.

There is therefore potential for confusion for complainants. The ombudsmen do have informal arrangements for ensuring that complaints are referred to the appropriate office, and there is the possibility of composite investigations. However, because of the legislation under which they each operate, they have little flexibility to develop such arrangements. Consumers may be further confused by the increasing number of internal complaints adjudicators within the public sector. The system for complaints handling and redress are thus complicated and fragmented.

Although a comparatively new problem, it had been recognised over 25 years ago that the wide array of ombudsmen could cause confusion[29]. The Parliamentary Ombudsman at the time noted the need for a consideration of how a more co-ordinated total system, more directly related to the interests of members of the public, could be brought about[30]. The matter was examined by the select committee in 1980[31], but no definite proposals for reorganising the existing arrangements were made. In 1988, Justice discussed the suggestion for an integrated service, under which all the ombudsmen would operate under the same legislation. It decided against recommending the creation of a single integrated service, as it was felt that the existing arrangements for composite investigations were working satisfactorily[32]. Ten years later, the select committee considered that there was need for greater coherence in the structure of the public sector complaints system, and it recommended a review, with a view to bringing the complaints authorities together[33].

---

[29]   D Williams *Maladministration: Remedies for Injustice* (1976) Oyez Publishing p 5.

[30]   Sir Alan Marre in his Annual Report 1975 (HC Paper 141 (1975–76)).

[31]   Second Report of the Select Committee on the Parliamentary Commissioner for Administration (HC Paper 254 (1979–80)) (The System of Ombudsmen in the United Kingdom).

[32]   Justice *Administrative Justice: Some Necessary Reforms* (1988) Clarendon Press p 40.

[33]   Third Report of the Select Committee on Public Administration (HC Paper 398 (1997–98)) para 89.

The Cabinet Office review was prompted by the public sector ombudsmen themselves. In 1998, the three Local Government Ombudsmen in England and the Parliamentary and Health Service Ombudsman presented a paper to ministers, suggesting that a review was timely. The review was announced in March 1999. Its terms of reference required it to consider whether the present organisational arrangements for the public sector ombudsmen were in the best interests of complainants and others, given the moves towards integrated provision of public services.

The major recommendation of the review is for an integrated system of ombudsmen in the public sector in England, a 'one-stop shop' as it is sometimes described. The recommendation is for a new commission to be established[34], combining the work of all three public sector ombudsmen in England, operating on a collegiate model. No ombudsman is to be subject to any other ombudsman, and no one ombudsman is to have an appellate function in relation to the decisions of the others. There is no prescription in the review about how the college should be structured, except to say that functional roles could be retained. The division of work would be an internal matter for the commission, and it could be done on a regional basis, as is the present Local Government Ombudsman system. One ombudsman would chair the commission. The chair would be responsible for reports to Parliament, management and external representation. In addition, the chair would be responsible for matters relating to the UK as a whole, and for reserved matters in Scotland, Wales and Northern Ireland[35].

The new commission is to be accountable to Parliament, and funded in the same way as the Parliamentary Ombudsman, whose funds are voted by Parliament, subject to the approval of the Treasury[36]. There is nothing in the review about the relationship of the new body to the select committee. However, the ombudsmen themselves have suggested that the new commission should be answerable to the select committee for the general conduct of its activities, but not for the investigation of individual

[34] *Review of the Public Sector Ombudsmen in England* (2000) Cabinet Office para 2.43.

[35] *Review of the Public Sector Ombudsmen in England* (2000) Cabinet Office paras 4.3–4.4. The model adopted for the Financial Ombudsman Service, where there is one chief ombudsman and a number of ombudsmen for particular sectors was rejected by the review.

[36] *Review of the Public Sector Ombudsmen in England* (2000) Cabinet Office para 5.13.

complaints[37]. The proposal is for the legislation affecting these changes to allow flexibility in the system. One of the problems of the present statutory framework, especially in relation to the Parliamentary Ombudsman, is that it is very prescriptive, allowing little scope for changes in working practices.

The review was published in April 2000. Its recommendations have been warmly welcomed by the public sector ombudsmen, who felt that its conclusions were 'broadly in line' with what they had advocated[38]. The Cabinet Office issued a consultation paper on the review in June 2000, asking for comments by the end of September. The select committee made some further suggestions for reform in July 2000, and endorsed much of what was in the review[39]. In July 2001, the Government announced its intention to introduce legislation to rationalise the system. There is now a consultation process with all the key stakeholders to decide how best to develop the proposals. It seems unlikely however that there will be legislation before 2003, and some are suggesting that there will be no change before 2005. The Parliamentary Ombudsman has declared that this lack of progress is 'deeply disappointing'[40] and notes 'with regret' that there is as yet 'no sign of the promised proposals'[41]. Where it is possible to make changes without legislative authority, in order to integrate the work of the offices, the ombudsmen are doing so. For example, there are plans to locate the three ombudsmen together in the same premises, and internally, systems are being devised to facilitate an integrated service within the limits of the statutory requirements. However, legislation is needed to create a single institution, and, importantly, remove the member filter.

A Coherent Ombudsman System?

The terms of reference of the Cabinet Office review were fairly restrictive. As noted above, they were concerned with whether the 'organisational

---

[37]   *Review of the Public Sector Ombudsmen in England* (2000) Cabinet Office p 83.
[38]   Parliamentary Ombudsman Annual Report 2000–01 (HC Paper 5 (2001–02)) pp 10–11.
[39]   Third Report of the Select Committee on Public Administration (HC Paper 612 (1999–2000)) (Review of Public Sector Ombudsmen in England).
[40]   Parliamentary Ombudsman Annual Report 2000–01 (HC Paper 3 (2000–01)) p 11.
[41]   Parliamentary Ombudsman Annual Report 2001–02 (HC Paper 897 (2001–02)) p 11.

arrangements' for the public sector ombudsmen were in the 'best interests of complainants and others' in an era of integrated provision of public services. The review provides detailed recommendations for procedural reforms of the system, which will make the ombudsman process more accessible, more flexible, and more able to cope with increased demand. These are laudable proposals, but overall the review is 'essentially a management exercise' rather than a rational and coherent body of reforms[42].

The review addresses the issue of the proliferation of other complaints-handling bodies within the public sector, but only suggests that working arrangements should be made between them and the new commission. In addition, it recommends that the public be made aware of the remits of these bodies, so that they can make an informed choice as to which mechanism to use. The review acknowledged that there were also other bodies, whose work would interconnect with the new commission. These include the ombudsmen in the devolved governments and the Information Commissioner[43]. The review suggests that protocols will need to be established, where there is overlapping jurisdiction[44]. There was no suggestion that this latter post be brought within the new commission. That such an issue was not addressed is unfortunate, as it is common practice in some countries to combine the roles of ombudsman and information commissioner[45].

Similarly, other ombudsman-like bodies were left out of the new arrangements, including the Police Complaints Authority and the

[42] See D Lewis and R James 'Joined-up Justice: Review of the Public Sector Ombudsman in England' (2000) 4 International Ombudsman Yearbook 109–140 p 119.'

[43] The Information Commissioner is the new name for the Data Protection Registrar. This new office will take over from the Parliamentary Ombudsman the handling of complaints from the public about access to government information.

[44] Protocols will also need to be established with the Standards Board for England, which deals with complaints about the conduct of local councillors. At present, there is a protocol between this body and the Local Government Ombudsmen.

[45] One of the problems with having a separate system for complaints about access to information is that mixed complaints to the Parliamentary Ombudsman, combining issues about a lack of information and general administration, are commonplace. In addition, the unreasonable withholding of information can be viewed as maladministration (see D Lewis and R James 'Joined-up Justice: Review of the Public Sector Ombudsman in England' (2000) 4 International Ombudsman Yearbook 109–140, p 119).

Independent Housing Ombudsman[46]. Again, this is unfortunate, as it will not result in there being one over-arching ombudsman for the public sector. The Prisons Ombudsman was specifically excluded from the new commission, on the basis that this was a 'niche' role that was 'properly part of the executive'[47]. When the office of the Prisons and Probation Ombudsman is eventually placed on a statutory footing, it will not be so easy to dismiss it in these terms. It is unfortunate therefore that the review was not used as an opportunity to assess the roles of these other bodies, and their relationship with the public sector ombudsmen. If there is to be a truly coherent public sector ombudsman system, serious consideration should be given to whether these bodies should be a part of it. If not, there is the risk of more jurisdictional problems in the future. There is also the possibility that other specialist ombudsmen will be called for to fill any perceived gaps, unless the new ombudsman system has a wide remit over the whole public sector.

The review made no suggestions about jurisdiction, except to say that the present bodies within jurisdiction should remain so[48]. There were no recommendations about other jurisdictional matters relating to the various exclusions in the three schemes. These were to be decided during the legislative process[49]. Disappointingly, whether the remit should be extended beyond maladministration was similarly not discussed. The review dismissed the idea that the ombudsmen's remit should be extended to allow own-initiative investigations. Essentially, it was accepted that the present role and function of the ombudsmen — primarily complaint handling — would remain. The reforms it suggests enhance this role, and thus the ombudsmen are steered away from an investigation and report. This may be appropriate, but the advantages and weaknesses of this model need to be fully addressed. Unfortunately, the review does not do this. It makes no radical suggestions, and does not discuss the potential for a new system.

---

[46] The Housing Association Ombudsman scheme in Scotland has been brought within the new integrated system there.

[47] *Review of the Public Sector Ombudsmen in England* (2000) Cabinet Office para 4.7.

[48] *Review of the Public Sector Ombudsmen in England* (2000) Cabinet Office para 5.4.

[49] *Review of the Public Sector Ombudsmen in England* (2000) Cabinet Office para 5.11.

Administrative Justice

Ombudsmen in the UK have been remarkably successful. They were established to provide remedies for administrative shortcomings and they thus provide redress which would not normally be available through the courts. Ombudsmen therefore provide an additional method for ensuring administrative justice. Although their remit is concerned in the main with issues of maladministration, this has proved to be a flexible concept, which has not reduced their ability to provide appropriate remedies. Not only do they provide remedies where none would be available through the courts, but they do so using methods that overcome many of the disadvantages of the court system. They have clear advantages over the courts in terms of procedures, and costs. Their style is inquisitorial. They have extensive powers to enable them to conduct thorough investigations. The investigation process is conducted in private. The service is free to complainants, and there is no need for professional advice. Overall then, the public sector ombudsmen have brought redress to thousands of citizens, and have proved themselves capable of performing the tasks for which they were appointed. Moreover, they have shown themselves to be adaptable enough to respond to the changing environment in which public services are delivered. This is evidenced by the emphasis on obtaining resolutions for complaints. It is not surprising then that they have been called a 'central plank of our system of administrative justice'[50].

Ombudsmen are one among a number of methods of controlling public bodies and one form of accountability mechanism available to citizens[51]. They are an integral component of a whole framework of dispute resolution operating in the public sector. They do not operate in a way that is unrelated to other grievance systems. Their work has therefore to be set in the context of these other mechanisms, and their relationship to them is important. Of particular importance is the relationship of the ombudsmen to the courts and administrative tribunals. These bodies should not be duplicating each others work. However, in order to avoid this, the

---

[50] D Lewis and R James 'Joined-up Justice: Review of the Public Sector Ombudsman in England' (2000) 4 International Ombudsman Yearbook 109–140, p 131.

[51] See generally, P Giddings, R Gregory, V Moore and J Pearson ('Controlling administrative action in the United Kingdom: the role of the ombudsman systems and the courts compared' (1993) 59(2) International Review of Administrative Sciences 291–309), who compare the ombudsman system, courts and tribunals as a means of exercising external control over administrative action and securing the redress of grievances.

appropriate roles of the courts, tribunals and the ombudsmen in dealing with citizens' grievances need to be addressed. These roles are not immutable, and the 'proper divide' between their relative jurisdictions 'must be defined and redefined as circumstances change'[52].

There have been calls for an integrated system of control mechanisms to protect fully citizens from abuse of administrative power, and to foster partnerships between judicial and non-judicial review[53]. The problem is that there is no single body charged with keeping the whole system of administrative justice under review. Administrative justice has developed in a fragmented fashion, as have the ombudsmen. Indeed, one of the criticisms of the original proposals to set up the ombudsman was that such a system was a poor substitute for a system of administrative justice[54]. The lack of a 'proper system of public law' was perceived to be the fundamental problem, and the establishment of the ombudsman was condemned as a 'perfect excuse for continuing inertia'[55]. Others warned against the idea that an ombudsman would cure all administrative ills, arguing that a whole variety of controls over administrative action was needed, as well as other reforms to plug the gaps in the system of administrative control[56].

These issues are still very pertinent. There have been calls for the reform of the system of public law[57]. In particular, arguments have been put forward for a Standing Administrative Conference[58] and a Standing

---

[52] H Woolf *The Protection of the Public — a New Challenge* (1990) Stevens p 123.

[53] H Woolf *The Protection of the Public — a New Challenge* (1990) Stevens p 92.

[54] J D B Mitchell 'Administrative Law and Parliamentary Control' (1967) 38 (4) Political Quarterly 360–374.

[55] J D B Mitchell 'The Ombudsman Fallacy' (1962) PL 24–33, pp 28, 24. In fact, the emergence of the Parliamentary Commissioner for Administration in 1967 was accompanied by a debate about the need to reform the system of administrative justice more generally. This was not done and thus the Parliamentary Ombudsman was seen as a weak concession in order to avoid a broader re-examination of administrative justice.

[56] D Rowat *The Ombudsman Plan: The Worldwide Spread of an Idea* (2nd edn, 1985) University Press of America p 58.

[57] See D Lewis 'The Case for a Standing Administrative Conference' (1989) 60 Political Quarterly 421; N Lewis and P Birkinshaw *When Citizens Complain* (1993) Open University Press; M Loughlin *Public Law and Political Theory* (1992) Oxford University Press.

[58] D Lewis 'The Case for a Standing Administrative Conference' (1989) 60 Political Quarterly 421; D Lewis 'Filling the Gaps: A Standing Administrative Conference

Conference on the Resolution of Citizens' Grievances[59]. This latter proposal has been made because of changes in the administrative landscape, including an increase in the number of tribunals, the advent of the citizen's charter, internal complaints mechanisms, and ombudsmen in the public and private sectors.

The time is now opportune to discuss an integrated system of administrative justice. In addition to the Cabinet Office review of ombudsmen, there has been a review of the hearing of administrative law cases in the High Court[60] and a review of the tribunal system[61]. These three reviews taken together could be used as a basis for discussing the system of administrative justice. It is only within the process of a broad examination of administrative justice that the ombudsman system can be fully evaluated. The place of ombudsmen within the system can only be done where there is an overall assessment of what that system is. Such an examination should address the issue of whether the ombudsmen's combined remits are appropriate within the context of other public law redress mechanisms. This would enable the ombudsman's role to be examined 'in the light of the whole system of administrative justice set against clear constitutional parameters'[62].

Conclusion

Ombudsmen throughout the world have proved to be a success story. They have increased and multiplied and, in doing so, have shown their remarkable adaptability to a wide range of political and constitutional contexts. From its Scandinavian origins, the concept has 'travelled remarkably well' and has developed into 'different shapes and sizes'[63]. The ombudsman system

---

for the United Kingdom' in M. Harris and M Partington (eds) *Administrative Justice in the 21st Century* (1999) Hart Publishing.

[59] M Partington 'A Standing Conference on the Resolution of Citizens' Grievances' (1999) 21(3) Journal of Social Welfare and Family Law 279–284.

[60] Review of the Crown Office List (2000) a report to the Lord Chancellor conducted by Sir Jeffrey Bowman.

[61] Tribunals for Users: One System, One Service (2001) report of the Review of Tribunals by Sir Andrew Leggatt.

[62] D Lewis and R James 'Joined-up Justice: Review of the Public Sector Ombudsman in England' (2000) 4 International Ombudsman Yearbook 109–140, p 111.

[63] P Giddings 'The Future of the Ombudsman' in R Gregory and P Giddings (eds) *Righting Wrongs: The Ombudsman in Six Continents* (2000) IOS Press p 471.

in the UK is an example of the flexibility of the concept. Originally established as an adjunct to Parliament, ombudsmen have 'played a central role in the shaping of administrative justice in the late twentieth century'[64]. Although some were sceptical when the concept was first introduced[65], others described the Parliamentary Ombudsman system as 'an important new addition to the armoury of democratic government'[66].

Ombudsmen in the UK have brought redress to individual citizens for administrative shortcomings. In addition, their unique role has enabled them to oversee administrative practice, and to encourage improvement for the benefit of all citizens. Criticisms of the system are centred around lack of knowledge among the population of their role. They are not widely used, and their processes are slow. There are also criticisms of their remit and jurisdictional coverage. Weaknesses in the system concern their relationship with courts and other complaint-handling bodies. There is a danger also that the new emphasis on resolution rather than report could recast them as little more than small claims courts.

Their advantages are clearly their extensive investigative powers which allow them to seek out systemic abuse in a way that the courts and tribunals are ill-equipped to do. This quality must not be sacrificed in the new emphasis on resolution. There is concern that the ombudsmen have not yet reached their full potential[67], but that is partly because there is no agreed position of what they should be doing. The Cabinet Office review, despite its drawbacks, does present opportunities for the ombudsman system to become more coherent, and raise its profile with the public. It ought to establish the system firmly as an integral part of the constitution and an essential part of the system of administrative justice.

---

[64]   P Birkinshaw *Grievances, Remedies and the State* (2nd edn, 1994) p 2.
[65]   See, for example, J D B Mitchell 'The Ombudsman Fallacy' (1962) Public Law 24–33.
[66]   D C Rowatt *The Ombudsman: Citizens Defender* (1968) George Allen and Unwin p 292.
[67]   The present Parliamentary Ombudsman, Sir Michael Buckley, notes: 'The institution of Ombudsman is of great value. The value has yet to be fully realised in this country' (Parliamentary Ombudsman Annual Report 2001–02 (HC Paper 897 (2001–02)) p 11).

Bibliography

Adam, C 'In Quest of the Ombudsman in the Mediterranean Area' (1968) The Annals 98

Allsop, J and Mulcahy, L *Regulating Medical Work: formal and informal controls* (1996) Open University Press

Amos, M 'The Parliamentary Commissioner for Administration, redress and damages for wrongful administration' (2000) Public Law 21–30

Aufrecht, S E and Hertogh, M 'Evaluating Ombudsman Systems' in R Gregory and P Giddings (eds) *Righting Wrongs: The Ombudsman in Six Continents* (2000) IOS Press

Austin, R 'Administrative Law's Reaction to the Changing Concepts of Public Service' in P Leyland and T Woods (eds) *Administrative Law Facing the Future: Old Constraints and New Horizons* (1997) Blackstone Press

Barron, A and Scott, C 'The Citizen's Charter Programme' (1992) 55 Modern Law Review 526

Bearup, R S and Palusci 'Improving Child Welfare through a Children's Ombudsman' (1999) 23(5) Child Abuse & Neglect 449–457

Bell, C and Vaughan, J W 'The Building Societies Ombudsman: a customers champion?' (1988) 132 Solicitors Journal 1478

Birds, J and Graham, C 'Complaints Mechanisms in the Financial Services Industry' (1998) Civil Justice Quarterly 313

Birkinshaw, P *Grievances, Remedies and the State* (2nd edn, 1994) Sweet and Maxwell

Blom-Cooper, L 'The Case for an Ombudsman' in D C Rowatt (ed) *The Ombudsman: Citizens Defender* (1968) George Allen and Unwin

Bradley, A W 'The Role of the Ombudsman in Relation to the Protection of Citizens' Rights' (1980) 39(2) Cambridge Law Journal 304–332

Bradley, A W 'The Ombudsman and the Protection of Citizens' Rights: A British Perspective' in G E Caiden (ed) *International Handbook of the Ombudsman: Evolution and Present Function* (1983) Greenwood Press

Bradley, A W 'Sachsenhausen, Barlow Clowes – and then' (1992) Public Law 353

Buckley, M 'Remedies, Redress and "Calling to Account": Some Myths about the Parliamentary Commissioner for Administration' 1998 Denning Law Journal 29–47

Buckley, M 'The Parliamentary Ombudsman' (1998) 68 Advisor 6–8

Caiden, G E 'The Institution of Ombudsman' in G E Caiden (ed) *International Handbook of the Ombudsman: Evolution and Present Function* (1983) Greenwood Press

Carnwath, R 'Welfare Services – Liabilities in Tort after the Human Rights Act' (2001) Public Law 210–219

Christoplos, I 'Humanitarianism, Pluralism and Ombudsmen: Do the Pieces Fit?' (1999) 23(2) Disasters 125–138

Clothier, C 'Legal problems of an ombudsman' (1984) 81 Law Society Gazette, 3108

Clothier, C 'The Value of an Ombudsman' (1986) Public Law 204

Compton, E 'The Parliamentary Commissioner for Administration' (1968) Journal of the Society of the Public Teachers of Law 101

Compton, E 'The Administrative Performance of Government' (1970) Public Administration 48

Consumers Association *Ombudsmen* (1997)

Cooper, D 'The Citizen's Charter and Radical Democracy: Empowerment and Exclusion within Citizenship Discourse' (1993) 2 Social and Legal Studies 149–171

Craig, P and Fairgrieve, D '*Barrett*, Negligence and Discretionary Powers' (1999) Public Law 626–662

Crawford, C 'Complaints, codes and ombudsmen in local government' (1988) Public Law 246–267

Crawford, C 'Reviewing the Local Ombudsmen' (1999) 2(2) Journal of Local Government Law 34–39

Crawford, C 'Rule of Law, Lawyers or Ombudsmen?' (2001) 4(4) Journal of Local Government Law 73–79

Cunneen, M and Harrison, J 'Framework for a New System' (2001) Legal Action (August) 6–8

Danet, B 'Toward a Method to Evaluate the Ombudsman Role' (1978) 10(3) Administration and Society 335–370

Davis, K *Discretionary Justice* (1969) Louisiana State University Press

Denning, A *Freedom Under the Law* (1949) Stevens

Drewry, G 'Revolution in Whitehall: The Next Steps and Beyond' in J Jowell and D Oliver (eds) *The Changing Constitution* (3rd edn, 1994) Oxford University Press

Drewry, G 'The Ombudsman: Parochial Stopgap or Global Panacea?' in P Leyland and T Woods (eds) *Administrative Law Facing the Future: Old Constraints and New Horizons* (1997) Blackstone Press

Drewry, G 'The Northern Ireland Parliamentary Ombudsman' in R Gregory and P Giddings (eds) *Righting Wrongs: The Ombudsman in Six Continents* (2000) IOS Press

Drewry, G 'Whatever happened to the Citizen's Charter?' (2002) Public Law 9–12

Drewry, G and Harlow, C 'A Cutting Edge? The Parliamentary Commissioner and MPs' (1990) 53 Modern Law Review 745–769

Elcock, H J 'Opportunity for Ombudsman: The Northern Ireland Commissioner for Complaints' (1972) Public Administration 87–93

Farrand, J 'Courts, tribunals and ombudsmen' (2000) 26 Amicus Curiae 3–8

Farrand, J 'An Academic Ombudsman' (2001) 9(1) Journal of Financial Regulation and Compliance 11–29

Fuller, L L 'The forms and limits of adjudication' (1978) 91 Harvard Law Review 353

Galligan, D *Discretionary Powers* (1986) Oxford University Press

Ganz, G 'Government and Industry: The provision of financial assistance to industry and its control' (1977) Public Law 439

Gellhorn, W *Ombudsmen and Others. Citizens' Protectors in Nine Countries* (1967) Harvard University Press

Genn, H 'Tribunal Review of Administrative Decision-Making' in G Richardson and H Genn (eds) *Administrative Law and Government Action* (1994) Clarendon Press

Giddings, P 'The Ombudsman in a Changing World' (1998) 8(6) Consumer Policy Review 202–208

Giddings, P 'The Parliamentary Ombudsman: a Successful Alternative?' in D Oliver and G Drewry (eds) *The Law and Parliament* (1998) Butterworths

Giddings, P 'The Health Service Ombudsman after twenty-five years' (1999) Public Law 201–210

Giddings, P '*Ex p. Balchin*: findings of maladministration and injustice' (2000) Public Law 201–204

Giddings, P 'The Future of the Ombudsman' in R Gregory and P Giddings (eds) *Righting Wrongs: The Ombudsman in Six Continents* (2000) IOS Press

Giddings, P 'The United Kingdom Health Service Commissioner Schemes' in R Gregory and P Giddings (eds) *Righting Wrongs: The Ombudsman in Six Continents* (2000) IOS Press

Giddings, P, Gregory, R, Moore, V and Pearson, J 'Controlling administrative action in the United Kingdom: the role of the ombudsman systems and the courts compared' (1993) 59(2) International Review of Administrative Sciences 291–309

Goldsmith, A and Lewis, C (eds) *Civilian Oversight of Policing: Governance, Democracy and Human rights* (2000) Hart Publishing

Goldsworthy, D 'The Citizen's Charter' (1994) 9 Public Policy and Administration 59

Gottehrer, D M, Fergusen, M D and Aufrecht, S E 'Ombudsman Officers in the United States' in R Gregory and P Giddings (eds) *Righting Wrongs: The Ombudsman in Six Continents* (2000) IOS Press

Graham, C, Seneviratne, M and James, R 'Publicising the Bank and Building Societies Ombudsman Schemes' (1993) 3(2) Consumer Policy Review 85

Graham, D, James, R and Seneviratne, M 'Building Societies, Consumer Complaints, and the Ombudsman' (1994) 23(2) Anglo-American Law Review 214

Gregory, R and Alexander, A 'Our Parliamentary Ombudsman (Part II)' (1973) 51 Public Administration 48

Gregory, R and Drewry, G 'Barlow Clowes and the Ombudsman' (1991) Public Law 192–214 and 408–442

Gregory, R and Giddings, P 'The Ombudsman and the New Public Management' in R Gregory and P Giddings (eds) *Righting Wrongs: The Ombudsman in Six Continents* (2000) IOS Press

Gregory, R and Giddings, P 'The Ombudsman Institution: Growth and Development' in R Gregory and P Giddings (eds) *Righting Wrongs: The Ombudsman in Six Continents* (2000) IOS Press

Gregory, R and Giddings, P 'The United Kingdom Ombudsman Scheme' in R Gregory and P Giddings (eds) *Righting Wrongs: The Ombudsman in Six Continents* (2000) IOS Press

Gregory, R, Giddings, P and Moore, V 'Auditing the Auditors: the Select Committee Review of the Powers, Work and Jurisdiction of the Ombudsman 1993' (1994) Public Law 207–213

Gregory, R and Hutchesson, P *The Parliamentary Ombudsman. A Study in the Control of Administrative Action* (1975) George Allen & Unwin

Gregory, R and Pearson, J 'The Parliamentary Ombudsman after twenty-five years: problems and solutions' (1992) 70 Public Administration 469–498

Griffith, J 'The Crichel Down Affair' (1955) 18 Modern Law Review 557

Gwyn, B 'The Ombudsman in Britain: a qualified success in government reform' (1982) 60 Public Administration 177

Hain, P, Humphrey, D and Rose-Smith, B (eds) *Policing the Police: Volume I, The Complaints System: Police Powers and Terrorism Legislation* (1979) John Calder

Hambleton, R and Hoggett, P 'Rethinking Consumerism in Public Services' (1993) Consumer Policy Review 102–111

Harden, I *The Contracting State* (1992) Open University Press

Harlow, C 'Ombudsmen in Search of a Role' (1990) 53 Modern Law Review 745

Harlow, C and Rawlings, R *Law and Administration* (2nd edn, 1984) Butterworths

Harris, M and Partington, M *Administrative Justice in the 21st Century* (1999) Hart Publishing

Harrison, J and Cunneen, M *An Independent Police Complaints Commission* (2000) Liberty

Hawkins, K 'The uses of legal discretion: perspectives from law and social science' in K Hawkins (ed) *The Uses of Discretion* (1992) Clarendon Press

Heede, K *European Ombudsman: redress and control at Union level* (2000) Kluwer Law International

Hill, L B *The Model Ombudsman: Institutionalizing New Zealand's Democratic Experience* (1976) Princeton University Press

Hirschmann, A *Exit, Voice and Loyalty: responses to decline in firms, organisations and states* (1970) Harvard University Press

Holland, T 'Legal Aid R.I.P.' (1999) 24(1) International Legal Practitioner 24–28

Hollingsworth, K and Douglas, G 'Creating a children's champion for Wales? The Care Standards Act 2000 (Part V) and the Children's Commissioner for Wales Act 2001' (2002) 65(1) Modern Law Review 58–68

James, R 'The Ombudsman for Corporate Estate Agents – Putting Half the House in Order' (1995) 3(5) Consumer Law Journal 188

James, R *Private Ombudsmen and Public Law* (1997) Dartmouth

James, R and Morris, P 'The New Financial Ombudsman Service Scheme' (2000) 1(2) Financial Services Bulletin 1, 3–5

James, R and Morris, P 'The New Financial Ombudsman Service in the UK' in C E F Rickett and T G W Telfer (eds) *International Perspectives on Consumers Access to Justice* (2002) Cambridge University Press

James, R and Seneviratne, M 'The Legal Services Ombudsman: Form versus Function?' (1995) 58(2) Modern Law Review 187–207

Jones, G and Grekos, M 'Great Expectations? The Ombudsman and the Meaning of "Injustice"' (2001) 6(1) Judicial Review 20–24

Jones, M 'The local ombudsman and judicial review' (1988) Public Law 608–622

Justice *The Citizen and the Administration: the Redress of Grievances* (1961) Stevens

Justice *Our Fettered Ombudsman* (1977) JUSTICE

Justice *The Local Government Ombudsman: a Review of the First Five Years* (1980) JUSTICE

Justice *Administrative Justice: Some Necessary Reforms* (1988) Clarendon Press

Kerrison, S and Pollack, A 'Complaints as Accountability? The Case of Health Care UK' (2001) Public Law 115–133

Kircheiner, HH 'The Ideological Foundation of the Ombudsman Institution' in G E Caiden (ed) *International Handbook of the Ombudsman* (1983) Greenwood Press

Laws, F G 'The Local Government Ombudsman: Contemporary Issues and Challenges' in N Hawke (ed) *The Ombudsman – twenty five years on* (1993) Cavendish

Le Sueur, A and Sunkin, M *Public Law* (1997) Longman

Lewis, C *Complaints Against the Police: The Politics of Reform* (1999) Hawkins Press

Lewis, C 'Entrenching Civilian Oversight' in A Goldsmith and C Lewis (eds) *Civilian Oversight of Policing: Governance, Democracy and Human Rights* (2000) Hart Publishing

Lewis, D 'Filling in the Gaps: A Standing Administrative Conference for the United Kingdom' in M Harris and M Partington (eds) *Administrative Justice in the 21st Century* (1999) Hart Publishing

Lewis, D and James, R 'Joined-up Justice: review of the Public Sector Ombudsman in England' (2000) 4 International Ombudsman Yearbook 109–140

Lewis, N 'The Case for Change in the Ombudsman Service' (1979) Municipal and Public Services Journal 597

Lewis, N 'The Case for a Standing Administrative Conference' (1989) 60 Political Quarterly 421

Lewis, N *The Classical Ombudsmen* (1992) University of Sheffield

Lewis, N and Birkinshaw, P *When Citizens Complain: reforming justice and administration* (1993) Open University Press

Lewis, N, Seneviratne, M and Cracknell, S *Complaints Procedures in Local Government* (1986) University of Sheffield

Logie, J G and Watchman, P Q *The Local Ombudsman* (1990) T&T Clark

Loughlin, M *Public Law and Political Theory* (1992) Oxford University Press

Maguire, M 'Complaints against the police: the British experience' in A Goldsmith (ed) *Complaints against the Police: the trend to external review* (1991) Clarendon Press

Maguire, M and Corbett, C *A Study of the Police Complaints System* (1991) HMSO

Manby, B 'The South African Independent Complaints Directorate' in A Goldsmith and C Lewis (eds) *Civilian Oversight of Policing: Governance, Democracy and Human Rights* (2000) Hart Publishing

Mankin, L D 'The Role of the Ombudsman in Higher Education' (1996) 51 Dispute Resolution Journal 46–49

Marshall, G 'The United Kingdom' in D C Rowat (ed) *The Ombudsman: Citizens Defender* (1968) George Allen and Unwin

Marshall, G 'Maladministration' (1973) Public Law 32–44

McFadden, J 'The Public Sector Ombudsman System in Scotland' (2001) 2(1) Scottish Constitutional and Administrative Law and Practice 16–20

Merricks, W 'The Jurisprudence of the Ombudsman' (2001) 41 Journal of Business Law 654–660

Mitchell, J D B 'The Ombudsman Fallacy' (1962) Public Law 24–33

Mitchell, J D B 'Administrative Law and Parliamentary Control' (1967) 38(4) Political Quarterly 360–374

Mitchell, J and Doane, D 'An Ombudsman for Humanitarian Assistance?' (1999) 23(2) Disasters 115–124

Monti, G '*Osman v UK* – Transforming English Negligence Law into French Administrative Law' (1999) 48 International and Comparative Law Quarterly 757–778

Morris, P 'The Banking Ombudsman' (1987) Journal of Banking Law 133

Morris, P 'The Banking Ombudsman – five years on' (1992) Lloyds Maritime and Commercial Law Quarterly 227

Morris, P 'The Revenue Adjudicator – The First Two Years' (1996) Public Law 309

Morris, P E 'The Insurance Ombudsman Bureau and Judicial Review' (1994) Lloyd's Maritime and Commercial Law Quarterly 358

Morris, P E 'The Ombudsman for Corporate Estate Agents' (1994) Civil Justice Quarterly 337

Morris, P E and Henham, R 'The Prisons Ombudsman: A Critical Review' (1998) 4 (3) European Public Law 345–378

Mulcahy, L, Lickless, R, Allsop, J and Karn, V *Small Voices Big Issues: An annotated bibliography of the literature on public sector complaints* (1997) University of North London

Nobles, R 'Keeping Ombudsmen in their Place – The Courts and the Pensions Ombudsman' (2001) Public Law 380–402

Northey, J F 'New Zealand's Parliamentary Commissioner' in D C Rowat (ed) *The Ombudsman: Citizens' Defender* (1968) George Allen and Unwin

O'Brien, N 'Ombudsmen: fly swatters or lion-hunters?' (2000) 14 The Ombudsman 11

O'Brien, N 'Justice by any other name' (2001) The Ombudsman 7–8

Oliver, D 'The Revenue Adjudicator: A New Breed of Ombudsperson?' (1993) Public Law 407–411

O'Loan, N 'The Police Ombudsman for Northern Ireland – an Introduction' (2000) 14 The Ombudsman 7

O'Loan, N 'Police Ombudsman for Northern Ireland' (2002) 8(2) Visiting Times 10–13

Oosting, M 'Essential Elements of Ombudsmanship' in L C Reif (ed) *The Ombudsman Concept* (1995) International Ombudsman Institute

O'Rawe, M and Moore, L 'Accountability and Police Complaints in Northern Ireland: Leaving the Past Behind?' in A Goldsmith and C Lewis (eds) *Civilian Oversight of Policing: Governance, Democracy and Human rights* (2000) Hart Publishing

Osmotherly, E B C 'Modernising the Ombudsman Service' (2000) Journal of Local Government Law 41–43

Page, A 'The Citizen's Charter and Administrative Justice' in M Harris and M Partington (eds) *Administrative Justice in the 21st Century* (1999) Hart

Partington, M 'A Standing Conference on the Resolution of Citizens' Grievances' (1999) 21(3) Journal of Social Welfare and Family Law 279–284

Paul, S 'Accountability in public services: exit, voice and control' (1992) 20(7) World Development 1047–1060

Poole, K P 'The Northern Ireland Commissioner for Complaints' (1972) Public Law 131–148

Pugh, I 'The ombudsman-jurisdiction, power and practice' (1978) 56 Public Administration 127

Rawlings, R *The Complaints Industry: a Review of Socio-Legal Research on Aspects of Administrative Justice* (1986) Economic and Social Research Council

Rawlings, R 'Parliamentary Redress of Grievances' in C Harlow (ed) *Public Law and Politics* (1986) Sweet and Maxwell

Rawlings, R 'The MP's Complaints Service' (1990) 53(1) Modern Law Review 22–42, and 53(2) Modern Law Review 149–169

Robb, B *Sans Everything* (1967) Nelson

Robertson, J 'The Ombudsman Around the World' in International Ombudsman Institute and L Reif (eds) *The International Ombudsman Yearbook 1998* (1999) Kluwer Law International

Rowat, D C *The Ombudsman: Citizens' Defender* (1968) George Allen and Unwin

Rowat, D C *The Ombudsman Plan: The Worldwide Spread of an Idea* (2nd edn, 1985) University Press of America

Ryan, M and Ward, T 'A Prison Ombudsman of sorts: The long road to reform' in N Hawke (ed) *The Ombudsman – twenty five years on* (1993) Cavendish

Scott, C 'Regulation inside government: re-badging the Citizen's Charter' (1999) Public Law 595–603

Scott, I 'Reforming the Commissioner for Administrative Complaints in Hong Kong' (1994) Public Law 27–38

Seneviratne, M *Ombudsmen in the Public Sector* (1994) Open University Press

Seneviratne, M 'Estate Agents, the Consumer and the Ombudsman for Corporate Estate Agents' (1997) Consumer Law Journal 123–133

Seneviratne, M 'The European Ombudsman' (1999) 21(3) Journal of Social Welfare and Family Law 269–278

Seneviratne, M *The Legal Profession: Regulation and the Consumer* (1999) Sweet and Maxwell

Seneviratne, M 'The European Ombudsman – The First Term' (2000) 22(3) Journal of Social Welfare and Family Law 329–337

Seneviratne, M '"Joining up" the ombudsmen – the Review of the Public Sector Ombudsmen in England' (2000) Public Law 582–591

Seneviratne, M 'Ombudsmen 2000' (2000) 9(1) Nottingham Law Journal 13–24

Seneviratne, M 'The Prisons Ombudsman' (2001) 23(1) Journal of Social Welfare and Family Law 93–101

Seneviratne, M 'Ombudsmen for Children' (2001) 23(2) Journal of Social Welfare and Family Law 217–225

Seneviratne, M '"Joining Up" the Scottish Ombudsmen' (2002) 24(1) Journal of Social Welfare and Family Law 89–98

Seneviratne, M 'Ombudsmen and Social Housing' (2002) 24(3) Journal of Social Welfare and Family Law (forthcoming)

Serota, B 'The Evolution of the Role of the Ombudsman – Comparisons and Perspectives' in G E Caiden (ed) *International Handbook of the Ombudsman: Evolution and Present Function* (1983) Greenwood Press

Shaw, S 'First thoughts of the Prisons Ombudsman' (2000) 14 The Ombudsman 5–6

Smith, G 'Police Complaints and Criminal Prosecutions' (2001) 64(3) Modern Law Review 372–392

Smith, G 'The Police Complaints Commission: Independent from Whom?' (2002) 47 Criminal Justice Matters 40–41

Stacey, F *The British Ombudsman* (1971) Clarendon Press

Stacey, F *Ombudsmen Compared* (1978) Clarendon Press

Taggart, M *Corporatism, Privatisation and Public Law* (1990) Legal Research Foundation

Thompson, B 'Integrated Ombudsmanry: Joined-up to a Point' (2001) 64(3) Modern Law Review 459–467

Topping, I 'The Police Complaints System in Northern Ireland' in A J Goldsmith (ed) *Complaints Against the Police: the Trend to External Review* (1991) Clarendon Press

Vincent-Jones, P 'Responsive Law and Governance in Public Sector Provision: a Future for the Local Contracting State' (1998) 61 Modern Law Review 362

Von Tigerstrom, B 'The Role of the Ombudsman in Protecting Economic, Social and Cultural Rights' in International Ombudsman Institute and L C Reif (eds) *The International Ombudsman Yearbook* (1998) Kluwer Law International

Ward, S 'Is it a Fair Cop?' (2002) 99(4) Law Society Gazette 20–21

Waxman, E J and Gadin, H 'A Breed Apart' (1998) 4 Dispute Resolution Magazine 21–24.

Wener, G *A legitimate grievance? A report on the Role of the Ombudsman in the Prison System* (1983) Prison Reform Trust

Wheare, K C *Maladministration and its Remedies* (1973) Stevens

White, C 'Enforcing the Decisions of Ombudsmen – the Northern Ireland Local Government Ombudsman's Experience' (1994) 45(4) Northern Ireland Legal Quarterly 395–402

Williams, D *Maladministration: Remedies for Injustice* (1976) Oyez
　　Publishing
Williams, T and Goriely, T 'A Question of Numbers: Managing Complaints
　　against Rising Expectations' in M Harris and M Partington (eds)
　　Administrative Justice in the 21st Century (1999) Hart Publishing
Woolf, H 'Public Law – Private Law: Why the Divide?' (1986) Public Law
　　220–238
Woolf, H *The Protection of the Public – A New Challenge* (1990) Stevens
Yardley, D 'Local Ombudsmen in England: Recent Trends and
　　Developments' (1983) Public Law 522

Index